WALL STREET'S THINK TANK

WALL STREET'S THINK TANK

The Council on Foreign Relations and the Empire
of Neoliberal Geopolitics, 1976–2014

LAURENCE H. SHOUP

MONTHLY REVIEW PRESS

New York

Shoup, Laurence H.
 Wall Street's think tank : the Council on Foreign Relations and the empire
of neoliberal geopolitics, 1976–2014 / Laurence H. Shoup.
     pages cm
 Includes bibliographical references and index.
 ISBN 978-1-58367-551-9 (cloth : alk. paper) 1. Council on Foreign
Relations. 2. United States—Foreign relations—1977–1981. 3. United
States—Foreign relations—1981–1989. 4. United States—Foreign
relations—1989– 5. World politics—1989– I. Title.
 JZ27.C6S56 2015
 327.73—dc23
                    2015017149

Typeset in Arno Pro 11/14

Monthly Review Press
146 West 29th Street, Suite 6W
New York, New York 10001

www.monthlyreview.org

5 4 3 2 1

Contents

The moment we . . . hesitate to tell the truth that is in us, and . . . are silent when we should speak, the divine floods of light and life flow no longer into our souls. Every truth we see is ours to give the world, not to keep to ourselves alone.

—ELIZABETH CADY STANTON

If there is no struggle there is no progress . . . Power concedes nothing without a demand. It never did and it never will. Find out just what any people will quietly submit to and you have found out the exact measure of injustice and wrong which will be imposed upon them . . .

—FREDERICK DOUGLASS

The truth is the whole.

—HEGEL

PREFACE

We may have democracy, or we may have wealth concentrated in the hands of the few, but we cannot have both.

—SUPREME COURT JUSTICE LOUIS BRANDEIS

The think tank of monopoly-finance capital, the Council on Foreign Relations is the world's most powerful private organization. The CFR is the ultimate networking, socializing, strategic-planning, and consensus-forming institution of the U.S. capitalist class. It is the central "high command" organization of the plutocracy that runs the country and much of the world. The Council is the most important U.S. and global center of "deep politics" and the "deep state" that rules behind the scenes, a way that the 1 percent conducts their unrelenting class war against the 99 percent. Despite pretensions to "democracy" and endless attempts at instructing the world, U.S. "democracy" is, in reality, largely a fraud, a hollowed-out shell, devoid of any substantive content. The fact is that the U.S. government—led behind the scenes by the CFR—is largely run in an anti-democratic fashion by and for the interests of a financialized capitalist class, their corporations, and the wealthy families that control and benefit from these corporations. No matter who is elected, people from the Council propose, debate, develop consensus, and implement the nation's key strategic policies. The deep state, in the form of the CFR, operates behind the scenes, making and enforcing important decisions outside of those publicly sanctioned by law and society. A focus on the Council on Foreign Relations is a key way to understand concretely the central sector of the ensemble of power relations in the United States and its informal global empire.

The globalized system that the Council operates within and influences the development of is monopoly-finance capitalism.[1] Neoliberalism is today's enabling and legitimizing ideology of monopoly-finance capitalism, helping the system grow and spread. We say "capitalist" because this system is mainly privately controlled and has as its primary goal constantly increasing profits and the use of these for the endless accumulation of capital. The plutocracy that dominates the system is centered in the United States, but has powerful allied branches in Western Europe and Japan especially. We say "monopoly" capitalist system because production is dominated by a relatively few giant multinational corporations able to exercise considerable monopoly power. We say "finance" capitalist system because financial speculation has become a key way that the stagnation tendencies of the system have been, at least temporarily, overcome. Banking corporations like JPMorgan Chase, Citibank, and Goldman Sachs, as well as nominally industrial conglomerates like General Electric, all enjoy financial super profits under this regime.

The CFR network of people and institutions at home and abroad is extensive and is a key factor in the ongoing forging of a transnational capitalist ruling class. What David Rothkopf (himself a Council member) calls the "superclass" and "Davos Man"—the six thousand individuals that he says run the world—has its main base in the CFR.[2] Studying and understanding the Council is therefore a critical way to know concretely how a dominant economic class has ruled in the past and continues to rule today. Council leaders recognize these facts, but prefer to remain behind the scenes and to label the CFR the world's "leading" or "most influential" foreign policy organization rather than most powerful.[3] This preference, along with its mode of operation, has resulted in the Council being less widely recognized than its real influence would suggest.

A big and complex organization, the CFR is unique because it combines a well-staffed, scholarly think tank with a large and active dues-paying membership. It has a long history, many faces, and multiple facets, including publishing *Foreign Affairs*, a magazine founded in 1922 that the *Washington Post* has called "the bible of foreign policy thinking." It has published tens of thousands of publications of various types—from books to blogs—during recent decades. During every decade, it holds thousands of membership meetings starring top political and economic leaders from a wide variety of nations, as well as many leading intellectuals. The Council's work since the mid-1970s has largely focused on creating, planning, promoting, and defending a U.S.-dominated, world-spanning neoliberal geopolitical empire that, due to the resulting mass poverty of billions of people, has been called "a criminal process of global colonization" by the Brazilian theologian Frei Betto.[4] Samir Amin labels the system as one that imposes a "lumpen development" model of pauperization and super-exploitation on the people of the South, the majority of humankind.[5] This imperialist empire is mostly an informal one, but its rule over and exploitation of a considerable part of the world and its people is nevertheless very real.

The CFR's connections to and relationships with economically and politically powerful people and institutions around the world mean that the neoliberal geopolitical worldview of its members and leaders matters a great deal. The Council's leaders select the intellectuals who set the agendas, shape the critical debates, and design the policies that serve the capitalist class. The CFR also works very hard to produce and disseminate ideas about which policies are best so that the Council/capitalist class view gains "commonsense" acceptance among the public. In this way the framework for policymaking and publicity on a variety of key issues is established. More often than not, CFR leaders and members are the "in-and-outers" who pass through the revolving door of the federal government to high positions of authority, no matter who is elected. The CFR helps unite the capitalist class community, making it not just a class in itself, but also a class for itself. It achieves this by promoting the exchange of information and policy opinions necessary to foster consensus among the rulers on what the goals and tactics of U.S. foreign, and increasingly domestic, policy should be. As Council people cycle into and out of government, policies are implemented that mostly benefit those at the top of the economic structure, creating the vast wealth and income inequality that exists today.

The need to conduct such planning efforts reflects the fact that capitalism is a system in dynamic disequilibrium, always in a process of breakdown and recovery, and so requires a think tank like the CFR as a strategic guide to map out new directions for the capitalist class and the government itself before the inevitable crises become too acute. The speeding up of change due to the capitalist globalization promoted by the Council and related organizations has added to the complexity of the issues that must be addressed. All of these aspects mean that understanding the behemoth that is the Council on Foreign Relations requires an effort. There are no easy shortcuts to fully understanding this complex organization and its policies.

This book has had a long genesis; it is the result of a decades-long research process, dating to the early 1970s. William Minter and I went to different universities for graduate study, and both decided, before we met, to study the CFR. Minter did his work in sociology; I did mine in U.S. history. Our dissertations on the Council complete, we decided to combine them, with additional research, in a book. In July of 1976, we put the final touches on *Imperial Brain Trust: The Council on Foreign Relations and United States Foreign Policy* (Monthly Review Press, 1977). Gerald Ford was president, Henry Kissinger was Secretary of State, and Alan Greenspan was Ford's chief economic adviser. The Soviet Union was a world power. The Internet, cell phones, personal computers, the financialization of capital accumulation, neoliberalism, the "Washington Consensus," and many other things that are commonplace today were either not yet fully implemented or had not been invented.

In 1976, we believed that U. S. foreign policy was a disaster, not only for the billions of working-class people in the poorest parts of the world who suffer the most exploitation and the hardest blows from the imperialism and empire characteristic of monopoly-finance capitalism but also for the vast majority of the people of our own country. We also believed that a main source of the problem was the top-down control of U.S. foreign policy by a relatively small group of capitalists and their in-house experts operating through many channels, central among them the Council on Foreign Relations. Our book received gratifying attention in some quarters, but overall was ignored or its views disputed by most experts and attentive publics. Imagine my surprise almost two decades later when I found the following words in the CFR's own *Annual Report* for the 1994 fiscal year:

> For much of this century, U.S. foreign policy was made by several hundred leading politicians and figures dedicated to public service from the professions of law, banking, business, the military and diplomacy. The Council was conceived by members of this professional class in the years immediately following World War I. For many decades, this same professional class gave the Council its cachet, energy, and influence, serving as its membership as well as its principal constituency.
>
> Particularly after the Kennedy administration, this traditional group was expanded by policy experts from the academy and the think tanks, mainly people with increasingly professional training in the foreign and defense policy fields that dominated the country's Cold War concerns. This enlarged foreign policy community joined the Council's ranks and, like its predecessor, gave us weight, reach, and intellectual strength.[6]

Here we had the CFR's own leaders, in their own publication, stating that U.S. foreign policy in the twentieth century was made by a "professional class" (their term for a ruling capitalist class) of only "several hundred" people, augmented by a number of "experts" beginning in the 1960s. Almost all of these people were members of the CFR, which actively promoted a foreign policy suitable to the U.S. capitalist class, while, of course, expecting the people of the United States and the world to pay for the results of these policies with their blood and treasure. William Minter and I had been right to stress these realities in *Imperial Brain Trust*, and, in a very real sense, even the Council and its leadership were open to stating this truth by 1994. CFR leaders have gone even further in recent years; the Council's president Richard Haass stated in 2007 that the CFR is "the leading foreign policy organization in the world."[7] This book represents an effort both to document this assertion and go beyond it.

To fully understand this power one must delve into the subject of class. With few exceptions, the dominant culture pretends that we live in a classless society, one where all—no matter what their wealth and income level, race or gender, type of employment or where they live—have common interests. The United States is, however, a racialized and gendered class society, one with sharp divisions and different interests, and one where a ruling class of monopoly capitalists control almost everything of importance, either openly or behind the scenes. Their class interest lurks behind the all-encompassing veil of what is labeled the "national interest." But this does not happen by accident: the capitalists are highly organized and pursue their class interests relentlessly. One of the key places they do this is at the CFR, which consequently makes this organization so important to understand in depth. Studying the Council in detail allows us to understand the goals, strategy, and tactics of the powerful, how and why they define the "national class interest" as they do; it shows how this organization develops new initiatives, forges unity around them, then shapes the public agenda and debate, including discussions among public officials, a large number of whom are CFR members. A focus on the CFR illustrates key abstractions like "capitalist class," "ruling class," and "ideological hegemony." It yields a deeper understanding of specific historical events like the U.S. war on Iraq and the rapidly evolving ecological crisis, pointing out the potential vulnerabilities of this ruling class.

The Council has been pursuing a world-spanning hegemonic project since it was founded in the 1918–1921 period. One critical ingredient of such a project has been the capacity to provide intellectual leadership. Such leadership combines knowledge, experience, and a collective worldview to create and spread its vision and have the power and legitimacy to implement it. The CFR's constant stream of interpretations, recommendations, and development priorities are meant to provide a framework for a capitalist-class agenda and a strategy that can be deployed through the vast Council network of political-economic and cultural influence at home and worldwide. In this way a particular worldview, agenda, and policy discourse become effective in the real world. A full-scale analysis of the overall CFR worldview and grand strategy of neoliberal geopolitical economics was not formally developed in *Imperial Brain Trust*. This worldview will be outlined in some detail in the second half of the present volume, including the Council's key role in the development of neoliberalism as an effective doctrinal and ideological cluster, a governing philosophy.

Following the publication of *Imperial Brain Trust*, I continued to be interested in the CFR, and, have, over an almost forty-year period, collected a large archive of data, useful in producing *Wall Street's Think Tank*. Today (early 2015), the Council on Foreign Relations has an individual membership of almost 5,000, a corporate membership of about 170, a staff of over 330, supported by an annual budget of about $60 million and assets of almost $492 million.[8] It remains the largest and most powerful of all U.S. private think tanks that presume to discuss and decide the future of humanity in largely secret meetings behind closed doors in the upper-class neighborhoods of New York and Washington. During the last four decades the CFR has not only successfully continued its central position as the most important private organization in the United States, one with no real peer in the country. It has clearly succeeded in expanding its key role, and remains at the center of the small plutocracy that runs the United States and much of the world.

The reader will kindly take note that no monied interests, foundations, universities, corporations, research institutes, or think tanks have in any way funded or otherwise influenced the production of this book. It is an effort of independent scholarship, by someone who believes that the current power structure is bankrupt and fundamental changes are needed if the great majority of humanity is to survive the ecosystemic catastrophe and violent conflicts that the One Percent and their monopoly-finance capitalist system are creating for life on our planet.

I would like to especially thank Suzanne Baker, Dr. Daniel D. Shoup, Dr. Paul W. Rea, and Jennifer Ho who all took out time from their busy lives to read parts of the book and make suggestions on ways to improve it. Thanks also to Michael D. Yates and Erin Clermont, my editors at *Monthly Review*, who worked hard making numerous corrections and offered many helpful suggestions. Any remaining shortcomings are, of course, my responsibility alone.

—LAURENCE H. SHOUP
March 2015

INTRODUCTION: THE EARLY
HISTORY OF THE CFR

The Council on Foreign Relations in recent decades has become a much different organization than it was when it was established and incorporated in the 1918–1921 period. Nevertheless, origins do matter, and the CFR's beginnings and first half-century of existence set key patterns that still exist today.

THE ORIGINS AND EARLY DEVELOPMENT OF THE COUNCIL

The Council had its origins in the uniting of two different fledgling groups during the post–First World War era. The first, established in 1918, was the New York club called the Council on Foreign Relations. It had only 108 members, dominated by high-ranking Wall Street financiers and international lawyers. Its aims were to explore the effect of the war upon business and promote commerce. Its means were networking conferences and dinners hosting prominent foreign visitors.[9] The second organization grew out of the postwar planning body—mainly made up of intellectuals—set up by President Wilson's aide Edward House with the help of Walter Lippmann and others for the benefit of the 1919 U.S. peace delegation at the Versailles Conference. This group was called "The Inquiry."

Attending the conference, the group of planners met separately with members of the British delegation and decided to continue the Inquiry by forming a permanent Anglo-American Institute of International Affairs with two branches, one in each country. The plan foundered on the American side, but the British group formed what became the Royal Institute of International Affairs (Chatham House). After almost dying, the long-term Inquiry project was revived by joining with the established Wall Street group. The result was the incorporation of the Council on Foreign Relations under the laws of New York in 1921. It represented a synergy of internationally oriented corporate business interests and university-based academics: men whose goal was capital accumulation and men focused on ideas. The new CFR became the sister organization to Chatham House and the

two organizations have had a close cooperative relationship ever since, each helping the other in "a hundred different ways."[10]

The new Council had a fifteen-man board of directors and an honorary president in the person of Republican Elihu Root, the leading Wall Street lawyer of the
era. Root had not only served as counsel for many leading corporations, he personally had advised powerful political and economic actors like Theodore Roosevelt,
Andrew Carnegie, Jay Gould, and E. H. Harriman. One of the early revolving-door
players, he had moved in and out of government and private law practice, serving as
a U.S. senator, as President McKinley's secretary of war, and President Roosevelt's
Secretary of State. In these capacities he had played a central role in designing colonial and neocolonial policies in places like the Philippines and Cuba as the United
States intensified its imperialist expansion during the end of the nineteenth and
first decade of the twentieth century. The president of the new CFR was John W.
Davis, an attorney for the leading finance capitalist of the age, J. P. Morgan. He was
later, while still president of the Council, the 1924 Democratic nominee for president.[11] The new vice president, Paul D. Cravath, and secretary-treasurer, Edwin F.
Gay, were also J. P. Morgan-connected. Cravath's law firm worked for Morgan, and
Gay, a former Harvard professor, was editor of the New York Evening Post, owned
by Morgan partner Thomas W. Lamont.[12]

Among the new directors of the Council was Archibald Cary Coolidge, a
Harvard professor who had been part of the Inquiry and was from a prominent
and wealthy Boston family, one that went back to involvement in the nineteenth-
century China trade. He was asked to become the editor of the CFR's new flagship
magazine, Foreign Affairs. He only consented to take the responsibility if he could
have a full-time assistant. Gay recommended one of his young reporters, Hamilton
Fish Armstrong, a Princeton man whose ancestors not only included Hamilton
Fish, President Grant's Secretary of State, but also Peter Stuyvesant, a major figure in the early history of New York City. Armstrong eventually took over Foreign
Affairs, serving as its editor from 1928 to 1972, as well as a Council director during
the same forty-four-year period.

Root, Davis, Cravath, Coolidge, and Armstrong were all representatives of the
old money/prominent families/high society set, and were all listed in the Social
Register (SR), long considered the definitive guide to who is in or out of the upper
class.[13] A very large representation of SR listees among its officers and directors was
a prime characteristic of the early CFR. All seven of the Council presidents during
the period 1921–1971 were from families listed in the SR, as were both honorary
presidents, the first three chairmen of the board (1946–85), and the first three vice
chairmen of the board of the CFR (1971–78).

Other leading capitalists, not listed in the SR, were also on the Council's founding board. Two examples are Otto Kahn and Paul M. Warburg, both major Wall

Street investment bankers with Kuhn Loeb and M. M. Warburg, respectively. Both were economic competitors with J. P. Morgan—Kuhn Loeb was considered the second most prestigious U.S. investment bank behind Morgan, for example—but they worked together with Morgan-affiliated men in the CFR. Kahn's wealth was legendary; in 1919 he had a 127-room castle built on his Long Island estate, then the second-largest private residence in the entire country.

Coolidge, Gay, and Professor Isaiah Bowman of Johns Hopkins University were the most prominent representatives of the Inquiry-affiliated and scholarly sector of the CFR on its first board of directors. But the professional-class intellectuals have never held the top office at the CFR, and have always been, down to the present, a minority on a decision-making board of directors dominated by members of the capitalist class. An interesting aspect of this upper-class control is the shift, in the early 1950s, in the top leadership of the Council. Until 1953 the final decision maker, president until 1946, then chairman of the board after then, was always Morgan-connected. For example, Morgan partner Russell Leffingwell was chairman from 1946 to 1953. Beginning in 1953 and continuing until 1985, the chairman of the CFR was Rockefeller-connected: first John J. McCloy from 1953 to 1970 and then David Rockefeller from 1970 to 1985. Both McCloy and Rockefeller also served as chairman of the Rockefeller-controlled Chase Manhattan Bank while they chaired the Council.

One area where the intellectuals had greater influence was the implementation of the long-standing CFR goal of guiding American opinion and political-economic strategy toward a large, even dominant role in world affairs. Gay expressed the general perspective as early as 1898 when he wrote: "When I think of the British Empire as our inheritance I think simply of the natural right of succession. That ultimate succession is inevitable."[14] In a Council-published history of the organization, written by member Peter Grose, CFR president Leslie H. Gelb stated that from an early date "Council members have shared the conviction that Americans must know the world and play a leading role in its affairs."[15]

THE CFR PROGRAM, 1921–1970

From almost the outset, the Council organized a meeting and study program, operating out of its headquarters on the prestigious Upper East Side of New York. The meetings program was mostly to create a "continuous conference" on world politics and U.S. foreign policy, hosting domestic and foreign leaders in mainly off-the-record sessions for CFR members. The first major meeting was the appearance by former prime minister Georges Clemenceau of France in November 1922. From 1921 to 1938, every U.S. secretary of state made at least one important foreign policy address at the Council.[16] When a new CFR headquarters building—a

house donated by the Pratt family whose fortune stemmed from Standard Oil—
was opened in April 1945, Secretary of State Edward Stettinius, a Council member, traveled to New York "to bear witness, as every secretary of state during the past quarter of a century, to the great services and influence of this organization."[17]

Central to this "service and influence" was the studies program, the CFR think tank. This was, over the years, its most important activity, providing ongoing strategic thinking about how to solve the practical problems relating to the expansion of U.S. economic and political power abroad. Here is where the theoretical ideas of Council scholars were applied to the needs of industrial and financial interests as well as the state. The work of the CFR gradually became "a program of systematic study . . . to guide the statecraft of policymakers."[18] The way that this worked was that representatives from key sectors of society—especially academic intellectuals, corporate leaders, and government personnel—would be assembled in a study group that would focus on an issue, a nation, or a region. Following regular meetings for a year or more, one member of the group would take responsibility to write a book or article, representing his own personal view, but also coming out of the collective work and thinking of the group. As an organization dominated by the largest and most powerful industrial and financial groups—first J. P. Morgan and Kuhn Loeb, later the Rockefeller economic empire—it was natural for the CFR to promote an expansionist American foreign policy, aimed at maintaining a status quo at home by expanding abroad. More specifically, the powerful saw an increase in trade and investment as the solution to domestic problems like unemployment. As CFR director Bowman expressed it in 1928, foreign raw materials, imports, and exports were required "if we are to avoid crises in our constantly expanding industries."[19] Not surprisingly, one of the very first Council publications aimed at encouraging economic expansion abroad. This was Foster Bain's 1927 volume, *Ores and Industry in the Far East*, which came out of a 1925–26 study group at the CFR.[20]

The Second World War and the War-Peace Studies

The Council and its program reached one of its historic peaks with its work on setting U.S. foreign policy and war aims during the Second World War. This war and the subsequent Cold War were decisive events, marking a turning point toward full-blown U.S. imperialism and beginning a process of organizing the global political economy in a top-down fashion with the United States as the hegemonic power.

The CFR, its leaders, and members were at the center of efforts that defined the monopoly capitalist class "national interest" during this era, working out the strategy to implement the ensuing policy goals. During the war, this work was conceived and carried out by a special Council study group, called the War-Peace Studies. Almost 100 men worked on this Rockefeller Foundation funded effort, engaging in organization, research, analysis, discussion, and writing from 1939 until 1945, producing a total of 682 memoranda for President Roosevelt, the State Department, and other branches of the U.S. government. Midway through the war, a number of the CFR planners were brought into the State Department part-time to help officials set postwar policy.[21] Collectively, the body of work produced by the War-Peace Studies defined the U.S. "national interest" in a status-quo fashion, based on the percentage of the world necessary for the country to prosper without fundamental changes in the capitalist property ownership and "free market" system. Not surprisingly, most of the world was seen as needed as economic living space for such a system, meaning that the United States would have to go to war with and defeat Japan and Germany and then begin to reorganize the world as an informal empire beneficial to American and allied capitalist interests.

Postwar Focus on Containing and Overthrowing the Soviet System

Following the Second World War, the continuing existence of the USSR and its allies stood as a partial roadblock to U.S. global ambitions, and for the following several decades, this challenge was always near the center of Council concerns. Furthermore, the organization had a key impact on U.S. policies. In his semi-official history of the Council, Peter Grose stated that in the postwar period the Council's study groups "served as an important breeding ground for the doctrines ... that guided American foreign policy for the years of the Cold War."[22] This guidance involved "public enlightenment" through varied channels, including CFR-linked committees in many cities around the country, but also service in government by the "in-and-outers," Council people who move in and out of high government office and their private endeavors in finance, business, law, academe, foundations, other think tanks, and the media. As the 1951 CFR *Annual Report* expressed it:

> In placing emphasis on public enlightenment, however, it is not intended to suggest that the Council has no function in the evolution of foreign policies themselves. ... The roster of Council members who now occupy high office is impressive. Many of them spent long hours in Council study and discussion groups when they were private citizens, and some still participate actively in the work of the organization.[23]

Whether in government or at the CFR, these "wise men of foreign affairs" think in terms of their own "national class interest" and resulting grand strategy for the U.S. government.

The CFR dedicated a large portion of its efforts to understanding and countering its Soviet opponent and actual or potential allies. For example, *Foreign Affairs* magazine printed no less than 248 articles on Russia and the USSR during the long tenure of Hamilton Fish Armstrong as editor, including the famous 1947 "containment" article on the "Sources of Soviet Conduct" by Council member George F. Kennan.[24] The general thinking behind the Marshall Plan, the key government figures putting the plan together, and the "citizens organizations" working to gain public support were all closely linked to the CFR.[25] Allen W. Dulles, a *SR* listee and a central figure in the U.S. government's anti-communist crusades of the 1950s and early 1960s as CIA director (a leader of coups in Iran and Guatemala, as well as failed attempts to overthrow the Cuban Revolution), was continuously a director of the CFR from 1927 until he died in 1969. He was also successively the Council's secretary (1933–44), vice president (1944–46), and president (1946–50). Allen's brother John Foster Dulles, Eisenhower's secretary of state, was also a CFR member, and chose the Council as the venue to announce the U.S. government's "massive retaliation" nuclear doctrine against the USSR on January 12, 1954. This doomsday policy evidently gave rise to some doubts within the Council, which convened a group to study the question. A young Harvard University academic named Henry A. Kissinger was invited to chronicle the work of the group and spent the 1955–56 academic year at the CFR.[26] The resulting famous 1957 book by Kissinger, *Nuclear Weapons and Foreign Policy*, suggested a modification of the Dulles-Eisenhower policy toward one that suggested gradual escalation, including the possible use of tactical nuclear weapons.[27] Kissinger himself later retreated from this doctrine, taking a more sober view of the dangers to humanity represented by nuclear escalation. The junior academic met the Rockefellers and other powerful men at the Council and was on his way toward later prominence. Kissinger and the CFR also played a central role in the shift in U.S.-China policy during the 1969–72 years, moving away from a more dogmatic anti-communist policy to a more flexible one in which China could be used as part of a complex geopolitical power game involving the USSR and other states.[28]

War over Southeast Asia and Vietnam

The U.S. invasion of Vietnam and the resulting foreign-policy disaster of 1964–73 also reflected the anti-Soviet perspectives dominant in the CFR. But more important, it involved the longtime interest of Council leaders and planners in Southeast Asia as an important geopolitical and geoeconomic region, one where U.S. "vital interests" were so involved that the area was strategically important to keep within the U.S. sphere of influence. The CFR was able to set the basic assumptions, alternatives, and framework for policy that gained capitalist-class consensus, eventually resulting in a U.S. military adventure with an immense loss of human life and treasure. Setting the framework for policy began with the War-Peace Studies in 1940–41, but intensified in the 1950s when the Council had no less than five different study groups focused on Southeast Asia. Typical was the 1959–60 study group headed up by CFR members Harlan Cleveland and Russell H. Fifield, whose conclusions were summed up by Fifield in a 1963 CFR book called *Southeast Asia in United States Policy*, stating that the area was "of great strategic, economic and demographic significance . . . of special significance in the world balance" because of the importance of its raw materials and markets.[29]

The U.S. government, led by Council men, naturally adopted the imperialistic CFR perspective and went to war based on this analysis and the resulting consensus view of the national capitalist class interest.[30] After several years of intense military engagement, and with the war not going well, the Council's inspired consensus began to fall apart, leading to a remarkable turnaround in U.S. policy in early 1968. CFR men, including Chairman John J. McCloy, were dominant in the private "Senior Advisory Group on Vietnam" that for several years had advised President Lyndon Johnson to escalate the war, but then in 1968 urged Johnson to de-escalate and seek a negotiated peace.[31]

THE PASSING OF THE OLD GUARD: FINE-TUNING THE CFR

By the late 1960s and early 1970s the CFR was facing an aging problem, as a number of key directors and a large number of members were near or past normal retirement age. Some length-of-service records of some of the directors, almost all of them members of the old plutocracy, were extraordinary: Whitney Shepardson was a director for 45 years (1921–66); Hamilton Fish Armstrong for 44 years (1928–72); Allen Dulles for 42 years (1927–69); Frank Altschul 38 years (1934–72); and William A. M. Burden for 29 years (1945–74). One CFR fellow wrote an article about the Council in *New York* magazine in 1971, focusing on how the organization—"the citadel of the establishment"—was increasingly out of touch:

> If you can walk—or be carried—into the Pratt House, it usually means you are a partner in an investment bank or law firm—with occasional "trouble-shooting" assignments in government. You believe in foreign aid, NATO, and a bipartisan foreign policy. You've been pretty much running things in this country for the last 25 years, and you know it.
>
> But today your favorite club is breaking up, just on the eve of its fiftieth anniversary. The same vulgar polarizations that have popped up elsewhere—young against old, men against women, hawks against doves—have at last invaded the secluded Pratt House and citadel of the establishment itself.... The Council's leaders, and most of its members, are affluent New Yorkers

from the financial and legal community—the establishment heartland. . . . Increasingly, they look and act like fossils. . . . The Council is stuffy and clubby and parochial and elitist, but it is a place where old moneybags and young scholars are able to sit down and learn something from each other. It is pomp-ous and pretentious, but it still draws men of affairs out of their counting-houses and into dialogue with men of intellect. It is quaint, but not quite yet a museum-piece. It would be a pity, I thought, if it should die.[32]

Although the CFR was hardly "breaking up," or in any way losing its power, there was an atmosphere of crisis during the early 1970s due to the dissent of some of the younger members against the Vietnam War, and the fact that the Council was still an all-male organization with a high average age among its members. With 1,467 members in 1970, the CFR was a large organization, but it was soon to become much larger, this being necessary to acquire younger members, admit its first women, and gradually create a more diverse Council.

The other central issue was bringing into the Council a representative group from the large *nouveau riche* plutocratic class that had rapidly grown up during the post–Second World War economic boom. This boom had greatly increased the number of millionaires in the United States, reportedly by as much as ten times between the mid-1950s and the mid-1970s. The Council is an organiza-tion of, by, and for the plutocracy—and, as indicated by its history, membership, and top leadership, very attuned to the need to incorporate the leading capitalist class families. Therefore the newly rich element of the United States had to be, as much as possible, brought into the fold. To be sure, in the 1960s and 1970s the top leadership of the CFR was still dominated by members of the old plutocracy, as measured by listings in the *SR*. The membership also had a large representa-tion from America's richest old plutocratic families. For example, a quick review of the Council's 1970 *Annual Report* finds four members of the Rockefeller family, and also top men from the Morgan, DuPont, Mellon, Vanderbilt, Cabot, Duke, Roosevelt, Whitney, Dodge, Milbank, McCormick, Payson, Houghton, Schiff, Reid, Guggenheim, Root, Watson, Harriman, Aldrich, and Dillon families.[33] These and other plutocratic families are the ones listed in the *SR* and discussed in such classic studies of U.S. wealth as Ferdinand Lundberg's *America's Sixty Families*,[34] as well as more recent works like *Millionaires and Managers* by S. Menshikov, *Wealth and Democracy* by Kevin Phillips, and *The Founding Fortunes* by Michael Allen. The newly rich tend to look up to and get their prompts from the old rich, so as the CFR organization was fine-tuned after 1970, much remained the same, the old and new plutocracy met, mingled, and merged at the Council, resulting in an organi-zation more representative of the U.S. plutocracy as a whole, and therefore more united, strengthened, and even more powerful.

This brings up a key, and still very relevant point, namely that the CFR is not only a place where the capitalist class meets to discuss its own and our planet's future; it is also a place where others outside the circle of great wealth, especially intellectuals, are brought into the dialogue and assimilated in order to assure capitalist-class hegemony. As this book will illustrate in depth, this blending together of leading men and women of wealth and economic power with men and women of brainpower is a central part of what makes the CFR unique and so important. The Council is both a membership organization and a think tank, marrying action and reflection. Its life and activities are made possible through a membership that is a delicately balanced combination of leaders of capitalist businesses, leaders of status-quo intellectual life, and leaders in government. If any of these three main components get too weak or too strong in the CFR, the organization begins to lose what it considers to be its true character. So as Council leaders managed the gradual changes needed to maintain and increase their power, prestige, and influence, they had to choose future leaders as well as new members accordingly.

The changes after 1970 also took place under the chairmanship of David Rockefeller, the epitome of an old plutocratic figure. The colossal wealth and resulting power of Rockefeller gave him, in the eyes of many, a supernatural aura. What Stewart Alsop wrote about David's brother Nelson (also a CFR member) applies to the entire plutocracy, and especially to David Rockefeller: "People who meet Nelson Rockefeller are always aware of the dollar sign that floats conspicuously above his head. It is there but one must not mention it. Having that invisible dollar sign hovering above his head tends to hedge a Very Rich man off from his fellows, as divinity doth hedge a king." [35]

Wall Street's Think Tank has two main sections. Part I will follow up on and deepen the sketch of the CFR offered above with one chapter on the Council as a capitalist-class organization and another that details the changes at the CFR beginning in 1970. The domestic and international networks of the Council will also be reviewed.

Part II will cover the CFR worldwiew and its central role in creating the current imperial neoliberal geopolitical world order, with an overview and a number of case studies, including a detailed examination of the U.S. war on and occupation of Iraq. The final chapter will discuss the dangers posed to our planet and humanity's future by the irrational national and global system of neoliberal geopolitics that the Council has been so important in creating and maintaining.

PART I

Wall Street's Think Tank
1976–2014

The CFR is a central element of a large network of people and institutions that organize the strategic planning and ideological control needed to maintain and expand the wealth and power of the U.S. plutocracy. The first chapter in this section will put the Council on Foreign Relations in its proper class context, as an organization of, by, and for the dominant sector of the U.S. capitalist class. The second chapter will illustrate how the Council operates as an organization, presented together with a detailed examination of its recent (since 1976) organizational history. The third chapter focuses on the CFR's domestic networks, elaborating the Council's links to the federal government, other major think tanks, top corporations, leading universities, important media, and lobbying bodies. The fourth chapter covers the organization's international networks, discussing its close ties to a variety of powerful individuals and groups that have influence in their home countries, regionally or globally.

Part I as a whole illustrates how the Council is indeed "Wall Street's think tank," an organization with great range and power, in service to a ruling financialized monopoly capitalist class.

1

THE U.S. CAPITALIST CLASS AND THE COUNCIL ON FOREIGN RELATIONS

The first revolutionary act is to call things by their true names.
—ROSA LUXEMBURG

The economic-owning class is always the political ruling class.
—EUGENE V. DEBS

In the realm of political economy, societal and state domination, powerful classes and the organizations they control have the most to hide about their great power and how the world actually works. In contrast, the emancipatory potential of social science resides in its honesty and truth-telling, in illustrating how such power actually operates for the benefit of the few and to the detriment of the vast majority of the people. This is its subversive effect, its resistance function. In the case of the Council on Foreign Relations, understanding the truth involves above all comprehending that this organization is run by and for a plutocracy, the capitalist class of the United States of America.

The United States is first and foremost a class society, a key fact often left out in educational, political, and media discussions about the country. Classes are socioeconomic and power groupings of people that have common relationships with one another and different relationships with other classes. In a capitalist-class society, wealth and income are key aspects of life: having or not having a well-paying, secure job and ownership or non-ownership of capital largely determine one's socioeconomic class. Access to capital and jobs has a huge influence on the daily existence and life chances of people in every societal group. From the time an individual is born, access or lack of access to wealth, capital, property, and employment affects family life, where he or she lives, with what possessions, and in what conditions. It influences the individual's educational opportunities and health including access to doctors, securing healthy food, and limiting exposure to hazards such as crime and pollution. The United States is a particular type of class society, a racialized one, where some groups are stigmatized as inferior because of their race, a belief spreading to all segments of society. Once this oppressive idea becomes widespread, the resulting divisions within the working class can be used by the rulers to divide and conquer, preventing unity among the workers. People with a darker skin color than Europeans are frequent victims of this discrimination. Gender is another point of division fostered by those with capital; women are routinely paid significantly less for the same work, for example, and are discriminated against in other ways, assuring that there is no equality in the workplace, and most women are, like people of color, kept in the lower ranks of workers generally. In this system, class realities are largely downplayed or completely avoided in public discourse, and racial and gender issues are highlighted. The capitalist class always wants to highlight differences and divisions within the underlying population. In this racialized and gendered class system, class, race, and gender are all central to people's lived experience.

The two great major classes in today's United States are a numerically small capitalist class and a very much larger working class. The capitalist class is characterized by ownership of large amounts of wealth, much of which is capital, obtained mainly through investment in and control of the corporations that organize production, distribution, and the financing of the economy. The working class lacks such ownership and needs to enter the labor market to secure employment. Since they are without significant capital, the worker must sell to others his or her ability to labor, usually to the capitalists, in order to survive on the resulting wages. This inequality of ownership does three things. It allows the capitalist to exploit the individual worker—profits are extracted from the laborer's efforts. It confers tremendous economic and political power upon the capitalist. And it generates overt and covert conflicts over wages, hours, working conditions, and sometimes the system itself. This conflict must of necessity take a collective form, which is class struggle. With these facts in mind, class can be summed up as a relationship of exploitation, dispossession, oppression, and conflict between owners and workers, while each class has a potential relationship of internal solidarity.

Although the capitalist-worker class relation is central in any capitalist society, there is another group, well-educated professionals, that is also important. This group, which stands between the two key classes, is usually and inaccurately called the "middle class," but will be called here the "professional class." These professionals, with their education, intellect, and skills, are very important to capitalists and they are often appropriately rewarded. Some of them even profit enough from their work and connections to gradually, step by step, rise to fill capitalist occupations and become capitalists themselves. Many others aspire to this status, subordinating themselves to the capitalist class, both as a technique of survival and in hope of gaining a measure of power and status with greater rewards.

The capitalist class of the United States is defined here as people and families with financial or productive assets of at least $10 million, or a position as a top officer or director of a Fortune 500 corporation, or as a principal of a major law firm. Such corporate and legal positions are very well paid, making it possible to rapidly accumulate assets and, if not already wealthy, join the capitalist class in a relatively short time. This group is a very small percentage of the U.S. population. Official wealth statistics show that the top 1 percent of U.S. households had an average wealth of $19 million in 2007, dropping to $14 million in 2009. In contrast, 37.1 percent of U.S. households had a net worth of less than $12,000, and 24.8 percent had a zero or negative net worth.[36]

At the $10 million level, or as a top corporate executive or law firm partner, an individual member of the capitalist class does not ever have to enter the labor market, hat in hand, to seek a job. If employed—an option, not a requirement for much of the capitalist class—he or she often works for the family corporation, or, through ownership and connections, gets a comfortable and well-paid corporate position. Some top capitalist-class institutions also use the $10 million figure as a cutoff point. The Private Wealth Management unit of the JPMorgan Chase Bank, for example, has decided not to include clients with less than $10 million in financial assets, since their coverage model, using an integrated team of specialist advisers to meet the client's investing, wealth transfer, credit, and philanthropic needs, is most profitable when limited to only high-net-worth individuals and families.[37]

Viewing the percentage of wealth (total net worth) owned and controlled by key groups is also instructive. In 2010 the top 1 percent owned about 35 percent of total U.S. wealth. The next 4 percent had 28 percent, and the 15 percent after that owned 26 percent. The top 5 percent thus had 63 percent, and the top 20 percent had 89 percent of total U.S. wealth. The top about 20 percent together make up the capitalist class and the professional class, with the dividing line difficult to determine as some individuals from the professional class are rising into the ranks of the capitalists. The bottom 80 percent of the population, approximately corresponding to the working class, owned only 11 percent of the wealth. Financial wealth is even more concentrated.[38]

The *World Wealth Report* by Capgemini and Merrill Lynch Wealth Management has recently estimated the wealth of the world capitalist class. In 2010, the wealth of the world's eleven million super-rich individuals stood at $43 trillion, or 70 percent of global gross domestic product.[39] The U.S. capitalist class held more of that wealth than any other national capitalist class. The 2011 Capgemini/Merrill Lynch *World Wealth Report* found that North America (United States and Canada) had 3.4 million high-net-worth individuals worth a total of $11.6 trillion. Forty thousand ultra-high-net-worth individuals, over half of them living in a few large cities, held the bulk of this wealth. The Asia-Pacific and European regions were second and third with $10.8 and $10.2 trillion held by high-net-worth individuals respectively. These three world regions, and especially the top nations and key cities within them, held the vast majority of the world's wealth. Among U.S. cities, New York, the headquarters of both finance capital (Wall Street) and the CFR, had by far the largest number of super-rich (roughly three times as many as second-place Los Angeles), with San Francisco, Chicago, Washington, D.C., Houston, and Dallas rounding out the top seven.[40] Although London is also important, New York is the top command center of the world economy, controlling a large percentage of the world's finances. It was ranked number one in 2012 and 2014 articles on the world's most economically powerful cities, with London in second place.[41]

The capitalist class of the United States is by far the most organized, class-conscious, and powerful segment of society. It has, in fact, more power than any ruling class in world history. It has its own expensive private schools for its children, such as college "prep" schools at the high school level, as well as the eastern "Ivy League" private universities, like Harvard, Yale, Princeton, and Columbia, and elite outposts around the nation like Stanford and the University of Chicago. It has its own luxurious "high society" culture and lifestyle. Families in this class tend to intermarry, strengthening their connections and economic and political power. They are also usually open to allowing well-educated members of the professional class to enter their ranks, as long as these newcomers want to be of service to the capitalist class and are willing to adhere to the cultural, social, and political norms of their betters. The CFR is one place where such ambitious outsiders meet and form alliances with members of the capitalist class. Just one example illustrates the possibilities: William Jefferson Clinton was not born into a capitalist-class family, but he was intelligent and ambitious, worked to become a professional by gaining a college education, and was awarded a Rhodes Scholarship in England. He ran for political office and was, with the help of capitalist-class member Madeleine K. Albright, able to become a member of the Council in the 1980s. The contacts he made at the CFR helped him get the favorable media attention, funding, and top advisers to validate his candidacy and successfully become president. He brought many fellow Council members into leading positions in his administration, and implemented a raft of pro-capitalist CFR policies. Once out of office, lucrative speaking engagements and book deals made him wealthy, a member of the capitalist class himself, with his own foundation. One estimate is that by 2014 he had $80 million in personal assets, another estimate puts the total at $38 million.[42] He was also able to bring his daughter Chelsea into the CFR, allowing her to expand her network to the rich, well-educated, and powerful people that she will meet at the Council. This is a common pattern: CFR members often bring relatives into the organization to promote individual and family agendas.

In the United States the capitalist class is numerically a large group, amounting to tens of thousands of extended families. These families usually maintain close ties with one another because their wealth is tied up in corporations with shared ownership and control, and inheritance generally depends upon blood relationships. Within wealthy circles, the age of the fortune is one key source of internal differentiation. Members of the old plutocracy, dominant in the CFR's early history, are usually included in the *Social Register*, a book that lists and promotes social relationship among the "prominent" families (that is, those wealthy for a long time) of the United States. These old plutocratic families have also, whatever the original source of their wealth, usually diversified it, especially into finance but also into other sectors of the economy. They are also more transnational: they and their corporations have invested significant amounts overseas. Newer wealth is usually more concentrated in one industry, such as manufacturing or trade. Newer wealth also tends to be more locally and nationally based. The capitalist class also supports both the Democratic and Republican parties, with the newer, more localized rich more strongly supporting Republicans and the financialized old rich more balanced in their support for both "moderate" Democrats and "moderate" Republicans. But all sectors of the U.S. capitalist class organize their economic power through the corporate system, which they control, as families and as a class. If the modern corporation is one of the key locations in which the power of the capitalist class is institutionally crystallized, another central place of capitalist-class power is the Council on Foreign Relations and its larger network of associated organizations. The activities of the CFR are one important way that this class organizes itself, develops a generalized unity, and projects itself and its special class interests (portrayed by the Council, of course, as the general interest) upon the national and world stage. The CFR's key role is to move the capitalist class from being a class in itself (the owners of the corporate-dominated economic system) to a class for itself (with consciousness, agency, and heightened power).

This chapter discusses the capitalist-class representation in the CFR during the 1976–2014 years. Since the Council has both individual and corporate membership categories, both individuals and corporate members are included. Professionals also appear, as they are important to the intellectual functioning of the Council, but it must be kept in mind that they are primarily present in an advisory role. Although many professionals may be on their way up the power and wealth ladder into the capitalist class, all final decisions are still reserved for their capitalist masters.

When examining the CFR leadership as a group, their close relationship to the federal government is striking. Many CFR leaders are "in-and-outers." These individuals often have a primary career, typically in finance, business, law, politics, or academic life, but are appointed to high political office by a given U.S. president, serve a few years, then return to "private enterprise," sometimes including non-profit work. These individuals often are a kind of access entrepreneur, who use connections acquired in government service to afterward do business or advance professionally. They may also maintain influence with their former colleagues in government, especially the ones who are also members of the Council. As we shall see in this and future chapters, this is an important pattern both for the CFR's top leadership and for the Council as an organization.

TOP LEADERSHIP

The Council on Foreign Relations is a corporation, and is organized in a top-down corporate fashion with a chairperson as the final decision maker, aided by the president and board of directors. The board of directors approve all new members and selects all of the top leaders. There is a pro-forma process set up for the membership to "elect" the board, but even the membership does not take the process very seriously, as almost all board members are chosen as a listed slate that the members vote for, so up to two-thirds of the members typically do not vote.

Between 1970 and 2007 there were only two chairs—David Rockefeller and Peter G. Peterson—and from 2007 to 2014 two co-chairs, Robert E. Rubin and Carla A. Hills. At the same time there have been seven vice chairs who served longer than one year: Rubin, Hills, Cyrus R. Vance, Douglas Dillon, Warren Christopher, Maurice R. Greenberg, Richard E. Salomon, and David M. Rubenstein. Through a discussion of these ten individuals, a detailed collective biography of the organization's top leadership can be developed. Vast personal and family wealth, finance capital careers, top corporate connections, and cabinet-level government service are their main characteristics, and they exemplify the Council's deep capitalist-class connections.

David Rockefeller, Chairman 1970–1985

David Rockefeller was born in 1915 into what is likely the richest family in human history (the European Rothschilds being their main rival for this title). His grandfather, John D. Rockefeller, at one time held an estimated inflation-adjusted equivalent of a hundred billion dollars or more in today's values, far outdistancing even the richest individuals of our era. David grew up in the largest private home in New York City, surrounded by an army of working-class employees: butlers, valets, drivers, gardeners, nurses, cooks, and chambermaids. He also spent significant time in coastal Maine and the Hudson River Valley, where his family had enormous houses and estates. He was educated at Harvard and earned a Ph.D. at the Rockefeller-founded and funded University of Chicago. He is now, in 2014, the last Rockefeller of his generation, the grandchildren of John D. Rockefeller Sr.

As a man who has epitomized the Establishment, David Rockefeller is, fittingly, also one of the two most important leaders of the CFR during the 1976–2014 years. As this is written in 2014, David Rockefeller is revered as the still living legend linking the Council's past with its present. It is difficult to exaggerate his importance in several areas, including as the CFR's all-time leading financial contributor. Though exact amounts are not available, consider that during every single year since 1976, he was always ranked in the top group of contributors in the CFR's *Annual Report* listings, and that he often gave special gifts, such as one for "$25 million and above" in 2007.[43] This last contribution led to the renaming of the CFR's study program as the "David Rockefeller Studies Program."[44] The 2007 *Annual Report* called Rockefeller "a guiding force in the Council for over half a century." He first became a member in 1941, served as a board member from 1949 to 1985, and was Chairman from 1970 to 1985. Although he is now almost 100 years old, he remains, in 2014, the CFR's Honorary Chairman.

At the beginning of the new century, David completed a full-length book on his life and times with a one-word title: *Memoirs*. Although he lists by name no less than ninety-five individuals—writers, researchers, archivists, and commentators—including twenty-five members of his "immediate staff," who helped him research and write the book, it nevertheless appears to accurately reflect his thinking, his philosophy, and cultural preferences. As could be expected, a close reading of *Memoirs* reveals a person with a strong sense of class and personal entitlement, illustrated by Rockefeller's recounting of his and his wife's attempt to limit their household spending just after the Second World War, a time when they acquired "three rather large houses" in only one year. As he put it: "This presented a serious financial challenge since I had no capital of my own and was dependent on the income from the trust that Father had established for me in 1934, which in 1946 amounted to slightly more than $1 million before taxes." "Making ends meet," as this section of the book is titled, on that level of trust income was difficult, Rockefeller states, because taxes were quite high and they gave $153,000 to charity that year, leaving them with "less than $150,000 in discretionary income." Since they wanted the furniture they purchased to be of "good quality," they had a problem, solved by finding a dealer who "helped us buy many fine pieces of eighteenth-century English furniture at prices we could afford." He was happy that his homes had "style and elegance" on an income level that was, in his opinion, "clearly modest."[45] Census data point out, however, that the average income of non-farm U.S. families was about $3,000 in 1946.

David points out he learned the neoliberal "free market" economic philosophy at an early date. The conservative Austrian economist Friedrich von Hayek tutored him at the London School of Economics in the late 1930s. He later recounted: "I found myself largely in agreement with [von Hayek's] basic economic philosophy."[46] This belief in the efficacy of the "invisible hand of the market" was later reinforced during his graduate work at the University of Chicago.[47]

Rockefeller often stresses his and the larger family tradition of "noblesse oblige," or "philanthropy," but this giving was tainted by the causes to which he donated to and the ruling-class aims of undercutting both the need for state intervention and people's movements for fundamental change, promoting reformist "solutions" instead. Another purpose was to improve the "public image" of the Rockefellers and their institutions like the Chase Manhattan Bank: "The manner in which an institution gives expression to its relationship with the community has an important bearing on its public image. I was eager to have Chase perceived as a modern, progressive, and open institution. To forge a new 'image' . . . I wanted to transform our uncoordinated corporate charitable giving into a broad-based and carefully conceived program."[48]

Memoirs also starkly reveals the culture of illegality, corruption, and extreme commodification that pervades the higher circles of U.S. society. There is a sense that money rules and can buy everything and everybody, and that the rich are above the law. For over a decade, 1969–80, David Rockefeller was the Chairman and CEO of Chase Manhattan, the Rockefeller family bank. David Brooks, a "moderate" Republican columnist of the *New York Times,* stated that Rockefeller, "the leading corporate statesman of his day . . . spent much of his career at Chase doing business with tyrants. . . . Rockefeller was soiled by his close embraces with these thugs."[49] One illuminating example of the practices of the Chase Manhattan Bank and the larger corporate ruling class comes from this period. When Nixon and National Security Adviser Henry A. Kissinger were establishing U.S. ties to China in 1971–2, Rockefeller was very interested in gaining a top position for Chase Manhattan Bank there as a key part of expanding the bank's presence in Asia. As Rockefeller recounted in *Memoirs*:

> I asked Henry Kissinger for advice on the best way to get permission to enter China. He told me to contact Ambassador Huang Hua, the PRC's permanent representative to the United Nations and the senior Chinese diplomat stationed in the United States. . . . It took more than a year to arrange an invitation. Henry's support was certainly crucial, but astute marketing by one of

the bank's officers also contributed significantly to my success.... Leo Pierre ... filled a suitcase with $50,000 in cash and spent all day in the lobby of the Roosevelt Hotel waiting for the Chinese delegation to arrive. When they finally turned up, he presented himself to the Ambassador, explained his purpose for being there, and handed over the suitcase, politely refusing even to accept a receipt for the instant loan. Huang was impressed by Leo's gesture, and soon afterward the Chinese mission opened an account with Chase.[50]

Rockefeller then went on to point out how this initial contact led to his trips to China and eventually a correspondent bank relationship with the Bank of China. He clearly encouraged and approved of bribery of foreign officials to successfully gain favor, despite the law and the supposed "moral code" of the Rockefeller family. This illustrates a current fact about the United States, namely that the top economic and political leadership consider themselves to be, and often are, above the law.

Rockefeller also recounts in *Memoirs* his long behind-the-scenes role as a semi-official representative of the United States and its capitalist class, acting as a "diplomatic go-between" in China and the Middle East, especially while chairman of both the Chase Bank and the Council on Foreign Relations. Prior to one of his many trips to China, he met with President Jimmy Carter, Secretary of State Cyrus Vance, and National Security Adviser Zbigniew Brzezinski and carried messages from them to the Chinese leadership.[51] Rockefeller also used the Council as a means to promote the interests of his Chase Manhattan Bank. In 1977 he was invited to visit China by the People's Institute of Foreign Affairs

in my capacity as chairman of the Council on Foreign Relations, with whom they wanted to establish closer ties. I accepted the invitation with the understanding that I would also be able to discuss banking matters with Chinese officials. Nurturing the relationship between PIFA and the CFR was important to me, but I was more interested in prodding the Chinese to be a bit more imaginative about Chase's operations.[52]

In the Middle East, where Chase had major interests due to "its close and long-time association with the major U.S. oil companies," Rockefeller often met with many of the dictatorial and repressive rulers of the regimes there, including King Faisal of Saudi Arabia, Nasser and Sadat of Egypt, and Saddam Hussein of Iraq, giving and taking back messages to President Nixon and Secretary of State Kissinger.[53] Rockefeller preferred this unofficial, behind-the-scenes role rather than entering the U.S. government in an official position. Both Nixon and Carter asked him to serve as treasury secretary, and Carter wanted to appoint him Federal Reserve board chairman, but Rockefeller declined all of these requests, although he did successfully recommend Paul Volcker for the latter job. Volcker had worked for Rockefeller and Chase as a vice president, as well as the New York Federal Reserve Board, and, of course, was a director of the CFR.[54]

Another topic discussed in *Memoirs* is the tensions within the ruling class between old and new money, between "self-made" (often with the help of the already rich) and inherited capitalist wealth. The latter group is often listed (as David and other Rockefellers are) in the *Social Register*. David recounts how John J. (Jack) McCloy, a key Wall Street lawyer for Millbank, Tweed, Hadley and McCloy, a law firm closely connected to the Rockefeller family and its interests for many decades, and who preceded Rockefeller as chairman of both Chase and the CFR, repeatedly told a story in public that, David wrote, "always made me feel uncomfortable." Rockefeller said that McCloy told this story "in my presence a hundred times, the last time . . . when I succeeded him as chairman of the Council on Foreign Relations." David felt that the story demonstrated "ambivalence . . . even latent hostility" toward Rockefeller and his family:

> Jack was born, as he often recalled, on the "wrong side of the tracks" in Philadelphia. His father died when he was quite young, and it was only by dint of hard work and exceptional ability that he made his way through Amherst College and Harvard Law School, and on to a distinguished career. Despite his own great achievements, Jack seemed wary, perhaps even resentful, of what I appeared to represent in financial and social terms. . . . He had worked his way through college and law school in part by tutoring during the summer and had traveled to Maine in the summer of 1912, three years before I was born, hoping to get a job on Mount Desert Island. One of the families he decided to contact was mine. Jack always imparted the story at great length—walking the quarter mile from the main road up to the Eyrie, knocking on the massive door, and explaining to the butler why he was there, only to be turned away.[55]

As a professional who had risen through hard work into the capitalist class, McCloy obviously did harbor some resentment toward those, like David Rockefeller, who were born into vast inherited wealth, and therefore had their path through life made relatively easy and trouble free.

In 2012 David was at the center of a significant event in Rockefeller family history, the formalization of the long-standing informal cooperation between two of the wealthiest families in world history, the U.S.-based Rockefellers and the European-based Rothschild family. In May of 2012, the Rothschild Investment Trust, RIT Partners, announced that it would purchase a 37 percent stake in Rockefeller &

Company, the Rockefeller family wealth advisory and asset management group, with $34 billion under management. Lord Jacob Rothschild joined the board of directors of the Rockefeller firm, on which David Rockefeller Jr. sits, and of which David Rockefeller Sr. is honorary chair. At the time of the Rothschild purchase, David Sr. stated: "Lord Rothschild and I have known each other for five decades. The connection between our two families remains very strong. I am delighted to welcome Jacob and RIT as shareholders."[56] The Rockefeller family also remains strong in the CFR; the Council's 2013 *Annual Report* lists David and four other Rockefellers, joining his daughter Peggy Dulany as members of the organization.[57]

Peter G. Peterson, Chairman 1985–2007

The second long-term chairman of the CFR was the "in and outer" Peter G. Peterson, who served even longer than David Rockefeller. Whereas Rockefeller is a third-generation billionaire, Peter G. Peterson did not inherit vast wealth; rather he served at the cabinet level in the federal government and engaged in various business enterprises, including especially the Blackstone Group, a private equity firm that he co-founded in 1985, eventually becoming a billionaire. Born in Nebraska in 1926, Peterson is the son of a Greek immigrant father who owned a small restaurant. After being expelled for cheating at MIT, he still attended and graduated from a top private university, Northwestern, near Chicago.[58] He was then able to land corporate jobs and move up the ranks due to his intelligence, work ethic, and, of course, conformity to the needs and desires of the corporate capitalist class. One of those key needs is always growth, the endless accumulation of capital. Early in his career, Peterson worked his way to the top of Chicago's Bell & Howell Corporation, saying in *Forbes* magazine that his company was "committed to growth."[59] His friendship with Charles Percy, the prior head of Bell & Howell, led to Peterson's coming into closer contact with leading members of the Rockefeller family. One event was the 1967 wedding of John D. Rockefeller IV, currently U.S. senator from West Virginia, and Charles Percy's daughter Sharon. Another contact was through the Bell & Howell and Chase Manhattan Bank relationship, whereby Peterson became friends with David Rockefeller. A little more than a year after the wedding, John D. Rockefeller III invited Peterson to Rockefeller family headquarters at Pocantico Hills in New York's Hudson River Valley for a meeting that included John J. McCloy, then chair of both the CFR and the Chase Manhattan Bank, and C. Douglas Dillon, another CFR leader, a close friend of John D., and head of the investment banking firm of Dillon Read. Rockefeller wanted Peterson to organize and lead a major commission that would propose "reforms" to head off looming congressional restrictions on the foundations of the super-rich. Peterson stated in his memoirs that with this meeting he, a "Greek country boy," knew that he had connected with the top tier of the "American establishment." As Peterson expressed it:

> But any look at American foundations necessarily involved the inner sanctums of what was then the American establishment. Indeed, Jack McCloy . . . was widely proclaimed by people in the know in corporate boardrooms, the business press, and the lush apartments on New York's Park and Fifth Avenues to be the unofficial chairman of the Establishment, of this network of elite Northeasterners. Doug Dillon was certainly on its executive committee, as were the Rockefellers. This establishment had great entrée to the corridors of power and used their access and control with quiet discretion and great effectiveness. Their grip on America's major philanthropic institutions was particularly strong. To call upon a forty-two-year-old Midwestern outsider indicated they saw a serious problem, one that required a set of fresh eyes from outside the Eastern establishment.[60]

Asserting his independence, Peterson declined to head the suggested Rockefeller-funded commission until he had had a chance to fully investigate the situation. After meetings in Washington with leading congressmen, he determined the situation was serious and required a different approach. He again traveled to New York for a meeting with Messrs. Rockefeller, McCloy, and Dillon, this time at Rockefeller Center. Peterson recounted what happened at this second meeting:

> I told them I was deeply flattered by what they wanted me to do, but I felt the problem foundations face went far deeper than they might have imagined. A commission on foundation reform, supported by foundation money and foundation staff, would have no credibility. If I were to chair the body they envisioned, it would have to raise its own, non-foundation money, hire its own staff, and not include members from the foundation world. Total independence was a must. I saw John D. blanch as I spelled out these requirements. I don't know if it shook him to hear how badly the foundations were viewed in Washington, or to hear me insist on an independent commission. He probably thought he had made a mistake to propose this brash young Midwesterner, that I was presumptuous to look his gift horse of a well-intended offer in the mouth. To that point, Jack McCloy had sat quietly. . . . Now he cleared his throat and spoke into the resulting silence. "John, I have to admit frankly I'm embarrassed," he said thoughtfully. "I believe this young fellow is proposing the wise course. I should have thought of these concerns myself." "Do you really think so, Jack?" John D. asked. "Yes, I certainly do." Doug Dillon quickly weighed in with Jack McCloy, and John D. made it

unanimous. We set about to name our organization: The Commission on Foundations and Private Philanthropy.[61]

Peterson's contacts, his success in the foundations work and in other instances, together with his Republican politics (he was a leader of Illinois citizens for Eisenhower-Nixon, for example) later brought him to the attention of President Nixon. In 1971 Nixon tapped Peterson to head up the cabinet-level Council on International Economic Policy, with advisory responsibility to the president. Peterson soon became known as the "economic Kissinger." Peterson's natural focus was on foreign trade, monetary policy, and U.S. economic expansion abroad. In January 1972 Nixon appointed Peterson to be Secretary of Commerce. In that post, he supported the general free-market approach to political economy, including increased government support for multinationals, relaxing antitrust laws, tax cuts, financing for exports, and business-oriented government-financed research and development. In his early career, he was active in both the "conservative" Committee for Economic Development and the "liberal" Brookings Institution. Working as a leader in both organizations he made additional important friends and contacts. In 1971 he applied for and was accepted into membership in the CFR.

Peterson became close friends and a political partner with Henry Kissinger, but clashed with the far-right Republicans in the Nixon administration, resulting in his exit from Washington.[62] When he left in 1973, he was brought into Lehman Brothers as vice chairman. Later the Wall Street firm became Lehman Brothers, Kuhn, Loeb, with Peterson as chair and CEO until the end of 1983. Two years later he was a co-founder, with fellow CFR member Steven A. Schwarzman, of the Blackstone Group, which soon became a prominent firm specializing in private equity, mergers and acquisitions, real estate, and investment (especially for pension funds). Blackstone also created a more liquid and speculative branch, a fund of hedge funds called Blackstone Alternative Asset Management. Peterson became a billionaire while serving as chairman of Blackstone. In 2007 alone, the year Blackstone went public, he was paid $1.85 billion. While at Blackstone, part of the largely unregulated but vast "shadow banking" system, Peterson also served as head of the New York Federal Reserve Bank from 2000 to 2004, as well as chair of the Council.

Over the years, Peterson developed very close ties to David Rockefeller and the Rockefeller family. He has served as a trustee or board member of at least three Rockefeller family–dominated organizations—the Japan Society, the Museum of Modern Art, and Rockefeller Center Properties, Inc. Consequently, Peterson has had only good things to say about the Rockefellers. John D. III was "dedicated to maintaining one of America's premier legacies and converting family wealth to public good."[63] David was "a special person. . . . He seemed to have met every famous person in the world, and he spoke of global political and economic matters with great command."[64] In addition, Peterson said, "I have always been a so-called Rockefeller Republican, a rapidly vanishing species. I joke that there are only two of us left, David Rockefeller and myself."[65] In addition, "I was no longer young when David Rockefeller asked me to chair the Council in 1985. . . . That I, the son of Greek immigrants from a small, rural town in Nebraska, could follow David was a rare privilege."[66]

For decades Peterson has been a strong advocate of reducing the federal budget deficit, even critiquing his own Republican Party for overspending, stating in 2004: "I remain a Republican, but the Republicans have become a far more theological, faith-based party, not troubling with evidence." He is the founding chairman of the Peterson Institute for International Economics, the Concord Coalition, and the Peter G. Peterson Foundation, donating large sums to each organization. These bodies, especially the latter two, focus on fiscal sustainability issues, especially trying to set the stage for cuts to what Peterson and other elements of the capitalist class call "entitlements." But these so-called entitlements are actually programs like Social Security and Medicare that rank-and-file workers have fully paid for with their taxes. The federal government has borrowed heavily from the Social Security trust fund, threatening the system by leaving only IOUs behind. Peterson and the organizations he has founded and funded are trying to kill these and other programs that help working people survive, drumming up hysteria about budget deficits as a means to try to accomplish this end. This hysteria also aims to lower taxes on corporations and the rich.

Robert E. Rubin, Vice Chair, 2003–2007, Co-Chair, 2007–Present

Born in 1938, Robert E. Rubin was born into a New York City Jewish household strongly influenced by the culture of law. His father and his mother's father were lawyers, and Robert at first followed the same path. After a Harvard BA in economics and a year at the London School of Economics, he attended Yale Law School. Upon graduation, he joined a Wall Street law firm. Attracted more to a career in finance capital, he soon quit the law firm and was hired by the Goldman Sachs investment bank as a securities trader, starting a lifelong Wall Street career. Soon he was specializing in the arcane world of risk arbitrage, and he was very good at it. Risk arbitrage is a type of hedge fund trading, gambling on commodities, foreign exchange, and stock price movements, the latter focusing on "spreads" between the existing stock price of a company and an offer price, which requires assessing the varied risks in mergers, acquisitions, and liquidations by and between corporations. Rubin's skill at risk arbitrage and the two dozen or so years he specialized in it led him to both great personal wealth and the top of Goldman Sachs by

1990, when he and Stephen Friedman, another CFR leader, became co-chairmen of Goldman Sachs. Along the way he applied for and was accepted as a member of the CFR in 1981.

It was while at Goldman Sachs that Rubin became a key player in the Democratic Party, illustrating that Council leaders are active in both of the two main U.S. political parties. He was part of candidate Walter Mondale's "brain trust," both as a fundraiser and as a strategist in 1984, and was also a major supporter of Michael Dukakis in 1988. Both of these Democratic presidential candidates were CFR members, as was William J. Clinton, whom Rubin served as a key economic adviser. Once Clinton was elected president in 1992, Rubin was chosen to lead the newly formed National Economic Council and became one of the key formulators of the North American Free Trade Agreement. In late 1994, President Clinton appointed Rubin to be the nation's 70th secretary of the treasury.[67]

As part of Clinton's inner circle, Rubin helped him win a second term in 1996. As treasury secretary, Rubin was a vocal supporter of the repeal of the 1933 Glass-Steagall Act, allowing commercial and investment banks to be unified.[68] He resigned in 1999 and was replaced by one of his protégés, Lawrence H. Summers, also a CFR member. That same year Rubin joined the board of directors of Citigroup, and also served as a senior adviser to the company. Citi was a main beneficiary of the financial deregulation that Rubin sponsored during the Clinton administration.[69] Rubin is reported to have received at least $126 million in cash and stock in the almost ten years he worked for Citi. He quit Citicorp in early 2009 as it was on the verge of collapse, which was only averted by a $45 billion federal government bailout.[70] After leaving Citi, Rubin became counselor for Centerview Partners, an investment and private equity firm. In 2012 Centerview was financial adviser to Rupert Murdoch's News Corporation dealing with its intention to pursue a separation of its publishing and its media/entertainment businesses into two distinct publicly traded companies. Murdoch is also a member of the CFR.

In 2000 Rubin was elected to the Council's board of directors, and became vice chairman in 2003. In 2006, he was a founder of The Hamilton Project at the Brookings Institution, the stated aim of which is to develop innovative policy proposals to foster growth in the U.S. economy. In June of 2007 he donated between $1 million and $5 million to the Council and that year was named its co-chair, a position he still held in early 2015.

In 2008 Rubin continued his role as a senior adviser to Democratic presidential candidates, this time helping Barack H. Obama. Varied news reports place Rubin as one of Obama's main behind-the-scenes economic advisers. Rubin also recommended a number of his protégés, such as Lawrence H. Summers and Timothy F. Geithner, both members of the CFR, as well as Jason Furman of the Brookings Institution, for high political offices in his administration. *Politico* writer Eamon

Javers stated that "behind the scenes, Rubin still wields enormous influence in Barack Obama's Washington, chatting regularly with a legion of former employees who dominate the ranks of the . . . administration's policy team."[71] He has been a director of Ford, and is a member of the Harvard Corporation, the governing body of this leading university and the oldest corporation in the United States. His views on class issues were illustrated in a 2011 interview, when Rubin defined "class warfare" as existing only when one used "inflammatory language," not when government policies are enacted that favor the rich, which he argued has nothing to do with "class warfare."[72]

Carla A. Hills, Vice Chair, 2001–2007, Co-Chair, 2007–Present

Carla Anderson Hills, like Peterson and Rubin, is an "in and outer." She was born in Los Angeles in 1934. Her mother was reported to be "socially prominent," and though her father was not, he became a business executive worth millions, as well as the president of the Hollywood Chamber of Commerce. Carla grew up in Los Angeles and Beverly Hills, attending the exclusive Marlborough School for girls, playing tennis and riding in horse shows with the high society set. She attended Stanford University, studying during one summer at Oxford in England. A bright student, she went on to Yale Law School, ranking high in her 1957 graduating class. Soon thereafter, she married Roderick M. Hills.

A Republican, Ms. Hills was able to land a job in the Justice Department in 1974 after a number of years in private law practice. Her work at Justice brought her to the attention of President Ford, who appointed her secretary of housing and urban development in 1975. She was only the third woman cabinet member in U.S. history. That same year, Ford appointed her husband head of the Securities and Exchange Commission.

After being back in private practice for some years, Hills was tapped by President George H. W. Bush to be U.S. Trade Representative in 1989, serving until 1993. She was a primary U.S. negotiator of the North American Free Trade Agreement, as well as for the Uruguay Round of the GATT. Again out of public office, she co-founded Hills & Company International Consultants. Hills, a member of the Council at least since 1993, was elected a director of the CFR in 1994, and has been a director ever since, also serving as a vice chair from 2001 to 2007. She has also been a director of major corporations like American Insurance Group, AOL Time-Warner, and Chevron and has served on the international advisory board of JPMorgan Chase, Coca-Cola, Rolls-Royce, and the Center for Strategic and International Studies. She is chair of both the National Commission for U.S.-China Relations and the Inter-American Dialogue, and a member of the executive committee of both the Peterson Institute for International Economics and the

Trilateral Commission. She has served on a number of CFR task forces, including the Future of North America and U.S.-India Economic Relations.

Her husband, who has been a member of the board of directors of twenty corporations, and was a co-chair of the Committee for Economic Development, partners with her in Hills and Company International Consultants. Their firm offers advice and other services to big corporate clients like Chevron, Boeing, Bechtel, AIG, Pfizer, Coca-Cola, and Procter & Gamble in identifying both risks and profitable economic opportunities abroad, as well as negotiating with foreign governments to implement aspects of the neoliberal economic program, such as reducing taxes, tariffs, regulations, licenses, and investment restrictions, especially in "emerging market economies."

Cyrus R. Vance, Vice Chair, 1973–1976, 1985–1987

Cyrus R. Vance was born in 1917 and died in 2002. He was from an upper-class family long active in the CFR. One of his relatives was John W. Davis, a Wall Street lawyer (Davis, Polk) who was one of J.P. Morgan's attorneys. As mentioned above, Davis was a longtime CFR director (1921–55) who also served as the Council's first president, from 1921 to 1933. Davis was considerably older then Vance, but their closeness is indicated by the fact that Vance was Davis's adopted son. Both Davis and Vance were listed in the *Social Register*.

As was normal for an upper-class youth, Vance attended an elite prep school, Kent, then Yale, where he was in the secret society Scroll and Key. After graduating from Yale Law School in 1942, he served in the U.S. Navy until 1946. After the war, Vance joined the prestigious Wall Street law firm of Simpson, Thacher & Barlett, working there for the rest of his legal career, interrupted by several episodes of government service.

A mainstream Democrat like his adoptive father, he was appointed by President John F. Kennedy to be Secretary of the Army. President Lyndon Johnson then promoted him to the position of Deputy Secretary of Defense. Vance, following the CFR consensus view, was at first a supporter of the U.S. war on Vietnam, but later changed his views and resigned, advising Johnson to end the war. Within a short time Vance was vindicated and was appointed a delegate to the peace talks in Paris.

Vance was elected to the CFR board in 1968, and vice chair in 1973. During the mid-1970s he was also active in the Trilateral Commission. He resigned these positions in 1976 to become President Jimmy Carter's Secretary of State, but of course he remained a member of the Council. In this office, Vance represented the "good cop" in the administration's foreign policy, stressing negotiations in general, and specifically with the USSR, China, and Iran, as well as between Israel and Egypt. Carter's more hawkish National Security Adviser, Zbigniew

Brzezinski, also a longtime active member of the CFR and former director, represented the "bad cop." Once Brzezinski's influence became dominant, Vance decided to resign, and did so once Carter ordered the 1980 failed attack on Iran to rescue hostages. Vance was again elected to be a CFR director in 1981 and served until 1987. During the final two years of his tenure, Vance again became vice chair of the Council.

Douglas Dillon, Vice Chair, 1976–1978

Born in 1909, Douglas Dillon was also educated at an elite prep school, Pine Lodge, together with three Rockefeller brothers. He became a close friend of John D. Rockefeller III. He went on to Groton and then Harvard University. He and his family are, like Vance and the Rockefellers, listed in the *Social Register*. Upon graduation in 1938, he joined his father's Wall Street investment banking firm of Dillon-Read, now part of United Bank of Switzerland (UBS). After service in the Second World War, he was elevated to the head of the firm and became active in Republican politics, serving as a major fundraiser for Eisenhower in 1952. The new president soon appointed Dillon to be ambassador to France, a reward for his fundraising. Reflecting the beginning of a transition to Democratic Party dependence on Wall Street funding, John F. Kennedy selected Dillon as his Secretary of the Treasury in 1961. Leaving government service in 1965, Dillon became a CFR director, serving until 1978. He was also chairman of the Rockefeller Foundation and Brookings Institution, as well as president of the Harvard University Board of Overseers during the 1970s.

Warren Christopher, Vice Chair, 1987–1991

The son of a bank manager, Warren Christopher graduated from the University of Southern California and Stanford Law School, going on to become a longtime partner in O'Melveny & Myers, a large and prestigious Los Angeles–based international law firm. Christopher became the chair of O'Melveny and Myers, whose clients included major monopoly corporations like Exxon Mobil, Bank of America, Enron, and Goldman Sachs. Late in his career he became Deputy Secretary of State in the Carter administration, then served as a CFR director from 1982 to 1991 and as vice chair during the later part of this period. He was Clinton's Secretary of State from 1993 to 1997. Besides his role in the CFR, he was also a director of the Trilateral Commission, a member of the Bilderberg Group, president of the board of trustees of Stanford University, and chair of both the Carnegie Corporation's board of trustees and the CFR-connected Pacific Council on International Policy. Born in 1925, Christopher died in 2011.

Maurice Greenberg, Vice Chair, 1994–2002, Honorary Vice Chair, 2002–Present

Son of a Jewish candy store–owner, Maurice "Hank" Greenberg was born in 1925. He earned a degree from the University of Miami and a law degree from New York University. In 1962 he was hired to work for American International Group (AIG), and soon rose to the top of the firm, where he worked for over forty years. He helped make AIG the world's eighteenth-largest public company and the largest insurance and financial services corporation. Greenberg has also been the chair and CEO of C. V. Starr & Company and chair and managing director of Starr International, a diversified financial services company. He also serves as chair of the associated Starr Foundation. By 2006 Greenberg was worth $3.2 billion and ranked number 214 on the *Forbes* list of wealthy individuals.

While chair and CEO of AIG, Greenberg developed a close relationship with the Rockefeller family and Henry Kissinger, whom he appointed to be on AIG's International Advisory Board and hired as an adviser on business possibilities in a number of nations. Greenberg was also selected to be a member of the Trilateral Commission, a trustee of the Asia Society, Rockefeller University (where he received an honorary degree), and the Museum of Modern Art, all four institutions founded and heavily funded by members of the Rockefeller family. He also served in executive positions at the New York Stock Exchange and the Federal Reserve Bank of New York, and has been a member of the Business Council and Business Roundtable. At the same time, he became active in the CFR, serving on the board of directors from 1992 to 2002 and from 2004 to 2009. In 2007, Greenberg helped arrange, through the Starr Foundation, a donation of between $10 million and $20 million to the Council.[73]

In 2005 New York State Attorney General Eliot Spitzer charged Greenberg and other AIG defendants with "fraudulent transactions designed to portray an unduly positive picture of AIG's loss reserves and underwriting performance."[74] Greenberg appealed, and the case was still in the courts in 2014. Greenberg's career at AIG was over, but he remains a leader at the CFR, which named its Center for Geoeconomic Studies after him.

Richard E. Salomon, Vice Chair, 2007–Present

Richard E. Salomon, an investment adviser, born in 1942, has been a CFR member for decades and a director since 2003. He is managing partner of an investment advisory firm, East End Advisers, but more important, he serves as senior adviser to David Rockefeller, and also works for other wealthy families. His ties to the Rockefeller family appear to be paramount since he is a trustee of Rockefeller

University and the Museum of Modern Art, both Rockefeller family institutions. He also serves as vice chair of the trustees and chairs the nominating and governance committees of Rockefeller University. He is a director of Boston Properties, a trustee of the Alfred P. Sloan Foundation, is on the board of the Peterson Institute, and chairs an advisory board of Blackstone. Since Salomon has no known special expertise in foreign policy, his presence as vice chair of the CFR reinforces the view that David Rockefeller, the Rockefeller family, and old wealth generally continue to exercise an important leadership role in the inner workings of the Council. Salomon's wife is a senior editor at the *Wall Street Journal*.

David M. Rubenstein, Vice Chair, 2012–Present

The youngest member of our group of CFR leaders, David M. Rubenstein, born in 1949, is a co-founder and managing director of The Carlyle Group, one of the world's largest private equity firms. In 2011, he had a net worth of $2.6 billion, and was ranked 148th richest American by *Forbes* magazine. He and his two co-founders of Carlyle shared a payout of $413 million in 2011 according to the *Financial Times*.[75] Rubenstein has all the trappings of a billionaire—mansions in Nantucket and Colorado, a Gulfstream private jet, and an annual income of $135 million in 2012.[76]

As illustrated by the *Financial Times*, in 2013 Carlyle was the most geographically diversified of the ten largest U.S. and European private equity firms.[77] This meant that among these top firms, Carlyle had the greatest need for intelligence about trends and events around the world, something with which the CFR can obviously help. As examples of the connections of the firm, former French president Nicolas Sarkozy's half brother Oliver is a partner at Carlyle, as is former conservative British prime minister John Major.[78]

Rubenstein's early life focused on the law, and he earned his law degree from the University of Chicago after undergraduate work at Duke University. During the 1970s and 1980s he practiced law with two leading firms in New York and Washington, and also served as a domestic policy adviser to Jimmy Carter. In 1987 he co-founded Carlyle. Today this firm manages $148 billion, with twenty-nine offices and employing over 500 investment professionals worldwide. Carlyle's structure as a trust means that, unlike other buyout firms that have gone public, such as KKR and Blackstone, whose leaders are also prominent in the CFR, shareholders do not have the right to elect board members or vote on executive compensation.

Rubenstein joined the CFR in 2004, became a director in 2005, and gave between $5 million and $10 million to the Council in 2007.[79] Several other top Carlyle officials are also CFR members, including former IBM chief Louis

V. Gerstner Jr., former Air Force chief of staff General John P. Jumper, former Securities and Exchange Commission head Arthur Levitt Jr., and former Internal Revenue commissioner Charles O. Rossotti.

Besides being a Council director and vice chair, Rubenstein also serves on the boards or advisory committees of a number of important institutions, among them Harvard University, University of Chicago, Stanford University, Asia Society, Brookings Institution, Peterson Institute, Center for Strategic and International Studies, World Economic Forum, Institute for Advanced Study, Trilateral Commission, and JPMorgan Chase.

SUMMARY

The ten top leaders of the Council discussed above, with the possible exception of the Rockefeller-connected Salomon, are all clearly part of the capitalist class and especially represent the financial sector known as Wall Street. They often have multiple connecting points with this class. David Rockefeller, Douglas Dillon, and Cyrus R. Vance, for example, are not only very wealthy representatives of leading "old" capitalist families, but are also in the *Social Register*. Peter G. Peterson, Maurice R. Greenberg, and David M. Rubenstein became billionaires more recently, but all are tied to the Rockefeller family through being invited to serve on the boards of one or more Rockefeller family institutions. Robert Rubin is very wealthy through the stock options and bonuses characteristic of those running top financial organizations like Goldman Sachs and Citigroup. Warren Christopher was the head of a leading law firm. Carla A. Hills has herself been a director of a number of top corporations, and her husband, Roderick M. Hills, during the past forty years has served on the board of directors of twenty different corporations and been the chair or CEO of a number of them. So at least nine of the top ten Council leaders during recent decades are clearly members of the capitalist class, and the remaining individual (Salomon) has made his career as an adviser to David Rockefeller and Rockefeller-connected institutions. Eight of the ten—all except Hills and Christopher—spent a majority of their careers on Wall Street in finance or law. In sum, these individuals illustrate how the top leadership of the CFR has an especially close connection to Wall Street and finance capital.

Also worth noting is an apparent evolution in the CFR top leadership from those involved in commercial and investment banking—such as Rockefeller and Dillon—to leaders focused more on financial trade and speculation, such as Peterson, Rubin, and Rubenstein. The typical activities of Chase Manhattan Bank and Dillon Read during the 1970s and 1980s are clearly different from Blackstone, Goldman Sachs, Citigroup, and Carlyle in the 1990s and 2000s. Rockefeller and Dillon and their banks often organized loans for capitalist development. The second group of men and one woman often engaged in speculative ventures, like hedge funds and buying and selling securities as well as entire firms or parts of firms. This difference reflects what is happening in the internationalized world of monopoly finance capital during the same era. The top leadership of the CFR has therefore reflected what is happening in the larger capitalist system.

Seven of the ten discussed above—Dillon, Peterson, Vance, Hills, Christopher, Rubin, and Rubenstein—were "in-and-outers," and six of them served as cabinet-level secretaries in five different administrations, then returned to private business. In addition, David Rockefeller was asked by two different presidents to serve as secretary of the treasury, but declined both times.

PRESIDENTS AND LONG-SERVING CFR DIRECTORS, 1976–2013

As will be discussed in detail in the next chapter, the top leadership, together with the board of directors, make the important strategic decisions in the CFR. The role of the presidents, on the other hand, is that of day-to-day manager of all Council activities. If it is clear that the top leadership of the CFR has been and is dominated by members of the capitalist class, what about the secondary leaders, the presidents and directors of the organization during this period? There have been a total of five presidents who served longer than one year: Bayless Manning, Winston Lord, Peter Tarnoff, Leslie Gelb, and Richard N. Haass. A brief biography of each of these five individuals follows. Additionally, there have been 167 CFR directors during the period 1976–2013. Biographies of all of these directors would be tedious, and unnecessary in any case. This is because there are two major categories of director that stand out, those clearly members of the capitalist class, and those best described as part of a class of professionals hired to serve the capitalist class. Below is a short list of the longest-serving directors, which will serve as a manageable sample illustrative of the whole. The Appendix includes a list of the CFR directors from 1921 to the mid-1970s, as well as the 167 directors who served during the 1976–2013 period.

Based on career patterns, the capitalist-class sector, consisting mainly of finance capitalists and corporate capitalists, make up almost two-thirds of the total number of directors. The second group is characterized by their professional knowledge, their connections, and their intellectual skills. They make up a professional class, specializing in developing creative solutions to the problems faced by capitalism and their system, and promoting the system's legitimacy. This latter group is divided, about equally, into two groups: first, career academics, and second, lawyers, government officials (including military officers) and journalists. Many of these professionals are in the process of being assimilated into the capitalist class, and their membership in and service to the CFR often assists their advance to that level of wealth and status. One key way is gaining invitations to serve on corporate boards, where high pay is the norm; another is setting up a consulting or other business that serves corporations and the wealthy. Of the 167, only three individuals were connected to organized labor: Lane Kirkland and Thomas R. Donahue, as salaried leaders of the AFL-CIO, and Glenn E. Watts, the head of the Communications Workers of America.

THE CFR PRESIDENTS

The role of the president of the Council, a paid position, is to manage the organization and its staff in accordance with the desires and will of the board of directors and top leadership. There are two striking things about the five CFR presidents as a group: their service in government and their professional-class status as organic intellectuals for the capitalist class. Only one, Winston Lord, could be called a member of the capitalist class prior to his tenure as president of the CFR. This illustrates a central aspect of the CFR, its role in marrying the intellect of a variety of corporate connected professionals with the power of the capitalist class, under the leadership of the latter.

Bayless Manning, President, 1971–1977

Bayless Manning served as Council president from 1971 to 1977. He was a Yale University graduate who later taught law at Yale, then became a law professor and dean of the Stanford Law School. His expertise was in corporate law. David Rockefeller and Cyrus R. Vance reportedly chose Manning to serve as CFR president. After he resigned this position, he joined the New York corporate law firm of Paul, Weiss, Rifkind, Wharton & Garrison.

Winston Lord, President, 1977–1985

Winston Lord succeeded Manning and was president of the Council until 1985. Lord's family is part of the old plutocracy; his mother, Mary Pillsbury Lord, was a Pillsbury of the flour fortune. He became an expert on China, going into the government as part of Henry Kissinger's staff at the National Security Council during the Nixon administration. He then became director of policy planning at the State Department in the mid-1970s and an adviser on China. While CFR president, he became President Reagan's ambassador to China from 1985 to 1989. In 1993 President Clinton appointed Lord an Assistant Secretary of State. He occupied that position until 1997. His wife, Betty Bao Lord, was a CFR director from 1998 to 2003.

Peter Tarnoff, President, 1986–1993

Peter Tarnoff was Council president from 1986 to 1993. Tarnoff had been a Foreign Service officer who rose through the ranks, becoming a special assistant to both Secretary of State Muskie and Secretary of State Vance. He later became the executive director of the World Affairs Council of Northern California. President Clinton appointed Tarnoff to the position of Undersecretary of State for Political Affairs while he was CFR president. He then resigned as CFR president to serve in the government from 1993 to 1997.

Leslie H. Gelb, President, 1993–2003

Leslie H. Gelb succeeded Tarnoff and served as Council president until 2003. Prior to becoming president of the CFR, Gelb had a career in both the State and Defense Departments, then was hired by the *New York Times* as a national security correspondent, editorial page editor, and columnist. In between government postings, he taught at the college level and was associated with the Brookings Institution and Carnegie Endowment. He wrote a number of books before and after serving as CFR president, including *Power Rules: How Common Sense Can Rescue American Foreign Policy.*[80]

Richard N. Haass, President, 2003–Present

In a feature article in the *Financial Times*, Richard N. Haass was called "one of the most prominent members of the US foreign policy establishment . . . president of the Council on Foreign Relations, the influential New York think tank." He and his wife live on the Upper East Side of New York, near the CFR headquarters and Central Park, and also have a 300-year-old country house north of Manhattan.[81] Haass was a Rhodes Scholar, and earned a master's and doctorate from Oxford University, later teaching at the college level. Prior to being named CFR president, Haass was in and out of government, first as Special Assistant to George H. W. Bush and as part of the National Security Council. He received the Presidential Citizens Medal for helping to develop plans for the first invasion of Iraq, Operation Desert Storm. During the Clinton years he was out of government, working as a senior associate at the Carnegie Endowment and as a vice president and director of foreign policy studies at the Brookings Institution. When George W. Bush took office, Republican Haass was again brought into government, this time as Director of Policy Planning at the Department of State and a close adviser to Secretary of State Colin Powell. He left that position to become president of the Council.

In 2007 Haass was asked to join the board of directors of the Fortress Investment Group, a global investment management firm with over a thousand institutional and private investors. According to *Forbes*, in 2011 alone he received $210,000 in compensation from Fortress, including stock grants. He is the author of eleven books on American foreign policy, including *The Opportunity: America's Moment to Alter History's Course*.[82]

Haass in April 2013 wrote positively about Margaret Thatcher, the British conservative leader, stating that the United States should "take to heart" how she got "Britain's economy back on track." Haass sums up the central elements of Thatcher's program that he favors as follows: "privatization, lower taxes on income, a reduced role for trade unions—in short, the successful trimming of the role of government in the economy."[83]

CFR CAPITALIST-CLASS DIRECTORS

One hundred and three, 61.7 percent, or almost two-thirds, of all 167 CFR directors during the 1976–2013 years have been capitalists: they had assets of over $10 million, were longtime officers or directors of major U.S. corporations, or a principal of a major law firm. They inherited or married wealth or made all or key parts of their careers as power wielders in the capitalist-class-dominated corporate world. A number of these individuals are also known to be billionaires or near billionaires. One pattern for capitalist-class CFR directors has been a close connection to one of the big New York or regional commercial or investment banks—Chase Manhattan/JPMorgan Chase, Citibank/Citicorp, Lehman Brothers, Goldman Sachs, Morgan Stanley, Manufacturers Hanover, Lazard Brothers, First Chicago, Dillon Reed, First Boston, Brown Brothers Harriman, American Express, and Bank One. A second important group of finance capitalists were involved in the lucrative "shadow banking" system of private equity, mutual funds, hedge funds, and other investment vehicles, especially the biggest ones such as the Blackstone Group, Carlyle, Blackrock, the Soros Fund, and Kohlberg Kravis & Roberts. A third group are the CEOs or directors of a variety of giant corporations, including oil, pharmaceuticals, foods, telecommunications, technology, news/information, airlines, utilities, hotels, and manufacturing. Another, less common relationship to the capitalist class was as an officer with one of the Federal Reserve Banks, the New York Stock Exchange, or a principal of a major law firm. Several were also directors of insurance companies, and some also worked as directors of both financial and non-financial corporations, in financial corporations or academia, then in and out of government.

THE PROFESSIONAL-CLASS DIRECTORS

The CFR also depends upon the expertise of well-educated professionals—academics, lawyers, consultants, journalists and government officials—to develop and implement the initiatives and strategies best suited to the continuation and strengthening of capitalist-class rule. There are many former professional-class directors of the Council whose knowledge, intellectual skills, and judgment have resulted in their assimilation into the capitalist class. The primary criterion for such status is directorships in top corporations or law firms, which brings great wealth. The CFR directors discussed in depth below include several examples. It is inevitable that others, due at least in part to their connections developed as CFR board members, will in the future be brought more directly into the top levels of the corporate capitalist class either as officers or directors of leading firms or as owners of their own businesses directly serving this world. As this occurs, they will more and more directly reflect the needs, interests, and ideology of the capitalist class, and will become fully assimilated into this class.

Below is a list of the twelve longest serving CFR directors during the 1976–2014 years. Six have already been profiled here as part of the top leadership. The other six, representative of both the capitalist class and assimilating professional class directors of the Council, are profiled below.[84]

1. David Rockefeller, commercial banker, 36 years, 1949–1985
2. Peter G. Peterson, shadow banker, 34 years, 1973–2007
3. Carla A. Hills, corporate director, business consultant, 20 years, 1994–
4. Karen E. House, journalist, publisher, 16 years, 1987–1998
    and 2003–2008
5. Maurice Greenberg, insurance executive, 15 years, 1992–2002 and
    2004–2009
6. Cyrus Vance, Wall Street lawyer, 15 years, 1968–1976 and 1981–1987
7. Paul Volcker, commercial banker, 15 years, 1975–1979 and 1988–1999
8. Martin Feldstein, Harvard professor, 16 years, 1998–
9. Robert Rubin, investment banker, 14 years, 2000–
10. Richard Holbrooke, investment banker, 13 years, 1991–1993, 1996–
    1999, 2001–2009
11. Robert Hormats, investment banker, 13 years, 1991–2004
12. Steven Stamas, oil company executive, 12 years, 1977–1989

Karen Elliott House

In the 1987 board election, the CFR directors chose eight names from a list of over two hundred individuals suggested by Council members for eight seats on the board. These were Karen Elliott House, Richard B. Cheney, Robert F. Erburu, Donald F. McHenry, Peter G. Peterson, William D. Rogers, Glenn E. Watts, and Walter B. Wriston. In the election held in April 1987, all eight were elected by the members.[85] House, who first became a CFR member in 1978, immediately began to serve on the membership committee of the board, a committee she frequently served on in subsequent years, but was also on the Executive and *Foreign Affairs* committees.[86] House also showed her support for the organization by frequently contributing between $1,000 and $10,000 (above and beyond regular dues) to the organization as part of the "Annual Giving" fund drive.[87]

House, who started out as a journalist with the hawkish, neoliberal *Wall Street Journal*—rising successively to foreign editor (1984), president of Dow Jones International (1995), and publisher of this newspaper in 2002—represents an example of the professional class rising into the ranks of the capitalist class. Her expertise was the Middle East, especially the oil giant Saudi Arabia, and for decades she wrote prize-winning stories and then a book on this part of the globe. Her knowledge and insight, especially into the inner workings of the powerful Saudi monarchy, was likely one of the things that made her valuable to the Council and its leadership. She also spent time as a senior fellow at Harvard's Belfer Center, endowed by CFR member Robert A. Belfer, part of the family that owned and controlled Belco Petroleum, which merged with another company to form Enron.

Paul A. Volcker

Educated at Princeton, Harvard, and the London School of Economics, Volcker spent his career as a banker, especially at the Chase Manhattan Bank where he reached the status of vice president, and within the federal government, mostly in the Treasury Department, but also as president of the Federal Reserve Bank of New York (1975–79) and chair of the Board of Governors of the Federal Reserve system (1979–87). He served as a CFR director before and after being head of the Fed. As chair of the Federal Reserve, he had an important role in the rise of neoliberalism, which will be discussed in chapter 5. He has had strong connections to the Rockefeller family for many years, working as an assistant to David Rockefeller at Chase Manhattan, then later as one of several trustees directly overseeing the Rockefeller family fortune. Volcker was also chair of the Group of Thirty, a founding member of the Trilateral Commission, and a longtime member of the Bilderberg Group.

Martin S. Feldstein

Feldstein is another example of an academic who recently successfully made his way into the capitalist class. He received his BA at Harvard and earned a PhD at Oxford. An economist, for thirty years he was president and CEO of the National Bureau of Economic Research, with time out to serve as chairman of Ronald Reagan's Council of Economic Advisers (1982–84). He was also a professor of

Economics at Harvard for many years. While serving in these public and private positions, he was on the boards of directors of several major corporations, among them JPMorgan, TRW, Eli Lilly, and American International Group (AIG). He served for twenty-two years on AIG's board and a decade on the Lilly board. Income plus stock options from his service on corporate boards together with his income from other sources, such as Harvard University, the Bureau of Economic Research, and the federal government, allowed his net worth to grow substantially over recent decades.[88] At the same time he was receiving large compensation packages from multiple sources, Feldstein, as a conservative economist, was avidly advocating the privatization of Social Security as part of "entitlement reform." Equally hypocritical, he was on the board of directors of AIG when it received a taxpayer-funded bailout from the federal government amounting to no less than $185 billion, at least some of which likely went into his own pocket in the form of a large compensation package. Feldstein is also well connected internationally, serving on the Trilateral Commission and Group of 30.

Richard C. Holbrooke

Holbrooke was initially part of the professional class, serving in the federal government. He then was recruited to top corporate boards in the financial sector, thereby rising into the capitalist class. He received his BA from Brown and immediately went into the Foreign Service, becoming an expert on Vietnam. During the 1962–69 years he worked on a variety of tasks as part of the U.S. counterinsurgency war, starting with rural "pacification" in the Mekong Delta, then "Operation Phoenix," which organized the murder of tens of thousands of Vietnamese. Holbrooke also advised the U.S. ambassadors in Saigon, as well as President Johnson, and he ended this period in his life with the Paris Peace Talks as well as writing a volume of the *Pentagon Papers*. During the 1970s he was a journalist and State Department official in the Carter administration. In 1981 he joined the financial capitalist world as a senior adviser at Lehman Brothers. Within a few years he was Managing Director of this firm, serving in that role until 1993. He also served on the boards of American International Group (AIG), Suisse First Boston (vice chair), and Perseus LLC (vice chair). He was also a Trilateral Commissioner. Holbrooke later returned to government service in a variety of diplomatic roles: ambassador to Germany, ambassador to the United Nations, Bosnian Peace Negotiator, and U.S. Special Representative for Afghanistan and Pakistan, which was his position when he died of a heart attack in 2010. During Bush's run-up to the war on Iraq in 2002, Holbrooke strongly favored attacking Iraq, and in secret meetings with congressional Democrats he advised them in no uncertain terms to support the coming war. In short, Holbrooke was a hawk his entire life.

Robert D. Hormats

Hormats attended private schools where he received his BA (Tufts) and MA and PhD (Fletcher School of Law and Diplomacy). His initial career line was in the federal government, at the National Security Council, working with, in turn, National Security advisers Kissinger, Brzezinski, and Scowcroft. Then he worked in the Department of State as an adviser on the international economy. He joined Goldman Sachs in 1982, working for the firm for over twenty-five years and rising to the position of vice chair. In 2009 he was chosen by President Obama to be Undersecretary of State for Economic Growth, Energy and the Environment, a position he held until 2013, when he left the government and became vice chair of Kissinger Associates, a private consulting firm headed by Henry A. Kissinger. He has also been a member of the Trilateral Commission.

Stephen Stamas

Stamas was a Harvard graduate who went on to be a Rhodes Scholar at Oxford University. He also earned his doctorate at Harvard. Following a brief stint with the federal government, he joined Exxon Corporation, eventually rising to become a vice president. He was also a vice chair of Rockefeller University and a trustee and chair of the American Assembly.[89]

CAPITALIST-CLASS MEMBERS OF THE CFR

In addition to the capitalist-class top leaders and directors of the CFR, many Council members belong to the capitalist class. The fact that the CFR has always been headquartered in New York, by far the richest city in the United States as measured by number of billionaires and multimillionaires, is telling when combined with other data. According to the 2014 CFR *Annual Report*, there were a total of 1,604 "business" members in the CFR in 2014, by far the single largest group.[90] Professors, fellows, and researchers composed the second-largest group with 896 members. Although some of the business group are lower-level staff members of corporations and smaller businesses, a large fraction are part of the capitalist class, but we do not know exactly how many or who they are. Members of the capitalist class tend to be secretive about their wealth, and with over 4,600 current members in 2012, and almost 5,000 in 2014, a study of every CFR member, his or her occupation, wealth, and corporate connections is hardly feasible.[91]

The CFR has a clear bias toward accepting potential members who are wealthy and is an organization where members can meet, network, and form alliances with others who are also rich and powerful, further reinforcing the unity of those at the peak of the U.S. class system. Again, it should be stressed that though a variety of capitalists are represented in the Council, there is a strong tendency for financial capitalists—those who own and manipulate capital in its most abstract forms, such as stocks, bonds, trusts, hedge funds, and insurance, what can be labeled "fictitious capital"—to be most prominent in the leadership and, most likely, the membership of the CFR. The holders of functioning capital, invested in the ownership of the factories and equipment that puts labor in motion to produce commodities, are also well represented in the CFR but are less central to the organization.

SUMMARY: THE NATURE OF THE CFR

This chapter has illustrated in detail some central facts about the CFR, and why it is Wall Street's think tank. First, in terms of its leadership, history, financing, and much of its membership, it is a top-down capitalist-class organization representing the system of monopoly finance capitalism. Second, finance capital plays a central role in the organization, especially in leadership and funding. Third, what is best called a professional class also plays an important part; most of the Council's presidents are from this class, along with a substantial minority of its leadership and a large part of its membership. This professional class, with its intellectual skills, includes some who are clearly on their way into the capitalist class through the connections available to CFR leaders (especially by being invited to join corporate boards), and others who apparently are satisfied with just their professional work. The next chapter will review the internal history of the CFR during the thirty-eight years from 1976 to 2014, illustrating what Wall Street's think tank actually does.

2

THE ORGANIZATIONAL HISTORY
OF THE COUNCIL, 1976–2014

You don't go to speak to the Council; you go to get advice.

—TIMOTHY F. GEITHNER

A very influential organization. . . . There isn't anything quite like the Council. . . .
It's unique in its scope and level of expertise and experience that members share.
. . . it's a good place to meet other people involved in making policy.

—JEANE KIRKPATRICK

On a January evening in 1999 the Council on Foreign Relations held a dinner at its New York headquarters in celebration of their new meeting facility. The organization's entire membership was able to participate through new videoconferencing technology. Peter G. Peterson, the CFR's chairman at the time, later described the night's central activities:

It was the kind of event only the Council on Foreign Relations seems able to stage. With our beloved Honorary Chairman David Rockefeller presiding, the following Secretaries of State, Council members all, glittered onto the video screen: George Shultz from San Francisco, James Baker from Houston, Warren Christopher from Los Angeles, Henry Kissinger and Cyrus Vance from New York, and Madeleine Albright from Washington. For good measure, President Clinton greeted us from Washington, Council Vice Chairman Hank Greenberg joined us from Hong Kong, and U.N. Secretary General Kofi Annan delivered the keynote address. All, as you would expect, did a splendid job of talking about new world challenges and opportunities and

answering questions from our members. It demonstrated the quality discussions the Council, almost uniquely, can generate. It showed as well the
technological possibilities now open to us for conversations among our
members.[92]

Chairman Peterson's comments highlight the close connections between top
government leaders and the CFR, but also the need to pay attention to the internal
relations within the organization and its network of members. Such relations are
central in determining the way that the capitalist class as a community recognizes,
articulates, organizes, unifies, and acts on its own interests as a class and engages
other classes and class fractions in relations of conflict and consensus. The CFR
has been a pioneering organization in opening the world to U.S. capital through
the influence of its board of directors and its membership, studies, and meetings
programs. These four fundamental features make up the essential organizational
foundation of the CFR.

THE CORPORATE BOARD

The CFR is a corporation, and it is governed, like other corporations, by its
board of directors. Council members are like small individual stockholders,
interested in what happens, but without much power to change anything. The
board is technically elected by CFR members, but these elections are carefully
managed by those in power and mainly exist to legitimate the self-perpetuating
rule of the board of directors.

In 1981 the CFR had twenty-four directors on its board, divided into three
groups of eight, with staggered terms of three years. Following the Council's bylaws, a small nominating committee set up by the board took the 150 names suggested by CFR members and selected nine nominees for eight seats. In the resulting election, there was an unusually high turnout, 56.7 percent of those eligible to
vote actually voted. The result shocked CFR leaders—Henry A. Kissinger, who
had been a director since leaving the government in 1977, was the sole nominee
who was *not* elected. President Winston Lord quickly pointed out that the CFR
would continue to depend upon Kissinger's "vast experience and wise perspective in the years ahead."[93] The 1981 *Annual Report* stated what happened next: "A
number of Council members expressed their concern with election procedures
and the results produced. . . . Members were constrained to vote for eight out of
nine names," adding that "many considered this undesirable both for the members
voting and the candidates running."[94] Obviously, giving the Council's membership
a slight choice was considered a dangerous excess of democracy when a favorite
of the CFR's inner power structure was voted out. Within a few years election

procedures were changed, and beginning in 1985 the nominating committee was required to "propose a slate of nominees equal to the number of vacancies in any election."[95] This gave the existing directors absolute power over who would serve on the board, with the membership simply ratifying the selections of the nominating committee. In 1994–95 another change took place in the board's election rules, whose effect was similar to the prior undemocratic setup. Since that point in time down to the present (2014), three board members are elected from a slate of six (or rarely seven) chosen by the nominating committee, and three or four more are selected by the board. Therefore, the three (or four) losing candidates in each election can be selected by the board, or the board can select different individuals. Thus, since 1985, with minor changes, power has been even more completely concentrated in the hands of the existing board, and the membership has been less and less involved in the overall election process, with typically only a little over a third of the members bothering to vote in a given "election." The number on the board has gradually been expanded, and as of 2014 there were thirty-six individuals serving on it, each with a five-year term.[96]

The 2011 board election at the Council was typical of elections since 1994–95; members chose three directors from a list of six candidates selected by the nominating committee, and three more directors were appointed by the board itself. Only about one-third of Council members (33.9 percent), bothered to vote, but this was considered acceptable and within the bylaws of the organization.[97] Elections held during 2012, 2013, and 2014 had similar results, low turnout of members, three individuals elected to the board, and four appointed.[98]

The Nature of Democracy within the CFR

The CFR board election process makes it clear that like the nation as a whole, the organization operates under a form of managed "democracy." Elections are a democratic formality without real choice, and half or more of all board directors are typically appointed by the existing board. There is a provision for CFR members to nominate additional candidates by petition, but this has been done only occasionally, and in every case the outside nominee or nominees lost. In sum, the choices offered to members in selecting the Council leadership are limited to capitalist-class insiders. Voting on candidates from a preselected list is not democracy, rather it is the hollowed-out illusion of democracy. The point of such farcical elections is simply to provide a veneer of legitimacy. But it is also clear that most members do not care and are satisfied to operate under the hegemony of the CFR's existing power structure.

THE MEMBERSHIP

The second fundamental organizational feature of the Council is membership. The CFR has two categories of members, individual and corporate, and thus will be discussed in that order. In 1984, then-president Winston Lord described CFR's individual membership as "our most important and vital resource and audience," pointing out that even a "casual glance" at the membership list illustrates the "quality and range of American leaders who have been elected to join the Council."[99] The Council's 2011 *Annual Report* expanded on this by stating that it is a membership organization whose "ranks include top government officials, renowned scholars, business leaders, acclaimed journalists, prominent lawyers, and distinguished nonprofit professionals" who are "unmatched in accomplishment and diversity in the field of international affairs" and "discuss and debate the major foreign policy issues." They "have unparalleled access to world leaders, senior government officials, members of Congress, and prominent thinkers."[100] The 2014 *Annual Report* became even more specific:

> CFR's members are and always have been its most valuable asset, a pillar of the institution's strength, and an indication of its influence. The roster today counts two former U.S. presidents and two vice presidents (there have been a total of seven of each in CFR's history); twenty-six Pulitzer Prize winners; nine Nobel laureates; ninety-six Rhodes scholars; fifty-two leaders of *Fortune* 500 companies; forty-two special envoys; and sixty-two admirals and generals in the U.S. armed forces. Since CFR's founding, thirty secretaries of state have served as members ... the caliber of CFR's members is one reason the organization is able to attract such prominent speakers. [101]

These quotes illustrate the CFR's unique essence as a powerful body that is both a membership organization and a think tank marrying action and reflection—people of "affairs" with people of "ideas." Its life and activities are made possible through a membership that is a delicately balanced combination of leaders of capitalist corporations, especially in finance but also industry, communications, and law; leaders of intellectual life, especially in top universities, but also in journalism and other think tanks; and leaders in government, especially the federal government, but also state and local government. If any of these three main components get too weak or too strong, the Council begins to lose what it considers its true character. For example, in 2011 membership was divided almost equally between men and women of "affairs"—from business, government and, law—and individuals of "ideas"—including university professors and administrators, nonprofit employees, and journalists—(49 percent and 42 percent respectively), with "other" making up the remaining 9 percent.[102]

Individual membership in the Council is by invitation only. U.S. citizens with the time, interest, connections, foreign policy credentials, and the ability to pay high annual dues can apply, but the membership committee of the board and the board of directors decides who to invite to become a member. Potential members must be recommended by a current CFR member and be seconded by three other individuals, preferably also Council members.[103] CFR membership is always growing; it has increased from 1,725 in 1976 to 4,900 in 2014.[104] Once in the Council, as a regular member, one normally stays in the organization for life, as long as the yearly dues are paid. These dues are high, and there is internal pressure to make an additional donation every year. Depending upon age, residence location, and profession (business or non-business) members currently pay dues from a low of $250 to a high of $3,610 a year.[105]

On rare occasions, a member will quit the organization. Chalmers Johnson, a University of California professor who late in life became disenchanted with the Council and U.S. foreign policy in general, called and told the female staffer on the phone that he wanted to cancel his membership. She answered, "Professor Johnson, I'm sorry, sir. No one cancels their membership in the Council on Foreign Relations. Membership is for life. People are canceled when they die." Johnson, not missing a beat, replied, "Consider me dead."[106]

During the late 1960s–early 1970s the CFR recognized that its membership policies were outdated and needed a serious overhaul. Consequently, membership was opened for the first time to women, and the body also became more open to minorities and younger people, three groups that had previously been largely invisible in Council membership and activities. A five-year "term" membership category for people thirty to thirty-six years old was established to continuously recruit and train the next generation of foreign policy experts and leaders. Many of those in the term membership program have gone on to become regular lifetime members of the CFR. In addition, Council leaders determined that a better geographical balance was needed between the historically dominant New York, the rising Washington, and the rest of the nation. The need for a delicate balance dictated a very gradual approach, and several decades would be required to create a newer CFR membership. In 1977 Council president Bayless Manning made it clear that while increasing diversity, maintaining the right balance within the membership was of the highest importance. For example, the number of academics in the CFR had to be limited to the correct ratio compared to those from business, law, and government because academics can more easily allocate time to CFR activities, which could result in a tendency for the Council to lose its unique character as an organization connected to real-world policymaking and "become over-academicized."[107]

In 1978, the Council's *Annual Report* stressed the need for continuing the "sustained emphasis on diversifying the Council membership," adding that fully 42 percent of the current membership had joined since 1972. New members in 1978 included neo-conservatives like Richard N. Perle, Richard E. Pipes, George F. Will, and Norman Podhoretz, representing the beginning of a wave of neocons entering the Council.[108] By 1980 Council leaders could proclaim that the drive for geographic membership diversity was beginning to result in the buildup of clusters in key cities like Cleveland, Minneapolis, Houston, Dallas, Tulsa, Phoenix, and Los Angeles.[109] This was combined with steady growth in membership and activities in Washington, where, beginning in 1977, regular general meetings for area members were held at the Carnegie Endowment's Conference Center. By 1980 there were 450 members in the D.C. area, a little over half the number in New York.[110] Diversification by gender was so slow that after almost a decade of admitting women, CFR membership was still only 7.5 percent female.[111]

During the early and mid-1980s Council leaders also stated that they were trying to add "more spice from the left and right" to the organization.[112] During 1981 and 1982 this meant particularly more "spice" from the right as more neoconservatives were added to the usual mix of establishment moderates and conservatives. The new neocon members during these years included Richard B. Cheney, Paul D. Wolfowitz, Jeane J. Kirkpatrick, John D. Negroponte, Casper Weinberger, and Francis Fukuyama.[113] Few if any additions from the left were added, although apparently CFR leaders believed that a relatively few liberals represented a kind of "left wing" in the organization.

The Case of Condoleezza Rice

The process of diversification of the Council and the potential payoffs for the capitalist class can be illustrated with Condoleezza Rice. The year 1984 saw the election to membership of this obscure junior academic who would later play a key role as National Security Adviser and Secretary of State in the George W. Bush administration. Rice, in 1984 an Assistant Professor at Stanford University, became one of 228 female CFR members, and part of the 65 percent of Council members that had been elected to membership during the ongoing diversity drive that had started during the early 1970s.[114] The rise to prominence of Condoleezza Rice took place to a large extent through her association with the CFR. This was reminiscent of Henry A. Kissinger's rise to power a quarter-century earlier. Kissinger, a Harvard professor, had worked at the Council in the 1950s, wrote a book there, became a member, met and worked for Nelson Rockefeller, then solidified his career as a key member of President Richard M. Nixon's foreign policy team, later commenting to the CFR's leaders, "You invented me."[115] In Rice's case, she became a member first, then was invited to become a Council International Affairs Fellow during 1986–87.[116] During that year she also presided at some CFR meetings and was selected to serve on the board of directors' term membership committee.[117] Clearly satisfied with her potential as a representative of a more diverse CFR, as well as her service to the organization, the board then selected Rice to chair a 1988 task force on increasing minority representation.[118] As revolutionary changes swept through Eastern Europe during the 1988–91 period, Rice, an academic expert on the USSR, was invited to speak on these changes at CFR programs in September of 1989 and April 1991.[119] During these years of activity at the CFR, Rice met many of the individuals who helped her get better connected to the capitalist class and she was appointed to corporate directorships at Chevron, Transamerica, and Hewlett Packard, to higher positions at Stanford, and met and mingled with members of the Bush family. As a trustworthy minority female, well trained in the Council's worldview, Rice's CFR connection put her on the road to power, fame, and fortune as an enabler and legitimator of that worldview during her later years in government. Notably, her memoir conveniently leaves out these early years and her long relationship with the Council.[120]

The true role of women and minorities in the CFR in the 1980s and early 1990s is illustrated by the fact that in 1990 the Council membership was still 87 percent male and 93 percent white. After almost two decades of stressing the need to diversify and increase the numbers of women and minority members, the numbers had reached only 13 percent and 7 percent respectively.[121] During this period, however, there was a high level of loyalty within this membership. Chair Peter G. Peterson reported in 1990 for example, that over one-half of all members made annual gifts (above and beyond dues), to the organization, a higher level than any national organization as far as he knew.[122]

Membership since the Early 1990s

The year 1992 was a banner year for the Council, its leaders, and members as William J. Clinton, a CFR member, was elected president of the United States. Chair Peter Peterson reported that "dozens of other Council colleagues were called to serve in cabinet and sub-cabinet positions, as many others were returning to private life. . . . These appointments testify to the value of maintaining a pool of leaders thoroughly informed about international issues and prepared to assume the burdens of office. That task is one of the hallmarks of the Council on Foreign Relations."[123] Warren Christopher, the vice chairman of the Council, was quickly selected as the new Secretary of State. Four CFR directors—Richard Holbrooke, Donna Shalala, Strobe Talbott, and Cliffton R. Wharton Jr.—resigned to enter the government, and among those who replaced them on the Council board was

Richard B. Cheney, a future vice president.[124] Peter Tarnoff resigned as CFR president to become undersecretary of state for political affairs. Leslie Gelb, the *New York Times* national security correspondent, replaced him as the Council's president. Gelb immediately remarked that there were many foreign policy membership organizations and many think tanks, but only one had the strengths of both. This continued to be a key source of the CFR's "uniqueness" and enabled it to play a "special role," as "the world's premier foreign policy organization."[125]

Under the leadership of Gelb, the CFR intensified its drive to diversify its membership and spread its reach across the United States and into the wider world. One example was the establishment of a joint venture with the Los Angeles–based Pacific Council on International Policy. CFR members, officers, and directors all had been involved in forming the PCIP in order to further Council expansion west of the Rocky Mountains. By 1994 there were 358 CFR members in this section of the country, and the PCIP's purpose was to tie them to both organizations and develop CFR-type meetings and programs, especially on the West Coast.[126] At the same time, the Council's "Committees on Foreign Relations," in existence in dozens of U.S. cities since 1938 in order to strengthen ties to local power wielders, were transformed into new "Council on Foreign Relations" committees. CFR members in each city directly controlled these committees. As had been the case for over a decade, about a third of all Council members now resided outside of New York and Washington, and a more comprehensive and ambitious national program was now pushed forward more vigorously by Gelb and the other CFR leaders.[127] At the same time, the Council program in Washington was expanded, giving the CFR three main venues for its activities—New York, Washington, and nationally in varied cities around the country. One member, lawyer Richard Mallery, remarked that the Council was now becoming "an umbrella organization for the country."[128]

During the mid-1990s the Council printed in its *Annual Reports* quotes from a number of members focusing on what the organization meant to them. This provides a window into the organization at the membership level, and illustrates that an important part of what happens at the CFR goes on privately and informally between members who network with each other in a variety of settings, including within the government:

> The Council has given me a tremendous range of important associations. When I was on Wall Street, the Council allowed me to interact in a non-pressurized setting. . . . It also broadened my thinking quite a bit. . . . It has been a very enriching experience, both in terms of the people with whom I have been able to build relationships and also in terms of ideas.
> —JEFFREY E. GARTEN, Dean, School of Management, Yale University[129]

The Council is sort of the land of opportunity for a junior scholar. You are immediately dropped into an environment where you have access to an incredible array of people from all the communities involved in policymaking in your field—-journalists, top academics, heads of corporations, and, of course, policymakers themselves.
—ELIZABETH ECONOMY, CFR Fellow for Chinese Studies[130]

Outreach is an attempt . . . to expand the influence of the Council. . . . There is a generation of people within the government who routinely talk to their friends at the Council. These are people who would not move on important issues before they checked with people they know who are members of the Council, because they know they will get a perspective, a certain wisdom that they are unlikely to get anywhere else. Now what you're trying to do . . . is to get younger people in government to place the same sense of value on the Council, get them familiar with people in the Council, privately, discreetly.
—CHARLES G. BOYD, General, U.S. Air Force (Ret.)[131]

The most important thing about the Council is that it is an assembly point for committed people in the United States about foreign affairs writ large, a wider range of society than people who are pursuing policy. And it provides a place for both government officials from the United States and, just as importantly, officials from other countries, to come and make a public/private statement of their views on issues.
—JOHN DEUTCH, former director, Central Intelligence Agency [132]

I am involved in investing abroad, conversations with Council members who work in the same countries in which I'm interested give me a different perspective on some of the issues I may be addressing.
—NANCY GOODMAN, Attorney, Winslow Partners, LLC[133]

Membership activities over the next nearly two decades, 1995 to 2014, focused on expanding numbers and diversity of members, activities in Washington, in the corporate membership sector, and nationally, while maintaining the Council's New York base. This process of change continued to be slow; by 2014 women still represented only about 27 percent and minorities only about 16 percent of CFR membership.[134]

In 1996 CFR director Robert B. Zoellick, later prominent in the George W. Bush administration and head of the World Bank, remarked on the importance of expanding the Council's influence beyond New York to Washington and the rest of the country:

A national organization must have a significant presence in the nation's capital as well as a major presence in the nation's financial center. Washington is clearly the heart of policymaking and the policymaking debate. We never really had a base in Washington, now we do. We have foreign officials coming through, we have Congress, we have Council fellows; each offers opportunities to reach people that New York does not regularly reach. Looking ahead, the real challenge for the Council will be what it can do beyond New York and Washington.[135]

Indicating that Zoellick's call reflected a much wider consensus, chair Peter Peterson reported in 1997 that the Council was attempting to transform "itself from a New York–based organization into a truly national body—one that better reflects the diversity of the American body politic and its concerns and interests. . . . Now we are reaching further into America."[136] At the same time that this outreach was ongoing, the CFR was building up its now twin bases—New York and Washington. A new building was completed and occupied in New York in 1997, one wired with the latest interactive video-conferencing technology. The CFR.org website was also established that year. In Washington, larger offices and meeting spaces were occupied in the new Carnegie Endowment building next door to the Brookings Institution. There was a large increase in meetings, and a new focus on Congress was inaugurated.[137]

An expansion of the "national program" was also projected during this period, aiming at building membership and programs in key cities, including Los Angeles, the San Francisco Bay Area, Chicago, Houston, Atlanta, Dallas-Fort Worth, Miami, and Boston, with Seattle and Minneapolis to be added in the near future.[138] The aim was to create a solid core of Council members in each city, part of a network that could provide "real input into all our intellectual work."[139] In 2001 the first CFR national conference was staged, a two-day event with seminars conducted by CFR senior fellows and kicked off with an opening presentation by President George W. Bush's new National Security Adviser, Condoleezza Rice.[140]

By 2005 the Council's national program had expanded to over ninety annual sessions nationwide. The program included meetings of CFR senior fellows with Council members to discuss current research and share book drafts, reports, and articles in order to spread the CFR worldview and receive feedback and insights. This both helped shape the final product and involve "national" members (those outside New York and Washington) in the CFR's core activities. The 2005 annual national conference, attended by over three hundred members, was at the CFR headquarters in New York and focused on the occupation of Iraq.[141] Two years later the CFR reported that it now had programs in fourteen different cities and 37 percent of its members lived outside New York and Washington (that is, these two cities still had 63 percent between them). This distribution was not too different than was the case in 1981, when 31 percent lived outside these two key cities.[142] What had really changed was the large expansion of members in D.C. with a resulting reduction in the percentage of New York members in CFR (although not in numbers, as the organization's overall number of members continued to expand). This growth was reflected in the Council's purchase of its own building in Washington—appropriately enough located very close to the White House and called the "Boss" Shepherd building, named for a former mayor of the District.[143] That same year, Council president Richard N. Haass, who had taken over from Gelb as president in 2003, began to refer to the organization he headed as "the leading foreign policy organization in the world."[144]

In recent years, information about the CFR membership's views on foreign policy has become available due to polling efforts by the Pew Research Center in association with the Council. In November of 2013 the Pew-CFR team sent a set of questions online to all CFR members. Almost 40 percent of the Council members, a total of 1,838, responded. At the same time, they conducted a series of telephone interviews using the same questions with 2,003 people representing a sample of the American public. The most interesting results were in the areas in which the results from the public diverged most radically from the views of the CFR members. There was a serious difference, for example, on the issue of the relative priority that should be given in foreign policy to protecting the jobs of American workers. Fully 81 percent of the public group wanted this to be a "top priority," whereas only 29 percent of the Council members did. Results for earlier years showed an even lower result, in 1997 for example, only 16 percent of CFR members interviewed thought that protecting the jobs of U.S. workers was a top priority.[145] Similarly, 73 percent of Council members believed that it was mostly helpful when U.S. companies set up operations overseas, whereas only 23 percent of the general public agreed.[146] On trade issues, fully 93 percent of Council members felt that "free trade" agreements like the Trans Pacific Partnership were good things.[147] CFR members who responded also overwhelmingly believed that National Security Agency surveillance and drone attacks on other nations made the United States safer, although the public at large had a much lower positive response on these two issues.[148] These results reinforce the general point that, even at the membership level, the Council predominately represents the views of the higher levels of the class structure, those who are part of, or allied with, the capitalist class, in contrast to the needs and perspectives of whose who depend upon wage labor for economic survival.

Corporate Membership and Program

Another key part of the CFR as organization and network is its Corporation Service Program, for corporations that, by annual subscription, become corporate members of the Council. This program was started in 1953 and offers to executives of subscribing companies (both domestic and foreign-based) a series of meetings, discussions, dinners, conferences, seminars, workshops, trips abroad, access to the CFR's reference service, advice from members of the CFR's fellows and research staff, and (to those corporations who subscribe at the highest level) use of the Council's "Harold Pratt House ballroom and library." Additionally, "Multiple executives may take part in the Corporate Conference, a yearly summit on geopolitical and geoeconomic challenges." Benefits vary depending upon the subscription/membership level, the annual price of which in 2014 ranged from $100,000 for "Founders" to $60,000 for "President's Circle," down to $30,000 for "Affiliates."[149] As could be expected, the corporations that subscribe and become corporate members of the Council are the biggest, wealthiest, and most internationally oriented of U.S. corporations. For example, eight of the thirteen top U.S. corporations ranked by market capitalization are corporate members of the CFR. These eight alone are worth several trillion dollars.

There were also ten "Founders" on the CFR's corporate membership list in 2014, each paying $100,000 a year for the benefits the CFR offers to them. In 2014 the Founders were conveniently divided into three groups, five finance capital corporations, three oil corporations, an industrial corporation, and a consulting corporation.[150]

- **Bank of America Merrill Lynch:** This company has been called the world's largest financial services company and wealth manager. The *Financial Times* lists it as number one, with almost $2 trillion of assets under management.[151] Other sources list it as having $2.2 trillion under management. In 2010 Bank of America was ranked by *Fortune* as first in equity and the fifth-largest U.S. corporation by revenue.

- **JP Morgan Chase:** The website quotes chairman and CEO, CFR member Jamie Dimon, as stating that the bank's "aim is to be the world's most trusted and respected financial services institution." Second in assets only to Bank of America, it holds over $2 trillion in assets, according to the website. It manages the investments of many thousands of "old wealth" U.S. and foreign families. In 2010 JP Morgan Chase was ranked by *Fortune* as second in equity and the ninth-largest U.S. corporation by revenue; the *Financial Times* lists it as third in dollar value of global mergers and acquisitions in 2011.[152]

- **Goldman Sachs:** Although smaller in amount of assets owned and managed than the above two, Goldman Sachs is a leading global investment bank, offering a varied menu of securities, investment, finance, and management services. It ranked fifth on *Fortune*'s list of top U.S. commercial banks, and first in dollar value in global mergers and acquisitions in 2011.[153] Its current chair and CEO,

Lloyd Blankfein, is a member of the CFR, as are several other board members, one of whom, Stephen Friedman, is currently on the CFR board of directors. Robert Rubin, a former co-chair and co-senior partner of Goldman, is currently co-chair of the CFR.

- **Citi**: Another leading multinational Wall Street bank, it dates back to the City Bank of New York, founded in 1812. It was for many decades the largest U.S. bank, expanding through many mergers and acquisitions, and going under varied names over the years, including First National City Bank, Citibank, and Citigroup. It has long been both politically active (campaign contributions and lobbying) and CFR connected.

- **Nasdaq OMX Group**: Called the "world's largest exchange company," it owns and operates the NASDAQ stock market and a number of other stock exchanges worldwide.

- **Chevron**: Formerly Standard Oil of California and therefore part of the Rockefeller oil empire, this corporation is one of the world's leading integrated energy companies. Its own growth, together with large-scale mergers with Gulf, Texaco, and Unocal, have made it the third-largest U.S. corporation by revenue.

- **Exxon Mobil**: Another former Standard Oil Company, it is also one of the world's largest oil companies. Exxon Mobil ranked first in profits ($19.3 billion) and market value ($314 billion) and second in revenues ($284.7 billion) in 2009.[154]

- **Hess**: Much smaller than Chevron and Exxon Mobil, it is still a large multinational oil corporation, one with close ties, current and historical, to the CFR. The company's current (2011) chair and CEO, John B. Hess is a member of the CFR as are several other directors of the company.

- **PepsiCo, Inc.**: This is an integrated multinational food and beverage corporation, with interests in the manufacture, marketing, and distribution of snack foods, beverages and other products. It employed 274,000 people in 2013, and was the largest food and beverage company in North America measured by net revenue.

- **McKinsey & Company, Inc.**: This company has been called "the world's most prestigious consultancy" by the *Financial Times*.[155] It is also a large organization, with over 1,200 partners and 9,000 consultants worldwide. It provides what is likely the most expensive advice that top corporate and government clients can buy. The 3,200 clients that it has reportedly served during the five years ending in 2011 included ninety of the top 100 companies worldwide. Its estimated revenues are about $7 billion a year. McKinsey also maintains a secretive and low-profile family of hedge funds and private equity firms collectively known as the "McKinsey Investment Office (MIO Partners)" for its own exclusive use, with over $5 billion under management. McKinsey received unwelcome attention in recent years due to the insider trading trial and conviction of hedge fund boss Raj Rajaratnam. Two McKinsey partners, one of them, Anil Kumar, an individual member of CFR, were accused of passing confidential insider information to Rajaratnam. Kumar plead guilty to the charge.[156]

CFR *Annual Reports* point out that the corporate program "helps distinguish the Council from other think tanks. . . . Corporate members are an integral part of the Council."[157] With about 175 (depending upon the year) corporations and their leaders involved, this represents a significant source of income for the CFR and "an extraordinary reservoir of hands-on experience in many of the countries and with many of the issues that the Council is studying."[158] These issues centered around how to expand profit-making opportunities for U.S. corporations abroad, sometimes by working to weaken or overthrow governments that were standing in the way of the expansion of corporate capital.

During recent years, the CFR corporate program has organized over a hundred events each year. The most important is the annual corporate conference. Such conferences, starring big-name speakers, typically explore issues at the intersection of international economics and foreign policy.[159] For example, Federal Reserve Board chairman Alan Greenspan, long active in the Council, spoke at the second annual corporate program conference in 2005.[160] The largest category of corporate members were those with an especially keen interest in what Greenspan had to say. Non-bank financial institutions made up the biggest group of corporate members during this period, with over 30 percent of the total, and banks were another almost 11 percent, making finance capital the leading sector of the corporate program with 41 percent of all corporate members. Almost 25 percent were in services, media, telecommunications, and technology and 22 percent were industrial, energy, and power corporations.[161] In 2010 the corporate membership program held 300 events, while over 500 events were held for the larger membership.[162] How the Council helps its corporate members is illustrated by one of the CFR's responses to the 2011 "Arab Spring," when the corporate membership program had three conference calls. These were geared to corporate executives to help them assess current geopolitical business risks and opportunities in the Middle East and possible effects of the "turmoil" on international energy markets.[163]

Outreach beyond the Council's Membership

In the 2008 *Annual Report*, President Haass discussed a new aspect of the CFR's work. For much of its history, the Council had concentrated on being a resource for its members—regular, term, and corporate—along with influencing powerful "elites," especially top government decision makers and mainstream media.

In recent years this agenda had been expanded to reach beyond these constituencies to new ones at least partly outside the CFR's membership in the "broader public": college administrators, professors, students, state and local officials, the religious community, and non-governmental officials. As usual when it comes to the Council's work, this new outreach program was robust, with an e-newsletter called *Educator's Bulletin* reaching 11,000 subscribers, plus conference calls, academic modules for professors based on CFR publications, and regular communication with about 5,000 state and local leaders as well as about 1,000 religious leaders.[164] By 2012 this program had "greatly expanded its work in the academic community. . . . The Academic Initiative connects educators and students at the college and graduate levels with CFR's research and analysis."[165] In 2014 the Council's president proposed a new focus including reaching "advanced high school" students.[166] A "Higher Education Working Group" of college, university, and community college presidents and "select foundation heads" also convenes regularly for briefings on the global economy, Asia, Europe, and the Middle East.[167] An "Educator's Workshop" was also first convened in 2012 "as a forum for academics to share ideas and to solicit feedback on the utility of our materials for the classroom."[168] Also a part of this continuing effort to go beyond traditional foreign policy circles was the continuing outreach to the religious community; in 2012 the Council organized its fifth annual "Religion and Foreign Policy Summer Workshop," with over 100 participants from sixteen different religious traditions.[169]

STUDIES: THE COUNCIL'S THINK TANK, 1976–2014

The 1978 CFR *Annual Report* described four purposes of the Council on Foreign Relations. First, break "new ground" in the consideration of international issues. Second, "help shape American foreign policy." Third, "provide continuing leadership for the conduct of our foreign relations." Fourth, inform and stimulate the CFR membership "as well as reach a wider audience."[170]

The serious intellectual work needed to achieve these goals is carried out in the Council's Studies Program, its "think tank." The CFR's long-term approach to shaping policy and building consensus is illustrated by the following description of the Studies Program: "The Council examines the key issues in U.S. foreign policy today, considers what challenges the United States will confront in the next five to ten years, and debates policy options."[171] The board of directors and staff decides the agenda or "policy options" to be considered. In 1996 CFR director Robert D. Hormats, later a top State Department official in the Obama administration, but then vice chair of Goldman Sachs International, discussed the think tank and the role of the Council's professional staff, most of whom are called "Fellows":

Among the Council's most important strengths are its membership and the Studies Program. The two interact with one another. Through the Studies Program, the Council generates new ideas about foreign policy for its membership and the broader public. In a way, it is the spark plug for the Council. Now the Studies Program is providing fresh insights into a whole new set of issues, and many of the fellows are at the forefront of this country's intellectual probing as the issues change and new challenges arise.[172]

That same year another CFR director, Robert B. Zoellick, later head of the World Bank, but then with Fannie Mae, stated: "A key goal at the Council has been to build up a Studies Program that is on the cutting edge of foreign policy thinking. The purpose is to draw ideas from the studies that will be the foundation for outreach to shape intellectual and public consideration of these topics."[173]

The Studies Program is made up of CFR employees who anchor the think tank. In 2013 there were 123 such employees: 14 administrative staff members headed by Senior Vice President and Director of Studies James M. Lindsay; 65 Fellows; and 44 members of the research and program staff, most of whom have the title "Research Associate."[174] Working both independently and organized into study groups, they operate under the guidance of the Committee on Studies of the Council's board of directors. This committee must review and approve all CFR publications, generally written by Council Fellows, other employees, or members.[175] As of the mid-1970s there were three main types of CFR study groups. The first is the Author's Study Group in which a Fellow writing a Council book works together with other Fellows to complete the publication. The second is the Survey Discussion Group that produces varied written products, such as articles, monographs, or opinion pieces. And finally, the Current Issues Review Group, a less formal type of group, meets irregularly as required by conditions.[176]

The key programmatic challenge faced by the Council during the 1970s was what its leaders called the "problem of outreach," that is, how to successfully market the CFR's work product and in this way spread its ideology, reaching "wider audiences" to "make a broad impact."[177] This was partly solved by preparing numerous radio programs for National Public Radio, reaching an audience "approaching one million" that year.[178] This represented a "significant extension of the Council's general program" and helped the CFR effectively inject ". . . its intellectual work product into the body politic of the nation."[179] By 1977 there were CFR programs on all 196 NPR stations with an estimated three million listeners.[180]

The Council's magazine *Foreign Affairs* (FA), founded in 1922, is another venue in which the organization's work product appears. It "has been the leading forum for serious discussion of American foreign policy and global affairs."[181] *Foreign Affairs* has frequently been called the "preeminent" or "premier publication in the field." *Time* has called it "the most influential periodical in print," and it own website, ForeignAffairs.com, states that its goal is "to guide American public opinion." It has a paid circulation of over 150,000 and is distributed throughout the world.[182] This readership includes the rich and powerful globally, with subscribers having an average household net worth of $1.4 million. As the *Foreign Affairs* website expressed it:

> For brands seeking to command the respect of today's Influential Elite, there is no media like *Foreign Affairs*. We are required reading in Congress, at G-8 Summits, in the C-suites of Fortune 500 companies, and at Davos. Our influence on policy can be seen in Congress and the White House, the Pentagon and the State Department, and ministries and boardrooms around the world. Our articles are written by today's most respected thinkers and most influential leaders. *Foreign Affairs* is the fuel that fires think tanks, a catalyst for economic change, and the intellectual capital that inspires businesses worldwide. For advertisers, we provide an unrivaled opportunity to have the undivided attention of the world's most influential minds in business and politics.[183]

The magazine's board of advisers is made up of CFR members who constitute a committee of the board of directors, which in turn appoint the editor, who in 2014 was Council member Gideon Rose. A substantial percentage of the authors who appear in *FA* are CFR members, staff, or Fellows, but there are also many authors who are not. It is a key place where the foreign policy ideas of the Council community are floated. In 1994 CFR president Gelb described one of the key roles of *Foreign Affairs* as "setting the agenda for policy debates."[184] Articles by CFR people sometimes get the attention of government officials in Washington, resulting in a call to government service. Such was the case with Admiral Stansfield Turner's article on the naval balance in the January 1977 issue. The article reportedly resulted in Turner being tapped for director of the CIA.[185] In 2000, *FA* was ranked by an independent survey as the "most influential of all print media among government decision makers."[186] By 2014 *FA* was expanding into social media and was reported to have 900,000 Facebook fans, as well as 300,000 Twitter followers and its own iPad app.[187]

In terms of actual content, the work of the Studies Program during the late 1970s and throughout the 1980s was especially focused on economics, "both directly and as components of relations with our allies, the developing world and the East."[188] Key programs included a "Soviet Project" and a two-year "Future of Canada and the U.S. Interest" project that began in 1980 and was at least one origin point of the North American Free Trade Agreement that was signed by a former CFR director, President George H. W. Bush, in late 1992.[189] NAFTA's goal and practice was to open up Canada and Mexico to neoliberalism and U.S. corporate economic penetration. As CFR chair Peterson stated in 1989, since the world was headed into a period characterized by "sea changes," the Council needed to be in the forefront, playing a "leadership role":

> Whatever we may believe the new foreign policy agenda to be, it is clear they are likely to be strikingly different from much of the post–World War period. And the Board of Directors and the staff of the Council have decided that this institution should play a leadership role in defining these new foreign policy agenda, the root causes of these profound forces. The end product of this effort might well be to help define new and broader meanings to the concept of the national interest. Quite beyond difficult and substantive policy questions that must be asked, equally demanding challenges must be faced in the process of making foreign policy.[190]

Peterson was correct—the 1990s turned out to be a transformational period both for the world and the CFR. By the mid-1990s the Studies Program had evolved into a much different set of study groups than had existed two decades earlier. In 1997–98 there were five organizational forms/study groups only one of which had existed in 1976. Authors' Study Groups were carried over from earlier years; this form was employed to help CFR Fellows and Adjuncts write books, scholarly monographs, and articles through joint research, dialogue, and critique. The way this usually worked was to have the Fellow or adjunct write an outline or book chapter, distribute it, then use these written materials as the basis for discussion and possible revision.[191] By 1994 Independent Task Forces (ITFs) were initiated to study and discuss a key foreign policy issue, reach consensus, then issue a report with recommendations to policymakers and the attentive public. CFR members typically dominate a given ITF. These study groups are called "independent" because, although the Council chooses the topic and those involved, each group can, in theory, come to whatever conclusions it wants, and thus are supposedly "independent" of the CFR, which "takes no institutional position on matters of policy."[192] This argument fails to convince, however, since, as we will see in detail in subsequent chapters, members of the capitalist class dominate the CFR, and members of this class have definite interests and policy positions. The Council also decides to admit certain members who have clear interests and perspectives, excluding others, and decides what topics will be studied, and the composition of the groups that will complete these studies. Its leadership decides to publish some works with definite policy positions, to publicize/promote these works, and to communicate to policymakers and larger publics certain views about foreign policy and economic, political, educational, and cultural matters. The excluded voices include serious leading world-class intellectuals (Noam Chomsky to name just one) who recognize that capitalism is playing a profoundly negative role in the world and the class that owns the capital is conducting destructive wars, exploiting billions of people, as well as impacting and destroying the ecologies upon which all life on earth depends.

The formation of the ITFs was clearly undertaken to get around the traditional Council prohibition on formally taking specific policy positions, allowing the CFR to become even more explicit about taking policy positions. In the 2001 *Annual Report* chairman Peterson said:

> About eight years ago, Board Vice Chairman Hank Greenberg, Council President Les Gelb, the other Board members, and I faced a challenge. How could the Council increase its impact on the real world, which by its nature involves making specific policy recommendations, without violating the Council's tradition of not taking institutional positions on policy matters?... One solution: The Council would periodically create and convene independent task forces on the top foreign policy issues of the day. Each independent task force, comprising current and former policymakers, academics, and leaders from the private sector . . . would meet over the course of several months to forge policy proposals that would help resolve or manage international problems on a nonpartisan basis. Today, the real-world impact of the independent task forces has exceeded our most fervent hopes.[193]

For the CFR leaders and members involved, the ITF process requires high-level, but basically status quo intellectual work on key policy issues. In 1997, Gideon Rose, first a Council Fellow and now a CFR member and editor of *Foreign Affairs*, wrote about the goals and process of ITFs:

> In Washington, the discussion of policy questions is so heavily politicized and so generally superficial that serious intellectual analysis is sorely lacking. In the academy, attention to policy matters is considered evidence of superficiality or excess practicality, so there you don't often get a chance to marry rigorous analysis and policy relevance. Task forces provide a way to bring several worlds together—representatives of the political world, the academic world, the think-tank world, the business world, the NGO world, the armed services, the diplomatic corps—and pool all their talents and expertise. That's not an experience you can get in many other places, and I think it's one of the best things the Council can do for its members and for society at large. The objective is to try to shape the discussion that takes place at the highest levels, both inside government and out. These projects can help put issues on

the agenda that might not have been there before, and they can help generate potential solutions and get policymakers to consider them.[194]

A few examples of the successful work of the Independent Task Forces include a 1994 ITF on China and Most Favored Nation chaired by former secretaries of state Henry A. Kissinger and Cyrus R. Vance. They communicated their policy recommendations directly to President Clinton in a "timely special letter."[195] The 1997 ITF chaired by Robert D. Blackwill on U.S.-Russian Relations reportedly "contributed toward the forging of a consensus on the steps that the Clinton administration took at Helsinki."[196] According to CFR chair Peterson, the ITF began to have an even greater "real-world impact," exceeding "our most fervent hopes," in 2000–2001. During a Council-sponsored trip to Cuba,

> every senior Cuban official we met cited proposals in the two reports of the Council-sponsored Independent Task Force on Cuba. Not that the Cubans were positive. . . . In our meetings, President Fidel Castro and other top Cuban officials pulled no punches in confronting our group with their objections to many of the task force's recommendations. But the point of the task force's work was never for Havana to like it. The object was to prompt new thinking . . . the task force did just that.[197]

Peterson also noted an ITF that recommended engagement with North Korea, a policy adopted by both President Clinton and Bush II.[198] An ITF on Brazil "had resonance of major proportions."[199] Among its recommendations was that the United States use Brazil as a focal point for its policy on South America. Brazil's foreign minister immediately requested a meeting at CFR headquarters with the task force members, and when the president of Brazil later visited Washington, the ITF "findings were a focus of his trip."[200] At the request of President Clinton and his Secretary of the Treasury, Robert Rubin (both CFR members), an ITF on global financial institutions and financial crisis was formed. Its recommendations were the subject of much debate and "mostly praise." Peterson crowed: "Any time the most senior officials of the United States suggest we form an independent task force to help them solve a problem, that's a sign that our task forces—like the Council itself—are making a genuine difference."[201] In the Cuban and Brazilian examples, it is telling to note that the involved foreign leaders immediately, and correctly, assumed that it was the CFR itself that was responsible for the recommendations of the "independent" task force and engaged directly with CFR leaders. Since the CFR leaders did nothing to counter this assumption, it is clear that the Council's supposed institutional neutrality is an illusion.

Another type of study group is the Council Policy Initiative, used when there are important but highly controversial issues about which it is unlikely a consensus can be reached. Clashing views are outlined as a summary of the choices available to the national leadership, then posted on the CFR website and debated in CFR circles around the country.[202] There are also Roundtables, informal discussion groups mainly composed of CFR members, led by a Council Fellow, to help members keep abreast of important subjects and provide ideas and information for Fellows to write short articles, such as op-ed pieces.[203] Finally, Council Fellows organize conferences that focus on a broad political or economic issue discussed over a one- or two-day time frame.[204]

During the years at the turn of the twenty-first century two more innovations in CFR studies practice took place. The first was the establishment of a "Center for Preventive Action." The idea was to recommend U.S. government actions that might prevent violent conflicts from even getting started, thereby limiting the need for further intervention. President Gelb pointed out that task forces focusing on specific places in the world would be "the means for developing ideas and selling the prevention plans to the proper authorities."[205]

The second new initiative can be traced to CFR vice chair Maurice Greenberg's belief that there was a "new centrality and power of economics in world affairs."[206] Key nations like China, Russia, Germany, and Japan were all concentrating on economic growth and Greenberg felt that the United States should make a similar transition. Following Greenberg's lobbying, the Council formally launched the "Maurice R. Greenberg Center for Geoeconomic Studies" in early 2002 with Vice President Richard B. Cheney as keynote speaker.[207] CFR president Gelb had stated in 2001 that the "geoeconomist" was the "next generation of foreign policy expert" who could link the study of economy and finance to traditional strategic issues in national security, country and regional affairs, science and technology, drugs, environmental issues, and health.[208] Geopolitical and geoeconomic thinking had, in truth, long been at the core of CFR and U.S. government thinking about foreign policy. The CFR's War-Peace Studies program of 1939–45 had a geoeconomic as well as a geopolitical focus, as did the CFR's 1980s Project during the mid- and late 1970s. Part II of this book will explore in depth this worldview that has long been a key aspect of Council thinking and the formulation and execution of U.S. foreign policy.

By 2005 the number of studies program staff (17) working at the Center for Geoeconomic Studies was second only to the number of staff at *Foreign Affairs* magazine (18).[209] The numbers of staff focusing on other aspects of U.S. foreign policy were all much fewer during that year: Asia 11; Middle East 10; Council Meetings 9; Global Health and Environment, Science, and Technology 9; Europe 8; Washington Program 7; U.S. Foreign Policy 7; Director of Studies Office 7; National Security 5; Center for Preventative Action 3; Africa 2; Latin America 2.[210]

These organizational changes at the Council were framed by dramatic events that put foreign policy front and center in the political and economic life of the

United States. Within a week of the September 11, 2001, attacks on the World Trade Center and the Pentagon, President Gelb formed an Independent Task Force on terrorism, consisting of fifty individuals with longtime leaders Carla A. Hills and Richard Holbrooke as co-chairs. The group, labeled the "centerpiece of the Council's work" during 2001–2002, met twenty times to define, debate, and discuss the key issues, then wrote a report that was submitted to members of the Bush administration.[211] The CFR's *Annual Report* for 2002 claimed a central role for the organization during this period: "This year, perhaps more than ever, the Council's independent task forces have played an important role in shaping foreign policy. Decision makers in government look to the Council's task forces . . . to help guide their decisions."[212]

The CFR's role in setting the framework for policy decisions leading to the U.S. invasion of Iraq was also substantial. CFR Fellow and Director of National Security Studies Kenneth Pollack took a leading role, advocating war to force regime change in Baghdad when he wrote what chairman Peterson called a "trailblazing" article in *Foreign Affairs* in early 2002 and a CFR book that same year called *Gathering Storm: The Case for Invading Iraq*.[213] The Council's key role in the decision to go to war and the implementation of U.S. policy in occupied Iraq will be the subject of detailed study in Part II of this book.

Gelb retired as CFR president in 2003, succeeded by Richard N. Haass. In the 2003 *Annual Report*, chairman Peterson paid tribute to Gelb, pointing out that during his decade-long tenure, CFR programs sharply expanded, with the overall number of full CFR Fellows jumping from ten to seventy, and the Washington program's Fellows going from zero to twenty-three. Study seminars in nine key cities went from zero to over fifty a year.[214] Independent Task Force reports were "having more impact than ever."[215] In 2003 ITFs were studying Iraq, homeland security, public diplomacy, terrorist financing, and other topics, resulting in over a thousand news stories by nearly every major newspaper and news organization in the United States. New government policies followed.[216]

The change in CFR's presidents was to some extent connected with the developing situation of the United States in its war and occupation of Iraq. In June 2003, Richard Haass left his position as director of policy planning at the State Department to become CFR president. The *New York Times* stated that unidentified "friends of Mr. Haass" believe that he, as a close adviser to Secretary of State Colin Powell, was frustrated about losing some Washington policy battles. But Haass told the *Times* that he was not leaving out of discouragement; rather it was because he was offered the important opportunity to lead the Council.[217] A few months later, however, the *Times* quoted Haass as being worried about translating U.S. power into "lasting influence. . . . It would be tragic or worse if history looked back at this period and said we did not use our power wisely."[218] The *Times* portrayed Haass as an "enthusiastic devotee" of Henry A. Kissinger, and as a "beleaguered multilateralist" within the unilateralist-oriented Bush administration, and felt out of place by the late spring of 2003, and suggested that this is one reason he resigned from his State Department position.[219]

By 2004, there was a somewhat changed mood in the CFR and within the larger U.S. capitalist class. Some movement was under way from a world hegemonic (and unilateralist) approach to foreign policy toward a more cautious balance of power perspective. CFR leaders were worried about the possible weakening of the NATO alliance system, because of growing strains over how to deal with the U.S. invasion of Iraq and an unstable Middle East. As a result, an ITF on "Transatlantic Relations" was organized, headed by Henry A. Kissinger and Lawrence H. Summers. The stated purpose was to

> revitalize the Atlantic alliance by forging new "rules of the road" governing the use of force, adapting the North Atlantic Treaty Organization to meet today's threats coming from outside Europe, and launching a major initiative to bring about political and economic reform in the greater Middle East. The Task Force, which included former senior government officials, business leaders, and policy experts from both sides of the Atlantic, generated significant media attention on the United States and Europe. In addition to briefings in the United States, Task Force members took their report on the road, holding meetings and press conferences in London, Paris, Brussels, and Rome.[220]

During this period, the CFR also conducted studies on the issue of global warming, one product being a Council Policy Initiative in the form of a book by CFR Fellow David G. Victor. Meant to foster dialogue on a critical issue rather than develop policy consensus, Victor's book, *Climate Change: Debating America's Policy Options,* appeared in 2004.[221] It offered three weak policy options. The CFR's overall policy on this important topic as well as Victor's book will be returned to in chapter 8 of this book.

By 2005, the tenth anniversary of the CFR's Independent Task Force program, over fifty reports had been completed. The 2005 *Annual Report* summed up this aspect of the Council's work as follows:

> As Task Forces are intended to help shape the public debate on critical foreign policy issues, the Council mobilizes its resources to maximize the impact of Task Force reports, both at the time of initial release and as developments warrant. In addition to media outreach, the Council supports the efforts of Task Force chairs and members to reach influential practitioners in the executive branch, in Congress, and beyond.[222]

Task force reports from the 2004–2005 period that appear to have had an important lasting influence include one on "Iran: Time for a New Approach" headed up by Zbigniew Brzezinski and Robert M. Gates, and another "In Support of Arab Democracy: Why and How" co-chaired by Vin Weber and Madeleine K. Albright.[223]

The year 2005 also saw the first discussion of a new type of CFR product, called a Council Special Report (CSR). Introduced in 2004, CSRs are concise policy studies that aim at contributing to an emerging debate or a rapid response to a developing crisis. They are produced in consultation with an advisory committee of experts chosen by CFR leaders and are published by the Council.[224]

After the Council's Studies Program was renamed the "David Rockefeller Studies Program" in 2007, it was focused on what the CFR considered to be the four "most significant" foreign policy issues facing the United States in the twenty-first century: conflict in the Middle East; rising powers in Asia (that is, China and India); globalization; and the formulation of U.S. foreign policy.[225] Council Fellows, representing what CFR leaders called the nation's "preeminent foreign policy organization," were busy briefing government officials—263 separate briefings were given during the 2006–2007 fiscal year, for example.[226] These briefings included eight given to many of the aspiring 2008 presidential candidates, including Barack Obama, Joseph Biden, Hillary R. Clinton, and John S. McCain.[227]

The 2008–2011 years have been characterized by a gradual increase in Fellows briefings to U.S. and foreign government officials: 333 in 2009, 348 in 2010, and 438 in 2011.[228] At the same time, media mentions of the CFR have skyrocketed from only about a thousand in 2003 to over 25,000 in 2008 and over 37,000 in 2010.[229] A small section of these were articles and op-eds written by CFR Fellows: 350 in 2008, over 500 in 2010, and 570 in 2011.[230] At the same time the Council's website, CFR.org, was expanding rapidly, in 2011 reaching an average of over 1.2 million page views and 450,000 unique visitors each month.[231] The Studies Program also added a new publication series, Policy Innovation Memoranda, which targets critical areas where the Council believes new thinking is needed.[232]

The year 2011 also saw a major new CFR program, the Renewing America initiative, a prime example of "mission creep," that is, the recent tendency for the Council to expand its focus of activity beyond foreign policy to the domestic realm. The CFR leadership believes that this new initiative is needed because the underpinnings of U.S. global power are weakening as unsolved problems grow within the country. The first problems to be examined as part of this program were trade policy and education reform, with ITF reports from two different study groups, one led by Thomas A. Daschle and Andrew H. Card, and another led by Condoleezza Rice and Joel Klein.[233] Other ITF reports were on "Global Brazil and U.S.-Brazil Relations," which endorsed the Brazilian bid for a permanent seat on the UN Security Council and "U.S.-Turkey Relations: A New Partnership," which encouraged a new and closer relationship between the leaders of these two nations.[234] In 2012 the Council published an ebook, *Iran: The Nuclear Challenge,* edited by Henry A. Kissinger and CFR Senior Fellow Robert D. Blackwill. This volume "maps objectives, tools and strategies for dealing with Iran's nuclear program. . . . The volume aims to provide clarity on policy choices."[235] Reflecting the gradual globalizing of the Council's work, a U.S.-India Joint Study Group was also formed in 2012, co-sponsored by the CFR and Aspen Institute India. Intellectual, business, and policy leaders from both nations participated in this study group.[236]

In the spring of 2012 the Council published a list of its think tank scholars, its *CFR Experts Guide,* a list of seventy-four Fellows and other experts working at the CFR who produce a key part of the intellectual output of the organization, including books, reports, articles, and op-ed pieces.[237] The experts are also active in giving briefings and media interviews. At least twenty-three of the seventy-four have been or are university professors, ten have been or are journalists, and six are or have been business executives.[238] The index covering the expertise of this group, together with their biographies, is instructive, indicating the current regional and issue foci of the Council. Geopolitical economics, a concentration on the most militarily powerful and resource-rich (especially oil) areas and nations, is a clear theme in terms of the interests and expertise of the seventy-four. Each scholar typically has a number of issues and areas of expertise, so the numbers below add up to much more than seventy-four. By region, the number of these Fellows and other experts is as follows, with the nations most commonly focused on in parentheses:

- Asia, 28 (India, Afghanistan, China)
- Middle East, 23 (Iran, Iraq, Israel, Egypt, Saudi Arabia)
- Europe/Russia, 16 (Russian Federation)
- Americas, 15 (United States, Mexico, Colombia)
- Africa, 12 (Nigeria, Algeria, Tunisia)
- Polar Regions/Antarctica, 1

By issue, the most common areas of expertise for these scholars are as follows:

- U.S. Strategy and Politics, 24
- Economics, 18
- National Security/Defense, 18
- Business and Foreign Policy, 16
- Defense/Homeland Security, 16
- Economic Development, 15

- Public Diplomacy, 14
- Defense Strategy, 14
- Terrorism, 14
- Trade, 13
- Democracy and Human Rights, 13
- Media and Foreign Policy, 13

A large majority of these seventy-four are "in-and-outers," experts who have spent significant time in the U.S. government. The largest group served in the State Department (20), followed by the National Security Council (16), the Defense Department or as a higher officer in the Armed Services (14), and in economic institutions such as the Treasury Department, the Fed, World Bank, Trade Representative's Office, etc. (8).

Output of the Studies Program

The CFR's Studies Program has resulted in a truly prodigious output of publications aimed at influencing private and public policy agendas on a wide range of issues at home and worldwide. Statistics compiled from the Council's website (CFR.org) offer a glimpse of this output. A total of 185 full-length books came out of the Council's work during the 1987 to 2014 period alone. There were 1,796 academic and journal articles published by CFR scholars during the 1993 to 2014 years and 4,457 op-ed pieces during the 1998 to 2014 years. Since Independent Task Forces were first established in 1995, seventy-six of them had completed reports by 2013. There have been sixty-six Council Special Reports (2004–2013); 1,311 Analysis Briefs (2006–2013); 1,552 interviews (2001-2013); 198 cases of testimony before Congress (1998–2013); 597 podcasts (2006–2013); 201 videos (2010–2013); eighty-three Expert Roundup reports as well as smaller numbers of Policy Innovation Memoranda (30) and Contingency Planning Memoranda (19). These figures alone add up to over 10,000 products during the years mentioned, many more if a longer period is included.

MEETINGS: THE CONTINUOUS CAPITALIST-CLASS CONFERENCE ON FOREIGN POLICY

The fourth major fundamental feature of the Council is its meetings program, which amounts to a continuous conference starring global political, economic, and intellectual leaders. Council members are invited to attend a session with an important figure, introduced by a Council "presider." The photos and lists of meeting participants in the Council's *Annual Reports* over the years are impressive. To name only a few meetings among many over the years since 1976: David Rockefeller, presider, hosted on different occasions former President Carter, President Salinas of Mexico, King Juan Carlos of Spain, President Anwar el Sadat of Egypt, President Sarney of Brazil, Jessie Jackson, and President Mugabe of Zimbabwe. Cyrus Vance, presider, hosted China's foreign minister and President Mubarak of Egypt. Henry Kissinger, presider, hosted the King of Morocco, Secretary of State Albright, and President Jiang of China. Peter Peterson, presider, hosted former British prime minister Margaret Thatcher, Alan Greenspan of the Federal Reserve, Prime Minister Koizumi of Japan, former president William J. Clinton, UN Secretary-General Kofi Annan, and Vice President Richard Cheney.[239]

There are also informal, often unreported meetings between CFR leaders and foreign officials, reflecting the knowledge among foreign leaders that the Council represents the key capitalist-class power wielders behind the U.S. government. Only occasionally does information get published about such encounters. One such instance was when CFR president Haass wrote in the *Financial Times* about his September 2013 discussions with Iran's new leadership, which had not yet met with President Obama: "In my two meetings with Mr. Rouhani and his foreign minister, I heard flexibility on the possibility of giving up uranium already enriched to higher levels—but not going back to the day when Iran had only a small number of centrifuges. So it is far from clear that what will be enough for Iran in the way of nuclear capacity will not be too much for Israel or the U.S."[240] Here is a case where the president of the CFR had two meetings with Iran's new president, while the president of the United States was limited to one telephone call.

In recent years the Council has organized almost a thousand meetings of different types each year, mainly in New York and Washington, but also in other large U.S. cities.[241] The meetings program amounts to an organized dialogue mainly within the United States and world capitalist class, connecting the powerful but also the expert from many nations. It is therefore also a dialogue that includes selected professionals, as well as foreign political leaders whose cooperation is viewed as desirable. The meetings consist of both formal presentations from the powerful or knowing and informal discussions, all part of the ongoing attempt to assure ideological hegemony by setting policy agendas and frameworks, influencing governmental actions at home and abroad and developing ideas that will be put forward in books, articles, or CFR reports.

The formal meetings are touted in CFR's *Annual Reports* as venues where Council members can interact and exchange ideas with world leaders, top U.S. policymakers, and opinion-shapers. This process is, in a sense, dialectical; ideas are presented, those present react to these ideas with either a critique or clarifying questions and propose alternatives leading toward a policy synthesis.

The informal meetings that take place between CFR leaders, fellows, and members on the one hand and foreign leaders on the other also have the deeper purpose of assessing personalities, co-opting leaders, and developing relationships. There is usually a gross power imbalance when a leader of a relatively small and weak nation travels to meet the leaders of what is the most powerful nation the world has ever known. A subtle type of informal negotiation often ensues in which access to the weaker nation's people and resources are exchanged for current or future political-economic-military support. This process encourages corruption: the foreign leader is pressured to adopt the interests and ideology of the more powerful nation and sell out his or her nation's sovereignty and national interests. This ongoing process in the context of corporate globalization and the empire of neoliberal geopolitics has resulted in the serious loss of sovereignty for numerous nations, and personal tragedies for uncounted millions of people.

The Council's meetings program has held thousands of meetings since 1976, too many to cover adequately here. The essence of the meetings program will be summarized through a brief review of meetings during four different fiscal years, each ten years apart. These years will be 1975–76, 1985–86, 1995–96, and 2005–2006. In addition, three of the Council's leadership trips to foreign countries will be covered to add further depth to our understanding of the CFR meetings program.

The 1975–1976 Meetings

The over a hundred meetings in the 1975–76 fiscal year all took place in New York City.[242] One of the highlights of that year was CIA head George H. W. Bush speaking on China. Soon chosen as a CFR director, in a little over a decade Bush would be elected U.S. president. Another high point was UN Secretary-General Kurt Waldheim who discussed the UN's role in the Middle East. Other important speakers included Paul A. Volcker, soon to take over as Federal Reserve chair, speaking on the international monetary system; Margaret Thatcher, future prime minister of Britain, on conservatism; King Juan Carlos I on Spain; future president of France François Mitterrand on his nation's foreign policy, and Italian industrialist Giovanni Agnelli on Western Europe.[243]

The 1985–1986 Meetings

The 1985–86 meetings program was also centered in New York City, but a few of the approximately 130 meetings were held in Washington and Los Angeles, illustrating the beginning of a long-lasting trend of expanding meetings to locations outside of New York.[244] Planning for the fiscal year's meetings began, as usual, in the spring, "assessing the areas and persons we hoped to include in a substantive, provocative and well-balanced program."[245] Council organizers also pointed out that an invitation to the CFR to discuss major issues in no way represented an endorsement of a person or a position, only a recognition that the individual represented a significant aspect of a given debate.[246]

This year saw a large spike in meetings on Africa, the result of the growing crisis in Southern Africa, as liberation movements—the African National Congress in South Africa and the Southwest African People's Organization (SWAPO) in Namibia—grew in strength in their fight to overthrow the oppressive apartheid regime. Closely connected with these struggles was the war in Angola, where efforts of Cuban military volunteers to protect the Angolan government against South African aggression had been successful. Many of the key players in this appeared at CFR meetings to discuss the situation, and twelve of the fifteen Africa meetings that year focused on what the CFR called the "critical situation in Southern Africa."[247] Among those who spoke to and interacted with Council leaders and members were President Jose Eduardo dos Santos of Angola, the Secretary-General of SWAPO, and Jonas Savimbi, the leader of the CIA supported National Union for the Total Independence of Angola (UNITA), then engaged in a civil war to overthrow the Angloan government. The 1986 *Annual Report* summed up the other meetings/discussions on Southern Africa as follows:

> We heard from Olusegun Obasanjo, former President of Nigeria and co-chairman of the Commonwealth Group of Eminent Persons which was formed to seek a non-violent solution to the situation in South Africa; from Samora Moises Machel, President of Mozambique, on the impact of the conditions in South Africa on the surrounding states; and from South African leaders in business, religion, education and politics.[248]

One key Council concern was to help manage a transition of power to the majority in South Africa that would preserve and even enhance U.S. and Western capitalist interests, an aim that was successfully achieved over the next decade.

The 1995–1996 Meetings

CFR meetings on October 23, 1995, illustrated the organization's impressive convening power: "The Harold Pratt House rang with many different voices all at once. On one single fall day, the Council hosted Cuban President Fidel Castro Ruz, PLO leader Yasser Arafat, Uzbekistani President Islam Karimov, and Czech Republic President Vaclav Havel."[249]

By this point in time, the CFR's meetings program had expanded to include three separate elements: the New York program, still the largest and most important; the corporate meetings program; and a smaller national meetings program. The major foci of the New York meetings during 1995–96 were twenty-four sessions on Europe/Russia. The high number of meetings was due to the need to focus on and take advantage of the transition to neoliberal "free market" capitalism going on in Eastern Europe and the nations of the former USSR. Highlights of the Europe/Russia meetings program included presentations by the president of Albania, the former head of the European Commission, the prime minister of Greece, the Minister of Foreign Affairs of Hungary, the former Economics Minister of Germany, the former Minister of Foreign Affairs for Russia, the former USSR ambassador to the United States, representatives to the United Nations from Yugoslavia, Croatia, and Bosnia Herzegovina, and Russian writer and poet Yevgeny Yevtushenko.

The 2005–2006 Meetings

By 2005 the Council had altered the format of its *Annual Report* to only sum up the meetings and other CFR programs, not cover them in detail. The New York meetings program held over 130 events with a "strong focus on Iraq and other developments in the Middle East, U.S. intelligence, and the war on terrorism."[250] The CFR's own summary of the key features of the year's New York meetings was as follows:

Fifteen heads of state and chief ministers offered Council members their unique perspectives on world events. Mexican President Vicente Fox presented his views on Mexico's economy and democracy. Turkish Prime Minister Recep Tayyip Erdogan assessed the recent history and current state of U.S.-Turkey relations. Nigeria's President Olusegun Obasanjo discussed corruption and other challenges facing his country; and Spanish Prime Minister Jose Luis Rodriguez Zapatero focused on Spain's commitment to fighting terrorism. Insights from the Middle East were provided by Saudi Foreign Minister Prince Saud al-Faisal, who made the case for fighting extremism, and Qatari Foreign Minister Sheikh Hamad bin Jassim bin Jabir al-Thani, who outlined his view of a strategic partnership with the United States....

Council members also had the opportunity to exchange ideas with numerous current or former U.S. government officials. Former president Jimmy Carter assessed obstacles and chances for peace in the Israeli-Palestinian conflict, Secretary of Defense Donald H. Rumsfeld outlined the challenges for U.S. forces in today's media age, Attorney General Alberto R. Gonzales engaged members in a discussion about the war on terrorism, and Secretary of Homeland Security Michael Chertoff reviewed his priorities for maritime, air, and land security. In addition, Director of National Intelligence John D. Negroponte discussed challenges for U.S. intelligence policy.[251]

The Washington meetings program of 2005–2006 focused on bringing CFR members and leaders together with representatives from the Bush administration, including President George W. Bush, who spoke to the Council on the progress of the war in Iraq; Congress (eleven sitting members of Congress addressed the CFR, including Senator Barack Obama), business leaders, and discussions with ambassadors from a number of nations.[252]

The National meetings program held 110 sessions across the country, events that included manuscript review seminars, roundtables, the National Book Club Series, a film series, and general meetings. In contrast to the New York program, only a few foreign leaders attended the National program events, which were mainly focused on presentations and discussions led by CFR leaders and experts, evidently aimed at educating and influencing CFR members and attentive publics in various cities.[253]

CFR CORPORATE PROGRAM AND ITS FOREIGN TRIPS

The CFR described the 2005–2006 Corporate Program as follows:

Executives of member companies and individual members in the private sector took part in over seventy events in New York and Washington, DC, including the C. Peter McColough Roundtable Series on International Economics, the McKinsey Executive Roundtable Series on International Economics, the Corporate Program Energy Roundtable, the China Roundtable, and the World Economic Update Series. Featured speakers included four past chairs of the Securities and Exchange Commission, European Central Bank President Jean-Claude Trichet, and Ambassador of Saudi Arabia to the United States Prince Turki al-Faisal.

A highlight of this past year was the Council's second annual Corporate Conference held March 9–10 in New York City. The conference explored the economic and political vulnerabilities in the global system through sessions on global energy supply, corporate governance and social responsibility, the economic threat of a flu pandemic, China, India, and Europe. The CEOs of Caterpillar, Electronic Data Systems, and Estée Lauder opened the conference with a lively panel discussion, and U.S. Trade Representative Rob Portman served as the event's keynote speaker. . . . The Corporate Program also offered over thirty interactive conference calls with business and foreign policy specialists, including fellows from the Council's Maurice R. Greenberg Center for Geoeconomic Studies and other experts. Corporate members exchanged ideas with Council scholars in other settings as well, such as roundtable discussions, exclusive dinners and receptions, and private meetings.[254]

During the 1987–90 period, the CFR's *Annual Report* offered specifics on three corporate program trips taken by Council leaders. Over the years there were many such trips, but most were merely referred to, not covered in detail, such as the CFR trip to Cuba mentioned in the 2001 *Annual Report*, when CFR chair Peterson only mentioned that the CFR group met with President Fidel Castro and other "top Cuban officials." [255]

The 1987 *Annual Report* stated that the CFR's corporate program sponsored a "Middle East Trip" from April 21 to April 29, 1987. Council participants were not listed, but these top leaders of the three nations visited held meetings with the CFR group:

- **Jordan:** King Hussein, prime minister Zeid Al-Rifai, and Minister of Foreign Affairs Taher Al-Masri
- **Egypt:** President Hosni Mubarak, Prime Minister Atef Sedki, Minister of Foreign Affairs Ahmed Abdel Meguid
- **Israel:** Prime Minister Yitzhak Shamir, Foreign Minister Shimon Peres, Defense Minister Yitzhak Rabin.[256]

The 1989 *Annual Report* offered even more details about a trip to Poland and Hungary from February 28 to March 8. This time the Council participants were also listed. David Rockefeller and Peter G. Peterson led the CFR delegation. Others on the trip included *Washington Post* owner Katharine Graham and John C. Whitehead, a close associate of the Rockefeller family, former Reagan State Department official and retired chair of Goldman Sachs and the Federal Reserve Bank of New York; CFR president Peter Tarnoff; William and Linda Dietel, he a former president of Rockefeller Brothers Fund; Richard and Isabel Furlaud, he a president of Bristol-Myers Squibb and Chair Emeritus of the Board of Trustees of Rockefeller University. Several experts on Eastern Europe were also included, among them Columbia University political science professor Seweryn Bialer and CFR Senior Fellow Michael Mandelbaum.[257] In sum, the group was a mix of CFR leaders, business executives closely connected to the Rockefeller family economic and cultural empire, and experts who could provide insights about the political, economic, and cultural situation in Poland and Hungary as these countries stood on the verge of big changes as the Soviet Union began to disintegrate.

On the Polish side, the CFR group met with fifteen of the nation's leaders, including the president of the Council of State, General Wojciech Jaruzelski, as well as the prime minister; Foreign Minister; Minister for Foreign Economic Cooperation; Finance Minister; Minister for Industry; and the Secretary of the Polish United Workers Party who was also a member of the Politburo. Besides government officials, the CFR group also met with opposition figures, including Lech Walesa, chairman of Solidarity; Professor Andrzej Stelmachowski, the chief Solidarity negotiator with the Polish government; and Cardinal Glemp.[258] Hungary's representatives who met with the CFR trip participants included the prime minister; the Minister of State; the Minister of Trade; the head of the Hungarian Socialist Workers Party, and the Secretary of the Central Committee of that party.[259]

The 1990 *Annual Report* provides specifics about a February 2 to 10 trip to the Persian Gulf, listing the CFR participants as well as those they met with in Saudi Arabia, Kuwait, and Oman. David Rockefeller and Peter G. Peterson again led the Council excursion, which was dominated by CEOs of leading firms. The business leaders who were part of the CFR group included James Burke of Johnson & Johnson; Albert Gordon of Kidder Peabody; Peter Haas of Levi Strauss; William A. Hewitt of Deere & Co.; William D. Mulholland of Bank of Montreal, Harris Bank, Upjohn and BMO Financial Group; John G. Smale of Procter & Gamble and General Motors; and billionaire Mortimer B. Zuckerman, real property and magazine owner and editor-in-chief of *U.S. News and World Report*. Also on the trip were four wives of the business leaders as well as Pamela Harriman, wife of W. Averill Harriman and a leading Democratic Party fundraiser whose career was soon to include appointment to the post of U.S. ambassador to France by President Clinton.

Besides Rockefeller and Peterson, CFR leaders on the trip included Richard W. Murphy, who after a thirty-four-year career as a Foreign Service officer, State Department official, and ambassador had become the CFR's Senior Fellow on the Middle East. As well as being an expert on that region, Murphy spoke Arabic. Two other Council leaders, President Peter Tarnoff, and Executive Vice President John Temple Swing rounded out the group.

The 1990 *Annual Report* stated that "participants met with top political, economic and cultural leaders."[260] They included the top leaders of Oman as well as the following:

SAUDI ARABIA
- King Fahd bin Abd al-Aziz Al Saud
- HRH Prince Sultan bin Abd al-Aziz Al Saud, Defense Minister and acting Minister of Foreign Affairs

- HRH Prince Abdullah bin Faisal bin Turki Al Saud
- HRH Prince Salman bin Abd al-Aziz Al Saud, governor of Riyadh Province
- Ali Naimi, CEO of Saudi ARAMCO
- The Ministers of Finance, Commerce, Petroleum and Natural Resources, Deputy Minister of Foreign Affairs, and the Secretary General of both the Saudi Chamber of Commerce and the Gulf Cooperation Council

KUWAIT
- Sheikh Jaber al-Ahmed al-Sabah, Emir
- Sheikh Saad al-Abdullah al-Sabah, Crown Prince/Prime Minister
- Sheikh Sabah al-Ahmed, Deputy Prime Minister and Foreign Minister
- Sheikh Salem Sabah al-Salem, Minister of the Interior
- Sheikh Ali Khalifa, Oil Minister
- Rashed al-Rashed, Minister of State for Cabinet Affairs
- Shiekha Hussa Sabah al-Salem, Patroness of al-Sabah Islamic Art Collection, National Museum
- Suhail K. Shuhaiber, Director, Department of the Americas, Ministry of Foreign Affairs

What is striking about each of these trips is the extraordinary access granted to the CFR delegation by the most powerful leaders in each nation. Obviously, the rulers of these countries are quite aware of the central role played by the Council in the policies of the United States. Just as the United States has experts on other nations who are consulted by those in power to help understand a given country, its leaders, policies, and goals, other nations have their own experts on the United States who conduct studies and analyses on the United States. The Meetings Program well illustrates that top world leaders and their expert advisers uniformly and strongly believe that CFR leaders and members are central to the structure of power in the United States, and as such are quite worthwhile meeting to discuss political and economic issues of mutual concern. No other single private organization in the United States comes close to consulting with the number and range of leading world decision makers year in and year out.

TOWARD THE FUTURE I: GLOBAL GOVERNANCE AND THE
COUNCIL OF COUNCILS, 2008–2014

In 2008 the CFR began another of its periodic world order initiatives, this one called the "International Institutions and Global Governance Program," a five-year program supported by a grant from the Robina Foundation. The initiative is seen as necessary and important because the present architecture of global governance reflects the world of 1945 more than it does the realities of the second decade of the twenty-first century. The Council aims to identify the institutional requirements—political, military, financial, developmental, and trade related—for effective multilateral cooperation in the future, taking into account the changes since the end of the Second World War. The full spectrum of CFR resources, its membership, studies, and meetings programs, are all expected to be brought into play to plan and implement the research and make recommendations to the Council leadership, government policymakers, and wider publics.[261]

In early 2012 the CFR added an international aspect to its global governance research, planning, and policy formulation program. This was the founding by the CFR of a "Council of Councils" network to directly connect the Council on Foreign Relations with twenty-one other "leading foreign policy institutes" from around the world. Additional details of the work of the Council of Councils will be covered in chapter 4. The work of this body will bear close watching in coming years.

TOWARD THE FUTURE II: THE RENEWING AMERICA INITIATIVE

In its 2011 *Annual Report*, the Council announced that as a part of its ninetieth anniversary, it was launching a new project, called its "Renewing America Initiative."[262] The purpose of this new, ongoing program is to

examine the slate of domestic challenges that have a direct impact on U.S. foreign policy and international leadership. Renewing America examines the domestic underpinnings of U.S. power as difficulties within the country increasingly limit what it can do outside its borders. The initiative focuses on six areas: infrastructure, education and human capital development, debt and deficits, corporate regulation and taxation, innovation, and international trade and investment. The scope of this initiative includes work by the David Rockefeller Studies Program; programming in New York, Washington and nationally; outreach to targeted constituencies, including government officials, business leaders, educators and students, religious leaders, and individuals active at the state, local, and community levels; publications, including *Foreign Affairs*; and the website, CFR.org.[263]

Thus as we move toward the CFR's hundredth anniversary, the organization is again conducting a wide-ranging grand strategic assessment of overall U.S. policy similar to their War and Peace Studies during the Second World War era and the 1980s Project during the 1970s. CFR is planning to come to conclusions and attempt to influence the government and wider circles of people through intensive targeted outreach. What is different this time is that the Council has a domestic as well as foreign policy focus. One reason for this is the recognition of a key contradiction of the system of capitalist neoliberal geopolitics the Council has helped create since the mid-1970s, which is that the system results in high levels of inequality, a relatively few very rich plutocrats, and large numbers of poor working-class people. Since the working class is needed to keep all aspects of the system functioning and could also decide to resist the class struggle being waged on them from above with rebellion and class struggle from below, the situation is one that CFR and the capitalist class believes needs attention, research, analysis, consensus building, and action.

Should economic problems and the erosion of its domestic base go unaddressed, it is feared that the United States "will gradually lose its ability to influence friends and adversaries, to shape international institutions, and ultimately to project . . . power to defend . . . national interests."[264] Therefore the Renewing America Initiative focuses on both the neoliberal and geopolitical aspects of U.S. grand strategy, set by the capitalist class and the CFR. Not surprisingly, the policies of the Obama administration strongly resemble the policies being advocated by the CFR in its Renewing America Initiative, including a stress on nation building at home, the pivot to Asia, privatizing schools, and cutting rank-and-file "entitlements."

As is the case with any of the larger Council programs, this one is producing numerous progress reports, working papers, round table discussions, backgrounders, policy innovation memos, scorecards, and blog posts, a full review of which would result in a book-length study. Short of such a study, the best window into this still developing body of agenda setting, policy planning, and policymaking is a 2013 book by CFR president Richard N. Haass: *Foreign Policy Begins at Home: The Case for Putting America's House in Order.*[265] Haass has been participating in and keeping track of the entire Renewing America Initiative effort, approving the posting of some of the results on the CFR website, for example, and his book represents, in many respects, an initial summary of the whole. We will review material from this book as appropriate during coming chapters.

3

THE CFR'S DOMESTIC NETWORK, 1976–2014

A meeting ground for powerful members of the U.S. corporate and foreign policy establishments. . . .

—DAVID C. KORTEN

The Council counts among its members probably more important names in American life than any other private group in the country

—THEODORE WHITE

The Council on Foreign Relations is the ultimate networking and socializing institution of the U.S. capitalist ruling class. But it does not operate in isolation; rather, it is at the center of an extensive network of key institutions in a number of interconnected realms of U.S. social life: politics, think tanks, finance and economics, higher education, philanthropy, media, and culture. The U.S. capitalist class has a core and a periphery. The CFR and its members are at the core of the dominant sector of this class, but the network extends broadly. The nearly 5,000 individuals who are members and leaders of the Council collectively have hundreds of thousands of ties—social, economic, and political relationships that bind them into a community of the powerful. This is one reason why so many people want to join and participate in the Council and its activities. Those at the core of the large clique that makes up the CFR's inner circle have common traits, access to the same general information, and mostly homogeneous opinions. They have close and frequent interactions—a daisy chain of connections to various organizations—resulting in strong ties and relationships with one another and powerful positions in their own groups, the political economy, and the larger society.

Those with less close links may reflect the phenomena of the "strength of weak ties." This phenomena points out the reality that to make new connections, gain new insights, and acquire new information, members of the core clique must look beyond it to others less closely attached. Such weak ties then become stronger. The end result is a verification of the folk wisdom in the statement that advancing in life is often based on "not what you know but who you know."

The approach in this chapter will be to compare lists of the key individuals, the decision makers, of what are widely considered to be central organizations in a given profit or nonprofit field, with the 2011 to 2014 CFR membership lists and the historical list of all Council directors. This procedure will document the vast number of interlocks between the CFR and most of the key institutions of U.S. society and political economy. Interlocks represent sociological anchors of a community of interest; they develop and cement the personal and institutional relationships that create the common ideology, cohesion, coordinated action, and unified political-economic influence and power of the capitalist class and its allies. At the same time, intra-ruling class conflict is reduced. Showing how the Council is at the center of a vast domestic network of the powerful, including a majority of the most important think tanks, represents additional concrete evidence that it is the most powerful organization in the United States and the world. Other think tanks around the globe have been established and grown up "under the shadow of American intellectual hegemony."[266] One recent work on think tanks elaborates as follows on this theme:

> The United States remains . . . the superpower of policy research: the prime exporter of concepts and intellectual frameworks, the most important source of transnational funding, the model that others take as their point of reference in the post–Cold War world. It is this intellectual "soft power" that leaves the USA "bound to lead" global political and economic order. . . . Across Europe, for example, students of foreign policy read the CFR journal *Foreign Affairs*, and take the arguments they find there as a starting point for their own work. . . . No European policy review attracts similar attention.[267]

The CFR is the world's most powerful private organization because it is the most influential U.S. think tank in a world under U.S. ideological hegemony and because it is a very active membership and meeting organization with close relationships to the U.S. government and a vast number of other powerful institutions. These characteristics magnify the power of the Council and the small percentage of the population it represents by intensifying the connections among the powerful, allowing them to reach consensus and unity on interests and strategic direction, and then to project their power into many institutions and sectors of American life.

INNER CIRCLE AND WIDER CIRCLE

Using interlocking directorate/network analysis, and 2011 and 2012 lists, but covering the entire 1976–2014 period in the case of government ties, we will review the connections with the Council's large inner circle of allied institutions within the United States, together with a less well-connected wider circle, reflecting the "strength of weak ties." The data developed from this network analysis will illustrate the central role played by the Council in bringing together a very powerful network of people and institutions that dominates both the United States and much of the world. Our next chapter will focus on the CFR's extensive transnational connections among the powerful worldwide. We will begin with the Council's close ties to the U.S. government since 1976.

The "In-and-Outer" and the Federal Government of the United States

Only three months after leaving the Obama administration, former treasury secretary Timothy F. Geithner, a newly minted Council senior "Distinguished Fellow," was on the lecture circuit, reportedly receiving $400,000 for just three lectures given to audiences at key finance capitalist meetings. Geithner offered his prognostications on topics such as Federal Reserve policy and geopolitical risk at three meetings organized by CFR finance capital corporate members: Deutsche Bank, the Blackstone Group, and Warburg Pincus.[268] Being rewarded by large sums of money for a few hours of talking are just one of the perks that flow to a group of people, the "in-and-outers," who circulate through what is, in effect, a revolving door into and out of public service and the private sector. Their value to the private sector, and hence the giant speaking fees, is based both on the knowledge of how things work at the top and ongoing relationships with those in charge.

Geithner had been active in the Council for years: he was a member by 1996, a Senior Fellow by 2001, joining the Chairman's Advisory Council by 2005.[269] Specifics of how being part of the CFR network influences key government policy behind the scenes surface occasionally in the mainstream media, and a recent example is an analysis of Geithner's diary while he was in office. In its analysis, the *Financial Times* found that during an eighteen-month period, while he was treasury secretary, Geithner's most frequent telephone calls were to leading CFR members. The most calls (49) were to Laurence D. "Larry" Fink, CEO of BlackRock, the world's largest money manager. Fink is a CFR member and became a Council director in 2013. Second was CFR co-chair Robert Rubin (33 calls), the next highest were Council members Jamie Dimon, CEO of JPMorgan Chase (17 calls), and Lloyd Blankfein, CEO of Goldman Sachs (13 calls). Also noted were "frequent conversations" with CFR members and former treasury secretaries Henry Paulson and Larry Summers.[270] Geithner's frequent calls to Rubin are consistent with the oft-repeated suggestion that Geithner is a Rubin protégé.[271] The larger point is that Council-connected people and the largest financial firms are those who have special relationships with and access to those holding state power.

Geithner and other former officials are part of a charmed network; they can open doors or pick up the phone and gain access to the powerful. This access is very valuable, because it allows one to put one's case directly to the policymaker. Geithner was soon hired as president of Warburg Pincus, making a large yearly income and large stock options a sure thing for the ex-secretary.[272] Geithner's activities point out the role and power of the "in-and-outers," individuals who trade on their connections. Though of questionable morality, such corrupt behavior is not illegal today.

THE COUNCIL AND PRESIDENTIAL ADMINISTRATIONS, 1977–2014

The CFR is a nation-state oriented organization in the sense that it successfully influences, even controls, through a variety of means, governments at all levels, but especially the federal government of the United States. A look at the high numbers of Council members who have occupied top- and also mid-level positions in the federal government, as well as advisory boards and "blue ribbon" policy commissions, produces concrete evidence of the pervasive influence of the CFR and the dominance of its favored policy perspectives in the federal government. The "in-and-outer" is a key part of this influence.

In the words of the CFR's *Annual Report,* 1977 was a year of "special transition." James E. Carter became president and tapped four members of the Council's leadership to serve in top positions in his administration. As Bayless Manning, then president of the CFR, expressed it: "Four members of its Board of Directors were called to serve in President Carter's administration and in consequence resigned from the Council's Board: Michael Blumenthal, Zbigniew Brzezinski, Cyrus Vance, and Paul Warnke."[273] These four men joined the Carter administration as secretary of treasury, national security adviser, secretary of state, and director of the arms control and disarmament agency, respectively.

By itself, this was not so remarkable, since it is a commonplace that CFR members and leaders are frequently brought into every new administration in leading positions. What is striking in this case is who replaced these four and two others who also gave up their positions on the CFR board at that time. The six who were elected as new directors in 1977 were: George H. W. Bush, Lloyd Cutler, Philip Geyelin, Lane Kirkland, Henry Kissinger, and Marina von Neumann Whitman. Thus as several key Democrats left the CFR board, they were replaced by other

Democrats (Kirkland was also an AFL-CIO leader), and some key Republicans, among them the outgoing secretary of state (Kissinger), and a future vice president and president (Bush). What was a "special transition" for the CFR signaled that business as usual was to be the order of the day both at the CFR and the U.S. government: individuals having much the same connections and worldview were switching positions in the realms of private and public power. This illustrates in a concrete way the close interconnections between the CFR and the U.S. government. In fact, the single institution that appears to be most interpenetrated with the CFR is the federal government of the United States, which has hundreds of members of the Council working in it. As of July 1, 2011, for example, the CFR had 529 of its members serving in "government."[274] Given the CFR focus on foreign policy, one can safely assume that the great majority of these members are working in the federal government. In its 1998 *Annual Report*, the Council itself pointed out that its members "include nearly all current and former senior U.S. government officials who deal with international matters."[275]

As shown in some detail below, CFR members and leaders have, in all administrations, dominated policymaking. Fully seventy-seven of ninety-six (80.2 percent) top federal government policymakers for foreign policy during these years were also, at some point in their careers, Council members.

The Carter Administration, 1977–1981

Democratic administrations are generally closer to the Council and its members than Republican ones. This pattern begins to show itself right at the beginning of our period with the administration of James E. Carter. All twelve of his top foreign policymakers were CFR members at some time in their careers. Walter Mondale, his vice president, was elected to membership prior to 1977 and continues as a member today. Carter's first secretary of state, Cyrus R. Vance, and National Security Adviser Zbigniew Brzezinski were both longtime members and directors of the CFR prior to holding their offices, and Vance was vice chairman of the Council for a number of years. Carter's secretaries of the treasury W. Michael Blumenthal and G. William Miller, Secretary of Defense Harold Brown, CIA director Stansfield Turner, and World Bank head Robert S. McNamara were all longtime members of the CFR prior to taking office, and Brown and Blumenthal also served as directors of the Council. Carter's two United Nations ambassadors, Andrew Young and Donald McHenry, also belonged to the Council, and both became CFR directors after leaving government. Carter's other secretary of state, Edmund Muskie, was also a CFR member for many years, but only after taking office. Carter himself only became a member of the CFR after he left office, but he has continuously been a member since 1983.

The Reagan Administration, 1981–1989

The pattern for Republican administrations was also established early in our period by President Ronald Reagan. Although not as close to the CFR in terms of top personnel, and Reagan himself was never a CFR member, there were nevertheless solid connections in that fourteen of nineteen top foreign policy officials were Council members. Vice President George H. W. Bush, who had been a member for a number of years,-was a Council director from 1977 to 1979. Both of Reagan's secretaries of state, Alexander M. Haig and George P. Shultz, were longtime members, and Shultz was a Council director immediately prior to assuming the role of secretary of state.

During his eight years in office, Reagan had a total of six national security advisers. Two of these, Colin L. Powell and Frank C. Carlucci, had been in the CFR prior to taking office. Three others, Richard V. Allen, William P. Clark Jr., and Robert C. McFarlane, became CFR members later. Only one, John M. Poindexter, was never a Council member. One of Reagan's two secretaries of the Treasury, Donald T. Regan, was in the Council prior to taking office and the other, James A. Baker III, joined after taking office. Similarly, both of this conservative president's secretaries of defense, Casper W. Weinberger and Frank C. Carlucci, were members of the Council, Weinberger joining while in office, Carlucci prior to being in office.

Both of Reagan's CIA directors, William J. Casey and William H. Webster, were longtime CFR members, as was one of his two ambassadors to the United Nations, Jeane Kirkpatrick, and she became a CFR director immediately upon leaving government.

Reagan's appointees to the World Bank, Alden W. Clausen and Barber Conable, were not Council members, nor was his second UN ambassador, Vernon Walters.

The Bush I Administration, 1989–1993

As mentioned above, George H. W. Bush had been a CFR member and director prior to becoming vice president under Reagan. During his own presidency, ten of eleven top foreign policymakers were Council members and four also had been CFR directors. Bush's vice president, Danforth Quayle, was not a member of the Council. Both of Bush I's secretaries of state were in the CFR, James A. Baker III after his service in government, and Lawrence S. Eagleburger before, during, and after. National Security Adviser Brent Scowcroft was a longtime Council member before taking office, and a CFR director immediately prior to taking office. Secretary of the Treasury Nicholas F. Brady, was a member of the Council prior to taking office, as was his secretary of defense, Richard B. Cheney, who also had been a CFR director. Lewis T. Preston and Robert M. Gates, World Bank and CIA heads respectively, were members prior to taking office. Finally, both of Bush I's UN ambassadors, Thomas R. Pickering and Edward J. Perkins, were Council members, and Pickering was later a CFR director.

The Clinton Administration, 1993–2001

Like the Carter and Bush I administrations, the Clinton administration was very closely connected to the CFR; fifteen of Clinton's top seventeen foreign policy officials were in the CFR and five had also been or were soon to be directors. William J. Clinton was himself a CFR member before he became president, although his vice president, Albert A. Gore Jr., was not a member. Both of Clinton's secretaries of state, Warren M. Christopher and Madeleine K. Albright, were longtime members; Christopher was a director and vice chair of the Council before joining the Clinton administration, and Albright became a CFR director after leaving government. Both of Clinton's National Security Advisers, W. Anthony Lake and Samuel R. Berger, were longtime members of the CFR.

Of Clinton's three secretaries of the treasury, the first, Lloyd M. Bentsen, was not a CFR member, but Robert E. Rubin and Lawrence H. Summers were, with Rubin later becoming a director and co-chair of the Council. All three of Clinton's choices for Secretary of Defense, Les Aspin, William J. Perry, and William S. Cohen, were CFR members, and Aspin and Cohen were directors. Cohen was a director when Clinton called on him to serve in the government.

Clinton appointed three directors of the CIA, all members of the CFR. R. James Woolsey and John M. Deutch were longtime members when appointed, and the third, George J. Tenet, became a member about the same time he became head of the CIA. Clinton's World Bank president, James Wolfensohn, and his three UN ambassadors, Albright, William B. Richardson, and Richard Holbrooke, were all Council members years prior to entering office, and Holbrooke was a CFR director.

The Bush II Administration, 2001–2009

George W. Bush was never a member of the CFR, but fourteen of the seventeen top foreign policy officials he appointed were or had once been Council members, and three were or soon became directors. His vice president, Richard B. Cheney, was a longtime member and was a two-time director between 1987 and 1995. Both of Bush's secretaries of state, Colin L. Powell and Condoleezza Rice, had long been members of the Council when they were appointed, and Powell became a CFR director in 2006, right after leaving government. National Security Adviser Stephen Hadley and one of Bush's secretaries of the treasury, Henry M. Paulson

Jr., were Council members. On the other hand, the other two Bush II secretaries of the treasury were not in the CFR.

George W. Bush had two secretaries of defense, Donald H. Rumsfeld and Robert M. Gates. Rumsfeld was a CFR member during the 1970s but later dropped out of the organization. Gates has been a continuous Council member since 1985. Bush's appointees to head the CIA, Porter J. Goss and Michael V. Hayden, were CFR members prior to entering office, as were both of his appointees to head up the World Bank, Paul Wolfowitz and Robert Zoellick, who had also been a Council director. Three of the four men Bush appointed to be UN ambassador, John D. Negroponte, John R. Bolton, and Zalmay Khalilzad, were CFR members prior to their appointments.

The Obama Administration, 2009–2014

Barack Obama's administration continues to exemplify a strong CFR presence in government. Obama has never been a member of the CFR, and his vice president, Joseph R. Biden, was only briefly a member in the late 1980s. All three of Obama's national security advisers, James L. Jones Jr., Thomas E. Donilon, and Susan E. Rice, have been CFR members. Both Donilon and Rice were especially close to the CFR. Donilon served for years on the Council Chairman's Advisory Council as vice chair, and upon leaving government service became a "distinguished fellow" at the CFR. Susan E. Rice, who also served as Obama's first UN representative, has been active in the organization for years. She was a term member by 1994, a regular member by 1996, and a speaker at CFR meetings by 1998.[276] From 2002 to 2004 she was on the Nominating and Governance subcommittee of the Council Board of Directors and was on the Chairman's Advisory Board of the CFR during 2003–2004.[277] Samantha Power, Obama's 2013 choice to replace Rice as U.S. ambassador to the UN, is not currently a CFR member.

Although Obama's first secretary of state, Hillary Clinton, is not a member, her husband, Bill, has been a member for more than twenty years, and their daughter Chelsea had become a member by 2013.[278] Obama's second secretary of state, John Forbes Kerry, became a CFR member in the early 1990s. He married his second wife, the near billionaire Teresa Heinz (who inherited the Heinz food fortune), in 1995, the same year she was elected to Council membership.[279]

Former secretary of the treasury Timothy F. Geithner has belonged to the Council for eighteen years, and Obama's second appointment to this office, Jack Lew, almost as long. Obama's first secretary of defense, Robert Gates, has been active in the CFR for over two decades, and he headed up a CFR Independent Task Force with Zbigniew Brzezinski on Iran and Iraq in the mid-1990s. Obama's second secretary of defense, Leon Panetta, who was also Obama's first CIA director, is not a CFR member, but Obama's second CIA director, General David H. Petraeus, has been a CFR member for at least twenty-eight years. His third CIA chief, John O. Brennan, is not a Council member, but on the other hand, Obama's third secretary of defense, Chuck Hagel, has been a CFR member for at least fifteen years, and his fourth, Ashton B. Carter, has been a Council member since 1984, and also served on the Trilateral Commission. The World Bank head during most of Obama's first term was Robert B. Zoellick, a CFR member for twenty-three years, who was also a Council director from 1994 to 2001, but Obama's pick to replace him, Jim Yong Kim, is not a CFR member.

Of the seventeen top foreign policymakers in the Obama administration, one (Zoellick) has been a CFR director and a total of eleven have been CFR members, with the exception of one, all prior to joining the Obama government.

So far, only the top foreign policy positions in a given administration have been discussed, but many of the other cabinet-level positions in a given administration have also been held by CFR people. In the Obama administration, for example, Janet A. Napolitano (Homeland Security), John E. Bryson and Penny S. Pritzker (Commerce), Ernest J. Moniz (Energy), Sylvia Mathews Burwell (Health and Human Services), and Mary Jo White (Securities and Exchange) are all Council members. Bryson and Burwell are former CFR directors, and Pritzker was a Council director when tapped for public office by Obama.

THE COUNCIL'S CONNECTIONS TO ADVISORY BOARDS AND BLUE RIBBON COMMISSIONS

Additional important examples of the close interpenetration of the CFR and the federal government are the composition of the advisory boards for the Department of State, Department of Defense, and CIA. In the case of the Department of State, its Foreign Affairs Policy Board was established in late 2011 to provide the Secretary of State and other top leaders with "bipartisan," and "independent, informed advice and opinion concerning matters of U.S. foreign policy."[280] In early 2013 it had twenty-five members, and twenty of them (80 percent) were CFR members, including six current or former Council directors. These six included one of the CFR's co-chairs, Carla Hills, current director Ann Fudge, and former directors Thomas R. Pickering, Anne-Marie Slaughter, Helene Gayle, and Laura Tyson. Several members of the group are also directors of leading corporations or are wealthy, so capitalist-class representation is also high.

The Defense Policy Board Advisory Committee first became famous during the years when longtime CFR member Richard Perle headed the committee and used his position to influence the decision to go to war on Iraq. In 2009 this policy board had twenty-five members, seventeen of whom (68 percent) were CFR members or CFR Fellows. These included former Council directors Harold Brown and Henry A. Kissinger, as well as CFR member Chuck Hagel, who became Secretary of Defense in 2013.

The CIA set up its own fourteen-member "External Advisory Board" in 2009, ten of whom (71.4 percent) belonged to the Council. These included former CFR directors Madeleine K. Albright, Warren Rudman, and Thomas R. Pickering.

Another example of the unequaled power of the broad Council network is the 2006–12 Project on National Security Reform (PNSR), a "nonpartisan non-profit" "blue ribbon" organization mandated by the U.S. Congress. Its purpose was to recommend improvements to the U.S. national security system in order to combat new threats by becoming more agile and efficient. Funded by Congress, foundations, and corporations, the PNSR saw itself, in the words of its website, as an "authoritative resource and trusted advisor that defines and develops the means to bridge the gap between the current state and needed future state of national security." No fewer than eighteen federal government departments and agencies, as well as twenty-seven think tanks and similar organizations, and a large number of universities, corporations, and law firms contributed to PNSR's work, which resulted in many recommendations to the government. The PNSR's website lists the names of the "Guiding Coalition" of "former senior fed-eral officials and others with national security experience. The bipartisan group sets the strategic direction for the Project, examines progress, discusses objec-tives, and reviews findings and recommendations . . . [communicating] the final findings and recommendations of PNSR to officials in government, the policy community and the public." Thirty-two individuals are listed as having been on the "Guiding Coalition" during its period of operation. Although not one of the thirty-two lists the CFR as one of their affiliations, fully twenty-one of the them (65.6 percent) were members of the Council. Several were even more active than mere membership would indicate; three (Joseph S. Nye Jr., Thomas R. Pickering, and Brent Scowcroft) were current or former CFR directors, and one, Robert D. Blackwill, was, in 2011, the Council's Henry A. Kissinger Senior Fellow for U.S. Foreign Policy.[281]

Finally, a 2011 book by Jordan Tama, a CFR member—*Terrorism and National Security Reform: How Commissions Can Drive Change During Crises*—lists all U.S. "blue ribbon" official U.S. government national security commissions dur-ing the period 1981–2006, a total of fifty-one.[282] Although the words "Council on Foreign Relations" do not appear in the index to Tama's book, he does list who chaired or co-chaired each of the commissions. Comparing the fifty-seven chairs/co-chairs of these government bodies to lists of Council members from 1981 to 2006 reveals that thirty-eight (66.7 percent) were members of the CFR. Eight of these heads of commissions were Council directors: Brent Scowcroft,

Henry A. Kissinger, Bobby Inman, Les Aspin, Harold Brown, William Crowe, John Deutch, and James R. Schlesinger.

In summary, fully seventy-seven of the ninety-six (80.2 percent) top government policy positions during the 1976–2014 years have been filled by CFR members, and twenty-two (22.9 percent) were also CFR directors. If we add representation on top advisory organizations and policy boards, we find another ninety-six positions of which sixty-eight (70.8 percent) were filled by CFR members. These are extremely high numbers, not approached by any other private organization in the country.

THE CFR AND THE LEADING NONPROFIT THINK TANKS AND POLICY GROUPS

The number of nonprofit think tanks in the United States has exploded since the 1970s, and they now collectively employ thousands of fellows and assistants whose intellectual output occupies a good deal of public space on the Internet, in newspapers, and magazines, as well as airtime on television and radio. Think tanks, especially the CFR, play a central role in developing new policy ideas and shaping key debates, setting agendas, and guiding both public and professional opinion.

The Think Tanks and Civil Societies Program of the University of Pennsylvania ranked the U.S. and other nations' think tanks in 2009, publishing the results in early 2010.[283] Among the "Security and International Affairs" think tanks, the CFR was ranked number 1 in the world.[284] But when domestic as well as foreign policy were included, James McGann, senior fellow and director of the program, ranked these thirteen think tanks at the top:

1. Brookings Institution
2. Carnegie Endowment
3. Council on Foreign Relations
4. RAND Corporation
5. Heritage Foundation
6. Center for Strategic and International Studies (CSIS)
7. Cato Institute
8. Woodrow Wilson International Center for Scholars
9. American Enterprise Institute
10. Hoover Institution
11. Peterson Institute for International Economics
12. Freedom House
13. Aspen Institute[285]

The mistake that caused McGann to rank the Council as the third most important U.S. think tank instead of number 1, is his failure to consider several key facts about the CFR. First, that it is a membership organization with almost 5,000 members, all of them paying dues and many of whom make yearly donations and participate in many of the CFR activities, including study groups and meetings. Second, this membership base, connected to an organized think tank with a large number of staff scholars, together with its corporate and government connections, is what gives the Council its unique strength as the world's most powerful think tank. The membership activities, think tank work, meetings program, corporate service, media work, and government connections all function together. In an earlier book about think tanks, McGann stated that in 2005 the CFR had a total of 185 research staff members, compared to Brookings Institution's 319, and Brookings had a slightly larger annual budget.[286] What he left out was that in 2005 the Council had as members 794 professors, Fellows, and researchers, 496 government officials, as well as 275 university and college administrators, completely dwarfing the numbers working with and for Brookings and also Carnegie, neither of which is a membership organization.[287] In his 2007 study, McGann asked the key executives (mainly presidents) of twenty leading think tanks to write essays about their own organizations, which he published in his book.[288] But McGann failed to check into the connections between the top leaders of these different organizations and the CFR. Had he done so, he would have discovered that twelve of the twenty top officials of the other think tanks were members of the Council as well. These included Edward P. Djerejian of the Baker Institute, Strobe Talbott of Brookings, John J. Hamre of Center for Strategic and International Studies, Ellen Laipson of the Stimson Center, John Raisian of Hoover, Herbert I. London of Hudson, C. Fred Bergsten of the Institute of International Economics, Dimitri K. Smies of the Nixon Center, and James Thomson of RAND.[289]

Returning to McGann's list of top think tanks above, we find that seven of the above-listed top think tanks—Brookings, Carnegie, CSIS, Wilson, Peterson, Freedom House, and Aspen—have extensive links with and are closely connected to the CFR, part of its inner circle. Three others—RAND, Hoover, and American Enterprise Institute—have fewer links and are most accurately considered part of Council's wider circle. The last two of this top group, Heritage and Cato, each have at least one connection to the CFR, but the links are relatively few.

McGann's list of leading U.S. think tanks totaled fifty. A discussion of the top twelve's connections to the CFR follows, then we will briefly examine the leadership of sixteen more of the think tanks, all among the top thirty-five on McGann's list. This will illustrate that the CFR has wide and deep connections to the great majority of top U.S. think tanks. At least twenty-six out of the top thirty-five are part of either the Council's inner or wider circle.[290]

1. **The Brookings Institution** traces its origins to 1916; it was the first private organization devoted to the analysis of public policy issues at the national level. Its 2011 *Annual Report* pointed out five main foci of its work: economic studies, foreign policy studies, global economy and development, governance, and metropolitan policy.[291] It had assets of $410 million (a little less than the Council's assets) and spent $88 million in 2010, more than the $55 million spent by the CFR in that year. It had over 300 resident and non-resident fellows. Brookings' *Annual Report* stated that it "strives for impact in at least three ways: designing policy recommendations, shaping critical debates, and setting the longer-term agenda."[292]

   Brookings is very closely interlocked with the CFR, indicating a strong commonality in ideology and political approach, and they occupy buildings that stand next door to each other in Washington. All five of its top leaders are Council members, including its chair, John L. Thornton. Its president, Strobe Talbott, is a former CFR director (1988–93). David Rubinstein, one of its vice chairs, is also vice chair of the CFR and a current Council director. Fourteen of its forty-five current trustees (31.1 percent) are CFR members, and two of them are current Council directors. Twenty of its forty honorary trustees (50 percent), are CFR members, and four of them are current or former CFR directors. Major funding sources in 2010 included the Rockefeller and Gates Foundations, the Carnegie Corporation, Microsoft, and ATT, all organizations with ties to the Council. There are also many historic and current connections between Brookings and CFR scholars. One of these scholars, Richard N. Haass, worked for the Council, then at Brookings, then at the Department of State, then became president of the CFR. In December 2002, when working as director of policy planning at State, he stated in a speech he gave at the CFR: "The Council remains the blue chip think tank in the field. I can say this in all honesty because when I worked next door at a fellow—some might say rival—institution we often measured success by how many of our scholars appeared in the pages of *Foreign Affairs* or participated in Council study groups and task forces."[293]

2. **The Carnegie Endowment for International Peace** was founded in 1910 as a nonpartisan international think tank dedicated to cooperation between nations. It now has offices in five world cities. Its funding comes from branches of the federal government—including the Departments of State, Defense, and Energy—foreign governments, individuals, leading corporations, and foundations, many of them closely connected to the Council. Seven of its twenty-six trustees (26.9 percent) are CFR members, including Stephen R. Lewis Jr., its vice chair and president, and Paul Balaran, its vice president.

3. **The RAND Corporation** was founded in 1948 as a spin-off of Douglas Aircraft Company. This nonprofit is focused on improving policy and

decision making through research, analysis, and development. Its national security and economic and social issues research work is funded by government agencies, foundations, and corporations. Two out of its twelve top leaders (16.7 percent) are members of the CFR, including Michael D. Rich, RAND's president and CEO.

4. **The Heritage Foundation** is made up of "policy entrepreneurs" whose mission is to "formulate and promote conservative public policies based on the principles of free enterprise, limited government, individual freedom, traditional American values, and a strong national defense." None of its twenty-three trustees are members of the CFR, but at least one of its top scholars, Kim R. Holmes, director of foreign and defense policy, is a longtime CFR member, accepted in 1995.[294]

5. **The Center for Strategic and International Studies** was founded near the height of the Cold War in 1962. It focuses on foreign policy and national security issues and, like the CFR, has a large number of former top government officials among its ranks. It is closely interlocked with the CFR; twenty-four of its forty trustees (60 percent) are also members of the Council, including chairman Sam Nunn, vice chairman David M. Abshire, and president/CEO John J. Hamre. Nine of the twenty-four CFR members who are CSIS trustees are also current or former directors of the CFR, including Carla A. Hills, one of the Council's current co-chairs, and David M. Rubenstein, the current CFR vice chair. Its budget for 2010 was $29.8 million, about 62 percent of what the CFR spent during that year.

6. **The Cato Institute** was founded in 1977. It is a libertarian think tank dedicated to "individual liberty, free markets and peace." None of its twenty trustees are members of the CFR, but at least one of its scholars, Ted G. Carpenter, is a longtime Council member, and has participated in a CFR study group.[295] This think tank advocates small government, and is, in general, supported by smaller corporations, which could be called the more competitive sector of U.S. capitalism. The major exception to this is the strong support given to Cato by the Koch brothers, who own and control large corporations and are two of the richest individuals in the world. Charles Koch is one of the founders of Cato and David Koch is on the board of trustees.

7. **The Woodrow Wilson International Center for Scholars** was founded as an "official memorial to our nation's 28th president," and its trustees are appointed to six-year terms by the president of the United States. The Wilson Center tries to "inform the nation's public policy debates" and bridge the world of academia and public policy. Two of its fifteen trustees (13.3 percent) are CFR members. At least some of its working committees are much closer to the Council. In 2008, for example, the Wilson Center formed an international committee to promote

"greater understanding" between the United States and China. The U.S. members included five current or former CFR directors: Henry A. Kissinger, Maurice R. Greenberg, Carla A. Hills, Robert E. Rubin, and George P. Shultz.

8. **The American Enterprise Institute** has been called the premier conservative think tank. It was established during the Second World War to lobby against the possibility that price and production controls would be continued as anti-depression measures after the war. Since then it has continued to promote its goals of "strengthening free enterprise" and "expanding liberty."[296] AEI focuses on both domestic and foreign policy. Three of its twenty-seven trustees (11.1 percent) are CFR members, including Lee R. Raymond, former head of ExxonMobil, who reportedly gave $1.6 million to AEI. Another trustee is a former Council director, former vice president Richard B. Cheney. There are also CFR-connected people among its senior scholars; Council members Norman Ornstein and Newt Gingrich are two examples.

9. **The Hoover Institution** is located on the campus of Stanford University in California, and most of its trustees are based in that state. Hoover stresses that it collects knowledge, generating and disseminating the ideas that "define a free society and free markets," including representative government and private enterprise. None of the eighteen trustees on its executive committee are in the CFR, but a number of their Hoover Fellows are, including former Council director George P. Shultz. At least seven other Council members are among the list of Hoover Fellows, including former secretary of state Condoleezza Rice, former national security adviser Richard V. Allen, and former secretary of defense William J. Perry.

10. **Freedom House** was founded as an interventionist group to counter isolationist sentiments in 1941. Later it became a bipartisan anti-Soviet organization that was also against McCarthyism. Today it focuses on promoting political freedoms, democracy, and human rights that it sees as vital to the U.S. "national interest." Its chair, William H. Taft IV, and both vice chairs, Ruth Wedgwood and Thomas A. Dine, are CFR members. Its thirty-nine-member board of trustees includes eighteen CFR members (46.2 percent), two of whom, Lee Cullum and Betty Bao Lord, have also served as Council directors.

11. **Peterson Institute for International Economics** was founded in 1981 by soon-to-be CFR chair Peter G. Peterson. This private nonprofit, nonpartisan organization studies and makes recommendations on the international economy. With an annual budget of about $10 million, it states that it has "helped provide the intellectual foundation for many of the major international financial initiatives of the past three decades." These include reforms of the IMF, international banking, currency and trade policies. Its forty-three-member board of directors includes twenty CFR members (46.5 percent).

Its leadership includes not only Peterson, but also other top CFR leaders like David Rockefeller, Carla A. Hills, Richard E. Salomon, and Maurice R. Greenberg, as well as a number of other current or former directors of the Council. Longtime active CFR member C. Fred Bergsten has been the Institute's director since it was founded.

12. **The Aspen Institute** is based in four locations in the United States with an international network of partners in other nations. Aspen's mission is to "foster values-based leadership" and to provide a "neutral and balanced venue" for discussion and action. It does this through seminars, fellowships, policy programs, and public conferences, bringing a "diversity of perspectives" together. Walter Isaacson, its president and CEO, and vice chair Henry E. Catto are both Council members. Twenty-four of its sixty-one (39.3 percent) trustees are also CFR members, a number that includes one current (Vin Weber) and one former (Madeleine Albright) Council director.

Sixteen Additional Leading Think Tanks and the CFR

- **The German Marshall Fund** is ranked number 15; its co-chairs, Guido Goldman and Marc Leland, are both CFR members.
- **The U.S. Institute of Peace is** ranked number 16; its chair, J. Robinson West, and its vice chair, George E. Moose, are both Council members.
- **The Center for American Progress** is ranked number 17; its list of fellows include Council member and former senator Tom Daschle, former CFR vice president Lawrence J. Korb, former CFR director Laura D'Andrea Tyson, and a number of Council members, including Harvard professor and former Obama economic adviser Lawrence H. Summers.
- **The Open Society Institute/Open Society Foundations** is ranked number 18. This "democracy promotion" think tank is also a foundation, with billionaire George Soros as its chair, founder, and chief funder. Soros was accepted as a Council member by 1988 and has also been a CFR director. President Arych Neler is also a CFR member.
- **The Center for Global Development** is ranked number 19; its board includes CFR members Timothy D. Adams, C. Fred Bergsten, Lawrence Summers, and Henrietta Holsman Fore.
- **The Center for Transatlantic Relations** is ranked number 20; its director, Daniel Hamilton, is a CFR member.
- **Human Rights Watch** is ranked number 21. Its chair is James F. Hoge, a Council member and former editor of *Foreign Affairs*. Its executive director (Kenneth Roth) and two of its vice chairs (Joel Motley and John J. Studzinski) are all Council members.

- **The Pew Center on Global Climate Change/C2ES** is ranked number 23. The Pew Center, recently renamed C2ES, has at least three CFR members on its board of directors: Theodore Roosevelt IV, Elieen Claussen, and Frank E. Loy.
- **The Stimson Center** is ranked number 24. CFR members Berry Blechman and Michael Krepon founded this organization in 1989. Its board includes Alton Frye, a former senior vice president of CFR, Thomas Pickering, a former CFR director, and Council member Lincoln Bloomfield.
- **The Carter Center** is ranked number 27. CFR member and former U.S. president Jimmy Carter founded this organization. Other trustees include Council members Richard C. Blum and Charlayne Hunter-Gault. Gault has also been a CFR director.
- **The EastWest Institute** is ranked number 28; its founder, president, and CEO is John Edwin Mroz, a member of the CFR.
- **The Atlantic Council** is ranked number 30. Historically, the Atlantic Council has focused on North American-European relations primarily, but today it is a broader organization that also conducts studies on Africa and on the Near, Middle, and Far East. It has a large board of directors, consisting of 147 individuals, sixty-two of them CFR members (42.2 percent). Twelve of its thirteen honorary directors (92.3 percent) and eleven of its fifteen lifetime directors (73.3 percent) are also CFR members. Looking at the total list of eighty-five CFR members among the leadership of the Atlantic Council, seven were or are CFR directors.
- **International Crisis Group** is ranked number 31. This organization has as its chair Thomas R. Pickering, a former director of the CFR. Its executive committee includes former Council director George Soros and member Morton Abramowitz. The chair of its advisory board is CFR member and leading Council donor Rita E. Hauser. Hauser, a Republican, is also chair of the International Peace Institute and was appointed to the President's Intelligence Advisory Board by both George W. Bush and Barack Obama.
- **Hudson Institute** is ranked number 32. Its chair emeritus is Council member Walter P. Stern. One of its vice chairs is CFR member Marie-Josee Kravis.
- **World Resources Institute** is ranked number 34. Its chair, vice chair, and two of its directors—James A. Harmon, Harriet Babbitt, Bill Richardson, and Theodore Roosevelt IV respectively— are all CFR members.
- **Center for New American Security** is ranked number 35. Eleven of its directors are Council members, including former CFR director Karen Elliott House.

THE CFR AND OTHER PRIVATE POLICY GROUPS

A number of other important organizations involved in policy formation do not appear on McGann's list of key think tanks but are within the CFR's inner circle of sister organizations. Thirteen of these are briefly reviewed below.

- **The National Committee on U.S. China Relations** is an organization important in the development and dissemination of U.S. China policy. All of the top leaders of the NCUSCR (president, chair, four vice chairs, treasurer, secretary) are CFR members, including chair Carla A. Hills, and twenty-seven of its forty-member board of directors (67.5 percent) were also in the Council, three of them (Albright, Kissinger, and Gerstner), former CFR directors. A number of these same people were part of a 2007 Independent Task Force on China policy organized by the CFR.

- **Foreign Policy Association** was founded in 1918. Its stated aim is to instruct the attentive public about foreign policy issues. It has a "great decisions" program with content that is placed in teacher's guides for schools and also used for television programs. In 2011, seventeen of it fifty-four directors (31.5 percent) were Council members. These directors included former CFR vice chair Maurice R. Greenberg, and former CFR executive vice president John Temple Swing, who is also the president emeritus of the FPA.

- **The Business Council** was formed by top corporate executives in 1933. At first it advised only the secretary of commerce, but it has expanded its role over the years, advising many branches of the federal government. It also provides personnel for special panels and committees that, in its words "help develop policy for the federal government." In 2012 four of the fourteen members (28.6 percent), of the BC's executive committee were CFR members. These included current Council directors Henry R. Kravis and James W. Owens. CFR member James Dimon chairs the BC and Council member Kenneth Chenault is also a BC executive council member.

- **The Business Roundtable** was established in 1972 as an association of CEOs of leading corporations. It aims to play an "active and effective role in the formation of public policy" by presenting government with "reasoned alternatives." Its members represent corporations that make up nearly one-third of the total value of the U.S. stock market. In 2012 four CFR members sat on the eighteen-member executive committee (22.2 percent) of the Roundtable. These included Dimon and Chenault, mentioned above, and also Ajaj Bunga and Randall L. Stephenson.

- **The Committee for Economic Development** was founded by corporate leaders during the Second World War to conduct research and formulate policy recommendations "designed to sustain long term growth" in the economy. Among other things, the CED favors a freer global trading system. As of 2012, six of its seventeen executive committee members (35.3 percent) were also in the CFR, among them the president and co-chair of the CED, Charles E. M. Kolb and Roger W. Ferguson Jr., respectively.

- **The U.S. Chamber of Commerce** stresses its small business connections, but this organization largely reflects the interests of its large corporate members. The top leadership of the Chamber is composed of very wealthy men with close ties to the biggest U.S. corporations. For example, the Chamber's current president and CEO (since 1997) is Thomas J. Donahue. He is also a director of the Union Pacific Corporation. At Union Pacific, Donohue's fellow board members include the retired chairman of Conoco Phillips, a general partner of Brown Brothers Harriman, the former chairman and CEO of Weyerhaeuser, and former executives from DuPont, Phelps Dodge, and Louisiana Pacific. The Chamber's board chairman, Thomas D. Bell Jr., has been a corporate executive at Ball Corporation (an industrial corporation with about 14,000 employees), Young and Rubicam (an advertising agency with about 16,000 employees), Gulfstream Aerospace Corporation, Norfolk Southern, and SecurAmerica. The U.S. Chamber of Commerce is (since 2004) a corporate member of the Council and its president Donahue and chair Ball are members of the CFR.

- **The Nixon Center/The Center for the National Interest (CNI)** was founded by Richard Nixon and was named for him until 2011 when it became he CNI. It publishes the bimonthly magazine *The National Interest*. Though not considered a leading U.S. think tank, this organization's leadership is very close to the CFR: every one of its top five leaders is a member of the Council, including two former directors, Maurice Greenberg and Henry Kissinger. Greenberg also served as a chairman of the Nixon Center. The president of the organization, the Russian immigrant Dimitri Simes, is a Council member. A number of its scholars are also in the CFR, including Geoffrey Kemp, General Charles G. Boyd, and Lt. General Wallace C. Gregson Jr.

- **The Project for the New American Century** was a short-lived (1997–2006) far right-wing neoconservative think tank that was especially influential in the George W. Bush administration. Its stated goal was to "promote American leadership" and "greatness" through "a Reaganite policy of military strength and moral clarity." This involved increasing the U.S. military budget to "retain its militarily dominant status" worldwide, and using the military threat and force "to shape a new century favorable to American principles and interests." PNAC pushed for a war on Iraq, sending a letter to President Clinton to that effect in 1998, and continued its efforts until success in 2003, when a number of its own people were leading policymakers—for example, Richard B. Cheney, Donald

Rumsfeld, and Paul Wolfowitz. (We will return to this organization in chapter 6 on the origins and war aims of the U.S. in Iraq.) Of the sixty-eight signatories or contributors to the PNAC's reports and statements, fully forty-three (63.2 percent) were CFR members as of the year 2000. These included four current or former CFR directors: Richard B. Cheney, Jeane Kirkpatrick, Vin Weber, and Robert B. Zoellick.

- **The Chicago Council on Global Affairs** has been called the "Midwest's leading think tank."[297] Its top leaders are CFR members: chairman of the board Lester Crown, vice chair Michael H. Moskow, and president Ivo H. Daalder. Among its top corporate contributors are JPMorgan Chase, Goldman Sachs, and the Boeing Company, all corporate members of the CFR. Its fellows include former CFR senior fellow Rachel Bronson, who is also a member of the Council. *Forbes* magazine called billionaire Lester Crown Chicago's richest man; he is a major stockholder of military contractor General Dynamics Corporation and sits on its board.

- **United against Nuclear Iran:** In July, 2014, the Obama administration confounded the legal community by successfully going to court to protect UNAI from having to defend itself in a private defamation lawsuit. The government argued that UANI, a private neo-conservative organization, should be shielded under the state secrets privilege, depriving a private citizen of his day in court. Although UANI is not formally connected to the American government, a review of the 42 leaders of the organization reveals many former intelligence and defense operatives from NATO nations and Israel. Seventeen of the 27 American citizens helping to lead UANI are CFR members (63%), and include a former Council president and four former directors.

- **International Rescue Committee** is a non-governmental relief, "human rights" and development organization, based in the United States but operating in forty countries, founded in 1933. Among its 2012 list of twelve officers and former chair are seven CFR members (58.3 percent). Its twenty-eightmember board of directors includes seven Council members (25 percent), one of which (Mary M. Boies) is a current director of the CFR. Among the IRC's Overseers are seven current or former CFR directors and a number of other Council members.

- **The Asia Society** was founded in 1956 by John D. Rockefeller III. It states that its mission is to promote understanding between Asia, especially China, and the United States. It conducts strategic, economic, educational, and cultural studies. Its financial statement shows $107.7 million in assets, a large proportion likely contributed by Rockefeller. Both of its co-chairs, Ronnie C. Chan and Henrietta H. Fore, are CFR members, as are fifteen of its fifty-two trustees (28.8 percent). A review of its trustees, officers, fellows, and experts found forty-five CFR members who are also part of the Asia Society.

- **The Japan Society** was founded in 1907, and, like the Asia Society, funded in part by John D. Rockefeller III. It has fewer but still substantial ties to the CFR, with ten Council members out of forty-three of its trustees (23.3 percent).

LEADING LOBBYING GROUPS

The dividing line between the work of think tanks, policy organizations, and lobbying groups can be fuzzy, but it is clear that lobbying groups generally focus on a narrower and more immediate agenda than think tanks. Three prominent lobbying groups are known to be connected to the CFR's network:

- **The Concord Coalition** is the most closely connected to the Council. Founded in 1992 by CFR chair Peter Peterson and Council member Senator Warren Rudman along with Senator Paul Tsongas, this organization aims at "educating the public" to support cutting "unsustainable entitlement programs" benefiting workers, such as Social Security and Medicare. In this way the taxes of the rich and corporations can be cut further. Concord uses patriotic language and imagery to try to convince people to support reducing an already too weak social safety net. Almost half of its thirty-one top officers and directors are CFR members, including its president (Peterson), co-chairs—Rudman and former Senator Bob Kerrey—and several vice chairs, among them Robert E. Rubin and Paul A. Volcker. The Coalition gives an annual "Economic Patriot" Award to those willing to sign on to and spread propaganda for its policies. In his memoirs, Peterson mentions six recipients of this award, all members of the CFR.[298]
- **Americans for Tax Reform** is led by its president and prime mover, CFR member Grover Norquist. The ATR is anti-government and wants to starve the government of resources by pressuring officeholders and candidates to commit in writing to oppose all tax increases. In the 112th Congress, 238 House members and forty-one senators have taken this pledge; at the same time at the state level thirteen governors and 1,249 state legislators have also pledged. Norquist is also on the board of the National Rifle Association, the Nixon Center, and the American Conservative Union.
- **American Israel Public Affairs Committee** is generally recognized as the most influential pro-Israel/Zionist lobbying organization in the United States. AIPAC focuses mainly on Congress, using funding and mass action to assure continued U.S. support for all Israeli policies, and to make sure that the U.S. national interest is defined in a pro-Israel way. It has a large, sixty-three-person board of directors. Four of these individuals (6.3 percent) are members of the CFR. These common members include two who are well known: Martin S.

Indyk, a former U.S. ambassador to Israel, and Dennis Ross, a longtime government "expert" on the Middle East.

THE CFR AND LEADING CORPORATIONS

The corporation is a central institution of capitalism. The ownership of shares, the
holding of high position in corporations, and the profits that are then received are
among the main sources of capitalist-class wealth and power in society. The question of ownership and control of the corporations is a complex and controversial
topic, and a full discussion is beyond the scope of the present work. It can nevertheless be said that the most detailed studies have convincingly shown that in most
cases each corporation has a group of cooperating major stockholders—extended
family-, bank-, or investment group-based or all of these together, often a kinship-
economic group—that make the key strategic decisions for the great majority of
large, medium, and small corporations.[299] Making such decisions is the function of
the board of directors of each corporation. Top professional managers are hired to
make day-to-day tactical judgments and often have input on the larger-scale strategic decisions. These super managers also receive very large salaries and perks
like gifts of stock in the company. This is part of the assimilation process into the
capitalist class, and top managers gradually join the society of the plutocracy and
become closely allied with the leading owners of a given corporation.

The state also generally protects, with taxpayer funds, these large, often Council-
connected monopoly corporations. The bailouts that took place in 2008 represent
examples of "too big to fail" corporations rescued by the government. Lehman
Brothers, for example, was a corporate member of the CFR at the highest level.[300]
It represented an exception in that it was allowed to fail, but massive government
bailouts were granted to a large number of other Council-related financial institutions. These bailed-out corporations included AIG, Citigroup, Bank of America,
JPMorgan Chase, Merrill Lynch, Goldman Sachs, and Morgan Stanley, all of which
were corporate members of the Council in 2008.[301] These same corporations control some of the world's largest investment funds. A *Financial Times* article in July
2013 lists the twenty top managers of alternative investments for pension funds.
Twelve of them were CFR corporate members in 2012, led by Goldman Sachs, the
Blackstone Group, BlackRock, UBS, Credit Suisse, and JPMorgan Chase. These
twelve Council corporate members alone had alternative assets under management of almost $1.2 trillion.[302]

The top 500 corporations of the United States are listed each year by *Fortune*
magazine. In 2010 *Fortune* listed the twenty-seven largest corporations by market
value and equity.[303] These tend to be the most transnational of U.S.-based corporations and collectively control trillions of dollars of assets. Of these, twenty-four

(88.9 percent) have some links to the Council, and eighteen of these have closer ties and could be considered part of the CFR's inner circle, and will be discussed below.

Many of other top 500 Fortune corporations, as well as smaller ones, are also well connected to the CFR as corporate members or through officers or directors who are CFR members. The section below will show that the CFR is, in general, most closely connected to the largest and most internationally oriented U.S. corporations; it does not list every leading corporation that is connected to the Council, for such a list would be very long. One limited measure of such relationships is participation in the CFR's corporate membership program.

- **Coca-Cola** is a "Premium" corporate member of CFR and has seven Council members among its seventeen directors. These members include Coke chair and CEO Muhtar Kent, also a Council director beginning in 2012, and former CFR director Donald F. McHenry (1984–93). Coke's largest single stockholder is Berkshire Hathaway, Warren Buffett's conglomerate, and Buffett's son, Howard G. Buffett, sits on the board of Coke.
- **IBM** is high among U.S. corporations when ranked by market value. IBM and its owning Watson family have long-standing ties to the CFR. IBM is a corporate member of the Council at the Premium level. Five of its fourteen directors are CFR members, including two former directors of the Council, Shirley Ann Jackson and Joan E. Spiro, and a current CFR director, James W. Owens.
- **General Electric** has long been among the top U.S. corporations in both market value and equity. GE is a Premium corporate member of the CFR, and five of its sixteen board members are also Council members. One, Ann Fudge, is a current CFR director.
- **ATT** is a Premium corporate member of the CFR. Its chair and CEO, Randall L. Stephenson, is a Council member, as are three other board members, one of which, Laura D'Andrea Tyson, is a former CFR director. ATT closely cooperates with the National Security Agency in its massive, unconstitutional program to wiretap and data-mine Americans' communications.
- **Citigroup** in 2010 was the third-biggest corporation by equity on the *Fortune* list. The Financial Stability Board has identified Citigroup as one of twenty-nine "Global Systemically Important Financial Institutions" (G-SIFIs) whose failure could trigger a global financial crisis. It has long had a close relationship to the CFR. In 2004, for example, eight of of its seventeen directors were Council members. In 2011 there was an almost entirely different group of directors, but still four of twelve were members, including chair Richard D. Parsons. Another Citi director, former President Ernesto Zedillo of Mexico, was previously a member of the Council's International Advisory Board.[304] Citi is among the "Founders" corporate members of the CFR.

- **Goldman Sachs** is another G-SIFI, and among the world's largest investment banks. In 2012 four of Goldman's twelve directors are also in the CFR, including its chair and CEO, Lloyd C. Blankfein. In 2004, three of nine were Council members, including CFR director Steven Friedman. Goldman is also one of the few among the top Founders group of CFR corporate members
- **Merck** is a Premium corporate member of the CFR. It has four directors who are Council members, including Kenneth C. Frazier, its chair and CEO. One of its directors, Thomas H. Glocer, is also a current director of the CFR.
- **JPMorgan Chase** is a G-SIFI, and ranks very high in equity and market value among U.S. corporations. JPMorgan Chase is one of the world's leading investment banks, with a full range of services, including asset management and private equity investing for wealthy clients. It is among the top of the Founders group of CFR corporate members. In 2004 six of its twelve directors, including its chair and CEO, were CFR members. In 2012, three of its twelve directors were also CFR members, and these included Jamie Dimon, the chair and CEO of the company.
- **Morgan Stanley** is another of the top tier of U.S. and world investment banks, a G-SIFI. It also has close ties to the Council. The CFR's current Chief Financial Officer and Treasurer, Kenneth Castiglia, is also CFO and Treasurer of Morgan Stanley. This corporation has three CFR members among its thirteen directors. One of these, Laura D'Andrea Tyson, is a former Council director, and another, James W. Owens, is a current CFR director. It is a CFR corporate member, at the "President's Circle" level.
- **American International Group** was historically close to the CFR under Maurice R. Greenberg, who was CEO of AIG for many years, and was at the same time vice chair of the Council. But since the current capitalist crisis, beginning in 2008, and the giant government bailout of the firm, a different group of directors now runs this firm. Whereas AIG was a corporate member of the CFR at the highest level in 2007, it has dropped its corporate membership and not renewed it. Three of its fourteen current directors are members of the Council, showing a continuing linkage, but not as central as before 2008.
- **Wells Fargo Bank** is one of the largest U.S. banks by both equity and market value, and is another G-SIFI. But Wells was also, in the words of the *Financial Times*, "the epitome of domestically focused American banking."[305] As a bank that generates only a small fraction of its $81 billion revenues from foreign operations, and only 2 percent of its 260,000 employees based outside the United States, Wells does not have the same keen interest in foreign affairs as the other major American banks, and consequently has much less interest and involvement in the CFR. This is obviously changing, since the

same *FT* article cited above states that Wells has big plans to expand abroad. Supporting this suggestion about Wells Fargo's likely evolution is the fact that in 2004 none of Wells fifteen directors were members of the CFR, but by 2012 three of its sixteen directors were members. Two of these, CFR members Elaine L. Chao and Frederico F. Pena, were former high federal government officials. Wells still has not joined the Council as a corporate member, but it has two corporate interlocks (and thus a kind of alliance) with Chevron, which is a CFR corporate member. Both Chevron and Wells Fargo are based in San Francisco, far from the traditional CFR centers of New York and Washington, but, as mentioned in the previous chapter, the Council has been working to expand its reach and become more active in the western part of the United States.

- **Johnson & Johnson** is one of the leading U.S. corporations in the health care sector. Three of its twelve directors are CFR members, as is Robert W. Johnson IV of the owning family. J & J is not, however, a corporate member of the Council.

- **Exxon Mobil** is near the top of the corporate ladder as measured by market value and equity. It is in the Founders group of CFR corporate members, and two of its 12 directors are members of the CFR. Lee Raymond, its former longtime chair and CEO, is also a Council member.

- **Chevron** is ranked near the top in both market value and equity among U.S. corporations. This oil giant is among the few Founders among the CFR's corporate members. Based in San Francisco, far from CFR headquarters in New York, Chevron nevertheless has two of its board members in the CFR.

- **Bank of America** was formerly San Francisco–based, but is now headquartered in North Carolina. This G-SIFI bank does not have the same long history of close ties to the CFR that several of the other inner circle banks have. Currently, only two of its thirteen directors are members of the Council, but by 2009 BofA had also joined the top Founders group of Council corporate members.

- **ConocoPhillips** is a major petroleum company, and a Premium corporate member of the Council. Two of this company's fourteen directors belong to the CFR.

- **Comcast**, a telecommunications firm, is not a corporate member of the CFR, but two of its board members are in the Council.

- **Proctor & Gamble**, one of the nation's largest companies by equity and market value, is not a corporate member of CFR. It does have one member of its eleven-person board who is a member of the Council, Kenneth Chenault, head of American Express, and another, former president of Mexico Ernesto Zedillo, who was on the CFR's International Advisory Board.[306]

PRIVATE EQUITY AND OTHER NON-BANK INVESTMENT FIRMS

Not listed among the Fortune 500 corporations, but important players in the U.S. and international economy, are the private equity and investment firms that are part of the large, powerful, and less-regulated "shadow-banking" system of non-bank financial institutions. The "shadow banking sector represents 25–30 percent of the world's financial sector," states one expert, European Commissioner Michel Barnier.[307] These firms engage in loans, take over corporations for profit, and speculate through hedge funds as well as structured investment vehicles. The big banks also engage in similar activities, but are under greater government regulation as well as protection. Another role played by the shadow-banking sector is to create new ways to expand and intensify capitalism, spreading commodification, exploitation, and dispossession into different sectors of the economy in order to broaden the scope and range of exchange value, increasing capital's profit at the expense of the broad working class. New speculative instruments like credit default swaps and the securitization of loans are invented. "Undervalued" firms are purchased, often with borrowed money, and made "more efficient." In practice this often means layoffs and speedups for the firm's workers, as more profits are squeezed out no matter what the effect on individuals and local communities.

The shadow-banking sector has grown tremendously over the past few decades of neoliberal financial globalization. Hedge fund industry assets were only a few billion dollars in the early 1990s, for example, but reached nearly $500 billion by 2000. Hedge fund assets then took off, more than doubling to over $1 trillion by 2005 and doubling again to over $2 trillion by 2012.[308] In 2013 private equity firms raised $485 billion from speculators and investors and had a record $1.7 trillion available for investment.[309] Much of this business represents gambling pure and simple, producing little to benefit society, yet producing vast wealth for a few. The lightly regulated and unregulated shadow-banking system, together with some overleveraged investment banks, was a key source of instability that helped lead to the 2008 financial crisis.

Following are the six private equity firms most closely connected to the CFR; these also are among the largest and most important.

- **The Blackstone Group** is a corporate member at the Premium level and has been close to the CFR since Blackstone was founded in 1983. In 2013 the *Financial Times* ranked it number one in the world as a manager of "alternative" investments—hedge funds, commodities, infrastructure funds, real estate funds, private equity—for pension funds.[310] One of its two founders, Peter Peterson, chaired the Council from 1985 to 2007 and the other, Steven Schwarzman, is a longtime CFR member. Its current vice chair, J. Tomilson Hill, is on the Council board and heads up the CFR's investment committee. Brian Mulroney, the former Canadian prime minister, is on the Blackstone board. He was also on the Council's International Advisory Board in 2007.[311] Blackstone has had a close cooperative relationship with Kissinger Associates, and the headquarters of both firms share a building in New York City. Blackstone manages $218 billion for wealthy investors, and also purchased about 40,000 single-family dwellings, many of them foreclosed properties, for over $7 billion in a major speculative move during 2012–13. Blackstone is renting many of these homes, "helping to diminish supply and drive up real estate values in some areas."[312] Such speculation increases prices for rank-and-file people, making it more difficult for them to afford to purchase a home. Blackstone, together with Deutsche Bank, Credit Suisse, and JPMorgan Chase, is also marketing a new bond, a security backed by the cash flow from the rental income of these dwellings. This is a new type of securitization, a "fresh asset class" in the words of the *Financial Times*, that has also been given a triple-A, nearly risk-free credit rating.[313] Schwarzman and others in the top leadership of Blackstone have made vast fortunes, and are billionaires. Schwarzman made $374.5 million in 2013 alone, for example.[314]

- **BlackRock** is the world's largest asset manager with over $4 trillion assets under management.[315] It has 120 investment teams working in thirty nations seeking out the highest returns, and its over 10,000 employees manage over 7,000 portfolios belonging to clients in over a hundred countries. It is a corporate member of the CFR at the "President's Circle" level.[316] BlackRock's chair and CEO is CFR member Laurence D. Fink, who also serves on the Council's board. Another CFR member, Jessica P. Einhorn, a former board member of the CFR, is also on BlackRock's board.[317]

- **The Carlyle Group**, founded in 1987, is a global investment firm that had 420 investment specialists working in nineteen nations with a total of $107.6 billion under management in 2011. It is a private partnership owned by senior Carlyle officials and two large institutional investors: Calpers, the California Public Employees Retirement System, which owns 5.1 percent, and Mubadala Development, owned by the Abu Dhabi government, which owns 7.5 percent. In 2004, four of the nine members of the senior management team running the company were CFR members, including current Council director and vice chair David M. Rubenstein, former CFR director Louis V. Gerstner Jr., and CFR members James Baker III (former secretary of state) and Frank Carlucci (former secretary of defense). Rubinstein made $250 million from Carlyle in 2013 alone.[318] Carlyle is majority owner of Booz Allen Hamilton, a CFR corporate member, and a major contractor for the National Security Agency. Booz was the former employer of Edward Snowden, and Booz is where Snowden got the information revealing the unconstitutional domestic and foreign surveillance activities of this agency. The connection between Booz, the NSA, and Carlyle likely allows the latter shadow bank to gain insider information about foreign and domestic corporations, data likely to be of great value in private equity purchases and on the trading floors of globalized casino capitalism.

- **Apollo Management** is a Premium level corporate member of the Council. Its top leadership, Leon D. Black, a founder and current chair, and CEO and managing partner Joshua Harris are both CFR members, as is another director, Paul Fribourg. Black reportedly made $546.3 million from his work directing Apollo in 2013.[319]

- **Kohlberg Kravis Roberts** is one of the largest in this group of firms, and is a corporate member of the CFR at the "President's Circle" level. KKR is closely connected to the CFR through Henry R. Kravis, one of its co-CEOs, and James W. Owens, a senior adviser. Kravis was a Council director (2006–12) and Owens began being a CFR director in 2006. KKR has a number of other connections with the Council. For example, CFR member and former general David H. Petraeus was hired by KKR in 2013 as chair of its "Global Institute," which functions as a kind of in-house think tank to develop the right investment response to emerging geopolitical, macroeconomic, and technological changes worldwide. Kravis made $150 million from KKR in 2013.[320]

  In March of 2013, the *Financial Times* reported that KKR and Apollo Management "have accelerated investments in companies using so-called hydraulic fracturing, or fracking to extract gas reserves."[321] Reporting on speeches by KKR co-founder and former CFR director Henry Kravis and Apollo co-founder and Council member Leon Black at a "SuperReturn" Conference in Berlin, the *Financial Times* stated that Kravis especially played down any negative impact that fracking might have. In regard to fracking, Kravis argued that "a large amount of study has gone into it and there is no proof yet that it's something that's going to hurt the water tables."[322]

- **Warburg Pincus** is a Premium corporate member of the CFR. Charles R. Kaye, one of the two co-presidents of this firm, is a Council member. Former secretary of the treasury Timothy Geithner, long an active CFR member, became president of this firm in 2013.

FOR-PROFIT STRATEGIC POLITICAL RISK AND
ADVISORY CORPORATIONS

Although think tanks like the Council handle large-scale strategic policy development and recommendations for action for the capitalist class as a whole, in our neoliberal era multinational corporations often feel the need for additional expert advice on best how to handle the specific issues and contradictions that arise as they expand their operations into other nation-states, pursuing profits and accumulation across geographic space. In order to meet this need, a number of strategic for-profit consulting firms have been founded since the mid-1970s, sometimes called political risk consultancies. In practice, these firms combine research and analysis, the past experience of their principals and staff, and connections with domestic and foreign leaders to develop recommendations on the risks and opportunities of a given course of action in a specific national political economy. They also develop strategies to meet or evade regulatory, customs, and tax requirements in various nations. These "in-and-outers" trade on their intellectual expertise and government connections at home and abroad to profit by serving the needs of major transnational corporate players. Ten such firms, all with close ties to the CFR, are reviewed below.

- **Kissinger Associates,** founded by Henry A. Kissinger and Brent Scowcroft with loans from Goldman Sachs and other banks in 1982, is known for its secrecy. Due to its prominence, however, enough research has been done to allow reporting in some depth about the organization. For a substantial price, Kissinger Associates (KA) will assist corporate clients on investment opportunities, potential strategic partners, and government relations in nations worldwide. Its list of strategic partners is known to include the Blackstone Group and the international law firm of Covington & Burling, where Eric Holder, President Obama's first attorney general, was a lawyer prior to assuming office. Key clients include American Express, American International Group, Freeport-McMoRan, Hollinger, and JPMorgan Chase. Other known clients include Atlantic Richfield, Coca-Cola, Heinz, Merck, Volvo, and Warburg Pincus. Among these fourteen corporations, only two—Hollinger and Volvo—were not corporate members of the CFR in recent years. At the level of individuals, both Kissinger and Scowcroft have been longtime members of the Council and have served on its board. CFR member Thomas (Mack) McLarty, a former White House chief of staff for Bill Clinton, joined KA in 1999 to open an office in Washington. Directors of KA have included other Council members such as William E. Simon, a former secretary of the treasury, and William D. Rogers, a former undersecretary of state. Foreign directors include several individuals active in the Bilderberg and Trilateral Commission meetings, such as Lord Carrington and Lord Roll of Britain, Etienne Davignon of Belgium, and Saburo Okita of Japan.

  Prominent KA staff over the years have included many CFR members, all of whom have also served in important roles as "in-and-outers" in the U.S.

government: Secretary of the Treasury Timothy F. Geithner, Secretary of State Lawrence Eagleburger, governor of New Mexico and energy secretary Bill Richardson, president of Federal Reserve Bank of Dallas Richard W. Fisher, Deputy Director of the CIA Jami Miscik, Ambassador and Assistant Secretary of State J. Stapleton Roy, member of the International Economic Advisory Committee of the Department of State Nelson Cunningham, and L. Paul Bremer, Director of Reconstruction in Iraq. In short, KA is very closely connected to the U.S. government as well as the CFR. Kissinger's personal views toward rank-and-file people, likely reflecting a wider CFR/capitalist-class perspective, were expressed when he once pointedly told his assistant, General Alexander Haig, another longtime member of the CFR, that "military men are dumb, stupid animals to be used . . ." as pawns in foreign policy ploys, including, of course, in wars.[323]

- **Albright Stonebridge Group,** founded by longtime CFR members Madeleine K. Albright (who has also been a Council director) and Samuel R. Berger in 2001, has worked in more than ninety-five different countries on six continents, with teams operating in at least a dozen major cities. Albright and Berger are still the co-chairs and are joined by three other Council members to make up a ten-person board of directors. They call themselves "a global strategy firm that helps corporations, associations and nonprofit organizations around the world meet their core objectives in a highly competitive, complex and ever-changing marketplace." The firm is also affiliated with Albright Capital Management, "an emerging markets investment firm led by a team of seasoned investment professionals." Under "capabilities" on their website, ASG lists six key aspects of their work: "navigate government regulations; assess market risks; develop regulatory strategies; create sustainable partnerships, seize growth opportunities; promote corporate citizenship." One 2014 example of its work was advising the Elliott Management hedge fund and other holdout creditors in their sovereign debt conflict with Argentina.[324]

Like Kissinger, Albright also has little regard for the lives of rank-and-file soldiers or, for that matter, innocent civilians. In the 1990s she favored a war on Saddam Hussein's Iraq and was looking for an excuse to start such a war. While UN ambassador, with the United States involved in enforcing a no-fly zone in Iraq, Albright had the following exchange with Chairman of the Joint Chiefs of Staff General Hugh Shelton, which he later recounted in his memoirs: "Hugh, I know I shouldn't even be asking you this, but what we really need in order to go in and take out Saddam is a precipitous event—something that would make us look good in the eyes of the world. Could you have one of our U-2's fly low enough—and slow enough—so as to guarantee that Saddam could shoot it down?" Shelton recounted that he was very angry at the question, but offered this reply: "Why of course we can, just as soon as we get your ass qualified to fly it, I will have it flown just as low and as slow as you want to go." Shelton added that he was shocked at the disrespect of Albright and told her: "Remember, there is one of our great Americans flying that U-2, and you are asking me to intentionally send him or her to their death for an opportunity to kick Saddam. The last time I checked, we don't operate like that here in America."[325]

As secretary of state, Albright also got critical attention with her answer to fellow CFR member Leslie Stahl's question as broadcast on *60 Minutes* on May 12, 1996. Stahl asked if the price of 500,000 dead Iraqi children due to U.S. sanctions was "worth it." Albright replied: "I think this is a very hard choice, but ... we think the price is worth it."

- **Hills and Company International Consultants** was formed by CFR co-chair Carla A. Hills with her husband, Roderick M. Hills, in 1993, immediately after Carla Hills had been George H. W. Bush's trade representative. Their corporate website states that the business was established to "help businesses expand trade and investment worldwide." They achieve this through developing a strategy for negotiation with the power players in a given nation. They then work to "persuade key figures in public and private sectors in a foreign market to take the steps necessary to accomplish the client's objectives." Building on Carla Hills's trade representative experience, Hills and Company stresses their expertise in the areas of World Trade Organization rules and procedures, bilateral and regional trade agreements, tax, tariff, health, regulatory, and product labeling matters, as well as customs classification and economic sanctions issues. They cite successes in working in China, Russia, Brazil, India, Japan, Pakistan, Argentina, Taiwan, Costa Rica, the Philippines, and Egypt. Hills and Company clients include Chevron, AIG, Boeing, Bechtel, Coca-Cola, Pfizer, Procter & Gamble, Novartis, Qualcomm, and Mars Incorporated.

  Carla A. Hills is the chair of Hills and Company, which has five principals, including Roderick M. Hills. Carla Hills has been a director of a number of large Council-connected corporations and her husband of even more. Another principal, vice chair Thomas R. Pickering, is a former Council director, and has been a U.S. ambassador both to the UN as well as to a number of countries. He also served as Undersecretary of State for Political Affairs in the Clinton administration. Hills and Company principal Alexander F. Watson is another CFR member, who, like Carla Hills, worked in the office of the U.S. Trade Representative and was also an assistant secretary of state.

- **Oxford Analytica,** a British-based corporate member of the CFR, calls itself "a global analysis and advisory firm which draws on a macro expert network to advise its clients on strategy and performance in complex markets." They claim a confidential contributor network of "over 1,400 leading scholars, former policymakers, regulators, and industry leaders, focused on geopolitical and macroeconomic issues. Most are based in top universities and research institutions around the globe." Founded in 1975, it is the oldest of the nine strategic consulting firms discussed here. Of the ten individuals listed as making up its board of directors in 2013, two former corporate executives, Lawrence C. McQuade and Tracy R. Wolstencraft, are members of the Council.[326] Additionally, five members of its international advisory board are also Council members, including former ambassador and undersecretary of state John Negroponte.

- **Control Risks Group** is also a British based-firm that is a CFR corporate member. Beginning as a professional adviser to the insurance industry, in the 1990s it expanded its focus to serve multinational corporations and now has thirty-four offices and over 2,000 employees around the world. It specializes in political, security, and integrity global risks. Its team of political risk analysts assesses how political risk issues might impact a specific business. Security risk involves providing threat assessment, security design, travel security, executive protection, and emergency crisis management. Integrity risk focuses on preventing corruption, including agent screening, managing whistleblower hotlines, and conducting investigations of malfeasance.

- **Eurasia Group** calls itself the "world's largest political risk research and consulting firm," with over 400 clients, a staff of 150, and a network of 500 experts in eighty nations worldwide. The Eurasia Group is recognized as the first risk consultancy to bring the discipline of political science to Wall Street in a systematic way, allowing them to rank the "top ten risks" on a yearly basis, and to apply both quantitative and qualitative risk assessments to measure stability in emerging markets. Their methodology is supposed to provide an early warning system, anticipating trends and predicting if a given country can withstand economic, political, security, and social shocks. The firm began in the 1990s with a focus on the nations of the former USSR and of Eastern Europe, but soon expanded worldwide, covering not just governance and security issues, but also regulatory ones, as well as regional relations and social trends. In 2011 Eurasia Group also launched a partnership with Bank of America to provide research to wealthy clients and use geopolitical analysis to develop investment portfolios. It also acquired Intellibridge, a strategic advisory firm founded by CFR members Anthony Lake and David Rothkopf.

  The top leadership of the Eurasia Group includes CFR members as well as foreign nationals. Its president, Ian Bremmer, and Cliff Kupchan, one of the members of its operating committee, both belong to the Council. On Eurasia's advisory board are former CFR director Thomas Pickering (also vice chair of Hills and Company); Enzo Viscusi, a vice president of Eni Corporation; Win

Neuger, vice chair of PineBridge Investments; and Edward L. Morse, managing director of Citigroup, all of them Council members.

- **GartenRothkopf** is a partnership of Council members Jeffery E. Garten and David Rothkopf. GartenRothkopf advertises itself as a cutting-edge "international advisory firm that helps leaders capitalize on transformational trends in energy, climate, risk and the global economy." With investor, executive, and official clients on four continents, they claim on their website a "distinct set of capabilities at the intersection of economics, markets, technology, and policy to systematically identify unforeseen risks and unconventional opportunities." Its largest areas of practice are in emerging markets and the rapidly developing field of energy choice and climate change.

  After working on Wall Street as managing director of Lehman Brothers and Blackstone, Jeffery E. Garten was the Undersecretary of Commerce for International Trade in the first Clinton administration. He then served for a decade as Dean of the Yale School of Management, then as a professor in the same school. He serves or has served on the board or advisory board of Aetna, Credit Suisse Asset Management, Toyota, Alcan, Calpine, and the Chicago Climate Exchange (a greenhouse gas trading exchange). He has also authored several books and a number of articles, including for *Foreign Affairs*.

  David Rothkopf is also an author of several books, including the 2008 work *Superclass: The Global Power Elite and the World They Are Making*, and over 150 articles. He served, as did Garten, as an undersecretary of commerce in the Clinton administration. After leaving government, he was the managing director of Kissinger Associates, then was co-founder and chairman of Intelibridge.

- **The Scowcroft Group** was founded by Brent Scowcroft, National Security Adviser to both presidents Gerald Ford and George H. W. Bush, besides serving as vice chair of Kissinger Associates. Later he founded and today manages TSG, which calls itself an "international business advisory firm" that develops and executes strategies carefully tailored to individual countries. Its website states that "our team of Principals brings extensive strategic planning and risk management experience in global business and government, coupled with extraordinary regional expertise in Asia, Africa, the Middle East, Western and Eastern Europe, Russia, and Latin America."

  The ten principals of the Scowcroft Group include five Council members, including its founder, who is a former CFR director.

- **RiceHadleyGates** is based in Silicon Valley and Washington, D.C. There are four principals in this firm, all CFR members. Condoleezza Rice, Steven J. Hadley, and Robert Gates all served in high positions in the George W. Bush administration, as National Security Advisers, as Secretary of State, and Secretary of Defense. Anja Manuel was a lower-level State Department official

in the same administration. Like the other firms of this type, it offers corporations "advice based on extensive experience in the international arena. We
work with companies to develop and implement their strategic plans and help
them expand in emerging markets, including in Asia, the Middle East and the
Americas." Two of their white papers, available on their website, discuss growth
opportunities in India and Sub-Saharan Africa.[327]

- **The Cohen Group** was founded by former Defense Secretary and CFR director William S. Cohen when he left the Clinton administration in early 2001.
The objectives of the firm are: "helping multinational clients explore opportunities overseas as well as solve problems that may develop. The Cohen Group
has the unique ability to provide our clients with truly comprehensive tools
for understanding and shaping their business, political, legal, regulatory, and
media environments."

The Cohen Group has a strategic alliance with the international law firm
DLA Piper, one of the largest law firms in the world. Both the Cohen Group
and DLA Piper have multiple connections to the CFR. Besides Cohen himself, Marc Grossman, a vice chair at the Cohen Group, is a Council member,
and former ambassador and undersecretary of state Nicholas Burns is both
a CFR member and a senior counselor at Cohen. Former Senator George J.
Mitchell, DLA Piper's former chairman, was a Council director, and former
U.S. senator and CFR member Tom Daschle is a policy adviser at this law
firm.

LEADING UNIVERSITIES

The Council is closest to seven of America's leading universities. Although it has
ties to many others, the seven that follow are most central to the CFR's work and
the training of future leaders and members of this organization.

- **Harvard and Yale** are the two richest, highest-ranked, and most prestigious
U.S. universities, and among the oldest. Harvard has the biggest endowment, for example, and Yale has the second largest. These two private schools
are also the "go-to" universities for the CFR. Top Council leaders are far
more likely to have attended Harvard and Yale than any other university:
Rockefeller, Rubin, and Dillon went to Harvard; Vance, Rubin, Hills, and
Salomon went to Yale. The same goes for staff members. The 1998 CFR
Annual Report offers detailed biographies of 36 CFR Fellows.[328] Among
them they list sixty-five earned college degrees (undergraduate and graduate). Twelve of these degrees were from Yale, ten from Harvard, six from
various schools in England (Oxford, Cambridge, King's College), and three

each from the University of Chicago and Stanford. Over half of all the earned degrees of these CFR Fellows were from these few key schools, with no other school having more than two.

Viewed from another perspective, Harvard and Yale's own leadership is also connected to the CFR. Two of ten fellows of the Harvard Corporation are members of the Council, and one of these is the CFR's co-chair, Robert Rubin. Of the thirty individuals on Harvard's Board of Overseers, four are members of the CFR. In the case of Yale, four of the seventeen Fellows of the Yale Corporation are members of the Council, and one of them, Fareed Zakaria, is a CFR director.

Finally, large numbers of professors from these two universities belong to the Council. A quick review of faculty lists of only four Harvard departments—Economics, Government, Kennedy School, and History—easily identified twenty-two members that were in the CFR. These included well-known names like Samuel P. Huntington, Stanley Hoffman, Ernest R. May, Richard N. Cooper, Kenneth S. Rogoff, Lawrence H. Summers, Joseph S. Nye, Graham T. Allison, and Stephen M. Walt.

- **The University of Chicago** was founded with funds from John D. Rockefeller Sr. Six out of forty-six trustees are CFR members. One of these, David M. Rubenstein, is a current Council vice chair, and another, Thomas J. Pritzker, also a CFR member, is the brother of Penny Pritzker, who was a CFR director prior to joining the Obama administration. David Rockefeller, who graduated from this university with a PhD in 1940, is Chairman Emeritus of this university. At least one top scholar in the field of international affairs, John J. Mearsheimer, is also a member of the CFR.[329]

- **Stanford University** has the third-biggest endowment among U.S. universities, behind only Harvard and Yale. Four of its thirty-two trustees were members of the Council in 2012, including former CFR director Penny S. Pritzker. Condoleezza Rice is also a professor at Stanford.

- **Princeton** has had a long relationship with the Council, even though only one of Princeton's forty trustees is a member of the CFR. Longtime CFR leaders Hamilton Fish Armstrong and Allen W. Dulles both graduated from this university, and its library holds their personal papers and a massive collection of the Council's historical archives. At least two top scholars in the field of international affairs, Robert Keohane and G. John Ikenberry, are Princeton professors and CFR members.[330]

- **Columbia University** has as its president, Lee C. Bollinger, who along with two other of Columbia's twenty-four trustees were CFR members in 2012. At least two top scholars in the field of international affairs, Kenneth Waltz and Robert Jervis, are Columbia professors and CFR members.[331]

- **Johns Hopkins** has four among its forty-five trustees who are members of the CFR, including Council vice chair David M. Rubenstein. Its School of Advanced International Studies (SAIS) has a large representation of Council members, Fellows and former Fellows. Vali R. Nasr, the dean of the SAIS, is a CFR member, and a former Council Senior Fellow for the Middle East. Kenneth H. Keller, the director of the Bologna Center of SAIS, is a Council member and former CFR Senior Fellow for science and technology. The fourteen Foreign Policy Institute Fellows at SAIS include six Council members, among them former CFR director Zbigniew Brzezinski and authors Francis Fukuyama and James Mann.

MAJOR FOUNDATIONS

Private philanthropic foundations represent a key way that the rich can avoid taxes and at the same time serve their own interests and gain recognition and legitimacy for their so-called charitable activities. Giving to charity undercuts the demand that government fully fund health and welfare programs that directly serve people's needs, which is what the state should be doing. Instead, private philanthropy creates dependency on the capitalist class. Support for educational activities also allows foundations, such as the Bill & Melinda Gates Foundation, to promote the privatization of education through charter schools and make donations of computers that over time directly expands the need for computers and the bottom line of Microsoft Corporation.

The educational activities of the CFR have been major beneficiaries of private foundations largess, representing a key funding source historically. In recent decades such funding has become less crucial, but still very useful to the CFR. Council funds come from a mix of older foundations, based on nineteenth- and early twentieth-century wealth, and newer foundations, based on mid- and late twentieth-century wealth. The National Endowment for Democracy is a special case, as it is funded by Congress. It is among the top tier of those institutions with the most links to the CFR. In this top tier are five private foundations that have at least six directors or trustees who are also members of the CFR. These collectively hold about $11.5 billion in assets.

- **The Rockefeller Foundation** is the private foundation most closely tied to the CFR. It had $3.5 billion in assets in 2012. Council member David Rockefeller Jr. is the chair of the Rockefeller Foundation's governing Board of Trustees. It consists of thirteen individuals, two of them not citizens of the United States. Of the eleven eligible for CFR membership, five are current (2012) members, and one more is a former CFR member, making a total of 54.5 percent former or current members.

- **Carnegie Corporation of New York** is also highly interlocked with the Council. It had $2.8 billion in assets, and nineteen trustees in 2012. Ten of them (52.6 percent) belong to the CFR. These include vice chair Kurt L. Schmoke, two university presidents, and former World Bank president James D. Wolfensohn.
- **The National Endowment for Democracy** is funded by the U.S. Congress. Founded in 1983, in recent years NED has spent about $100 million annually on over 1,000 projects of non-governmental organizations in over ninety nations. A large percentage of these projects are to foster the neoliberal geopolitical capitalist penetration of these countries, under the cover of promoting democracy. In the year prior to the 2014 conflict in the Ukraine, for example, it spent millions on sixty-five different projects in that nation, including $359,945 to fund a "Center for International Private Enterprise," at least partly to build up the lobbying power of Ukrainian businesses. Many of the Ukrainian projects are to train local activists, including election-related training. The twenty-three-member board of directors of NED include ten CFR members (43.5 percent). Two of them—Vin Weber and Robert B. Zoellick—are former or current Council directors and two—Elliott Abrams and Stephen Sestanovich—are CFR Senior Fellows.
- **The Bloomberg Philanthropies** were organized and funded by CFR member and billionaire Michael Bloomberg. They have $4.2 billion in assets, and eight on their twenty-two-person board of directors (36.4 percent) are Council members.
- **The Rockefeller Brothers Fund,** with nearly $1 billion in assets, has nineteen trustees. Six (31.5 percent) are CFR members. These include the fund's president, Stephen Heintz, and two members of the Rockefeller family: David Rockefeller Jr. and Nelson's son Steven, both members of the Council.

LEADING MEDIA

Most Americans get the information they need to think and act politically directly or indirectly from leading media. The most influential print media were ranked in 2004–2005 by Erdos & Morgan, a business-to-business research firm. Using a representative sample of over 450,000 U.S. opinion leaders the survey documented the print media leaders used to get the information needed in their work. Erdos & Morgan then ranked the top ten "most influential media." Ranked first was the CFR's own magazine, *Foreign Affairs.* The top eight on the list are:

1. *Foreign Affairs*
2. *CQ Weekly*
3. *New York Times*
4. *Wall Street Journal*
5. *The Economist*
6. *Harvard Business Review*
7. *Washington Post*
8. *New York Times Sunday Edition*

As is the case for large American corporations, it is not possible, within space limitations, to cover all the Council's connections to other influential media. But it can be said that the CFR has a multitude of connections with a wide range of media in the United States, ranging from the major television networks to magazines to news services to scholarly publications. [332]

- **CQ Weekly and *The Economist*.** These two leading media enterprises are both majority owned by British capital, the Economist Group. This Group is in turn owned by the *Financial Times (FT)*, along with the Rothschild, Cadbury, and Schroder family interests. Almost all of the Group's board of directors are British citizens and thus not eligible for CFR membership. One exception is group director Lynn Forester de Rothschild, who is a U.S. citizen and a CFR member. At least a few Council Fellows have a close relationship with the *FT*. Senior Fellow Sebastian Mallaby is a contributing editor to the *FT*, and Senior Fellow Edward Alden is a former Washington Bureau Chief of the *FT*. The *FT* also often prints op-ed articles from CFR leaders like Richard N. Haass.
- *The New York Times* has long had a close relationship with the CFR. At least three members of the Sulzberger-Oakes owning family of the *Times* have been members of the Council in recent decades: C. L.Sulzberger, John B. Oakes, and John G. H. Oakes.[333] One of the *Times*'s current directors, Robert Denham, out of ten, is a member of the CFR. A number of top staff members also belong to the CFR, such as Opinion Editor Andrew M. Rosenthal, Assistant Managing Editor Craig R. Whitney, Foreign News Editor Susan D. Chira, White House Correspondent David E. Sanger, and leading columnists or editorial writers Thomas L. Friedman, Nicholas D. Kristof, David C. Unger, and Andrew Ross Sorkin.
- **News Corp (Fox News and *Wall Street Journal*)** have a number of connections to the Council, beginning with Rupert Murdoch, billionaire chair, key owner, and CEO of News Corp, and a member of the CFR. Murdoch is a controversial figure even in corporate ruling-class circles. Philip Stevens, a *Financial Times* commentator, stated in 2011 that News Corp was guilty of criminality

on an "industrial scale," a "family fiefdom" that was "... out of control—devoid of even the most basic ethical standards."[334] Two other Council members also sit on the News Corp board, former Goldman Sachs banker John L. Thornton and investment banker Stanley S. Shuman, who is a director emeritus. The Deputy Managing Editor of the *Wall Street Journal*, Alan S. Murray, is also a CFR member, as are *Journal* writers Daniel Henninger and Peggy Noonan, who was Ronald Reagan's primary speechwriter. Prior to Murdoch's takeover of the *Journal*, CFR members Peter R. Kann and Karen Elliott House were the chair/CEO and president/publisher of the *Journal* until they retired in 2006. House is also a former director of the Council.

- *Harvard Business Review*'s editor-in-chief, Adi Ignatius, is a member of the CFR.
- The *Washington Post* also has key connections to the Council. Four CFR members are directors of this media group, including Ronald L. Olsen, a former Council director. Some of the Post's leading writers are also CFR members, such as Walter Pincus, Jim Hoagland, and David R. Ignatius. In 2008 the *Post* purchased *Foreign Policy* magazine from the Carnegie Endowment for International Peace. Two Council members, Samuel P. Huntington and Warren D. Manshel, were among the founders of this magazine in 1970, and CFR members have been central figures in its operation since then.

SUMMARY

Although this chapter does not include every single organization concerned with the U.S. political economy and foreign policy, it has shown in detail that the CFR is connected to a very large number of leading institutions across a wide swath of U.S. political, economic, media, and intellectual life. This highlights a central reality, namely that the CFR is unique: it stands at the center of a vast network of the most powerful people and institutions of the United States. There is no other organization in the nation with even nearly its level of connections. Its inner circle is very large and often deep, and it also has a wider circle of influence beyond that inner circle, making the totality of its network truly impressive. The Council is thus able to acquire information, communicate ideas, and coordinate the formation of top-level opinion on what should be the foreign and economic policies and strategy of the United States, the framework for discussion and debate. The CFR becomes the formal expression of an exclusive community of, by, and for the capitalist class. It is the central place where this community debates and develops their common worldview, spreading it far and wide through its many members and allied organizations, so that their views become accepted wisdom. The Council's activities are thus a key way that the ideological hegemony of the capitalist class is established and maintained, while developing and implementing the policies that make this class a ruling class, a class for itself.

There are only a relatively few important domestic institutions not connected or minimally tied to the Council, and those are generally on the far-right side of the political spectrum. One example is the Koch Brothers economic and political empire. What those on the right generally have in common is an ideological opposition to the state having a large role in the political economy of the nation. The CFR, on the other hand, strongly favors a powerful state, and its leaders and members directly and indirectly influence it, benefiting from government protection, intervention, and largess. Those outside the CFR circle that are at least a little left of center, such as most of today's labor movement, are apparently considered increasingly irrelevant by the Council.

4

THE INTERNATIONAL
CONNECTIONS OF THE CFR

The transnational equivalent of the CFR is the Trilateral Commission.

—ARUNDHATI ROY

Although national power structures persist and remain dominant, over the past few decades a small but increasingly integrated transnational capitalist class has gradually been developing. There is now in some respects a worldwide ruling class, a tiny percentage of the population that dominates the lives of billions. The core group is mainly made up of corporate businessmen: billionaires and multimillionaires, most of them living in the United States, Europe, the larger Asian nations, and the Middle East, making up a financialized international capitalist class. In her book *Plutocrats,* Chrystia Freeland argues that the members of this capitalist class, led by the U.S. contingent, are closely connected internationally: "America still dominates the world economy, and Americans still dominate the super-elite. . . . The rise of the 1 percent is a global phenomenon, and in a globalized world economy, the plutocrats are the most international of all, both in how they live their lives and in how they earn their fortunes."[335]

The CFR is one of the central organizations that consolidates this developing capitalist class network; it provides a key link between the financialized capitalist class of the United States and the rest of the world's globalizing plutocracy. In this chapter the Council's wide-ranging international connections and relationships with the foreign plutocracy are explored through examination of the close ties between the Council and a number of different organizations: the Bilderberg Group, the Trilateral Commission, the annual World Economic Forum meetings at Davos, the Group of Thirty, the International Crisis Group, the CFR's own

International Advisory Board and Global Board of Advisors, the Council's foreign corporate members, and a newer organization, the Council of Councils.

THE BILDERBERG GROUP

In a sense, the Council on Foreign Relations has always been well connected internationally, dating to its founding during the First World War era. Its sister organization was then, as now, the Royal Institute of International Affairs, also known as Chatham House, a body mainly of the British nobility and that nation's industrial, commercial, and financial plutocracy. Since the mid-1950s the CFR's international ties have greatly intensified. The initial spark for this development was the founding of the European-based Bilderberg Group, a secretive discussion and consensus-seeking organization that in 1954 began meeting for a long weekend once a year. The point of the original meetings was to call together a Western European–U.S. forum to begin to articulate a common program of cooperation and coordination, including NATO-related issues, developing European unity, and containing the left, the Soviet Union, and communism. Over time, additional concerns such as relations with the varied nations of the third world, including the Middle East, and more general world economic questions around trade, investment, and development also became major foci of discussion. The official Bilderberg website explains the origins, name, and method of operation of the organization:

> Bilderberg takes its name from the hotel in Holland where the first meeting took place in May 1954. That pioneering meeting grew out of the concern expressed by leading citizens on both sides of the Atlantic that Western Europe and North America were not working together as closely as they should on common problems of critical importance. It was felt that regular, off-the-record discussions would help create a better understanding of the complex forces and major trends affecting Western nations in the difficult postwar period. . . . At the meetings no resolutions are proposed, no votes taken, and no policy statements issued. . . . Invitations to Bilderberg conferences are extended by the Chairman following consultation with the Steering Committee members. . . . There are usually about 120 participants of whom about two-thirds come from Europe and the balance from North America. About one-third is from government and politics, and two-thirds from finance, industry, labour, education and communications. Participants attend Bilderberg in a private and not an official capacity.[336]

The somewhat defensive tone of this official description, stressing that there are no resolutions, votes, or policy statements was likely prompted by attacks on

Bilderberg by some on the far-right wing of the U.S. political spectrum, which has tried to impose its own bizarre worldview onto the topic, arguing that the Bilderberg meetings (and the CFR's for that matter) are a conspiracy aiming to create a "New World Order" of global socialism.[337] This only begins to make any sense if "socialism" is defined as government; that is, the collectivization of necessary modern-day functions, such as building and maintaining roads, water and sewer systems, schools, regulation of utilities, and so on. It is certainly true that the Bilderberg Group and the Council want pliable, capitalist-dependent national governments that protect them with police, jails, and military forces, that develop infrastructure, including financial infrastructure, and help capitalists with bailouts, corporate welfare, government contracts, conquering new markets, and much more. This hardly represents socialism, which is more accurately described as a new, more advanced form of civilization, a fully egalitarian and participatory democratic political economy and society of, by, and for the overwhelming majority of the people, the workers.

As stated above, the key leaders of the Bilderberg meetings are the chairman and steering committee members, who select the participants and agenda for each meeting. A review of the biographies of the seven chairmen who have served since 1954 reveals an interesting fact: six of the seven are from the European nobility. In addition, Joseph Retinger, a Pole whom David Rockefeller stated was of "aristocratic origins," was the one who urged Prince Bernhard, a prime early organizer and first chairman (1954–76), to form the Bilderberg organization to promote cooperation and coordination among the "Atlantic community."[338] The Bilderberg Group and its meetings are therefore best viewed as a project organized and led by the European nobility.

German-born HRH Prince Bernhard was the husband of Queen Juliana of the Netherlands. Bernhard was born into a landed noble family in 1911. His family lost some of their estates and their associated revenue after the First World War, but retained other lands, and Bernhard spent much of his youth on a family estate in East Prussia, an area now part of Poland. Bernhard was briefly a member of the Nazi Party while a university student in the 1930s, but left it after he graduated. In the mid-1930s he worked as Secretary of the Board of Directors of IG Farben, then one of the world's largest monopoly corporations. His life dramatically changed when he married then Princess Juliana in 1937. Various Nazis, both family members and friends, reportedly attended the wedding, but henceforth Bernhard was loyal to the Netherlands. This meant he was opposed to the Nazis and German domination of Europe. Even though his brother was a German officer in the Second World War, Bernhard fought with the British, flying both fighters and bombers in missions against his former country. By 1944 he was the well-respected commander of the Dutch Armed Forces.

After the war, Bernhard continued in military roles and served on numerous corporate boards, including that of KLM Royal Dutch Airlines. After over twenty years as chair of the Bilderberg meetings, Bernhard had to resign in 1976 due to a scandal. As Inspector General of the Dutch armed forces, in 1974 he sent a letter to Lockheed Aircraft Company demanding a "commission" of $1.1 million in exchange for arranging the purchase of Lockheed airplanes by the Dutch government. The bribe was paid, but once it was exposed in 1976, Bernhard had to resign as chair of Bilderberg, creating a temporary crisis in the organization.[339]

Bernhard was succeeded as chair by the president of West Germany, Walter Scheel, who had been a Luftwaffe pilot in the Second World War, then in turn foreign minister, chancellor, and president. Scheel served only a few years as chair of Bilderberg. The next three Bilderberg chairmen were all members of the British landed nobility, an earl and two barons. The first was Alec, the 14th Earl of Home, a Conservative leader of the House of Lords, the heir to extensive family estates in the English countryside, and a Knight of the Order of the Thistle. The second was Baron Eric Roll of Ipsden, a banker who became director of the Bank of England. The third was Peter, the sixth Baron of Carrington, also known as Baron Carrington of Upton. He was a Knight in the order of St. Michael and St. George and also served as chancellor of these two Orders. A Conservative Party politician, Carrington entered the House of Lords in 1940. He became Defense Secretary in 1970, chair of the Conservative Party in 1972, Foreign Secretary in 1979, and Secretary-General of NATO in 1984.

The most recent two chairs have been Etienne François Jacques Davignon, Viscount Davignon of Belgium, and Henri de la Croix de Castries of France. Davignon was the chair of the top Belgian bank Société Générale de Belgique as well as Brussels Airlines and was also a director of several other large multinational corporations. Castries, the current chair, is a member of a French landed noble family from Languedoc in southern France. The Castrieses are "Nobles of the Sword," and a family member (General Christian de Castries) was the commander at the decisive 1954 battle of Dien Bien Phu in Vietnam. Henri de Castries is the chair and CEO of AXA, the French multinational insurance company, with 1.1 trillion euros currently under management.

Bilderberg steering committee members, together with a small group listed as "Honorary Secretaries-General" past and present, include an impressive number of chairmen and CEOs of leading transnational banks, investment companies, conglomerates, media outlets, and industrial firms, together with some politicians and think tank leaders. By 2011 a few top leaders from China and Russia were also attending the meetings, but no one from these nations is on the steering committee or listed as Honorary Secretary-General. In both 2011 and 2012 current CFR co-chair Robert E. Rubin participated in the meetings. Although women have been severely underrepresented, in 2011 both the Queen of the Netherlands and the Queen of Spain attended, indicating that women are all right in Bilderberg circles (as long as they are queens). David Rockefeller and Boston Brahmin Senator John Forbes Kerry also attended in 2011, but Rockefeller is omitted from the 2012 list of participants, likely the first meeting he failed to make since 1954.

A comparison of the fifty-two U.S. citizens participating as top leaders in the Bilderberg meetings (on the steering committee or listed as an Honorary Secretary-General) with CFR membership lists reveals the striking fact that 48 of them (92 percent), have been members of the CFR. This includes thirteen who were also directors of the Council: Joseph E. Johnson, Kenneth W. Dam, Arthur H. Dean, Louis V. Gerstner, Winston Lord, Charles McC. Mathias, George J. Mitchell, Bill D. Moyers, David Rockefeller, Gabriel Hauge, Richard C. Holbrooke, Henry A. Kissinger, and Marina von Neumann Whitman. Hauge, whom President Eisenhower sent to Bilderberg meetings as his personal representative, was also a longtime treasurer of the CFR; Lord was also president; and of course Rockefeller was chair of the Council for fifteen years.[340] Clearly, the Bilderberg Group, organized by some of the leading nobles of Europe, together with their multinational corporate allies, consider the CFR to be the U.S. organization to be in consultation with when discussing and attempting to develop mutual understanding and consensus on what they consider the key issues of the future.

THE TRILATERAL COMMISSION

In 1972 CFR leaders David Rockefeller and Zbigniew Brzezinski attended the Bilderberg meeting in Belgium. The two had concluded that because of Japan's increasing global economic power, it was essential to have Japanese participation in international forums like Bilderberg. They proposed to the Bilderberg leadership that Japanese leaders be invited, but they were, in Rockefeller's words, "politely but firmly told no."[341] After the Bilderberg meeting was over, Rockefeller, Brzezinski, and several other Council members decided to establish a "trilateral" organization that would bring together leaders and key thinkers from Western Europe, North America, and Japan. Rockefeller then convened a large meeting at his country home in the summer of 1972, which included representatives from all three regions. Brzezinski agreed to serve as the director of the new organization, with Rockefeller as the North American chair. Thus the Trilateral Commission (TC), a private, by invitation-only, international agenda-setting and policy-planning organization, was founded with many Bilderbergers involved.[342] It soon became a part of the processes that resulted in the eventual birth of our present neoliberal geopolitical world order.

In the case of the Bilderberg meetings, European nobility are in charge, with help from the leaders of the biggest transnational corporations and the CFR.

In the case of the TC, U.S. and especially Council leaders have been in control. Another difference is that whereas both groups have only one formal meeting a year, the TC organizes small ongoing policy study groups with representatives from all three regions, the purpose of which is to consider a key problem and write a report outlining the issues and the common solution. In this, the TC is a lot like the CFR, except it has trilateral instead of only U.S. participation in studies. At a deeper level, the establishment of the TC involved recognition that Europe and Japan had fully recovered from the disaster of the Second World War, and therefore a more shared form of leadership and a wider system for the management of contradictions within the global capitalist class and among the leading capitalist nations, including Japan, was necessary.

Since that time, the TC has continued to attempt to marry the influential with the intellectual, identifying the central ideological and programmatic problems of the larger U.S. alliance system (roughly corresponding to the U.S. informal empire) and formulating neoliberal policy proposals to address them. These proposals included a concerted offensive against third world revolution by pursuing the integration of the neocolonies into the international capitalist system and developing a common front against challenges from the left. The TC, like the CFR, privately brings together key capitalist-class leaders, especially those representing transnational finance capital and their professional-class allies to identify and handle developing conflicts and develop consensus on maintaining and expanding the system. This includes assuring economic growth, influencing government leaders, and educating the attentive publics in each nation so that overall public opinion and governmental policies will come to reflect their private consensus. In the specific case of the TC the purpose is to promote the ideological outlook of the largest multinational corporations and engineer an enduring consensus among the ruling classes of the three main geopolitical centers of world power to "manage interdependence," safeguarding mutual interests in a rapidly changing and globalizing world. Its practice consists of regular meetings and a series of publications, most of them pamphlet-size, but some book-length.

One of the TC's early books, *The Crisis of Democracy: Report on the Governability of Democracies to the Trilateral Commission* (1975), drew unwelcome attention. As was usual for a TC publication, it was co-authored by three people, one each from North America, Europe, and Japan. The author from North America was Harvard professor and CFR member Samuel P. Huntington. Huntington wrote the section covering the United States. Recognizing the reality that capitalism always desires less democracy and that, in fact, genuine capitalism can best be achieved when all forms of democracy are abolished, Huntington wrote that U.S. citizens were at fault for taking democracy seriously and that there was an ongoing problem of an "excess of democracy," a "democratic distemper" in the United States.[343] This, he believed, had been caused by an "internal democratic surge" during the 1960s, and the solution was a "greater degree of moderation in democracy" in order to, among other things, reduce government expenditures as a percentage of Gross Domestic Product, thus weakening government so that private capitalism could play a larger role.[344] The bluntness of Huntington's assessment and direct advocacy of the neo-liberal gospel violated a taboo among the powerful of U.S. society, namely that the rhetoric of the United States as a wonderful and exceptionally democratic society should never be openly challenged. As a result, there was a controversy over the book, even within the Trilateral Commission itself.

The flavor of more recent TC concerns can be captured by a review of the sessions held at one of the Commission's annual meetings, held in Tokyo in April 2012, which was also addressed by Japanese prime minister Noda. The meeting's ten sessions were on the following topics:

1. Governance Challenges in Japan
2. Geopolitics of the South China Sea
3. Future Regional Architecture for East Asia
4. European Financial and Economic Crisis
5. Long-term Solutions for Global Economic and Financial Crisis
6. G-20
7. Changing Middle East
8. Impact on Global Economy of China's Economic Policy
9. Role of Business in Global Affairs
10. U.S. Presidential Politics and Economic Policy

The initial purpose of the TC was to bring together key players from the three main centers of the capitalist world economy, areas that were also the key global geopolitical power centers: North America (Canada and the United States), Western Europe (members of the European Union), and Japan. At first, the TC had about 180 members, with the largest number from Western Europe and the smallest number from Japan. By 1986 this number had grown to 330, and by 2011 the total number of Commissioners reached 408: 168 Europeans, 128 North Americans, and 112 from Pacific-Asia. By 2011 its scope had also expanded to include many more nations, especially in Asia, including China and India, but also in Eastern Europe and Mexico.[345]

A review of the 2011 list of the North American Group of the TC found that 92 were U.S. citizens, 23 were Canadians, and 13 were Mexicans. Of the 92 U.S. citizens, 68 (74 percent) were also CFR members. The North American chair was CFR director Joseph S. Nye Jr., and eighteen other Commissioners were or had been at one time directors of the Council. These included Harvard professor and former assistant secretary of defense Graham T. Allison Jr.,, former secretary of defense Harold Brown, Sylvia Mathews Burwell of the Gates Foundation, journalist Lee Cullum, former Reagan chief of staff Kenneth M. Duberstein, David Rockefeller's daughter Peggy Dulany, John Hopkins University Dean Jessica P. Einhorn, Harvard Professor and former Reagan economic adviser Martin S. Feldstein, former ambassador and speaker of the house Thomas S. Foley, CFR co-chair Carla A. Hills, journalist Karen Elliott House, former secretary of state Henry A. Kissinger, former CFR president Winston Lord, former CFR chair David Rockefeller,CFR vice chair David M. Rubenstein, and former Fed chair Paul A. Volcker.[346]

These extensive connections between the Council and the TC illustrate that they and CFR work closely together to pursue their common interests and ideological agenda. The Bilderberg group has also been well connected to the Commission, especially through Rockefeller, Kissinger, and Lord, all of whom have been key leaders of all three organizations, and Conrad Black of Canada, active in both the Commission and Bilderberg. A number of the European members of Bilderberg have also been leaders of the TC, such as Mario Monti and Giovanni Agnelli of Italy, Viscount Etienne Davignon of Belgium, Lord Roll of Ipsden representing Britain, Baron Edmond de Rothschild of France, and Peter Sutherland of Ireland.

The key behind-the-scenes influence of the TC is further indicated by the fact that after Barack Obama became president in 2009, he tapped a large number of Trilateral Commissioners, all but one of them CFR members, to be part of his administration. The one exception was soon voted onto the Council's membership roll. These Commissioners included secretary of the treasury Timothy F. Geithner; UN Representative Susan Rice; national security advisers James L. Jones and Thomas E. Donilon; special representative for Afghanistan and Pakistan Richard Holbrooke; deputy secretary of state James B. Steinberg; director ot the National Economic Council Lawrence H. Summers; secretary of defense Ashton Carter, Health and Human Services secretary Sylvia Mathews Burwell, and director of policy planning at the Department of State Anne-Marie Slaughter. This continued a tradition started by former president James E. Carter, who, like presidents George H. W. Bush and William J. Clinton, were members of both the CFR and the TC and staffed their administrations with numerous members of both organizations.

The European Group of the TC was originally dominated by five NATO nations: Germany, France, Italy, the United Kingdom, and Spain. In the 1990s and early 2000s, it was expanded to include Cyprus and nations formerly part of the Soviet bloc: Poland, Hungary, the Czech Republic, Slovenia, Estonia, Bulgaria, and Romania. The makeup of the twenty-five-nation European Group is complex, including former top officials, academics, journalists, think tank leaders, industrialists, and many finance capitalists. The latter include at least three leaders of the Rothschild banking empire and several representing Goldman Sachs, as well as the heads of a number of national banks (Poland, Belgium, Romania, Finland, Netherlands) and top officials of several private banks and investment companies. Some Commission members also entered public service as president (Estonia), minister of foreign affairs (Denmark), minister for defense (Norway), and other lesser offices in different countries.[347]

The behind-the-scenes role of the Commission is also important in a number of European countries. When Italy was facing a political/economic crisis in November 2011, for example, its leaders tapped Mario Monti, chair of the European group of the TC, as the new president of the Italian council of ministers. Monti, a former Goldman Sachs banker and a Bilderberger, had been active in the TC for at least two decades. An unelected leader, Monti was described in the mainstream press as a "technocrat," leaving out his close connections to ruling monopoly finance capitalist-class circles in Europe and the United States through the activities of Bilderberg and the TC. Jean-Claude Trichet, former president of the European Central Bank and chairman of the Group of Thirty (see below), replaced Monti as the chair of the European group of the TC. Similarly, when Greece also needed an unelected technocrat to control a crisis situation, Greek leaders chose another Trilateral Commissioner, Lucas Papademos, a former vice president of the European Central Bank.

The Asian contingent of the TC also has seen great changes since the TC was founded in 1973. In 2000 the Japanese Group was renamed the Pacific Asian Group and by 2009 had expanded to thirteen nations, including the People's Republic of China, India, South Korea, Australia, New Zealand, Indonesia, Malaysia, the Philippines, Singapore, and Thailand. The chairmanship remained in Japanese hands, and all five of the Pacific Asian Group's topmost leaders have been Japanese, three of them from leading monopoly financial/industrial corporate combinations, Fuji/Xerox, Mitsui, and SONY. China still apparently plays a limited role; in 2011 only nine Commissioners were from China, whereas 49 were from Japan and 16 from South Korea (out of 112 total).

A review of available information on the funding of the TC's work confirms the general perception of the organization outlined above. Mainly U.S.-based multinational corporations and ruling-class foundations supply the overwhelming majority of its funding. During the 1982–85 years 53 percent of funding was from major monopoly corporations (among them Coca-Cola, Atlantic Richfield, Exxon, Boeing, GM, Mobil, Phillips Petroleum, Squibb, Deere, Xerox, and Weyerhaeuser), and 32 percent from large foundations (including Ford, Hewlett, Rockefeller, GM, Shell, Heinz, the Rockefeller Brothers Fund, the Chevron Fund, the Annenberg Fund). The remainder came from wealthy individuals like David Rockefeller.[348]

THE WORLD ECONOMIC FORUM/DAVOS

The World Economic Forum (WEF), held every year in Davos, Switzerland, with additional meetings at regional locations, is an independent transnational capitalist-class organization of corporate, political, intellectual, and civil society leaders. It started in 1971 as a forum and platform for European business leaders only, then was gradually expanded to include other interest groups and regions of the world, and now has a global scope. Its "Foundation Membership" is limited to 1,000 of the foremost global corporations.[349] It is a key place for a global capitalist class to convene, gain access to key people, network, and cultivate relationships. This is done through dialogue at varied types of meetings, and through initiatives, programs, and taskforces that set global, regional and industry agendas. The motto of the WEF is being "committed to improving the state of the world."

The central figure in the WEF from its beginning has been Klaus Schwab, a Swiss-born engineer, businessman, and intellectual with a distinct philosophy, a set of ideas that are at the center of the WEF's public presence and propaganda. At the core of Schwab's philosophy is the key concept of the "stakeholder" in corporate economic life. For Schwab, corporations must respond to and serve not just the shareholders, creditors, and top managers of a given firm, but also employees, customers, suppliers, the state, and society at large. The problem is that the corporate participants do not adhere to these concepts. A large number of WEF member corporations or their top leaders have often been involved in illegal and unethical activities, such as mortgage fraud, fixing LIBOR rates, insider stock trading, bribery, municipal bond fraud, and environmental crimes. Even under a lax regulatory and enforcement regime, they have been forced to pay tens of billions of dollars in fines. It is thus obvious that as a group they can hardly be said to be following the core "stakeholder" responsibility ethic that the WEF is supposedly promoting. The attempt by the WEF to prettify capitalism and imperialism so as to appear humane and legitimate has clearly failed, because this system, by its very nature, is inhumane and cruelly destructive of the very things the WEF presumably is trying to uphold. Unmentioned in the hallowed halls of Davos are the exploitation of workers, imperialist wars like that of the United States in the Middle East, and the fact that global corporations are behind the rapid destruction of the ecological systems that form the basis of life on earth.

"Public private partnerships," "social entrepreneurship," "mutual responsibility," "communitarian spirit," "global corporate citizenship," and "organic community" are buzzwords used at the WEF to attempt to put a "progressive" gloss on the neoliberal world of austerity, exploitation, dispossession, and destruction imposed by the globalized capitalist class on the people and ecologies of our planet.

In early 2010, Schwab expressed disappointment at how the values inherent in the "stakeholder" philosophy were being ignored by many business leaders who were only trying to maximize profit and shareholder value in the short term, treating people as replaceable objects, creating selfishness. Schwab recommended a rethinking of "morals and ethics," warning that as "social peace" is undermined, "social crisis"—that is, the class struggle—awaits.[350] But it turns out that when push comes to shove Schwab himself acts like a businessman trying to maximize profit, not as a stakeholder with a concern about protecting the community and society at large. In the official history of the WEF, published in 2009, it states that during the WEF meetings of 2007, just before the "great recession" struck,

Klaus Schwab grew increasingly concerned about the likelihood of a major global recession after listening to the voices of experts such as New York University Economics Professor Nouriel Roubini and global investor George Soros. An opinion piece in the *Financial Times* in March by frequent Davos participant and Forum friend William Rhodes, the Senior Vice Chairman of Citigroup and CEO and President of Citibank, prompted Schwab to conclude that, if an insider such as the veteran banker was worried, he had to act. The Forum moved to restructure its investment portfolio, the Foundation's reserves, to shift mainly into Swiss government bonds. This was a fortuitous decision. It saved the Forum from experiencing the fate of so many foundations that lost substantial parts of their endowment when the financial markets slumped in the autumn of 2008.[351]

This illustrates that the WEF is subject to capitalist laws and acts like any other business interested in short-term preservation. What is actually needed, and the WEF is unwilling to consider, is a different system, one less unstable and not subject to the ups and downs of the capitalist business cycle. The WEF aims to preserve the existing dog-eat-dog capitalist system with a bit more trickle-down and a bit more "responsibility" on the part of the big capitalists. But the nature of the system assures that even Klaus Schwab will quickly drop existing WEF investments for secure Swiss government bonds, leaving others, especially those less well connected, to take the losses—including unemployment and austerity—when their unstable system falls into recession.

The two experts Roubini and Soros, and the banker Rhodes mentioned above are all members of the CFR, and Soros was a Council director. While no lists of all WEF participants could be located, and in any case would be quite lengthy, the official history covers the highlights of the WEF from 1971 to 2009. At least two-dozen Council members and leaders are mentioned as having an important role in the WEF over these years. A number of them were also CFR directors, including

Henry A. Kissinger, Martin S. Feldstein, Robert Zoellick, Richard C. Holbrooke, Richard B. Cheney, Fareed Zakaria, and Colin Powell. Others, like Condoleezza Rice, John F. Kerry, Henry M. Paulson, William J. Clinton, and Michael Bloomberg, though not Council directors, have been both active Council members and WEF participants.[352]

Leading global monopoly corporations play a big part of the WEF as "industry partners" and "strategic partners." The top-level "strategic partners" pay almost $700,000 to send five executives to attend the annual meeting.[353] The "industry partners" pay a smaller, but still stubstantial amount to attend. These corporations spend large sums of money to attend Davos because it is the biggest high-level global business conference, a place where top executives can meet and network with a large number of partners, clients, potential clients, and top government officials in the space of a few days.[354] Many of the attending organizations are corporate members of the CFR and part of the Council network. For example, there are 100 corporate "Strategic Partners" of the WEF as of 2009 and listed in its official history. Of these 100, twenty-eight are also listed as corporate members of the CFR in its 2010 *Annual Report*.[355] The twenty-eight active in both the CFR and WEF include such leading corporations as Bank of America, Barclays, JPMorgan Chase, Goldman Sachs, ATT, Chevron, BP, Credit Suisse, Deutsche Bank, Coca-Cola, McKinsey, News Corp, Standard Charter Bank, UBS, and Volkswagen.

THE GROUP OF THIRTY (G30)

Based in Washington, the G30 was founded in 1978 on the initiative of the Rockefeller Foundation, which also provided the initial funding. It is a private, nonprofit international body of senior representatives from the private and public sectors of the financial capitalist world. They meet twice a year to discuss important developments and also organize study groups that issue policy papers. As of 2012, the G30 had thirty-two listed members, the two extra participants being the chair emeritus, Paul A. Volcker, a former director of the CFR, and the executive secretary, Geoffrey Bell of the United Kingdom. The thirty regular members include twelve from Europe, seven from the United States, and five from Asia. Six of the seven U.S. members are also members or former members of the Council. Two, Jacob A. Frenkel of Israel who chairs the G30's board of trustees, and Ernest Zedillo of Mexico, have also been on the CFR's International Advisory Board (discussed below). Other members of the G30, such as Volcker; Zedillo; E. Gerald Corrigan, managing director of Goldman Sachs; William C. Dudley, president of the Federal Reserve Bank of New York; Martin S. Feldstein of Harvard; and Roger W. Ferguson Jr., former vice chair of the Board of Governors of the Federal Reserve, are all also members of the Trilateral Commission.

THE INTERNATIONAL CRISIS GROUP (ICG)

This private nonprofit transnational organization is based in Brussels, with field offices all over the world. It is mainly made up of representatives of NATO nations, with the United States having by far the biggest numerical national representation among the ICG's leadership. Founded in 1995, in 2012 the ICG had forty-five trustees, fourteen from the United States, fourteen from Western European nations, three from Canada, and the rest from varied other countries. Eleven of the fourteen U.S. ICG trustees (78.6 percent) are members of the CFR, and four of these are current or former members of the Council's board of directors. The chair (2012) of the ICG is CFR member and former Council director Thomas R. Pickering, a former U.S. ambassador to a number of nations, including El Salvador during the Reagan administration. CFR co-chair Carla Hills is a trustee of ICG, and former Council director George Soros is a trustee and one of the founders of the ICG. The ICG's senior advisers also include former CFR director and Trilateral Commission co-founder Zbigniew Brzezinski plus seven individuals who also have served on the CFR's International Advisory Board.

The ICG touts its role as a supposedly "independent" and "nonpartisan" organization "committed to preventing and resolving deadly conflict." Its actual role is to promote "humanitarian intervention" in the affairs of third world nations, often to further attempts to control them and successfully impose neoliberal globalization. Kosovo, North Korea, Venezuela, Iran, Somalia, Sudan, Zimbabwe, Haiti, and Colombia have been among the nations singled out for the ICG's attention.[356] The ICG, however, played no humanitarian role nor spoke out in favor of protecting people from military attacks when NATO intervened in Afghanistan in 2001 or when the United States and its allies invaded and occupied Iraq in 2003. These were two so-called deadly conflicts of which the ICG evidently approved.

The ICG's funding helps explain its practice of ignoring some deadly conflicts. Over 50 percent of its $20 million annual budget comes from governments, mostly NATO members; about 25 percent from big foundations like Ford, Gates, Carnegie, Hewlett, Merck, Mott, and Open Society (which is mainly funded by George Soros); and the rest from corporations, such as Chevron, BHP Billiton, and Royal Bank of Scotland, and capitalist-class notables like Soros.

THE INTERNATIONAL ADVISORY BOARD OF THE CFR AND ITS SUCCESSOR, THE GLOBAL BOARD OF ADVISERS

Established in 1995 with David Rockefeller as chairman, later led by Peter G. Peterson, the Council's International Advisory Board (IAB) held meetings annually "to offer perspectives on a broad range of matters of concern to the Council.

IAB members . . . comment on institutional programs and strategic directions, and on practical opportunities for collaboration between the Council and institutions abroad. They also provide invaluable international insights into U.S. foreign policy."[357]

The IAB was in existence from 1995 until at least 2009. Information about its deliberations and recommendations is unavailable to those outside the Council, and references to it disappear from CFR annual reports after 2009. Then, three years later in 2012, the Council announced the formation of a new international advisory board with the same essential goals, this one called the Global Board of Advisers. The CFR's website had this to say about the new group:

> The Global Board of Advisers (GBA) consists of prominent individuals, including business leaders, noted academics, and former government officials from developed and emerging-market countries. The prestigious group provides CFR with insight about their regions and also offers a mechanism for members of the GAB to join discussions on international relations and the U.S. role in the world. The GAB is chaired by David M. Rubenstein, CFR Board vice chairman.[358]

Rubenstein is the CFR's logical choice to chair the GBA. As a key owner and managing director of the giant private equity firm the Carlyle Group, he has a strong personal interest in information about international economic and political developments in many nations, regions, and worldwide. Such information can help guide Carlyle's global investments, including acquisitions.

The representatives on the IAB and GBA together total eighty-eight individuals from forty-three nations. They come from Europe (34.1 percent), Asia (26.1 percent), the Middle East (17 percent), Africa (10.2 percent), Latin America (9.1 percent), and Canada (4.5 percent). This geographic breakdown is indicative of where the CFR sees its geopolitical priorities, a topic that will be developed further in chapter 5.

A group of ninety individuals from forty-three nations is too big a group to adequately discuss in one chapter. However, about 60 percent of them come from the fifteen nations with the most representatives (three or more), indicating that these are the key nations with which the CFR most wants to consult and network. These consist of seven European nations, three Asian countries, two Middle Eastern ones, plus Nigeria, Mexico, and Canada. Below, we will discuss two individuals from each of these fifteen nations, in order to provide ample and accurate illustrations of the kinds of people the Council has chosen for its global dialogue.[359] These are first and foremost individuals who are multinational capitalist leaders, often heading the largest corporations, and neoliberal-oriented politicians. Secondarily, the ranks of the IAB and GBA have included political insiders of mainly middle-of-the road ideological persuasions, people who can offer insights into national and regional trends.

Britain

Two individuals, one a major corporate capitalist-class leader and one a leading political figure, can stand for the British direct connection to the Council. Both are nobles and members of the House of Lords. Baron Edmund John Philip Browne of Madingley was chief executive of British Petroleum from 1995 to 2007 and one of the most highly paid executives in the United Kingdom. He was also a director of Goldman Sachs. BP is involved in over eighty nations and is one of the top European corporations by revenue. Not only is it an oil major, BP is also involved in the fields of petrochemicals, biofuels, solar power, and wind farms. Blackrock is a major shareholder of BP.

Peter Carrington, Baron Carrington of Upton, has also been a leader of the Bilderberg Group and Secretary-General of NATO. He was discussed earlier in this chapter in the section on the Bilderberg Group.

Germany

Two individuals, one a major corporate capitalist-class leader and another who was a noble and a neoliberal political figure, illustrate the kinds of people the CFR connects with from Germany. Gerhard Cromme, whom the *Financial Times* called "Germany's most influential industrialist," has been on the board of directors of a number of Europe's biggest multinationals, including ThyssenKrupp, Siemens, GDF Suez, Volkswagen, Lufthansa, and BNP Paribas Bank.[360] Cromme was also chair of the European Roundtable of Industrialists from 2001 to 2005. This fifty-person body of corporate leaders is a powerful lobbying force in the EU.

Count Otto Lambsdorff was from a family that had estates in the Baltic countries and was part of a historic group of conquering colonists known as "Baltic Germans." After the Second World War, the family lost its lands and Otto went into politics, becoming an elected member of the Bundestag and a leader of the neoliberal Free Democratic Party, which began to reject Keynesianism as early as 1977. He was Federal Minister of Economics in the early 1980s, but had to resign for accepting bribes from the Flick industrial combine, in exchange for arranging tax breaks. A Bonn State Court also convicted him of tax evasion. These ethical and legal lapses did not prevent the CFR from inviting him to join their advisory board, and he was also made a top leader of the Trilateral Commission in the 1980s and 1990s, serving on the executive committee and as European chair.

Russia

Two of the Russians who have served on the IAB/GBA are well-connected, afflu-
ent individuals. Vladimir Potanin's wealth was estimated at $17.8 billion by *Forbes*
in 2011, much of it in a controlling ownership interest in the formerly state-owned
nickel mining giant Norilsk Nickel. Potanin gained control of this enterprise during the Yeltsin era when Potanin organized loans to the new, post-Soviet Russian
government, receiving first mining leases, then shares in return. This turned out to
be a form of privatization, the transfer of state-owned property to Potanin and his
insider partners, for a very low price. Norilsk Nickel operates the world's largest
heavy metals smelting complex in Siberia, ranked by one source as one of the most
polluted sites in the world. The area around the complex is an ecological disaster
area, and workers as well as about 130,000 local residents are exposed to high levels of air pollution, which, together with acid rain, has killed all of the forests for
miles around the industrial site. Life expectancy of workers there is ten years less
than the Russian average.[361]

The other Russian, Mikhail Fridman, was recently ranked twentieth on Forbes's
list of the world's billionaires. His wealth is new, dating to the 1990s privatization
schemes following the fall of the USSR. During this period, Fridman helped form
the Alfa Group, which was able to take over and consolidate a diverse set of properties in the fields of oil, retail, telecom, and banking, and even acquire holdings in
nearby nations like Turkey, Uzbekistan, and Ukraine. He has political connections
to the Kremlin and President Putin, and political favoritism likely figures largely
in his newfound billionaire status. In October 2014 the *Financial Times* reported
that Fridman has attracted very high profile advisers for his oil investment projects,
including Lord Browne of BP (discussed above) and Morgan Stanley.[362]

France

A member of one of the most prominent families of France, Christophe de
Margerie, was chair and CEO of Total SA, which operates in 130 countries and
is one of the world's six oil and gas supermajors. Among other ventures, Total is
currently investing in an oil shale/tar sands mining venture in Utah's Uintah Basin.
De Margerie, the grandson of the founder of the Taittinger champagne and luxury
goods house, died in a plane crash in Russia in October 2014. He was also a member of the European Roundtable of Industrialists, and was on the board of directors of Vivendi, a transnational mass communications corporation based in Paris.

The second French representative, Michel Rocard, was that country's prime
minister from 1988 to 1991, was part of the right wing of the French Socialist Party.
He opposed President Mitterrand's initial program of nationalization, generally

had poor relations with Mitterrand, and was forced to resign. He later became a member of the European Parliament.

Italy

Two Italians who have served on the IAB/GBA are major multinational corporate capitalists. Giovanni Agnelli, the richest man in modern Italian history, was the principal stockholder and longtime chairman of Fiat. The Agnelli family has been labeled "Italy's royal family," and Giovanni, also called Gianni, was known for many years as the true "king of Italy."[363] His grandfather founded the company and his mother came from a noble family from Perugia. During the Second World War Agnelli wore the black shirt of fascism and was wounded twice fighting for the German Nazi armies against the USSR on the Eastern Front. He was on the steering committee of the Bilderberg Group and was a participant in their meetings beginning in 1958. He was close to David Rockefeller, and served for years on both the International Advisory Committee of the Chase Manhattan Bank and on the Trilateral Commission.

Paolo Scaroni, the former CEO of Eni, the Italian oil and gas giant, was educated in the United States (MBA, Columbia), and worked for Chevron and McKinsey prior to taking over as head of Eni. He is a member of the powerful European Roundtable of Industrialists. In 1992, he pleaded guilty to a bribery charge and was sentenced to one year in prison, but never served the sentence.[364] He was paid 4.6 million euros as his salary for 2010. Under Scaroni's leadership, Eni is reportedly planning to continue its history of operating in nations that other major oil and gas majors find too difficult. Scaroni stated in May 2013, for example, that the countries that his company is now most interested in expanding into include Vietnam, Indonesia, Myanmar, and Pakistan.[365] Eni operates in 79 nations, and besides oil and gas is involved in contracting, energy, nuclear power, mining, chemicals, plastics, textiles, and news media. In 2014 Scaroni was appointed the deputy chairman of the Rothschild financial advisory group.

Sweden

Both of the Swedes who have served on the IAB, Percy Barevik and Jacob Wallenberg, are businessmen connected to the Wallenberg family, a family known as "the Rockefellers of Sweden." They play key roles is what is said to be Europe's largest family-run business empire, estimated to control, directly or indirectly, about a third of Sweden's entire GDP. Barevik and Wallenberg have been on the board of directors of the large transnational conglomerate known as ABB (Asea Brown Boveri). Based in Switzerland, ABB is one of the world's largest transnational conglomerates, with 135,000 employees and operations in over a hundred countries. Barevik was the CEO and chair of ABB between 1988 and 2002. He was called one of the world's most respected business leaders in 1998, a "visionary executive" whose aim was to globalize his company and world capitalism.[366] Barevik explained that his "vision was to create a truly global company that knows no borders, has many home countries, operates with mixed nationality teams and offers opportunities for all nationalities."[367]

One of ABB's largest stockholders is the Wallenberg family investment company, Investor AB, which owns a controlling interest in several large Swedish corporations and smaller positions in a number of other firms. Its chair is Jacob Wallenberg, a leading member of the royal family of Swedish business. Educated in the United States at the Wharton Business School, Jacob was the president and CEO of Stockholm's Enskilda Bank, another key part of the Wallenberg empire. He is also a director of Coca-Cola, a Knight of the Order of Seraphim, and sits on the current steering committee of the Bilderberg Group. Jacob is also a member of the European Roundtable of Industrialists. A brother, Peter Wallenberg, is a Trilateral Commissioner.

Spain

Juan March Delgado, one of the richest men in Spain, is part of the March family, the "Rockefellers of Spain." Juan March Delgado is the grandson of the founder of the family's wealth, Juan March Ordinas, who was already one of the richest men in Spain during the Spanish Civil War of 1936–39. During that struggle, the March family were key backers of the fascist military rebellion led by General Francisco Franco. March Ordinas is even reported to have arranged Franco's flight from the Canary Islands to Spanish Morocco to organize the rebellion, and personally financed the airlift of the African-based troops to Spain. The family wealth is organized around their Banca March, headquartered in Mallorca. This bank, although relatively small, is known to be one of the most strongly capitalized in the world and placed first in the European Union during the stress tests of 2012.[368] Juan March Delgado has served as a director of Banca March and other family enterprises (the March Group) for several decades, and has also been chair of the family foundation and the Juan March Institute for Advanced Studies in the Social Sciences. The March Group of enterprises, controlled through the Banca March, operates in construction, services, metallurgy, and security.

Javier Solana de Madariaga is from a well-known Spanish noble family. Presently affiliated with the Brookings Institution, he is a former Secretary-General of both the European Union and NATO. He has also been a member of the Trilateral Commission.

India

Mukesh D. Ambani has been the chair, CEO, and largest stockholder of Reliance Industries Ltd., a key part of the Reliance Group, an energy, industrial, and materials conglomerate and India's most valuable company by market value. Reliance operates in five major segments: exploration/production, refining/marketing, petrochemicals, retail, and telecommunications. It is a corporate member of the Council. Ambani is India's richest individual, ranking high on the *Forbes* list of the world's billionaires. He has also been on the board of directors of other Reliance corporations, as well as Bank of America, has been a co-chair of both the World Economic Forum in Davos, and the India-China Chief Executives Forum.[369] *The Economist* reports that Ambani and Reliance Industries also has an "uncomfortable degree of clout" in the Indian government, quoting a former cabinet minister who states that Ambani's "influence is huge. Whatever is happening he knows. He is able to post [bureaucrats] to positions and get ministers appointed who are favorable to him."[370]

Ambani is also famous as the owner/builder of his home in South Mumbai, called Antilia, that cost about $1 billion and is one of the largest and most expensive personal residences in the world. This mansion is twenty-seven stories high, has 400,000 square feet of space, and employs a full-time staff of over six hundred. It has three helipads, an air traffic control facility, spaces to park 168 cars, three floors of hanging gardens, a theater, swimming pool, ballroom, yoga studio, and health spa. Ratam Tata, another top Indian capitalist leader (the Tata Group is also a CFR corporate member), criticized Ambani as a kind of new maharajah, lacking empathy for the poor. Tata should not talk, however, since the Tata Group's Global Beverage arm owns a controlling interest in twenty tea plantations in Assam, where 30,000 mostly illiterate plantation workers work long hours for extremely low pay—the average is $24 a month—and suffer from abject poverty, a lack of union rights, poor housing and health conditions, including unsafe pesticide use.[371]

A second Indian representative is Anand Mahindra, a Harvard Business School MBA. His Mahindra Group is a multinational conglomerate with operations in a hundred nations worldwide. Mahindra's business is wide-ranging and includes finance, insurance, aerospace, industrial equipment, information technology, leisure, hospitality, real estate, retail, agribusiness, construction equipment, energy; it is also India's largest manufacturer of tractors and utility vehicles. *Forbes* estimated his net worth at $825 million in 2011.

China

Zhang Xin was educated in England, and has an MA from Cambridge University. She worked for financial institutions like Barings, Goldman Sachs, and Travelers

Group, then returned to China, founding a commercial real estate development company called SOHO. She is now a billionaire, ranked number fifteen among the richest Chinese on *Forbes* list with $3.6 billion. *Forbes* and *Fortune* rank her among the world's most powerful women.

Hong Kong's C. H. Tung is a graduate of the University of Liverpool and inherited the family shipping company, Orient Overseas, from his father. A conservative businessman with strong connections to the Chinese government, he became the first head of government in Hong Kong after the transfer to China.

Japan

Two of Japan's representatives on the IAB/GBA, Yorihiko Kojima and Toyoo Gyohten, are connected to Mitsubishi, a key monopoly finance capitalist corporation. Mitsubishi is what the Japanese call a *keiretsu*, a conglomerate whose companies and shares are interlocked with a bank playing the central coordinating role. The Mitsubishi Bank—part of the larger Mitsubishi UFJ Financial group; it merged with the Bank of Tokyo in 1996, and acquired a 21 percent stake in Morgan Stanley in 2008—has this central role for Mitsubishi. Mitsubishi consists of dozens of companies, employing about 350,000 employees. Some of their economic activities include mining, shipbuilding, telecommunications, heavy industry, oil and gas, real estate, food and beverage, chemicals, steel, and aviation. Yorihiko Kojima is the president, chair, and CEO of Mitsubishi. He has served as vice chair of the Japan Association of Corporate Executives and is a former board member of Sony. Toyoo Gyohten has had a career as a private finance capitalist (Goldman Sachs and senior adviser, Bank of Tokyo) and also in government (Japanese Ministry of Finance, IMF, Asian Development Bank, Organization of Economic Cooperation and Development, Group of Thirty). He has also been a member of the Trilateral Commission.

Saudi Arabia

Saudi business families have historically played a key role in the country, one business source states that a few families, organized as corporate conglomerates, have accounted for 90 percent of all companies in the Kingdom.[372] Among these top wealthy and powerful families are the Al Olayan and Alturki clans; both have been represented on the IAB/GAB.

Lubna Sulaiman Al Olayan was educated at Cornell and Indiana University, receiving an MBA from the latter institution. Following work for Morgan Guaranty in New York, she returned to Saudi Arabia, becoming the CEO and president of Olayan Financing Company, which was founded by her father. Olayan Financing is one of the top businesses in Saudi Arabia and is the holding company for the Olayan Group's operations worldwide. This conglomerate consists of over fifty companies engaged in manufacturing, distribution, and services. Olayan Financing also has hefty stakes in various multinational corporations, including MetLife, First Boston, AIG, and Credit Suisse. It reportedly has a 3.6 percent ownership stake in Credit Suisse, for example. The Olayan family's net worth is reported to be $12.4 billion.

The Olayan Group grew powerful through partnerships with key U.S. multinational corporations: JPMorgan Chase, Morgan Stanley, Goldman Sachs, Coca-Cola, Blackstone, Bechtel, Kimberly-Clark, General Foods, Pillsbury, Hunt Wesson, Cummins Engine, and others. Lubna Al Olayan is also a board member or an adviser for a number of foreign multinational corporations, including Schlumberger, the Saudi Hollandi Bank, Citigroup, and the Rolls-Royce Group. Listed among the world's most powerful women by both *Time* and *Forbes*, she co-chaired the World Economic Forum in Davos in 2005. Her husband, John Xefos, is a senior partner in the Texas law firm Baker & McKenzie, where former secretary of state James Baker is another senior partner. Her sister, Hutham S. Olayan, operates the U.S. branch of the Olayan Group. She has become a U.S. citizen and became a member of the CFR in 2012.[373]

Khalid Ali Alturki of Saudi Arabia is the chairman of his family's Trading and Development Company, with offices in Shanghai, China, and Riyadh. Another conglomerate, the company operates in a large number of fields, including consulting, investing, trading, manufacturing, construction, renewable energy, real estate, power, and telecommunications.

Israel

Council leaders consider Israel to be a key strategic geopolitical asset of the United States. So naturally Israel is among the nations with the largest number of individuals who have served in the IAB/GBA. Two examples are discussed here, and there is more discussion about the CFR's connection to Israel in chapter 7.

Jacob A. Frenkel was born in what was then the British Mandate of Palestine in 1943. Following schooling in Israel, he attended the University of Chicago, receiving a master's and PhD in economics. He was part of the faculty of this Rockefeller-connected university for nearly a decade and a half as the David Rockefeller Professor of International Economics. He then directed research at the International Monetary Fund for several years prior to beginning two terms as governor of the Bank of Israel. Serving in this position from 1991 to 2000, he successfully promoted a neoliberal program, including liberalizing Israel's financial markets and integrating the Israel economy into the global financial system. He then returned to work in the United States, first as chair of Merrill Lynch

International. Currently chair and CEO of the Group of Thirty, he has also been a vice chair of AIG and chair of JP Morgan Chase International. He has also been a member of the Trilateral Commission, and serves on the board of the Peter G. Peterson Institute for International Economics.

Idan Ofer has been called "Israel's richest man, co-heir to a shipping fortune and majority owner of its largest listed company, Israel Corp."[374] The *Financial Times* tallies his net worth at $6.5 billion. Israel Corporation is a strategic investment company, with stakes in many global businesses, including shipping, chemicals, Chinese autos, energy in South America, and even Silicon Valley electric car charging stations. Ofer was recently involved in a controversy over his move to join other family members and live in London, where taxes are lower than in Israel.[375]

Nigeria

Nigeria is the only African nation that has had as many as three representatives on the IAB/GBA. It is not hard to see why, since Nigeria is the biggest oil producer in Africa and one of the largest in the world. This translates into a major source of wealth and power, as well as to the CFR desire for a connection. The first of these links is Obusegun Obasanjo, the military dictator of Nigeria from 1976 to 1979 and the elected president of the country from 1999 to 2007. A noble from the clan of Yorubaland, he has also chaired the Africa Leadership Forum.

The Council's second connection is Hakeem Belo-Osagie, a Harvard Business School MBA and a trained petroleum economist. He set up an oil consultancy in Nigeria, worked as a presidential adviser, and took advantage of the country's neoliberal privatization process to purchase a majority stake in United Bank of Africa from the Nigerian government, later selling it for a huge profit. He now chairs a telecommunications provider called Etisalat Nigeria. He is listed by *Forbes* as the 40th richest man in Africa.

Mexico

Ernesto Zedillo Ponce de Leon began his education in Mexico, completing it with a PhD in economics from Yale. Following service at the Mexican Central Bank and in the Mexican federal government, he was elected president of Mexico, serving from 1994 to 2000. He was president during the 1995 Mexican financial crisis and bailout by the IMF and United States. The terms imposed required the implantation of a number of pro-corporate neoliberal measures, including wage reductions for workers, cuts in government spending, and a speed-up of the privatization of state-owned enterprises. This increased foreign ownership and control of the Mexican economy, especially the banking sector. The Zedillo administration also socialized large amounts of bad banking debt, "saving" the banking system but vastly indebting and weakening the Mexican state.

Once out of office, Zedillo moved to the United States, became a professor and director of the Center for the Study of Globalization at Yale. He was also invited to join the boards of leading U.S. multinational corporations, apparently a kind of reward for neoliberal services rendered while president of Mexico. He has been a director or on the advisory board of Citigroup (a major bank owner in Mexico), Union Pacific, Coca-Cola, Procter & Gamble, Alcoa, Electronic Data Services, Rolls-Royce, the Gates Foundation, and the Albright Stonebridge Group. He is also a member of the Group of Thirty.

Jose Antonio Fernandez Carbajal is a Mexican businessman with close U.S. connections. He is the chair and CEO of FEMSA, the largest beverage company in Latin America and is on the board of Coca-Cola and Heineken International. He is also on the U.S.-Mexico Foundation board and co-chair of the advisory board of the Woodrow Wilson Center.

Canada

One of the Canadian representatives on the IAB/GBA has been Paul Desmarais Jr., current chair and co-CEO of Power Corporation of Canada. He is the eldest son of the French-Canadian financier Paul Desmarais Sr., the fourth-richest Canadian with an estimated net worth of $4.4 billion. Desmarais Sr. controlled Power Corporation of Canada, which grew into a giant conglomerate, with branches in energy, utilities, construction, minerals, wine and spirits, media, pulp and paper, and financial services. The corporation has holdings in Canada, France, Belgium, Germany, and the United States.

The Desmarais family and its economic empire represents a prime example of the evolving transnational capitalist class, connecting North America and Europe. They operate in an alliance with the Frère family of Belgium. Baron Albert Frère is Belgium's richest man and, with the Desmarais family, controls Groupe Bruxelles Lambert as well as the Pargesa Group, both European-based conglomerates with major holdings in corporations like the French energy giant Total and the French multinational utility Suez.[376] The two families also have economic ties to the Agnelli family of Italy.[377] Paul Desmaris Jr. sits on the board of Suez, and both he and his father have been on the board of Total. The Desmarais family reportedly also works with the Carlyle Group, Dessault industries, and the Rothschilds. It has many political connections at the top of the Canadian political structure and has also been active in the Bilderberg Group and Trilateral Commission.[378]

A second Canadian on the IAB/GBA has been Brian Mulroney. Mulroney was a lawyer working for Paul Desmarais Sr., then became politically active as part of the Progressive Conservative Party. Elected to Parliament in 1983, he became prime minister the next year. The Progressive Conservative Party was a neoliberal party with privatization on its agenda; it merged with the Conservative Party in 2003. During Mulroney's years in office, a large number of government-owned crown corporations, including Air Canada and Petro-Canada, were privatized. In 1993, during his last years as a member of Parliament, Mulroney accepted at least $225,000 in cash bribes from the German-Canadian businessman Karlheinz Schreiber, who was trying to influence the Canadian government's decisions on the purchase of aircraft and military vehicles. Mulroney initially denied that he had taken the bribes, and did not admit to the facts, declare the income, or pay taxes on it until many years later, when Schreiber's activities were under investigation in Germany and his bribes to Mulroney were in danger of being exposed. After leaving public office, Mulroney was invited to become a corporate director, serving on a large number of transnational corporations like Barrick Gold, Archer Daniels Midland, and AOL Latin America, as well as on the International Advisory Board of leading financials like JPMorgan Chase and China International Trust and Investment Corporation.

INTERNATIONAL MEMBERS

Finally, the IAB and GBA have had two members that could be labeled international because of their importance to key international institutions. The first, Peter D. Sutherland, a former attorney general of Ireland, was the chair of GATT, then the Director-General of the WTO for many years, resulting in him being called the "father of globalization." He was appointed by Kofi Annan to be the UN Special Representative for Migration. He has served as chair of British Petroleum, chair of Goldman Sachs International, and on the corporate boards of ABB, Koc Holding of Turkey, Allianz, B.W. Shipping, Royal Bank of Scotland, as well as Eli Lilly's advisory board. He has been on the steering committee of the Bilderberg Group, the Foundation Board of the World Economic Forum (Davos), the vice chair of the European Round Table of Industrialists, and was the European chair of the TC for many years.

The second, Kofi Annan, was born in Ghana into an aristocratic family; both of his grandfathers and an uncle were tribal chiefs. He attended college in Ghana and the United States, eventually receiving a master's degree from the Sloan School of Management at MIT. He worked for the World Health Organization and in United Nations peacekeeping operations prior to serving as undersecretary general in the mid-1990s. He then became UN Secretary-General from 1997 to 2006. He was awarded a Nobel Peace Prize in 2001.

FOREIGN CORPORATE MEMBERS OF THE CFR

The over thirty international corporate members of the Council include some of the world's largest and most globally oriented multinational corporations. Although British and European multinational corporations are most numerous, Japan is also well represented. These include six giant foreign-based banks, five European and one Japanese, that are on the Financial Stability Board's list of "Global Systematically Important Financial Institutions," ones that could trigger a global financial crisis if they failed. These are Barclays, Credit Suisse, Deutsche Bank, Group Credit Agricole, UBS, and Mitsubishi.

Corporate members based in the United Kingdom include Anglo-American, one of the world's largest mining corporations, Standard Charter Bank, British Petroleum, *The Economist* magazine, and Indus Capital Partners, a London-based hedge fund focused on Asia. Italian and French members include oil giants Total and Eni, as well as financial outfits like Banca d' Italia, Intesa Sanpaolo, and Rothschild. DeBeers, the diamond monopolists, Airbus, Shell Oil, and the Spanish telecommunications giant Telefonica round out the European list. The only German representation is Deutsche Bank, which is Germany's largest and most powerful bank.

Japan's corporate members of the Council include large conglomerates like Mitsui, banks like the Japan Bank for International Cooperation, such auto companies as Toyota, traders like Marubeni and ITOCHU, and tech giants Hitachi and Sony.

Two of India's biggest corporate conglomerates are also CFR members: Reliance Industries (its leading executive, Mukesh D. Ambani, is discussed above) and the Tata Group. Tata, chaired by Ratan Tata for over two decades, became the first Indian corporate group to earn $100 billion in revenue. In late 2012 it was labeled "India's most global business."[379]

Within the Western Hemisphere, two Venezuelan corporations, Banco Mercantil and the Cisneros Group of Companies of Venezuela (Gustavo Cisneros was a member of the IAB) are Council corporate members, as is the Canadian Imperial Bank of Commerce. A final notable corporate member is Aramco Services, a subsidiary of the giant Saudi Arabian Oil Company.[380] Additional details on the IAB and GBA members can be found at laurenceshoup.com.

THE COUNCIL OF COUNCILS

In 2012 the CFR convened what it calls the "Council of Councils" to forge cooperative responses to what they define as the world's most pressing challenges and opportunities. For the inaugural meeting in Washington, the CFR called together representatives from many of the world's leading think tank representatives from twenty key nations, roughly conforming to the Group of 20. The two main speakers were both former CFR directors, Robert Zoellick, president of the World Bank Group, and Robert Hormats, former Goldman Sachs official and then U.S. Undersecretary of State for Economic Growth, Energy and the Environment. Three main emerging trends were identified at this initial gathering. First, national governments alone cannot meet the challenges now facing the world. Second, domestic politics increasingly shape international conditions and determine the prospects for coordinating multilateral approaches to transnational issues. Third, emerging powers, with their economic strength, will fundamentally alter geoeconomics and geopolitics, making it necessary to revamp international institutions and initiatives.

The mission that the Council of Councils has since articulated is to work toward consensus—"common ground"—on global governance and multilateral cooperation and "inject remedies into the public debate and policymaking processes of member countries."[381] It was intended that practical ideas and solutions would be generated at an annual conference, as well as ongoing exchanges on research and policy collaboration. A comprehensive agenda was envisioned, dealing with a full range of issues: economic, energy, environmental, political, and security.

The nations and institutes that are a part of the Council of Councils network, which amounts to a partial who's who of the world's leading think tanks in international affairs, are:[382]

- Australia, Lowy Institute for International Policy
- Belgium, Center for European Policy Studies
- Brazil, Getulio Vargas Foundation
- Canada, Center for International Governance Innovation
- China, Shanghai Institute for International Studies
- France, French Institute of International Relations
- Germany, German Institute for International and Security Affairs
- India, Centre for Policy Research
- Indonesia, Center for Strategic and International Studies
- Israel, Institute for National Security Studies
- Italy, Institute of International Affairs
- Japan, Genron NPO
- Mexico, Mexican Council on Foreign Relations
- Poland, Polish Institute of International Affairs
- Russia, Institute of Contemporary Development
- Singapore, S. Rajaratnam School of International Affairs
- South Africa, South African Institute of International Affairs

- South Korea, East Asia Institute
- Turkey, Global Relations Forum
- United Kingdom, Royal Institute of International Affairs and the International Institute for Strategic Studies
- United States, Council on Foreign Relations[383]

By the summer of 2013 one additional think tank had been added, Egypt's Al-Ahram Center for Political and Strategic Studies.

The CFR has a number of relationships with these think tanks. It has long had "sister institute" relationships with the Royal Institute of International Affairs, the French Institute of International Relations, and the Mexican Council on Foreign Relations.[384] Council directors have been involved in the Lowy Institute (Rita Hauser) and the Center for International Governance Innovation (Anne-Marie Slaughter). Members of the Council's IAB are also leaders at China's Shanghai Institute and Turkey's Global Relations Forum. There are undoubtedly other important connections as well.

One apparent long-term goal of this effort is to promote ideological hegemony by influencing the development of economic and strategic thinking in these rising nations along neoliberal geopolitical lines. This aims to ensure that, as the relative weight of the United States in the world declines, these nations will be close allies of the United States and its world hegemony goals. Note that all of the top national economies and geopolitical players of our current world are included in the above list of countries, with especially heavy representation from Europe (seven of the twenty-two) and East/Southeast Asia (six). North America and the Middle East each have three nations on the list.

SUMMARY

This chapter has demonstrated that the CFR is at the center of a large and very impressive network of national and transnational capitalist-class organizations and key individuals who participate in meetings to set agendas and study groups to seek consensus. The collective function of this effort, led by the Council and the United States, is to develop a climate of opinion and ideological hegemony about strategic directions for the world plutocracy. Its collective worldview is neoliberal geopolitics, a topic to which we now turn.

PART II

The Empire of Neoliberal Geopolitics

As a capitalist-class-dominated organization, the Council has been since its founding, during the First World War era, dedicated to the promotion of the expansion of U.S. economic power abroad. Since the mid-1970s this has been done by attempting to create pro-capitalist utopias for U.S. corporate investment and trade, nations where capital is unrestrained and low-cost resources and labor could be acquired, allowing high profits that could be repatriated to the United States. The term "neoliberal geopolitics" is used to characterize the world-spanning system that the CFR and its allies, including the U.S. federal government, have created over the last few decades. Included in this term is the subject of geoeconomics, which is properly seen as a subset of neoliberal geopolitics.

The Council's version of neoliberal geopolitics focuses, first and foremost, on the wealthiest and most powerful regions of the globe's political economy, the so-called triad: North America, Western Europe, and East Asia. Secondarily, regions adjacent to these key areas—the Middle East, Southeast and Southwest Asia—are also seen as especially important. Other parts of the world, though less central, are nevertheless valued as places where specific resources can be acquired, and markets penetrated.

Chapter 5 outlines in detail the origins and nature of the neoliberal geopolitical worldview and how it grew out of the thoughts and actions of a number of CFR leaders and members. Chapter 6 illustrates how the war on and occupation of Iraq had as its twin goals a long-term shift in the world balance of power in favor of the United States and the creation of a neoliberal utopia for Western capitalism. Chapter 7's short case studies collectively show the great range of the Council's grand strategic and tactical planning. Chapter 8 reviews the numerous studies the CFR has conducted on the issue of climate change during the years 1990–2014, with the ultimate conclusion to continue business as usual. The final chapter reflects on what the central role of the CFR means in terms of democracy and the public interest, asserting that its designs will inevitably fail due to multiple reasons, including declining American hegemony and the fact that CFR policies worsen a rapidly developing planetary ecological crisis. Part II closes with a call to action: the world's people must overthrow monopoly finance capital and its global system of neoliberal geopolitics in order to end the serious threat they pose to the ecological foundations of life on earth.

5

THE CFR'S WORLDVIEW, GRAND STRATEGY, AND TACTICS, 1976–2014

The need of a constantly expanding market for its products chases the bourgeoisie over the whole surface of the globe. It must nestle everywhere, settle everywhere, establish connections everywhere.

—KARL MARX AND FRIEDRICH ENGELS

Capital needs the means of production and the labor power of the whole globe for untrammeled accumulation.

—ROSA LUXEMBURG

T he Council on Foreign Relations is, above all, the place where the ruling capitalist class, together with its professional class allies, develop the grand strategy and tactics of creating empire: United States' global hegemony. Grand strategy must have goals, a vision appropriate for policy formulation, but also must be flexible enough to understand the unpredictability of historical developments and the need for collective planning, as well as the occasional reappraisal of tactics. The Council is organized to do this necessary research, thinking, debating, and planning to make such collective decisions under the auspices of the capitalist class. Over a period of decades, the CFR has—through its many programs and activities—gradually but successfully developed and implemented a coherent vision of global capitalist development to replace older ideologies and practices, especially Keynesianism. What has come out of this effort is the current world system, the informal empire of neoliberal geopolitics. This CFR worldview and grand strategy—the defining political and economic paradigm of our era—is neoliberal, "free market," corporate globalization, together with a combination of geographically oriented political and economic thinking and action at the level of global power politics, summed up by the term *geopolitics*. For the purpose of analysis in this chapter, the neoliberal and geopolitical policy frameworks are kept distinct, but they are united in actual practice as neoliberal geopolitics. At the level of grand strategy and goals, neoliberalism as a system of exploitation and as an ideology, the history of how the CFR and its members helped create neoliberalism, and the geopolitical and geoeconomic strategies for global implementation as outlined by key Council intellectuals, will be discussed. At the level of tactics, the role of "small wars," "soft power," and the U.S. government as Goliath will be examined.

Although the number of Council publications and communications, including books, periodical articles, videos, blogs, op-eds, interviews, and speeches is vast, a review of this literature allows a selection that will illuminate the CFR worldview, its definition of the capitalist-class interest, as well as its imperialist grand strategy and tactics during the 1976–2014 period. Many of the central economic and political policies of the United States and a number of other key world powers are influenced and framed by this Council/capitalist-class worldview. It has become a pervasive force, powerful in many nations and arenas, giving concrete meaning to the term "ideological hegemony."

One of the overall core functions of the CFR is a no-holds-barred ongoing effort to facilitate the expansion of opportunities for capital accumulation for the U.S. capitalist class and its corporations. Such expansion in search of investment and profit opportunities everywhere faces a variety of barriers, a key one being territorially organized state power. The world is organized as national units, each with a complex power structure and socio-politico culture, often with conflicting interests and ideologies, reflected in ruling classes, liberation movements, and class, ethnic, and gender struggles. As Marx and Engels observed well over 150 years ago, capital desires free-flowing movement, and thus penetrating state frontiers to conduct business, exploit human and material resources, and accumulate capital becomes a central focus. There is a contradiction between internationally oriented capital in the form of multinational and transnational corporations and the territorially organized state system, with each nation having the potential or actuality of sovereignty. John Bellamy Foster, Robert W. McChesney, and R. Jamil Jonna have described this conflict and its implications:

> Just as, nationally, any state programs that aid the working-class majority are targeted by neoliberalism, so internationally, the primary goal is to remove—in the name of "free trade"—any limits on the power of multinational corporations exercised by nation-states. This mainly hurts the weaker states, where such rules are more stringently imposed by international

organizations . . . and where there is less capacity to resist the intrusion of global corporations.[385]

Historically, military conquest and occupation, informal and formal colonialism, and economic efforts through such organizations as the IMF and World Bank have all been ways to overcome this key contradiction and open the way for the expansion of capital. These methods continue into our present historical epoch, but other, subtler means are also at work.

THE NEOLIBERAL SYSTEM OF EXPLOITATION

Every historical system that aims to be world-spanning has had its own unique deep structure: mechanisms for human and natural resource control, exploitation, and dispossession as well as legitimation of the system. This was true of ancient Rome; fascism in Germany, Italy, and Japan during the 1930s and 1940s; the British Empire of the nineteenth century; Keynesian liberalism; and the globalized monopoly finance capitalist–dominated neoliberalism of today.

Ancient Rome had vast emperor-directed military operations that conquered resource-rich lands, violently dispossessing and enslaving peoples who were then mercilessly exploited to benefit an agriculturally based small dictatorial ruling class. Fascism, taken to an extreme in Nazi Germany, was also based on the strong state and conquest of foreign lands to gain territory, resources, and slave labor. Additional central aspects of fascism included the destruction of trade unions and other workers' organizations, and the belief in an extreme form of Social Darwinism—supposedly superior races and individuals should ruthlessly rule over and exploit those who were not considered part of the self-defined "master race."

The later British Empire system had a more indirect capitalist dispossession and exploitation at home, accumulation through extraction of surplus value from wage labor although workers struggled to gradually achieve some limited rights. This was combined with more brutal exploitation and dispossession in their colonies. Elements of the British system served as a model for the Keynesian system of New Deal demand management. In their Keynesian scheme, unions for workers were accepted with the "class compromise"; state-imposed regulations restrained some actions of capital; taxes on corporations and the wealthy were relatively high; state planning, industrial policy, and state ownership existed in many cases; and there was some attempt at achieving full employment and a level of social welfare of rank-and-file citizens through varied forms of social security.[386] This system has been replaced today in economic thought and action by the doctrinal cluster of ideas called "neoliberalism," formally dedicated to the free movement of capital and goods worldwide (free markets), and multinational and transnational corporate globalization, promoted and enforced by state power. This is capital's default position, the direction that the system always pushes toward, taking into account the level of class struggle from below. Besides being an economic prescription, the corporate liberation project of neoliberalism also represents an ideological attack on the ideas of collective property (socialism), national development (national liberation), and social solidarity (trade unionism and community). Instead, individualism is exalted. David Harvey has offered a useful short definition of neoliberalism:

> A theory of political economic practices that proposes that human well-being can best be advanced by liberating individual entrepreneurial freedoms and skills within an institutional framework characterized by strong private property rights, free markets, and free trade. The role of the state is to create and preserve an institutional framework appropriate to such practices. The state has to guarantee, for example, the quality and integrity of money. It must also set up those military, defense, police, and legal structures and functions required to secure private property rights and to guarantee, by force if need be, the proper functioning of markets. Furthermore, if markets do not exist (in areas such as land, water, education, health care, social security, or environmental pollution) then they must be created, by state action if necessary. But beyond these tasks the state should not venture.[387]

Neoliberal corporate globalization operates through global management institutions, such as the World Trade Organization, International Monetary Fund, World Bank, and United Nations, and through nation-states and private, for-profit corporations. These are all powerful organizations that are hierarchical/dictatorial, bureaucratic, potentially perpetual, and have limited liability. These interacting institutions have created a new world system where the powerful nations, especially the United States, still have sovereignty, but for many other countries real sovereignty and state autonomy have been severely weakened. For these latter nations, state power has been transferred to investors/speculators, corporations, markets (especially financial markets), international bodies, and the more powerful nations, especially the United States. The power of individual large multinational corporations often exceeds the power of individual smaller states of the world. The steady increase in globalized corporate power thus poses a key question: Is this power now on a par with the strength of even the largest of states, such as the United States itself? The freedom of capital to move wherever and whenever it desires has often meant the loss of rights to employment for workers, since capital will be drawn to where labor is cheaper and regulations more lax. Such freedom for capital has also allowed the undermining of community-controlled political structures in favor of corporate-run ones. Precariousness for workers through dispossession—of union and job rights, property through foreclosures, rights to health care and education, and destruction of communities—is a frequent result.

In the globalized, neoliberal corporate system of exploitation the world capitalist class uses its monopoly of liquid capital, especially its control of finance, to exploit much of the world's land, natural resources, and workers, funneling much of the resulting accumulated riches to a relative handful of wealthy individuals and families in the empire's urban power centers (New York City being a key one). The spread of this system has been the overarching goal of the CFR and its allied network of institutions in the period under consideration here, 1976 to 2014. As will be illustrated, this has created a world-spanning investment, production, trade, and speculative system, an informal global political-economic empire whose dominant power is the United States, its corporations, and its financialized capitalist class. Neoliberalism represents both the national capitalist-class interest of the United States, as well as the interest of this U.S./multinational financial oligarchy, and has been vigorously promoted by leaders and members of the Council. Agreement on the goals of neoliberal corporate globalization is, in effect, with few exceptions, a prerequisite for CFR membership today. As shown in prior chapters, the membership selection process mainly brings in strong supporters of neoliberalism, and generally limits critics to those who disagree on the tactics needed to implement this worldview, not its fundamental premises.

A Capitalist-Class Project: The Practice of Neoliberalism

The actual practice of neoliberalism—adopted by the political parties of the right, center, and center left worldwide—is sharply different from its theory. This is because neoliberalism is first and foremost a capitalist-class project and ideology led by the CFR together with an internationalized and financialized U.S. capitalist class allied with key European and Asian capitalists. Its bottom-line goal is to increase the wealth, income, and power of capital, especially international finance capital, by any means necessary. This is an aspect of the fact that capital markets are now an extremely powerful force, representing the concentrated power of the financialized world capitalist class. Some, like CFR member and former deputy secretary of the treasury Roger Altman, argue that these markets, together with the capitalists who are investing in them, are now "the most powerful force on earth."[388]

The principles of neoliberalism have both ideological and concrete aspects. First is the formal ideology of neoliberalism which promotes the theory of the small weak state with low taxes and weak regulations as a means to destroy Keynesian social welfare liberalism and free capital from any restraint. In actual concrete practice however, government must operate at the service of the financialized transnational capitalist class, assisting its efforts to accumulate capital. This means that neoliberalism promotes the big, powerful, coercive activist state for the capitalist ruling class and the small weak state for everyone else. More specifically, in the arena of capital accumulation, neoliberalism means a "good business climate": large police and military forces, including repression and prisons in order to protect private property and expand the free movement of capital and the global circuits of capital accumulation, as well as controlling or even conquering nations with natural resources and/or an inexpensive, exploitable labor supply. Capitalists want help from the state, including bailouts by the trillions of dollars, when economic crisis inevitably develops. They want the state to expand the domestic investment market through the commodification, financialization, and privatization of everything possible, including people and ecologies, converting once public assets and spaces like public education into their private realm, infusing market logic everywhere and embedding it in capitalist social relations.

The capitalists want government contracts and subsidies. They want export promotion activities, such as taxpayer-supported foreign aid tied to purchases of U.S. products. Freed from regulation, finance and speculation—hedge funds, futures, options, derivatives, swaps, computer-generated trades, and so on—take over. Capital, freed from nation-state restrictions, roams the globe looking for the easiest profits; vast fortunes are rapidly acquired by insiders with connections, including private equity corporations, hedge fund operators, and other speculators. All are aspects of a monopolistic system, far from the ideology of "free markets." As we saw during the financial crisis of 2007–2008, when capitalists needed massive bailouts from the state and taxpayers, capitalist-class interest came to the fore, trillions of dollars suddenly became available, and neoliberal ideology was rapidly dumped.

At the same time, the financialized U.S. and transnational capitalist class wants neoliberalism to mean the destruction of the Keynesian/New Deal welfare state and the substitution of the small and weak state for the vast majority: the workers. Unions and safe working conditions are undermined or destroyed; health and safety laws gutted; wages, Medicare, Social Security, pensions, as well as ecological protections, come under attack and are reduced or eliminated. The diminished capacity of the smaller states in Africa and the Third World has proved to be dangerous to humanity, because viruses like Ebola are more apt to get out of control when the health sector is cut back or privatized in order to increase the avenues of profitability for private corporations in this sector.

Under the regime of neoliberal geopolitics, unemployment and underemployment have increased to near depression levels, with no serious countervailing government programs, since the government supposedly lacks resources. Austerity is the program for the working class, along with sharp competition between working classes in different countries, resulting in static or falling wages, though there is always plenty for the capitalist class. One predictable outcome has been a massive increase in inequality with much higher levels of wealth and income concentration at the top, together with severe deprivation for the poorest nations and peoples. The capitalist press is filled with examples of this vast increase in inequality. To cite just one, the *Financial Times* reported in 2014 that 110 Russian billionaires now control 35 percent of Russia's total wealth.[389] In the United States, the richest nation in the world, this meant a return to 1920s levels of disparity by the early 2000s.[390] The top 1 percent of U.S. families now average about $1 million income a year, while the bottom 90 percent average $29,840. The top 10 percent of wealth holders in the United States own 73 percent of the nation's wealth, while the bottom 60 percent own less than 5 percent.[391]

Viewed on a global scale, the situation is even more unequal. There are 29.6 million financial millionaires in the world, one half of 1 percent of the world's people. Assets of over $100 million are held by only 29,000 ultra-high-wealth individuals, the largest number by far living in the United States, which controls almost 30 percent of the world's total wealth and where over 40 percent of the world's millionaires live.[392] The richest 2 percent of the world's people hold 50 percent of the planet's wealth, and the top 10 percent own 85 percent. Wealthy people living in North America, Europe, and the richer part of Asia, amounting to only a small part of the globe's population, control 88 percent of the world's wealth.[393] The eighty-five richest individuals on the planet own the same amount of wealth as the 3.5 billion poorest people.[394] These billions of poor people live and die in dire poverty, with little or no chance to live a healthy life or fully develop their human abilities, a massively immoral crime. Statistics from the Credit Suisse bank show that the bottom 68 percent of the world's adults hold only 4.2 percent of the world's wealth.[395] The main achievement of neoliberalism worldwide has been to redistribute wealth upward, not generate new wealth.[396] One proof of this is a statistic from the United States: fully 95 percent of total income growth during the 2009–12 years has gone to the top 1 percent.[397]

In the United States both mainstream parties, the Republicans and the Democrats, are heavily influenced by elements of the financialized U.S. capitalist class and are neoliberal parties at their core. The Republican leadership is made up of hardcore neoliberals who are fixated on speeding up capital accumulation and believe that the source of all problems is government failure and the supposed excesses of Keynesian style liberalism. To them, excessive taxation, mistaken government intervention in the housing market, in the health care industry, in management of the money supply, and the promotion of social welfare are the key problems. At the same time, inequality, racism, sexism, unemployment, and poverty, the existence of a giant and very expensive military, a repressive prison system, the denial of rights to many people, and corporate welfare at taxpayer expense are not seen as issues.

The Democratic leadership consists of soft-core neoliberals. They argue that the main problem is that the neoliberal deregulation of the banks, which they themselves implemented in 1999 with the repeal of the Glass-Steagall Act, went too far, as did allowing housing loans to those who could not afford them. Mild adjustments in regulations are thus needed. Otherwise, despite some rhetorical flourishes to satisfy their base of rank-and-file supporters and some concern about the need to legitimate the system, policies of the Democratic leadership are also neoliberal. There are many examples. Democrats support NAFTA, the Trans-Pacific Partnership and other pro-corporate trade policies; they agreed to deregulation, then imposed only weak reregulations for much of the financial sector; they repealed welfare policies while refusing to sponsor a government-run full employment program when unemployment and underemployment have been at crisis levels. Democrats have also compromised with Republicans on their attempts to cut Social Security and Medicare; they have not even attempted to try to pass the Employee Free Choice Act to help unions organize workers who want to be in unions; they have maintained a privately controlled health care system instead of socialized medicine or a single-payer system; they have continued welfare programs for corporate agriculture and other wealthy vested interests; they have spent vast sums on militarism and war; and they have voted for trillions of dollars of bailout money for Wall Street.

GRAND STRATEGY: THE CFR AND THE HISTORICAL DEVELOPMENT OF NEOLIBERALISM

CFR leaders and members have had a central role in the development of globalized neoliberal ideology and practice since its origins in the early 1970s. Because neoliberalism is detrimental to the needs and interests of the overwhelming majority of the earth's people, it has to be imposed by force after a societal shock like a civil war or economic crisis, or imposed more gradually through secrecy, lies, deception, and trickery.[398] Neoliberalism has been a worldwide phenomenon and there have been many national roads to it, but the fountainhead of its ideology and practice has been in the United States, and the CFR and its network have played key roles in its origins and expansion.

A Key Point of Origin: Neoliberalism in Chile

Augusto Pinochet's dictatorship in Chile was the first large-scale implementation of neoliberalism. In September of 1973, Salvador Allende's democratically elected government was overthrown, followed by a one-sided civil war against the left, with estimates of over 3,000 activists known to have been murdered, over 30,000 tortured, over 80,000 arrested, and millions of people terrorized. Varied people's movements were destroyed and a path opened to unopposed privatization, union destruction, cuts in social spending, deregulation, and so-called free markets.

The U.S. government had sought and organized such a coup since September 15, 1970, when President Richard M. Nixon, a former member of the CFR, ordered CIA director and Council member Richard Helms to foster a government overthrow in Chile. Nixon characteristically ranted: "That son of a bitch Allende. We're going to smash him."[399] National Security Adviser Henry A. Kissinger and his assistant Alexander Haig, both CFR members, discussed promoting a coup on October 15, 1970. The next day the CIA station chief in Santiago, Chile, received Kissinger's orders via CIA headquarters: "It is firm and continuing policy that Allende be overthrown by a coup. . . . It is imperative that these actions be implemented clandestinely and securely so that the USG [U.S. Government] and American hand be well hidden. . . . This imposes upon us a high degree of selectivity in making military contacts."[400] The U.S. ambassador to Chile at the time was CFR member Edward M. Korry. Illustrative of the hostility with which the CFR community and broader U.S. capitalist class viewed Allende's free election as president of Chile is what Korry said when he heard the Allende had won: "Not a nut or bolt shall reach Chile under Allende. Once Allende comes to power we shall do all within our power to condemn Chile and all Chileans to utmost deprivation and poverty."[401]

Those pushing the U.S. government to sponsor a coup against Allende were other members of the CFR community such as Council member Harold S. Geneen, the president of International Telephone and Telegraph Company, which had investments in Chile.[402] After the bloody overthrow and destruction of Chilean democracy, *Foreign Affairs* ran an article by a Princeton professor who naively argued that those who suspected that the U.S. government had a role in the coup were wrong, since a U.S. Senate subcommittee had investigated and "concluded that there is no evidence of any U.S. role whatever."[403]

Once in power and his violent system of terror was in place, dictator Pinochet brought in a group of Chilean economists who had studied with Milton Friedman at the Rockefeller-founded and funded University of Chicago. Called "the Chicago Boys," they implemented a full neoliberal program in Chile, including privatizing many sectors of the economy and society, including public utilities, health care, parts of the education system, and pensions; dramatically cut government social services; and opened the nation to "free trade." The oppressed Chilean people had absolutely no say in the matter. The results of the program were very harmful to workers; unemployment reached 33 percent in 1982 and by 1988 almost half of Chileans were living in poverty, while the income of the richest 10 percent had increased by 83 percent. Under Pinochet and neoliberalism, Chile had become one of the most unequal nations in the world.[404] The Chilean people eventually rebelled and at great sacrifice overthrew the military dictatorship, resulting in a serious modification of neoliberal policies but far short of an egalitarian, just society run by and for the working class and peasant majority.

During the mid-1970s, as Pinochet was implementing neoliberalism in Chile, the Council was conducting its "1980s Project." One of the largest CFR projects ever, the multiyear project was started in 1974 and by late 1975 it was in full swing having received major funding from the Ford, Rockefeller, and Mellon Foundations, the German Marshall Fund, and the Lilly Endowment.[405] Council member and project director Richard H. Ullman described the size and scope of this planning effort as follows in the 1976 CFR *Annual Report*:

> During the period November 1975–June 1976, the 1980s Project sponsored 38 full-day meetings of ten issue-related working groups and of the central Project Coordinating Group; 318 persons, half of them members of the Council, took part in the discussions. Eighty papers—each specially commissioned to address terms of reference worked out by the Project staff— formed the background to the discussions. Many of these papers, and others not yet completed, will appear next year in a series of thirty or so books to be published for the Project by the McGraw-Hill Book Company.[406]

The substance of the 1980s Project was also impressive, a serious effort at integrated forethought with a transnational emphasis. As Ullman and 1980s Project staff member Edward L. Morse (also a CFR member) related in 1978:

> The 1980s Project had its origins in the widely held recognition that many of the assumptions, policies, and institutions that have characterized international relations during the past 30 years are inadequate to the demands of today and the foreseeable demands of the period between now and 1990 or so. Over the course of the next decade, substantial adaptation of institutions and behavior will be needed to respond to the changed circumstances of the 1980s and beyond. The Project seeks to identify those future conditions and the kinds of adaptation they might require. It is not the Project's purpose to arrive at a single or exclusive set of goals. Nor does it focus upon the foreign policy or national interests of the United States alone. Instead, it seeks to identify goals that are compatible with the perceived interests of most states, despite differences in ideology and in level of economic development.
>
> The published products of the Project are aimed at a broad readership, including policy makers and potential policy makers and those who would

influence the policy-making process, but are confined to no single nation or region. The authors of Project studies were therefore asked to remain mindful of interests broader than those of any one society.[407]

Some of the CFR studies conducted during this effort represented an initial embrace of neoliberalism. One that was especially relevant to the developing neoliberal perspectives was the 1978 *Rich and Poor Nations in the World Economy*, a CFR book published by the Council and McGraw-Hill. The lead author was Council member Albert Fishlow, who summed up his perspective on the future of the economic world system as follows: "In short, a truly interdependent new order must rely on symmetrically freer market forces, not on immediate national advantage." The "highest priority" in this global market system would be "freer trade," in order to "engage all nations within a freer market." Fishlow also advocated larger private financial flows, loans, and investment to poorer nations, stating that the "expansion of private-sector activity is consistent with the greater scope for market influence that has been advocated."[408] Building on the importance of private foreign investment, Fishlow links it to the spread of technology, and that in turn to monopoly power:

> The private sector of the developed countries has been the most prominent means of transferring technical knowledge and managerial capacity and diffusing modern industry. That know-how has been disseminated throughout the world in unprecedented fashion through the workings of the market.... Monopoly power is the rule rather than the exception for foreign enterprises. It is the rare firm that invests abroad without some control in that market.... Few firms possess absolute market power, however. There are other transnationals with similar products and skills, competitors that are increasingly of different nationalities.[409]

One 1980s Project publication advocated for a new international organization to promote neoliberal capitalist-oriented world production and trade, suggesting, at an early date, what became the World Trade Organization a decade and a half later. Miriam Camps, the primary author of a 1980s Project book, *Collective Management: The Reform of Global Economic Organizations*, called the proposed new organization a "Production and Trade Organization," but its purpose was the same as what later became the WTO.[410]

Five Prominent CFR Directors Promote Neoliberalism

While the policy ideas of the 1980s Project, including neoliberal "free market" perspectives, were circulating among top officials and intellectuals globally and as the world's first fully neoliberal experiment was being forcibly imposed on the Chilean people, five free marketers, all directors or former directors of the CFR—Walter B. Wriston, Alan Greenspan, Paul A. Volcker, Martin S. Feldstein, and Robert Rubin— were reaching the top levels of economic policymaking in the United States.[411] Collectively this group, representative of the Council's worldview, successfully launched the first great wave of neoliberalism in the United States, using the power of the state to implement, step by step, the capitalist goal of unrestricted freedom for corporations and capital at the expense of popular forces. This amounted to brutal class struggle from above, targeted at ordinary people, aiming at the cutback and elimination of government services and workers' rights leading toward austerity and the destruction of a social safety net built up in the United States over previous decades. These five men were key players in the implementation of neoliberal corporate globalization at home, a process that closely aligned the U.S. social formation with the ongoing expansion and reproduction of global transnational capitalism. A brief review of their careers and actions as power wielders helps deepen an understanding of how neoliberalism developed at home and abroad.

In 1967 Walter B. Wriston became the head of what was then called First National City Bank of New York, today's Citigroup. His father Henry, president of Brown University, had been a longtime (twenty-four years) director of the CFR and president of the Council for thirteen years in the 1950s and 1960s. Walter was also a director of the CFR from 1981 to 1987.[412] During this same period he was widely regarded as the most influential commercial banker of the time. Walter B. Wriston's driving passion was undoing the federal regulations of the financial industry that had been established during the Great Depression to protect the nation against financial speculation and market crashes. He wanted to make First National City a one-stop financial center for consumers and investor/speculators with everything under its wings: savings accounts, mortgages, credit cards, mutual funds, insurance, and brokerage. This required a loosening of federal regulations, multiplying the risks of financial collapse, which, of course, came in due time.[413] In his role as a leading banker, and as chairman of Reagan's Economic Policy Advisory Board from 1982 to 1989, Wriston put constant pressure on the Federal Reserve and policy makers to loosen regulations and allow for free markets, competition, free lending and borrowing, and speculation. He even published books to try to influence the public debate. One, *Risk and Other Four-Letter Words*, was a rant against "bigger government and more regulation, which inevitably lead to the loss of individual liberty."[414]

In 1974 Alan Greenspan, a longtime close friend and follower of laissez-faire libertarian Ayn Rand, was sworn in as the head of President Gerald Ford's Council of Economic Advisers. Greenspan had Rand standing next to him with Ford when he took the oath of office. Much earlier, Greenspan recounted, he had "decided to engage in efforts to advance free-market capitalism as an insider."[415] A member of the CFR, Greenspan counted among his New York friends CFR leaders David Rockefeller, Henry Kissinger, and Felix Rohatyn.[416] President Ford faced "stagflation," a combination of unemployment and inflation characteristic of late capitalism in many nations, and under Greenspan's tutelage decided to attack the problem with a program of tax cuts and deregulation. One expert on the Ford administration later stated: "In time, Greenspan would have more influence on Ford than any other economic adviser," pointing out that "deregulation came naturally to Ford, and his deregulatory inclinations were reinforced by his economic advisers, most prominently Alan Greenspan."[417] Greenspan later called Ford's deregulatory program the administration's "great unsung achievement." The Ford administration was a short-lived one, however, and Greenspan was soon temporarily out of power. But the Carter administration continued and got credit for the "deregulation initiative that had begun under Jerry Ford."[418] David Rockefeller had also called for a cut in the "excessive government regulation" of business in 1978, and Carter obliged. Carter also cut business taxes, something called for by his treasury secretary, former CFR director W. Michael Blumenthal.[419]

Business Week warned in the spring of 1978 that inflation was a threat to the "basic structure of American society."[420] Carter recognized it as a serious problem, searched for a cure, and came up with both the right man and ideas for the cure in the person of Paul A. Volcker. Volcker had been educated at Princeton, where the Austrian free market school of economics (Friedrich von Hayek et al.) was dominant, and this was important to the development of his economic theories. He joined the Chase Manhattan Bank in 1957 and soon was a special assistant to David Rockefeller. A few years later Volcker was brought into government, serving in the Treasury Department during the early Kennedy-Johnson years, returning to Chase in 1965 to again work as an aide to Rockefeller. Nixon brought him back into Treasury as its number three man in 1969.[421] Out of the Treasury again and back at Chase and also a director of the CFR in 1979, Volcker's name came up as a possible appointment to head the Federal Reserve. Carter, as Greenspan put it, "didn't even know who Volcker was." But Wall Street bankers and CFR directors David Rockefeller and Robert Roosa urged Carter to appoint Volcker "as the necessary choice to reassure the financial world."[422] In short, Volcker was the "candidate of Wall Street."[423] At the behest of Wall Street, Volcker took over as the "world's most powerful economic policy maker" during the summer of 1979.[424]

Once in office as the head of the Federal Reserve, Volcker followed the University of Chicago's neoliberal monetarist program, destroying inflation through restricting the money supply, driving up interest rates to 20 percent, which resulted in a recession with increased business failures and high unemployment. It is generally believed that Volcker's anti-inflation program lost Carter the election and helped open the way for the neoliberal deregulation policies that followed.[425]

President Ronald Reagan retained Volcker, and his tight money policy was continued, with unemployment reaching nearly 11 percent by late 1982. Volcker supported Reagan's anti-union policies; he believed that union wage contracts were inflationary, and wanted to break the back of union-inspired wage increases.[426]

The key background to the monetary policies that both Carter and Reagan followed during the 1979–82 years was the stagnation in the world economy and the fear of a low-growth trap, combined with the danger that high inflation posed to both established wealth and economic growth. A 1980 *Foreign Affairs* article, "The Continuing World Economic Crisis," by two Citibank vice presidents, one of them, Harold van B. Cleveland, a CFR member, discussed the central need to overcome stagnation and balance of payments problems through a neoliberal program of controlling inflation, together with "market discipline."[427]

Reagan's chief economic adviser during his first term was CFR member and later a Council director, Martin S. Feldstein. Feldstein had been president and CEO of the National Bureau of Economic Research, a private nonprofit organization. He became the head of the Council of Economic Advisers in 1982 and was said to be a chief architect of Reagan's neoliberal economic policies. Feldstein and Reagan saw four key areas where reductions were called for: rate of inflation, tax rates, size of government, and regulations of the private sector. Volcker's policies had inflation on the run. According to Feldstein, top income tax rates were cut from 70 percent in 1980 to 28 percent in 1986, the country's non-defense discretionary spending cut by one-third from 1980 to 1988, and regulations were reduced in a wide range of industries, including air transport and in the financial sector.

Connected to this deregulation and the creation of a more flexible workforce with fewer rights for workers was Reagan's destruction of the Professional Air Traffic Controllers Organization (PATCO) in 1981, one of the key events in late twentieth-century U.S. labor history. This union had gone on strike for better pay, working conditions, and fewer working hours due to the stress involved in their work. Invoking the 1948 Taft-Hartley Act, Reagan ordered the union's members back to work. When 11,345 stood firm, refusing to return without achieving at least some of their goals, Reagan fired and blacklisted them all. While still Federal Reserve Chair, Alan Greenspan later pointed out that Reagan's action "gave weight to the legal right of private employers, previously not fully exercised, to use their own discretion to both hire and discharge workers."[428] Indeed, Reagan's action encouraged private employers to take a hard line against unions and workers and, given the lack of fighting spirit among the leadership of many U.S. unions, the result has been a weakening of worker power and serious long-term decline of union membership. In congressional testimony in early 1997,

Greenspan reinforced this hard line while discussing Federal Reserve Board inflation goals in the context of workers' increasing fears of layoffs. Greenspan approvingly observed that "restraint on compensation increases has been evident for a few years now and appears mainly the consequence of greater worker insecurity."[429] Such "worker insecurity" is a key goal of neoliberalism, as it inhibits worker demands for better pay, benefits, and conditions—demands that could impact the power of capitalists to make super-profits and increase their class power.

By 1985 the Reagan administration had a comprehensive program to renew growth in the world economy, called the Baker Plan, after Secretary of the Treasury James A. Baker III. This was a fully neoliberal plan, calling for "market-oriented policies for growth," that is, structural adjustment, but it was not successful in gaining widespread agreement. A later plan, called the Brady Plan after CFR member and Secretary of the Treasury Nicholas F. Brady, was successful in developing a measure of international consensus. In typically neoliberal fashion, it linked debt relief to assurances of neoliberal economic "reforms" and trade openness in the less developed, less sovereign debtor nations.

At the same time during the 1980s, the World Bank was implementing structural adjustment policies, tying them to loans to poorer nations. All of the chief economists planning these policies at the World Bank during this era—Hollis B. Chenery, Ann O. Krueger, Stanley Fischer, and Lawrence Summers—were members of the Council on Foreign Relations. Krueger, later second in command at the IMF, was called a "famously neoliberal" thinker by Leo Panitch and Sam Gindin.[430]

Reagan also appointed Alan Greenspan, then a director of the CFR, to replace Volcker as Fed chief in 1987. Volcker was then brought back onto the Council board he had left in 1979, in effect replacing Greenspan.[431] Unlike Volcker, who was a Democrat, Greenspan had been an avid supporter of Reagan during the 1980 presidential campaign. As a free market ideologue, Greenspan was against unions and cheered Margaret Thatcher's attack on and defeat of the coal miners and other unions in Britain through a big-business government alliance in 1984–85.[432] Greenspan was to serve as the chairman of the Federal Reserve for almost two decades, longer than any other head of the Fed. Since Fed chief is the nation's highest economic office and Greenspan was the most widely admired chairman in Fed history, "he had more influence than any other figure over the direction the nation took during the 1987–2007 years."[433] Naomi Klein argued that while Greenspan headed up the Fed, he was "probably the single most powerful economic policy maker in the world."[434] Greenspan reportedly ran the Fed in a top-down, dictatorial fashion, even ordering his staff to produce studies with the conclusions he wanted.[435]

In 1989, just after the end of the Reagan years, the term "Washington Consensus" was coined. The term was used to capture the neoliberal interface between the U.S. Treasury Department and the Fed on one hand and the IMF and World Bank on the other. All were promoting neoliberal corporate globalization. In terms of the flow of capital abroad, the results were spectacular, whereas only about $170 billion in U.S. private sector capital moved to the private sector of developing nations in the 1980s, it increased to $1.3 trillion in the 1990s. In their book *The Making of Global Capitalism*, Leo Panitch and Sam Gindin summed up the new reality as follows: "It was a measure of how far the project for a global capitalism had been realized by 1995 that these private flows now dwarfed the bilateral and multilateral state loans that had provided most of the capital flows to developing countries in earlier decades."[436]

Neoliberal policies became further entrenched in the 1990s under Presidents George H. W. Bush and William J. Clinton, both CFR members. Bush began the process of creating the North American Free Trade Act (NAFTA) between Canada, Mexico, and the United States. Carla A. Hills, a Council member and later CFR co-chair, was Bush's trade representative and chief NAFTA negotiator. NAFTA was ratified during the Clinton administration due to his support and the vote of many Democrats. Robert Rubin, later co-chair of the Council, was a top Clinton economic policy adviser as assistant to the president for economic policy and strongly supported NAFTA.

Largely created by CFR members and leaders, NAFTA helped establish the template for the rules of the emerging global economy, a kind of socialism for the corporations and global competition for labor, a world where important state-enforced benefits would flow to capital at the expense of workers. Part of this was that NAFTA granted corporations extraordinary protections against national laws that might threaten their profits, and set up special courts, staffed by pro-corporate experts, to judge corporate suits against all levels of government. NAFTA also strengthened the ability of U.S. employers to force unions and their workers to accept lower wages and benefits by threatening to move their operations to Mexico. Besides undermining labor's bargaining power, NAFTA impacted U.S. environmental regulations, limiting government's ability to stop pollution, since this might limit profits. NAFTA was thus a key step in the global "race to the bottom." This term refers to the fact that the neoliberal world order creates "free market" competitive relationships between companies and countries resulting in cuts in wages, benefits, and conditions for workers in order to attract investment into a corporation or nation. This creates a negative downward economic cycle globally for the people and communities affected. NAFTA was also used to further lock in Mexico as a neoliberal nation, which had, according to a leading Mexico City newspaper, enriched thirteen super-wealthy families while impoverishing about 80 million Mexicans.[437]

Neoliberal corporate globalization, with its massive level of trade and largely unregulated free flows of capital, proved difficult to control. Marx and Engels, writing in the *Communist Manifesto*, were prescient about "modern bourgeois society" when they said that it "has conjured up such gigantic means of production and of exchange, [and] is like the sorcerer who is no longer able to control the powers of the nether world whom he has called up by his spells."[438] The crises tended to come in the nations like Mexico that were models of capital mobility and free trade. Extraordinary efforts were needed to contain these crises. When the Mexican government was threatened with default in 1995, President Clinton's new secretary of the treasury, Robert E. Rubin, and his team immediately put together a rescue plan worth $40 billion, an unprecedented amount. The goal was to fully reassure transnational capitalists and their markets that there would be no default ever. The result furthered neoliberal corporate globalization by assuring capitalists that they would be bailed out no matter what risky speculative bets they made. Meanwhile, flows of private capital to emerging markets continued to accelerate.[439]

During Rubin's and his protégé Lawrence Summers' tenures as secretary of the treasury, the further institutionalization of the neoliberal variant of capitalism took place. The World Trade Organization (WTO) was created in 1995 to further eliminate barriers to world trade. With Council member Timothy F. Geithner as U.S. negotiator, in 1997, over 150 nations in the new WTO acquiesced to a financial services agreement that applied "free trade" rules, formerly applicable to goods in international commerce, to the operations of banks, securities, and insurance companies, while reducing regulations, thus greatly stimulating their expansion abroad. With full assistance from the financial community, in 1999–2000 Rubin and Summers also steered through Congress the Financial Services Modernization Act, removing regulatory barriers and allowing the consolidation of commercial banks, investment banks, insurance firms, and securities companies. This repealed parts of the Glass-Steagall Act of 1933 and opened the way for both increased financial speculation and the growth of "too big to fail" financial institutions. The size of financial conglomerates was no longer limited by the federal government.

One final act of the Clinton administration was the Commodity Futures Modernization Act, signed by the president in December 2000, just before he left office. This law deregulated financial products known as over-the-counter derivatives. Such derivatives, especially credit default swaps, would later be a central factor in the financial crisis of 2008. The President's Working Group on Financial Markets, established by Clinton in 1999, made the recommendation to deregulate. Three of its four members were longtime CFR members: Treasury Secretary Lawrence Summers; Fed chair Alan Greenspan; and Securities and Exchange chair Arthur S. Levitt. The fourth was the existing regulator, William J. Rainer of the Commodity Futures Trading Commission. Meanwhile, Clinton's gift to the working class was austerity. In 1995 he signed the Republican-passed law that "reformed" welfare at a time when there was a chronic lack of jobs paying decent wages, driving many people deeper into poverty.

Under the presidency of George W. Bush, Greenspan "stepped far from the traditional duties of a Federal Reserve chairman" by endorsing Bush's neoliberal income tax cut proposal of $1.6 trillion over ten years. After that "nearly 90 percent of the benefits of the Bush tax cut went to the top 5 percent of earners in the nation."[440] This piece of capitalist policy increased the inequality characteristic of the era. Greenspan also encouraged various types of unregulated securities trading, speculative binges that were enabled by treasury secretaries Rubin and Summers during the Clinton years.[441] One result was the 2008 financial crisis, yet the same techniques, such as tax cuts and an increase in liquidity, were used to pump up a new economic "recovery."

Results of Neoliberal Globalization

The policies of neoliberalism, carried out for a number of decades, have increased the already substantial disparities in worldwide wealth and power. Helpful in illustrating this is the *Global Wealth Data Book*, produced in recent years by the Credit Research Institute of the Switzerland-based transnational bank Credit Suisse. One of the most striking findings in this 2010 study is that adults in the nations of the three allied developed capitalist "trilateral" regions of the world—North America, Europe, Japan—owned and controlled almost 75 percent of the world's wealth, with the United States controlling more wealth by far (28.6 percent), than any other single nation. Overall, adults in Europe had 31.8 percent, North America 31.1 percent, and Japan 10.8 percent of global wealth. By contrast, China controlled only 8.5 percent, Australia 2.6 percent, and India 1.8 percent of the world's wealth. In 2010, 49 percent of the world's billionaires lived in North America (mainly in the United States), and another 23 percent resided in Europe. At the millionaire level, 40.5 percent of the world's millionaires lived in the United States, and another 9.7 percent resided in Japan. Another 28.2 percent lived in four European nations (France, Italy, the United Kingdom, Germany) and Canada. Thus, as of 2010, 78.4 percent of all the world's millionaires resided in only seven nations, which collectively make up only about 10.7 percent of global population. Credit Suisse also presents a "global wealth pyramid," illustrating that the top 0.5 percent of the world's wealth holders held 35.6 percent of global wealth, and the top 8 percent held fully 79.3 percent. Conversely, the bottom 68.4 percent of the world's adults, basically a majority of the world's working people, held only 4.2 percent. The middle group, mainly professionals, who were 23.6 percent of the adult population, held 16.5 percent of the wealth.[442]

Statistics on U.S. foreign direct investment add to the picture of where the world's wealth is held and invested and possible implications for foreign policy. In terms of outward flows of direct investment capital, cumulative U.S. investments abroad are in Europe (55.6 percent), the Caribbean and Latin America (19.5 percent), Asia/Pacific (14.6 percent), and Canada (7.9 percent). In terms of inward flows, cumulative foreign direct investments into the United States have come from Europe (70.8 percent), Asia/Pacific (mainly Japan) (16.1 percent), and Canada (8.5 percent).[443] These central facts help set the context for the geoeconomics and geopolitics of the CFR, its leaders and members.

A GRAND STRATEGY FOR WORLD HEGEMONY: CHENEY, BRZEZINSKI, GEOECONOMICS, AND GEOPOLITICS

The importance of property and wealth as reflected in the statistics above is never far from the minds of the capitalists and their intellectual helpers at the Council. Therefore the study of geoeconomics—the relationship of geography and economic power—as well as how this relates to political power has long been a major CFR interest, helping to frame policymaking. On February 15, 2002, Vice President Richard B. Cheney was the featured speaker at the launch of the Council's new Maurice R. Greenberg Center for Geoeconomic Studies, the expressed goal of which is to train the next generation of foreign policy leaders in modern geoeconomics—the interrelationships among neoliberal economics, globalization, and foreign policy. CFR chair Peter G. Peterson introduced Cheney as a man who has been practicing geoeconomics for "many years," a man of

> great good sense, honesty and success . . . among his career high points was his service as Director on the Board of the Council on Foreign Relations—on two separate occasions. Those of us who worked with him on the Board and in all his other capacities know how lucky our nation is to have him where he is. Indeed, I, and many others, sleep better knowing he is there.[444]

The CFR has, for over three decades, made neoliberal geoeconomics a hallmark of its ideological orientation and worldview. This thinking is combined with a realist and idealist geopolitical theory based on military strength and the balance of power in world politics. Geopolitics focuses on the security of the nation-state and the imperial grand strategies required to achieve world power. The long-term geopolitical goals of the CFR and the larger U.S. power structure since 1941 have aimed at global military hegemony. Geopolitics, also called "power politics," therefore goes hand in hand with geoeconomics and the spread of neoliberalism on a world scale—all usually discussed in ruling-class circles under the headings of "multilateralism," "globalization," and "internationalism." A key part of geopolitics is locating and evaluating natural and economic resources and their relation to sea power and land power. In this way key spaces on the earth's surface can be identified along with the existing balance of forces at any given moment, leading to potential actions: military buildups and wars of conquest, attempts to shape the world power environment through alliances and offshore balancing, as well as diplomatic engagement. Geopolitical analysis thus tends to be nationalistic and era-specific and changes with shifts in the relative power and ambitions of the world's key nation-states.

Two basic geopolitical eras are considered here: the Cold War era (1976–90) and the post–Cold War era (1991–2013). A key CFR geopolitical thinker throughout both eras has been Zbigniew Brzezinski, a Council member for at least forty years, often a participant in Council study groups, a CFR director from 1972 to 1977, and a frequent writer for *Foreign Affairs*.[445] He has had a close relationship with David Rockefeller, and was a co-founder, with Rockefeller, of the Trilateral Commission (1973). He has also long been a counselor with the Center for Strategic and International Studies at Georgetown University. His views often reflect the consensus perspective of those in power due to his close relationships to the CFR and other ruling-class organizations.

Brzezinski was born in Warsaw of Polish nobility, escaping the fate of much of this old ruling class by the luck of living in Canada with his diplomat father during much of the Second World War. He became a cold warrior specializing in Eastern Europe and the USSR, teaching at Columbia and Johns Hopkins universities. As a Democrat but a hawk on Soviet-U.S. relations, his governmental positions have been in Democratic administrations, most prominently as Carter's national security adviser (1977–81), where he famously clashed with the secretary of state, the less hawkish Cyrus Vance, but also as a Department of State policy planner during the Vietnam War, which he fully supported. On the other hand, he was strongly critical of Bush II's invasion and occupation of Iraq. He has written extensively on geopolitics. *Game Plan: A Geostrategic Framework for the Conduct of the U.S.-Soviet Contest* (1986) and *The Grand Chessboard: American Primacy and Its Geostrategic Imperatives* (1997) are his two most important works in this field, and will be focused on here.[446]

Game Plan

During the 1976–90 period, a central concern of the Council and the larger U.S. ruling class was winning the U.S.-Soviet contest for hegemony over Eurasia. Brzezinski's *Game Plan* developed out of this concern and laid a framework for U.S. imperial grand strategy. Its focus was "the geopolitical struggle for the domination of Eurasia, but it also examines its peripheral and diversionary aspects as well as the rivalry on the oceans and outer space that is an extension of the struggle for earth control"[447] The area that Brzezinski defined as Eurasia ran from Britain and Spain in the west to the Soviet Far East, China, and Southeast Asia in the east. This Eurasia region included, in the mid-1980s, over 70 percent of the world's population, 60 percent of the globe's GDP, and nearly 40 percent of the land area.[448] People in this area held the overwhelming bulk of the world's wealth outside of North America. Eurasia was seen as the geopolitical prize, the central priority of the U.S.-Soviet contest, which Brzeziniski himself called a clash of rival imperialisms. Brzezinski described the struggle and possible outcomes as follows:

> For the United States, the prevention of Soviet domination over Eurasia is the precondition of achieving an acceptable outcome to the contest. For the Soviet Union, expelling America from Eurasia through a political or a military breakthrough on the three central strategic fronts remains the precondition of decisive success in the historical conflict. The struggle on the three central fronts principally involves a political competition buttressed by military power.[449]

The three fronts referred to by Brzezinski were the far western, involving an industrialized Western Europe controlling the key outlets to the Atlantic Ocean; the far eastern, Japan, the Koreas, China, and Southeast Asia controlling the main outlets to the Pacific Ocean; and southwestern, the greater Middle East with its energy resources.[450] The immediate conflict between rival imperialisms over control of Eurasia grew out of the conflict over Western Europe at the end of the Second World War in 1945, but it had deep historic roots echoing the ideas of historic geopolitical thinkers like Ratzel, Mackinder, Haushofer, Mahan, Spykman, and others:

> The struggle between Russia and America was joined when it became clear that the United States would not disengage from Europe and that it was prepared to oppose any demands Moscow made in excess of what the Soviet Union effectively controlled by 1945. This opposition was a historical milestone. In effect, it represented the beginning of the latest phase in the age-old struggle for the domination of the world's most active continent—a struggle that had raged from the time of the collapse of the Mediterranean-centered Roman Empire, through successive attempts to organize a Holy Roman Empire encompassing all of Europe, to protracted conflicts between oceanic empires, like Great Britain, and predominantly land-based powers, like Napoleonic France, Nazi Germany, and Russia. Now this struggle put the

two successful survivors of the Second World War—the dominant transoce-
anic power and the dominant power on the central landmass—on a collision
course.[451]

Besides Western Europe, the collision manifested itself in the Far East, a key
area, argues Brzezinski, because it is the "world's fastest-growing economic region,"
adding that it is central for a stable U.S.-controlled "trilateral" world system:

> The trilateral relationship between the states of the Pacific Basin in the Far
> East, North America, and Western Europe has emerged as the basis for a
> new non-Eurocentric international system sponsored by the United States.
> Cooperation among these three economically vital and politically demo-
> cratic regions has become central to the maintenance of international stabil-
> ity and to the development of the third world. Anything that would unhinge
> either the far eastern or far western connection from the United States—par-
> ticularly a Soviet political or military breakout—would contribute directly
> to the destabilization of these largely American-sponsored international
> arrangements.[452]

The "third front" was the Middle East, where the United States had long been
interested in controlling and profiting from the area's immense oil deposits. The
conflict of the 1970s in Afghanistan, and the Soviet involvement there, intensified
the importance of this front as an area of active great-power conflict and led to the
Carter Doctrine of January 23, 1980, promulgated while Brzezinski was National
Security Adviser: "Any attempt by any outside force to gain control of the Persian
Gulf region will be regarded as an assault on the vital interests of the United States
of America and such an assault will be repelled by any means necessary, including military force." The United States became more actively involved, due to the
key role of oil in the world economy and the danger that the Soviet move into
Afghanistan could lead to Soviet dominance of the larger Middle East region,
threatening to "unhinge the international system." In Brzezinski's words:

> With 56 percent of the world's proven oil reserves, the Persian Gulf states . . .
> continue to be a vital strategic interest of the West. Given Western Europe's
> and Japan's dependence on Middle Eastern oil, domination over this region
> would place the Soviet Union in a position to blackmail both Western
> Europe and the Far East into political accommodation on terms favorable
> to Moscow.[453]

For Brzezinski, the final result of the political, military, and economic struggles for control of each of these three strategic fronts depended on which side gained or retained power over the "linchpin states" in each region:

These linchpin states are Poland and Germany on the far western front; South Korea and the Philippines on the far eastern front; and either Iran or the combination of Afghanistan and Pakistan on the southwestern front. Soviet domination over Poland is central to Moscow's control over Eastern Europe, and the subordination or seduction of West Germany would tip the balance in Europe in Russia's favor. Soviet domination over South Korea and the Philippines would encircle China, directly threaten Japan's security through Korea, and potentially endanger Japan's main maritime lifeline from the Philippines. Soviet domination over either Iran or both Afghanistan and Pakistan would give Moscow control over access to the Persian Gulf or a presence on the Indian Ocean from which Soviet power could be projected at vulnerable areas to the southwest and southeast.[454]

This analysis and the actions that developed from it were key parts of the successful U.S. strategy of undermining Soviet control over Eastern Europe and preventing Soviet success in Afghanistan, one cause, among many, leading to the demise of the USSR itself. This led to a corresponding expansion of the U.S. informal empire and a hegemonic influence in Eurasia and much of the rest of the world.

The Grand Chessboard

A few years after the fall of the Soviet Union and most of the socialist bloc, Brzezinski updated the analysis he had put forward in *Game Plan* in the 1997 *The Grand Chessboard: American Primacy and its Geostrategic Imperatives.* In this book and in an article in *Foreign Affairs* he repeats his earlier perspective that Eurasia is central.

Eurasia is home to most of the world's politically assertive and dynamic states. All the historical pretenders to global power originated in Eurasia. The world's most populous aspirants to regional hegemony, China and India, are in Eurasia, as are all the potential political or economic challengers to American primacy. . . . A country dominant in Eurasia would almost automatically control the Middle East and Africa. With Eurasia now serving as the decisive geopolitical chessboard, it no longer suffices to fashion one policy for Europe and another for Asia. What happens with the distribution of power on the Eurasian landmass will be of decisive importance to America's global primacy and historical legacy.[455]

Brzezinski's strategic conclusion from this analysis was that in the short run the United States should "consolidate and perpetuate the prevailing geopolitical pluralism on the map of Eurasia." Beyond promoting division among a number of the key Eurasian states, in the middle term the United States should forge "broader strategic relationships with Europe and China" since this will determine Russia's future role and shape "Eurasia's central power equation." In this power configuration, U.S. global geopolitical hegemony would be anchored in Europe and NATO on the western edge of Eurasia, and China on the eastern edge. A strong democratic Europe will lure Russia into cooperation, and a deepening strategic understanding with China would divert this rising power into "constructive regional accommodation." Japan must be diverted into wider international partnerships as a U.S. ally, but not as America's principal military partner or offshore ally against China, as this would prevent the needed strategic consensus with China. Brzezinski's long-term vision involved developing a trans-Eurasian security system, beginning with an expanded NATO linked to cooperative security agreements with Russia, China, and Japan and with India included in a standing committee that encompassed all of these major players. The United States would then play the "decisive role as Eurasia's arbitrator."[456]

TACTICS: MAX BOOT AND SMALL GEOPOLITICS

Brzezinski's geopolitical perspective continues to provide the CFR's model for political grand strategy: U.S. hegemony over key world regions, especially on the borders of great-power rivals like the former Soviet Union (now Russia) and today's China. A series of other Council thinkers have focused on providing tactical ideas about how to promote and manage the informal U.S. empire. One of these is a more aggressive posture toward smaller nations around the world. In fact, the CFR and top U.S. leaders generally view these weaker nations through an imperialist lens; they are places and peoples that can be conquered, bullied, controlled, and exploited. A prime promoter of this tactical policy approach today is the Council's Jeane J. Kirkpatrick Senior Fellow for National Security Studies, the neoconservative Republican Max Boot. Boot, who also writes columns for the *Wall Street Journal* and *Los Angeles Times*, has been a CFR member since 2000 and a senior fellow at the Council since 2003.[457] Boot's most important work, *The Savage Wars of Peace: Small Wars and the Rise of American Power*, was published in 2002 when he was already a CFR member, but just before he was first listed in Council *Annual Reports* as a Senior Fellow.[458] In his book, Boot acknowledges and thanks by name a number of Council leaders and members, including president Leslie H. Gelb, former Director of Studies Nickolas X. Rizopoulos, and Managing Editor of *Foreign Affairs* Gideon Rose for their assistance, indicating the important input leading CFR people had in the creation of this work, and how it can be seen as reflecting the dominant perspective of the Council itself.[459]

In *Savage Wars of Peace*, Boot characterizes the "small wars" he studies as "adventures abroad" that "might well be called imperial wars . . . of the American empire." For Boot, as for Brzezinski, this empire includes an "inner core" of North America, Western Europe, and Northeast Asia. But outside this core the empire is in turmoil: "Violence and unrest lap at the periphery—in Africa, the Middle East, Central Asia, the Balkans, and other regions teeming with failed states, criminal states or simply the state of nature." The use of the terms "adventures" and "teeming with failed states" betrays the cavalier attitude Boot brings to his study of the destruction—human, property, and ecological—imposed upon smaller, less powerful nations and their peoples by the imperialist wars of the United States. These wars and related attacks by drones and Special Operations Forces make up some of the tactics used to impose neoliberalism on these small nations. Boot argues that if the "interests of the United States" are "placed in jeopardy" in these areas the civil government in control might have to be replaced through violent U.S. intervention. This can be done, according to Boot, because "the cost of intervention in small states has always been low. Economists call it a yield curve: when the cost is low, demand is high." In this regard, Boot approvingly quotes Thomas Friedman, another CFR member, who also advocates violence to protect perceived U.S. interests in small states: "The hidden hand of the market will never work without a hidden fist. McDonald's cannot flourish without McDonnell Douglas, the designers of the U.S. Air Force F15."[460]

In the final chapter, "In Defense of Pax Americana: Small Wars in the 21st Century," Boot argues that the United States should be the world's "benevolent hegemon" to prevent "chaos or worse" internationally. Part of his argument is what he calls the "price of nonintervention," citing as examples what he considers the premature withdrawals of U.S. troops from Nicaragua in 1925 and from Russia in 1919, the latter a supposedly missed opportunity, since he believes that "the Whites could have won" the civil war against the Bolsheviks. He mentions the experience of Britain in the nineteenth century as an example that "any nation bent on imperial policing will suffer a few setbacks." Boot added that Britain wanted "vengeance" after its defeats in Afghanistan (1842) and in the Zulu War (1879), and argues: "If Americans cannot adopt a similarly bloody-minded attitude, then they have no business undertaking imperial policing." Boot concludes his book with the following call to arms: "America should not be afraid to fight the 'savage wars of peace' if necessary to enlarge the 'empire of liberty.' It has done it before."[461] George W. Bush and his neocon advisers ordered the invasion and conquest of Iraq less than a year later, a topic discussed in detail in chapter 6.

JOSEPH S. NYE JR. AND THE TACTIC OF SOFT POWER

Neoliberal geoeconomics and the geopolitics of military power are both forms of hard power. They are "hard" because they involve the allocation of scarce resources and employ economic incentives/disincentives and violence/coercion to affect the behavior of others to achieve the larger goals of power and profit. The concept of "soft power" is, on the other hand, a tactic to gain compliance without resorting to force. This concept was developed by Harvard political science Professor Joseph S. Nye Jr. in two books, *Bound to Lead: The Changing Nature of American Power* (1990) and *Soft Power: The Means to Success in World Politics* (2004).[462] Nye, who comes out of the professional class, has been a member of the CFR for over thirty-five years and also served as a Council director during the 2004–13 years, indicating that he is in the top leadership and his views regarding the usefulness of this tactic are representative of an important sector of the Council.[463] In the acknowledgments of his 2004 book, Nye thanks nine different CFR members by name for their "special help" or "valuable assistance" in putting together the book.[464]

Soft power has to do with attraction, seduction, admiration, moral authority, cooperation, co-optation, setting a positive example, encouraging participation and emulation, having legitimacy, setting agendas, and developing institutions, which all lead to voluntary agreement or at least acquiescence. Soft power is rooted in an attractive culture, as well as positive political values and policies if they are viewed as legitimate and having moral authority. Promoting these aspects of international relationships, Nye asserts, shapes the preferences of others and is more effective in the long run than economic or military coercion, although he believes that these are also necessary at times.[465] Furthermore, nations that ignore and act contrary to soft power imperatives soon find themselves feared and hated and on the road to serious negative consequences. Hitler's Germany during the years 1941–45 is cited as an obvious example. Only interested in hard power, Hitler and Germany found themselves on the wrong side of a large and righteous coalition and soon suffered a massive and horribly costly defeat, with tens of millions of lives lost and major sections of the country destroyed. Nye, while recognizing the necessity of military power, applied lessons of the past to the "dark side" of neoliberal globalization and Bush's war on terrorism, then being waged, when he wrote in *Soft Power*:

> Americans—and others—face an unprecedented challenge from the dark side of globalization and the privatization of war that has accompanied new technologies. This is properly the focus of our new national security strategy, and is sometimes summarized as a war on terrorism. Like the Cold War, the threats posed by various forms of terrorism will not be resolved quickly, and hard military power will play a vital role. But the U.S. government spends

four hundred times more on hard power than on soft power. Like the challenge of the Cold War, this one cannot be met by military power alone. That is why it is so essential that Americans—and others—better understand and apply soft power. Smart power is neither hard nor soft. It is both.[466]

Nye stresses that the concept of soft power—the ability to get people to voluntarily do what you want them to do—depends upon context and relationships. In today's world, both of these can rapidly change, leading to serious problems for static thinkers. Nye likens international politics to a three-dimensional chess game, with raw military strength at the top. At this highest level the United States is supreme. The next level down the scale is economic power, and, in this realm, an increasingly transnational multipolar world exists with the United States also on top, but increasingly sharing influence and importance with a number of other players, especially Europe, China, and Japan. At the lowest level of the three dimensions are a number of issues involving both state and non-state actors in which power is widely and chaotically distributed. These include climate change, terrorism, international crime, and the spread of infectious diseases. Nye aimed his argument at the Bush administration, pointing out that the last set of issues

is now intruding into the world of grand strategy. Yet many of our political leaders still focus almost entirely on military assets and classic military solutions—the top board. They mistake the necessary for the sufficient. They are one-dimensional players in a three-dimensional game. In the long term, that is the way to lose, since obtaining favorable outcomes on the bottom transnational board often requires soft power assets.[467]

Nye stated that due to the perceived lack of legitimacy of Bush's actions in Iraq the soft power necessary to win a peace after the victory was largely lacking, creating a major problem for the United States and its allies, adding that "attraction can turn to repulsion if we act in an arrogant manner."[468] The Bush administration largely ignored Nye's views until near the end of its second term. The Obama administration, like Bush, has actively used hard power forms, but has paid more attention to the necessity of at least some soft power rhetoric and actions.

THE TACTIC OF THE U.S. GOVERNMENT AS "BENEVOLENT" HEGEMON: *THE CASE FOR GOLIATH*

Another example of CFR thinking on the tactics suitable to U.S. grand strategy and its neoliberal geopolitical empire comes from the book by Michael Mandelbaum called *The Case for Goliath: How America Acts as the World's Government in the 21st*

Century.[469] Mandelbaum has been a member of the Council for almost forty years, and a CFR Senior Fellow for at least seventeen of those years (1986–2003).[470] He has also been a professor of foreign policy at Johns Hopkins University. He dedicates the book to former Council president Leslie H. Gelb and two other CFR members who served as Carnegie Corporation presidents (he completed the book while on a Carnegie Scholar's Program). He also thanks in his acknowledgments former CFR director and Johns Hopkins Dean Jessica P. Einhorn for facilitating a leave of absence to finish the work.[471] On the book's back cover four Council members, two of them CFR directors, praise the book's "lucid prose" and describe it as "thoughtful," "provocative," and as offering a "compelling and important argument."

Mandelbaum's perspective on U.S. grand strategy and world geopolitics—written, interestingly enough, while the United States military was invading, occupying, and laying waste to Iraq and its people—is that first, following the end of the Cold War, the "enormous power and pervasive influence of the United States was universally acknowledged to be the defining feature of world affairs."[472] Secondly, the United States, although the world's hegemon, has been and is a benevolent one, functioning in an exceptional manner as the world's government with a role similar to the sun's in our own solar system. Mandelbaum's stress on the beneficence of the U.S. government promotes a clear ideological agenda, a tactic in the struggle for political consciousness at home and abroad:

> In the eyes of many, American supremacy counted as a great misfortune. The foreign policy of the world's strongest country, in this account, resembled the conduct of a schoolyard bully who randomly assaults others, steals the lunch money of weaker students, and generally makes life unpleasant wherever he goes. The United States was seen as the world's Goliath. . . . Although the United States looks like Goliath, however, in important ways the world's strongest power does not act like him. If America is a Goliath, it is a benign one. . . . This book explains other countries' acceptance of the American role in the world by painting a different and more benign picture of that role than the one implied by the comparison with Western civilization's archetypal bully. As portrayed in the pages that follow, it has something in common with the sun's relationship to the rest of the solar system. Both confer benefits on the entities with which they are in regular contact. The sun keeps the planets in their orbits by the force of gravity and radiates the heat and light that make life possible on one of them. Similarly, the United States furnishes services to other countries, the same services, as it happens, that governments provide within sovereign states to the people they govern. The United States therefore functions as the world's government.[473]

In the chapters that follow, Mandelbaum covers the American role in providing "necessary services" to the world, "acts of charity" flowing from a sense of "compassion" and "international responsibility." Security is achieved through deterrence and reassurance, including the use of military force in "preventive war," "humanitarian intervention," and "nation-building." Added to this are economic tasks, including the enforcement of contracts, protection of property, assurance of access to oil, and supplying the money needed for global economic transactions, as well as sustaining a high level of consumption to assure global production and trade.[474]

Mandelbaum's central thesis stresses that three great ideas provide a consensus for the global dominance of the United States, which has "embraced and espoused them." These three ideas are peace, democracy, and free markets.[475] Later in the book, Mandelbaum has a long section justifying a string of U.S. "preventive" wars and "humanitarian" interventions in the period 1991–2005, including in Iraq, Somalia, Haiti, Bosnia, and Afghanistan. Mandelbaum portrays these wars, with the hundreds of thousands of resulting dead, as part of a selfless United States attempt to make the world a better place for all:

> Preventative war and humanitarian intervention not only defended American interests and protected American values, they also served the wider international community. Indeed, these practices did more for others than for Americans, who were not exposed to the depredations of the regimes the United States removed from power and to whom the rogue states that were the objects of the doctrine of preventive war posed lesser threats than they did to their immediate neighbors. Americans certainly believed that they were acting on behalf not only of themselves but also of other countries for the purpose of making the world they shared a safer and more humane place.[476]

While accusing other "rogue regimes" of being "detached from the normal constraints of decency and prudence,"[477] he also claimed that American humanitarianism precluded using brutal tactics to rule its conquests:

> Nor, finally, could the United States employ the tactic that had done most to reduce the costs of ruling rebellious subjects in the past: brutality. . . . The regimes that the post–Cold War American interventions unseated often maintained their grip on power by murdering large numbers of their own citizens, thereby intimidating the rest. But the standards of political propriety and decency that prevailed in the United States, as well as one of the purposes of these interventions—to replace vicious, oppressive governments with kinder, gentler ones—precluded the American use of this tactic.[478]

In the next chapter we will examine in some detail the "propriety," "decency, and prudence" of the U.S. government's war and occupation of Iraq, led by the CFR and its members. Here it suffices to simply mention the obscene amounts of American military spending in a needy world and refer to the longer historical record, going back further to the U.S. war on Vietnam, with its millions of victims, and to covert wars waged by the CIA and Special Operations Forces, including against Cuba, Guatemala, Colombia, El Salvador, and Nicaragua, as well as U.S. military invasions of sovereign states like Panama and Granada resulting in unknown numbers of dead and wounded. From this record we can conclude that in recent history there is no country that is anywhere nearly as aggressive and warlike as is the United States under the hegemony of the CFR and its members.

The second and third of the central ideas of *The Case for Goliath* claim that the U.S. government promotes "democracy" and "free markets." In the view of capitalist-class intellectuals like Mandelbaum, the concept of "democracy" is limited to the right to choose which faction of the ruling capitalist class will rule for a specified time, before rank-and-file voters are allowed to choose a different faction of the same ruling capitalist class, all of whom follow similar economic and other policies favoring the wealthy. Mandelbaum himself admits that in this current world, ruled by the supposedly benevolent U.S. hegemon, "more than 1 billion people live on less than $1 per day, while another 1 to 2 billion live on less than $2 per day."[479] It may be reasonably asked: what is the quality of "democracy" and "free markets" in such circumstances? In none of the countries conquered and reorganized by the United States in recent decades has a real functioning democracy actually been established, if by that we mean rule by and for the people, with a substantial increase in equality and social justice.

Regarding democracy at home, Mandelbaum admits to a clearly undemocratic practice in the United States, stating that a "relatively small foreign policy elite . . . sets the general course of foreign policy . . . [and] many different issues . . . are usually decided by members of the elite with little or no input from the wider public." What he refers to as an "elite" is actually a capitalist ruling class led by his own organization, the CFR. Regarding democracy abroad, Mandelbaum briefly recounts the history of U.S. support for dictatorships such as the Saudi monarchy, which grossly suppresses human rights, especially the rights of women. The supposed U.S. belief in "democracy" and its promotion is not mentioned in this context, which focuses on value and profitability of oil, the usefulness of "Saudi oil abundance" and how it "formed the basis for the partnership with the United States."[480]

Mandelbaum's book, which exults and celebrates the American government, is additional verification of the CFR's promotion of a central role for the powerful state, together with the Council itself, as organizer and enforcer of the neoliberal geopolitical empire. This is in sharp contrast with the more reactionary sector of the U.S. capitalist class, as represented by non-CFR big capitalists like the Koch brothers and "libertarian" think tanks like the Cato Institute that favor, promote, and work for a weaker central state with a much smaller domestic and global reach.

MEAD AND U.S. GRAND STRATEGY FOR THE TWENTY-FIRST CENTURY

In 2004 during the early phase of the U.S. occupation of Iraq, the CFR's Henry A. Kissinger Senior Fellow in U.S. Foreign Policy, Walter Russell Mead, completed his book, *Power, Terror, Peace and War: America's Grand Strategy in a World at Risk.*[481] Mead's book attempts to be a comprehensive guide and summary of U.S. "grand strategy," the overarching goals and long-term tactical policies needed to assure U.S. world hegemony in the twenty-first century. In this book Mead presents the Council view of how to use all of the strategic and tactical policies discussed above as a totality.

Mead was elected to Council membership in 1997, and became a Senior Fellow for U.S. foreign policy in 1998.[482] He continued as Senior Fellow until 2010, after which he became a professor of U.S. foreign policy at both Bard College and Yale University. A Democrat, Mead supported the U.S. war on Iraq in 2003, voted for Barack Obama in 2008, and remains a CFR member. In the acknowledgments for his book, Mead thanks the many Council leaders, staff, and members who contributed to what was the "complicated social endeavor" of writing it. Special thanks went to the current CFR president, Richard Haass, and former president Leslie Gelb, as well as Director of Studies James Lindsay. Mead also mentions no less than sixty-two CFR members and staff who aided him in various ways with the book, including financial supporters, research associates, reference librarians, study group members, reviewers, and document searchers.[483] Although Mead's own ideas and efforts no doubt predominated, it is clear that the views he expresses closely reflect the collective perspective of a large segment of the Council's membership and top leadership, likely what Mead was referring to by his comment about the book being a "social endeavor." The book is labeled "A Council on Foreign Relations Book" on the title page and the Council is also mentioned on the copyright page, reflecting that Mead was a paid employee of the CFR when he wrote the book.

In the book's introduction, Mead states that he starts "with the idea that there is an American project—a grand strategic vision of what it is that the United States seeks to build in the world," adding that he writes as an "advocate" of this project. He further asserts that "American foreign policy may be the most complex subject in the world," touching on a great number of academic disciplines, and that U.S. grand strategy can only be fully understood from the historical record, "what we have done in the past." This leads to two key generalizations: first, the United States has always been a globally oriented power; and second, in the twentieth century the United States took over from Britain and "built our own version of the British world system, and took on Britain's old job of acting as not quite the policeman of the world, but at least the gyroscope of world order."[484]

Four Types of Power and the United States Empire

For Mead, there are four foundational aspects of U.S. grand strategy and global power, leading to hegemony and an informal world empire. He discusses them in this order: "sharp power," military/geopolitical; "sticky power," economic/ geoeconomic; "sweet power," soft; with all three together synergistically forming "hegemonic power," an empire imposed by American power, but one in which many nations have a stake.[485]

In his discussion of "sharp power," Mead follows Brzezinski and the CFR/capitalist-class consensus on the power centrality of Eurasia, especially the eastern and western fringes of this vast super-continent. He repeats the adage that if one nation controls all of Eurasia its power would potentially exceed American power and thereby threaten the United States. Also, like Brzezinski, Mead sees the Middle East and its oil as a "vital concern" due to both U.S. long-term oil requirements and the need to assure the hydrocarbon supplies of our allies. This in turn connects with control of the world's sea lanes for trade and commodity delivery and prevention of oil insecurity among our allies. Actual oil insecurity might lead other nations to boost their independent military capacities and duel with each other for influence in the Middle East, a situation that could be explosive and therefore should be prevented. The entire United States global neoliberal geopolitical empire is solidified through a system of military alliances and bases, especially in Europe, Asia, and the Middle East, to "promote stability." This has resulted in the vast and incredibly expensive (costing more than the next dozen of the globe's top militaries put together), and resource-wasteful (the largest single consumer of hydrocarbons in the world) U.S. military machine, which has as its purpose maintaining potential or actual geopolitical control of the world's economically and politically key regions. This is the "solid foundation of the American system."[486]

Mead defines "sticky power" as the set of global economic institutions and policies that attract others into the U.S. capitalist system with incentives that make it difficult for them to leave. He illustrates how this works using China as an example. The hope is that the rewards of integration into the global economy continue to be attractive enough to keep China cooperative and within the system. Certainly, powerful Chinese families have benefited enormously from the U.S.-created global trade, investment, production, financial, and legal system during our modern era, with their prosperity growing spectacularly and some of it shared with the larger population. Mead argues that American willingness to reduce trade barriers and open United States markets to imports from nearly all nations also helps create a level of prosperity benefiting especially those at the top of the world's class structure. Strong incentives for maintaining the existing system are also created in other nations when their wealthy families invest in the real property and vast number and type of financial instruments that exist in America.[487]

In defining "sweet power" Mead closely follows Nye's ideas. Positive values, ideals, and cultural precepts, such as women's rights and humanitarian assistance, peacefully draw others into support for the U.S.-dominated system. Immigration and foreign students studying in the United States also help.

The final type—that of hegemonic power, empire—brings the other three together. This creates a whole bigger than the sum of its parts, resulting in consent and legitimacy. Hegemonic power also includes the ability to set the agenda, determining the framework for discussion and debate, something strived for by the CFR itself. The resulting "Pax Americana" also has an aura of inevitability due to its synthesis of military, economic, and soft power, making it very difficult for most nations and leaders to resist and follow another path.[488]

The End of "Fordism" and the Rise of "Millennial Capitalism"

Mead also discusses the transition from what he calls the "Fordist" era of capitalist development dominant from the 1910s to the 1970s to our current era of what he calls "Millennial Capitalism," almost entirely avoiding the more useful and accurate terms "Keynesianism" and "neoliberalism." The term "Fordism," as used by Mead, is simply the policy of certain capitalists, one of the first being Henry Ford, to pay their mass production workers enough to purchase the goods they, the workers, produce. Mead does not mention the intense and costly class struggles that workers engaged in over many decades to achieve even some level of unionization and the resulting higher wages, better working conditions, and benefits in a given industry. He simply presents it as a given that eventually some capitalists accepted unions, resulting in a more administered, regulated, and stable socioeconomic system, characterized by some state planning, a level of class compromise and less income inequality.[489]

Mead points out that Fordism/Keynesianism "has gradually been yielding to . . . a new, more vigorous form of capitalism," which is now being invented and explored. He discusses two very different views of neoliberalism, what he calls "Millennial Capitalism." Both perspectives, he admits, are "partly true":

> For some, the shift from Fordism to millennialism is a rake's progress: the end of a system that produced peace, justice, mass prosperity, and social security and

the rise of a grotesque new system of inequality, instability, and bare-knuckled competition in a hideous, neoliberal dog-eat-dog world. For others, the shift represents the glorious triumph of technology and entrepreneurial spirit over a decadent and stagnant era, and the new and more dynamic capitalism offers opportunities to eliminate poverty and transform the human condition.[490]

Despite this recognition of serious potential and actual problems and injustices, Mead, representing the dominant strain in the Council on Foreign Relations thinking, remains a firm advocate of "millennial capitalism," what we have labeled neoliberalism. Mead's summary near the end of his book is a strong statement for a globalized neoliberal finance capitalism and against a renewal of what was a slightly more benign Fordism/Keynesianism:

> Nostalgic Fordists would like to bring back the welfare state, closed national markets, heavily regulated financial markets, and a greater state role in economic planning and policy. This seems to me to be as unfeasible as it is undesirable. The third quarter of the twentieth century was admirable in many ways, but I cannot believe that it represents the acme of human potential. . . . I do not believe that the genie of millennial capitalism can be forced back into the Fordist bottle. The quest for greater efficiency, productivity, and dynamism is not a feature of capitalism that can be dispensed with; it is the essence of capitalism, not an excrescence, and come what may it will find ways to fulfill itself.[491]

Mead's Council on Foreign Relations book represents a distillation of the consensus within the CFR about what American grand strategy and tactics should be in the early twenty-first century. It puts forward a clear argument for a continuation of the global system that the Council has created over the past several decades.

FOREIGN POLICY BEGINS AT HOME

In 2011 the CFR began another of its periodic, years-long comprehensive reviews of its grand strategy in the world, this one called the Renewing America Initiative. In 2013 President Richard N. Haass wrote a book based on this CFR review, *Foreign Policy Begins at Home: The Case for Putting America's House in Order*.[492] It begins with the following assertions about the dangers facing a United States now in decline:

> The biggest threat to America's security and prosperity comes not from abroad but from within. . . . For the United States to continue to act

successfully abroad, it must restore the domestic foundations of its power. Foreign policy needs to begin at home, now and for the foreseeable future. . . . Many of the foundations of this country's power are eroding; the effect, however, is not limited to a deteriorating transportation system or jobs that go overseas. . . . Shortcomings here at home directly threaten America's ability to project power and exert influence overseas, to compete in the global marketplace, to generate the resources needed to promote the full range of U.S. interests abroad, and to set a compelling example that will influence the thinking and behavior of others.[493]

A central part of Haass's book is an analysis of the current global power situation, with the conclusion that it looks more like the nineteenth than the twentieth century; what, in fact "distinguishes our era is the sheer number and variety of entities with global reach." He believes that the United States is no longer the world's only superpower; rather it is the "first among equals."[494] He identifies those entities he sees as major powers (key nation-states), as well as the lesser ones (international organizations, state governments, cities, transnational corporations, media, movements and political organizations, and NGOs):

What makes this era different for those that came before it is the number of actors in the world that have real impact. In addition to the major countries or cluster of countries (the United States, China, European Union, Russia, Japan and India) are numerous regional powers, including Brazil . . . Chile, Argentina, Venezuela, and Mexico in Latin America; South Africa and Nigeria in Africa; Egypt, Iran, Israel and Saudi Arabia in the Middle East; and Pakistan, Australia, Indonesia, South Korea . . . in Asia. . . . A good many organizations would be on the list, including those that are global (the UN, International Monetary Fund, World Bank), regional (the Organization of American States, African Union, the EU, NATO, the Association of Southeast Asian Nations, the Arab League, and many others) and functional (including OPEC, the World Health Organization, the International Energy Agency, and the Shanghai Cooperative Organization).[495]

Haass then reviews the policies of these key actors, focusing on the key nation-states beginning with China, concluding that none of them has the capacity or inclination to challenge U.S. global power and leadership, and that some cooperation is possible between the largest powers. This means that America has the strategic respite needed to carry out what he calls "Restoration" at home and abroad. The "goal is to increase the number of Americans who can hold their own in an increasingly competitive marketplace, shore up the economic and physical resilience of the country, and ensure that sufficient resources are available so that the United States can do what it wants and needs to do both at home and abroad." Haass concludes that because there is no "existential threat" internationally, "restoration" is possible as the basis for U.S. policy for a long time going forward, although "there would certainly continue to be wars of necessity."[496] He summarizes his policy recommendations as follows:

> Under Restoration, the United States would increase the resources devoted to internal as opposed to international challenges, so as to address critical domestic needs. The aim is to rebuild the foundation of this country's strength. . . . Second, a foreign policy informed by Restoration would eschew a . . . focus on the Middle East and any more large-scale wars for the purpose of remaking other societies. Instead, the priority of U.S. foreign policy would be to shape the behavior of the other principal powers. In addition, U.S. attention and effort would be more broadly distributed—in particular, to the Asia-Pacific region, the part of the world most likely to influence the course of this century. U.S. attention would also be directed more to the Western Hemisphere. This is consistent with both the region's centrality to America's economic and energy future and the reality that stability in Mexico and in the Western Hemisphere more broadly is of vital importance to America's own security. Third, Restoration would rebalance the implementation of foreign policy, in the process placing less emphasis on military instruments and more on economic and diplomatic tools and capabilities.[497]

The final section of Haass's book outlines his approach and, by extension, that of the CFR's Renewing America Initiative to restoring U.S. power at home. He lists specific policies in a number of fields that would allow America to exert soft power and return to a position of leading by example.[498] The first of these policies is federal debt reduction, needed, in his view, to increase economic growth. Leaving out military spending as a source of debt, Haass focuses on so-called entitlements like Social Security and Medicare for the aged that must be

> brought under control. The trajectory of Social Security spending can be reined in through a mix of gradually increasing the retirement or eligibility age . . . reducing the fast-growing area of disability payments, and altering the formula by which annual payments are adjusted for inflation. . . . Significant savings could be realized from raising the age for Medicare eligibility, requiring increased co-payments, limiting malpractice torts, means testing and introducing . . . administrative reforms.[499]

Later in the book Haass gets more specific about how long the retirement age should be extended, stating that when people turn sixty they will still be "facing as many as ten to twenty years of work." Such "reform" of "entitlements"—which are actually not gifts but the earned savings from the labor of millions of workers, held in trust by the federal government—will, in Haass's view, help America "present a model of political and economic competence that the world will want to emulate."

Haass also has chapters on education, infrastructure, immigration, and politics. Education is failing and can best be changed by tying teacher compensation to performance, curbing public sector unions as a "special interest," and cutting back on teachers' pensions and health care plans; infrastructure, though not failing, rates only a C grade at best. Immigration is a complex situation, solved by strengthening border security to prevent illegal entry, normalizing the status of those already here, and establishing a rating system for visas that reflects the "market needs" of corporations. As for politics, Haass sees the main problem as gridlock and drift leading to a crisis that could be avoided by various measures to "strengthen the center," even if a new political party of conservative Democrats, moderate Republicans, and Independents has to be formed.[500]

Haass argues that public sector unions should be "curbed" and health care and pension benefits cut, policies that are being carried out in the private sector by leading CFR- connected monopoly corporations that have been in the forefront of recent attacks on workers and unions. This is to be expected, given the Council's base in the capitalist class. The worldwide triumph of neoliberal geopolitics has emboldened capitalists, and they are waging a war on workers generally and unions specifically. Recent examples include the policies of three top U.S. multinational corporations—Boeing, General Electric, and Caterpillar. All three are corporate members of the Council.[501] They also have numerous other connections to the CFR. Five of GE's directors, three of Boeing's, and the former CEO and one other Caterpillar director are all Council members, and two of these corporate directors have also been Council directors. Despite being very profitable companies, these three corporations have been attacking the unionized segments of their workforce, demanding pay cuts, take-backs, pension concessions, and a two-tier wage structure, with lower wages for new hires. If workers do not agree and try to defend their living standards and collective futures, these corporations threaten to close plants and move them to lower-wage industrial locations at home or in other countries, carrying out this threat when necessary. Recent articles covering this development are explicit: "Caterpillar to Unions: Drop Dead," and "GE to Unions: Drop Dead."[502]

Another aspect of foreign policy that begins at home is the position of the United States as the new energy superpower, encouraged and welcomed by the Council. In the March/April 2014 issue of *Foreign Affairs*, an article titled "America's Energy

Edge: The Geopolitical Consequences of the Shale Revolution" focused on the strategic thinking going on regarding fracking. The two authors of this article, each a longtime active Council member, are Senior Fellows at the CFR. Robert D. Blackwill is the Henry A. Kissinger Senior Fellow for U.S. Foreign Policy and Meghan L. O'Sullivan, a professor at Harvard's Kennedy School of Government, is an adjunct Senior Fellow. Blackwill and O'Sullivan both served in the George W. Bush administration as strategists for an attempted victory in Iraq. As individuals who have worked in important roles in the federal government and at the CFR, their grand strategic ideas reflect forward thinking among the higher circles in the U. S. capitalist class.

The Blackwill-O'Sullivan article focuses on the advantages accruing to the United States as it becomes the world's number one energy superpower due to the successes of the fracking revolution. Competitors, with the possible important exception of China, will in general decline in power, including industrial power, due to the fossil fuel price advantage that the United States will increasingly enjoy. Blackwill and O'Sullivan believe that American geopolitical leverage worldwide will increase, and the traditional oil and gas producers—among them Russia, Iran, Mexico, Venezuela, and Nigeria—will lose power and may even undergo regime changes due to declines in economic growth and budget reductions, leading to mass dissatisfaction among their populations. This "will grant the United States a greater degree of freedom in pursuing its grand strategy."[503] The United States will be empowered to exploit the strategic vulnerability of other nations, pursuing a kind of petro-machismo with renewed imperialistic adventurism abroad. Here we see how geopolitical calculations connect with neoliberal capitalist ones, since the U. S. "grand strategy" focuses on the spread of American-style free market capitalism with its commodification and ecological destruction globally. Needless to say, large-scale fracking—together with mountaintop removal for coal, strip mining the land for tar sands, and deep sea drilling for oil—is yet another illustration of the fanatical drive by capitalists and their intellectual allies to gain geopolitical advantage over other nations as well as increasing their profits by tearing the earth apart, all to achieve a guaranteed doom through more rapid climate change, ocean destruction, and other ecological impacts.

SUMMARY: EMPIRE OF LIBERTY OR EMPIRE OF EXPLOITATION, VIOLENCE, AND CHAOS?

The Council on Foreign Relations, representing the larger U. S. capitalist class, especially its financial sector, has since the mid-1970s played a central role in renewing "the essence of capitalism," an exploitative, dog-eat-dog "free market" system. This has been developed, intellectually and in practice, as part of a

Council-inspired, neoliberal geopolitical empire characterized by the destruction of unions and working-class communities, privatization, speculation, grotesque economic inequality, ecological destruction, and the mass violence of war and conquest. The structures of domination have largely been hidden, the solidarity mechanisms of working-class people have been undermined, and debate about alternatives has been limited, omitting the fact that a different socioeconomic project—one worthy of humanity's best thoughts and feelings—is possible. The neoliberal geopolitical world is presented as an empire of liberty, but in reality it is an empire of exploitation, violence, and chaos. The following chapters offer some specific examples of how and why this is so.

6

IMPERIAL NEOLIBERAL
GEOPOLITICS IN ACTION: THE CFR
AND THE WAR ON IRAQ, 1982–2013

In the outskirts of the world the system reveals its true face.

—EDUARDO GALEANO

The invasion and occupation of Iraq represents the single most significant event in U.S. foreign policy since the war on Vietnam in the 1960s, and because of its scale and outcome, an event of international importance. As could be expected, the Council on Foreign Relations, as an organization and community, as well as its leaders, staff, and members, played a central role in all phases of the war on and occupation of Iraq, from 2003 to 2011. The CFR was involved in the development of an overall climate of opinion on the Middle East prior to 2003, in lobbying for the actual decision to go to war, in the development and implementation of imperialist war aims, including the brutal suppression of the Iraqi resistance movement, and in the ultimate decision to partly reverse course and withdraw American troops.

The Council's overall grand strategy in south-central Eurasia from its beginning in the 1980s represented a new development in the recent history of imperialism. The imperialist grand strategy in the conquest of Iraq represented a major break in the norms of conduct that have governed international relations since the end of the Second World War because it aimed at global domination. The more traditional geopolitical balance of power approach long favored by the

U.S. capitalist ruling class was overturned in favor of an unlimited, worldwide hegemonic goal of an American imperium through the control of the vast oil resources of the Persian Gulf. This region and surrounding areas like the Caspian Sea basin contain two-thirds of the world's oil and has thus been a main center of world geopolitical/geoeconomic power and competition during the late twentieth and early twenty-first century. Iraq holds a central geopolitical position in this region. Comparing Iraq to Vietnam, the CFR's vice president and Director of Studies James M. Lindsay expressed the Council perspective in an October 11, 2005, interview: "It was always hard to sustain the argument that if the United States withdrew from Vietnam there would be immense geopolitical consequences. As we look at Iraq, it's a very different issue. It's a country in one of the volatile parts of the world, which has a very precious resource that modern economies rely on, namely oil."[504]

The attempt to permanently embed American military power in south-central Eurasia was a global power play, as it would assure that the United States would control access to this oil whenever it wanted, shifting the long-term world balance of power even more in favor of the world's already dominant military, economic, and political power. This power play was carried out against not only the opposition of many of Iraq's people but against the major powers of Europe and Asia, because they depend upon the Persian Gulf region for their vital energy needs. This was a key part of the strategic plan for the war: if you control the energy supplies that Europe, Japan, and China need, then they are outflanked in the struggle for world power.

After the successful invasion of Iraq, the attempt to make it a neo-colony, embedding the American military in major bases there, was combined with neoliberal political and economic policies in a bid to reshape Iraq's political economy. After the invasion, exploitative neoliberal economic policies, along with a pseudo-democratic American-style political system, were imposed upon Iraq by military force. CFR policymakers, in and out of government, assumed that the supposedly superior results of such policies would successfully integrate Iraq, its resources, and people into the global international capitalist order that is largely run by the United States. In turn policymakers believed that this would strengthen the existing capitalist system at home, due to the resulting flow of profits/capital back to the United States. The imperialist policies that the war on Iraq represented were therefore ultimately aimed at creating additional global living space for the development of an expansionist capitalist system, the goal of which was to foster rapid capital accumulation, especially on behalf of an American and transnational capitalist class whose main policymaking and consensus-forming organization was, and continues to be, the CFR.

CREATING A CLIMATE OF OPINION: THE GEOPOLITICAL
ECONOMICS OF OIL, 1982–1989

Council publications during the Cold War and immediately thereafter helped set a future agenda for defining the national class interest of the United States by establishing the central importance of oil and what it labeled the "Oil Heartland," the Persian Gulf/Middle East part of Eurasia, to the future of the United States and the Western world. CFR books stressed that the area was a vital and crucial geopolitical interest of the consuming nations because it held approximately 70 percent of the world's known petroleum supply, because oil was a key strategic commodity, and because the control of the area by any other hegemonic power would be a disaster for the United States and the West. In short, this part of the world was seen as a center of gravity of the evolving American empire. Excerpts from two CFR publications during this period illustrate the key points. The first comes from a 1982 book by Council member Melvin A. Conant, who was a counselor for Exxon Corporation and an administrator with the Federal Energy Administration. The book and this policy perspective developed out of a CFR study group called "The Oil Factor in U.S. Foreign Policy." Conant was the chairman of this group, which had two co-directors, Council member and former Director of Studies John C. Campbell and CFR Assistant Director of Studies Janice L. Murray.[505] Conant's Council book on the *The Oil Factor in U.S. Foreign Policy 1980–1990* discussed oil as a central strategic interest, with the future of Eurasia at stake:

> No longer only a commercial commodity, oil is now vested in the highest strategic interest of nations. It is a key factor in the overall power balance between superpowers and a vital need for all industrial states and many states of the developing world. . . . In 1979 . . . the United States obtained 30 percent of its supply from the volatile Gulf region, Europe 62 percent, and Japan 72 percent, . . . Proximity to the Oil Heartland has not yet given the USSR an unusual energy advantage . . . in affecting supply to Europe, Japan, or the United States. . . . Exploiting such a position would give the USSR unprecedented leverage; it would be a critical step . . . [in the] literal immobilization of Europe and of Japan that could lead to a decisive Soviet influence over the whole of Eurasia.[506]

A second perspective was put forth in another book resulting from a 1980s Council study group, this one chaired by former CIA director and Defense and Energy Secretary James R. Schlesinger, a CFR member. Council Senior Fellow Paul Jabber, also a CFR member, and Council member Gary Sick wrote in the CFR book *Great Power Interests in the Persian Gulf*, which came out of the study group:

The interests of the West and Japan in the Persian Gulf area are both unambig-
uous and vital. For much of the 1980s, these interests have also been clearly
at risk. They revolve mainly around the critical issue of energy security, as
they have for some four decades. The region is by far the largest remaining
world source of cheap hydrocarbons in a global economy that continues to be
oil-based.... The emergence of any hegemonic power in the Gulf—whether
local or external to the region—capable of substantially directing, let alone
controlling outright, the oil production and pricing policies of the key producing states ... could be disastrous for the West. ... The interests of the
United States in the Persian Gulf region have been very simple and consistent: first, to ensure access by the industrialized world to the vast oil resources
of the region; and second, to prevent the Soviet Union from acquiring political or military control over those resources. ... The Reagan administration
adopted the Carter Doctrine and over the following seven years succeeded
in putting more substantial military power and organization behind its words
... [organizing in 1983] a unified command known as Central Command
(CENTCOM), based at MacDill Air Force Base in Tampa, Florida, with ear-
marked forces totaling 230,000 military personnel from the four services.[507]

This stress on the strategic importance of the oil in the Persian Gulf region and
the fact that whoever controls this resource has immense potential and actual power
over the key industrial economies of the world, was reflected in then Secretary of
Defense Richard B. Cheney's 1990 testimony before the Senate Armed Services
Committee. Cheney, a longtime CFR member and a director when the study
group on "Great Power Interests in the Persian Gulf" was meeting, adopted the
same perspective, stating to the senators that whoever controlled the flow of this
oil had a "stranglehold" over the American economy and "on that of most of the
other nations of the world as well."[508]

During the same period, in 1991–92, immediately following the demise of the
Soviet Union, a "Defense Planning Guidance" document was drafted, mainly by
four of Cheney's Pentagon subordinates, all CFR members: Paul D. Wolfowitz, I.
Lewis Libby, Zalmay Khalilzad, and Andrew W. Marshall.[509] Their draft document
was leaked to the *New York Times*, causing an uproar, since it clearly stated the
aims of a Pax Americana: the United States should make sure that it remained the
world's only superpower, which required that "we endeavor to prevent any hostile power from dominating a region whose resources would, under consolidated
control, be sufficient to generate global power." To make things even clearer, the
draft document further stated: "In the Middle East and Southwest Asia, our overall
objective is to remain the predominant outside power in the region and preserve
U.S. and Western access to the region's oil."[510]

WARMONGERING AND "PREVENTATIVE" WAR:
THE PNAC AND THE CFR, 1997–2003

During the Clinton administration and first years of the George W. Bush administration, there was a warmongering lobby constantly working to push the United States into invading Iraq in order to assure that the United States would dominate the Persian Gulf region and therefore the evolving world order of the twenty-first century. Two organizations were foremost in this lobbying effort, the hard-line imperialist Project for the New American Century (PNAC), founded in 1997, and the softer-line, more mainstream imperialism of the CFR itself, whose membership included most of the PNAC leadership.

The PNAC was a far-right neoconservative think tank that became influential in the Bush II administration before becoming inactive in 2006 after its policies in Iraq had failed and been partly discredited. Its initial stated goal was to "promote American leadership" and "greatness" through "a Reaganite policy of military strength and moral clarity." This involved increasing the U.S. military budget to "retain its militarily dominant status" worldwide and using the military threat and force "to shape a new century favorable to American principles and interests." Twenty-five individuals were listed as signers to the 1997 founding "Statement of Principles." These twenty-five included sixteen CFR members (64 percent of the total), among them Dick Cheney, Paul Wolfowitz, I. Lewis Libby, and Zalmay Khalilzad. One former Council member, Donald Rumsfeld, was also among the signatories.[511]

In January of 1998 the PNAC wrote an open letter to President Clinton, arguing that Iraq's leader, Saddam Hussein, and his regime must be removed from power, something requiring "a full complement of diplomatic, political and military efforts." Otherwise U.S. "vital interests in the Gulf," including "a significant portion of the world's supply of oil" would be endangered. Eighteen individuals signed the letter, nine of whom had also signed the 1997 "Statement of Principles." Of the eighteen, a total of twelve were CFR members (67 percent), who included former CIA head and Council member R. James Woolsey, CFR director Robert B. Zoellick, Wolfowitz, Khalilzad, Elliott Abrams, Richard Perle, and Paula Dobriansky (who was also a vice president, Washington office director, and a Senior Fellow at the CFR).

Finally, an analysis of the sixty-eight signatories or contributors to the totality of PNAC reports and statements as of the year 2000 found that fully forty-three (63 percent) were CFR members. These included four current or former CFR directors (Richard B. Cheney, Jeane Kirkpatrick, Vin Weber, and Robert B. Zoellick). The overlap of the CFR and the PNAC personnel during this period was therefore quite substantial—as were the strategic and practical policy orientations they represented.

Important elements within the Council itself were also engaged in at first subtle, and later overt, lobbying for a war with Iraq, beginning with general statements in 1997–99, then more forcefully advocating for war in 2001–2002. CFR member Richard N. Haass, a Council Fellow in 1994–97 who then became vice president and Director of Foreign Policy Studies at the Brookings Institution, wrote a number of books and articles outlining what American foreign policy should be. His perspective is especially important considering that he was the head of policy planning at the Department of State from 2001 to 2003 and became president of the CFR in July 2003.

In his CFR-published book, *The Reluctant Sheriff: The United States after the Cold War* (1997), Haass defined the geopolitical economic basis of U.S. foreign policy, calling for

a continued orientation of U.S. national security toward the Persian Gulf, the Asia-Pacific, and Europe. The United States has a vital interest in a favorable balance of power in these three regions of great economic and military resources. . . . We must act to maintain acceptable balances through countering or offsetting any imbalance as it occurs, be it from a local state or an emerging great power.[512]

Writing more specifically on the Middle East and the Persian Gulf, Haass stressed the "pressing vital interest of maintaining access to oil."[513]

In 1999, Haass, in an article for *Foreign Affairs*, stated that America must shoulder "an imperial role" in the world, the key question being

how to exploit its enormous surplus of power in the world. . . . American foreign policy must project an imperial dimension . . . [and] organize the world along certain principles affecting both relations between states and conditions within them. The U.S. role should resemble that of nineteenth-century Great Britain . . . [although] coercion and the use of force would normally be a secondary option.[514]

In late 2001 an article in *Foreign Affairs* expressed the assumption that there was to be a U.S. war on Iraq. CFR member and Johns Hopkins University professor Fouad Ajami (who was to start a decade-long term of service as a Council director in 2002) wrote:

In thwarted, resentful societies there was satisfaction on September 11 that the American . . . triumphalism that had awed the world had been battered. . . . We know better now. Pax Americana is there to stay in the oil lands and in Israeli-Palestinian matters. No large-scale retreat from those zones of American primacy can be contemplated. American hegemony is sure to hold—and so, too, the resistance to it. . . .

Now there is the distant thunder of war. The first war of the twenty-first century is to be fought not so far from where the last inconclusive war of the twentieth century was waged against Iraq. The war will not be easy for America in those lands. The setting will test it in ways it has not been tested before.[515]

The push for war by key Council individuals became more overt in early 2002, when *Foreign Affairs* printed Kenneth M. Pollack's article "Next Stop Baghdad?"[516] At the time, Pollack was a member, Senior Fellow, and director of national security studies at the CFR. Before joining the staff of the Council, Pollack had, during the Clinton years, served as director for Gulf affairs at the National Security Council and as a CIA military analyst specializing in the Persian Gulf region. His article reflected the growing consensus for war at the CFR and among ruling-class leaders, and was turned into a full-length volume: *The Threatening Storm: The Case for Invading Iraq*, a CFR book published by Random House later that year.[517] In the acknowledgments, Pollack offers his "deepest thanks" to CFR president Leslie Gelb and other leaders at the CFR who "made the book possible" with paid time off, a foundation grant, and the "full resources of the Council, and particularly its world-class experts."[518] Additionally, Pollack offered thanks to Gelb and eleven other CFR members and leaders who made comments and criticisms aimed at improving the work. CFR leaders Gideon Rose (then managing editor of *Foreign Affairs* and a former Senior Fellow) and Fareed Zakaria (formerly a managing editor of *Foreign Affairs*) gave lavish advance praise for the book, and in his introduction to the CFR's 2002 *Annual Report*, Council chairman Peter G. Peterson expressed his pride and endorsement of both the CFR's magazine and Pollack's work: "*Foreign Affairs* has burnished its position as the world's premier international affairs journal with trailblazing articles such as Ken Pollack's 'Next Stop Baghdad?'"[519] In short, it was in an important sense a collective work, and the disclaimer at the beginning of the book that the CFR "is host to the widest possible range of views, but an advocate of none" was, as is usually the case, nonsense.

Pollack's conclusion in both his article and book was that the situation was similar to Europe in 1938, and "the United States has no choice left but to invade Iraq itself and eliminate the current regime."[520] In both writings, Pollack focused on the building tactical case for invasion, discussing, as if a fact, that weapons of mass destruction were a big danger; that both containment and deterrence were inadequate; and that an invasion and defeat of Saddam's regime had advantages;

it would be an "enormous boon to U.S. foreign policy."[521] The "boon" that Pollack envisioned was that the threat of Saddam Hussein controlling "global oil supplies" would be ended, and the United States would be free to pursue other items on its foreign policy agenda, including the "opportunity to build a new Iraq."[522] In his book Pollack elaborated on this theme:

> The final advantage of an invasion. . . . Imagine how different the Middle East and the world would be if a new Iraq were stable, prosperous, and a force for progress in the region. . . . Imagine if we could rebuild Iraq as a model of what a modern Arab state could be. . . . Imagine if there were a concrete symbol demonstrating that America seeks to help the Arab world rather than repress it. Invading Iraq might not be our least bad alternative, it potentially could be our best course of action. If we are willing to accept the challenge and pay the price, we could end up creating a much better future for ourselves and all of the peoples of the Middle East.[523]

Pollack also stressed—and turned out to be greatly mistaken—that in reconstructing Iraq, U.S. costs would be minimal because "Iraq itself, with its vast oil wealth, would pay for most of its reconstruction. . . . It is unimaginable that the United States would have to contribute hundreds of billions of dollars and highly unlikely that we would have to contribute even tens of billions."[524] The alternative, for Pollack, was to allow Saddam Hussein, due to Iraq's strategic position in the "vital Persian Gulf region" and its own great oil resources to "hold the economy of the world in the palm of his cruel hand."[525] In a follow-up 2003 *Foreign Affairs* article, under the heading "It's the Oil, Stupid," Pollack elaborated on why the Persian Gulf was so vital, and why the United States and not Saddam (or Iran or any other nation than the United States for that matter) should control it:

> America's primary interest in the Persian Gulf lies in ensuring the free and stable flow of oil from the region to the world at large. . . . The reason is simply that the global economy built over the last 50 years rests on a foundation of inexpensive, plentiful oil, and if that foundation were removed, the global economy would collapse. . . . The Persian Gulf region has as much as two-thirds of the world's proven oil reserves, and its oil is absurdly economical to produce. . . . But the United States is not simply concerned with keeping the oil flowing out of the Persian Gulf; it also has an interest in preventing any potentially hostile state from gaining control over the region and its resources and using such control to amass vast power or blackmail the world. And it has an interest in maintaining military access to the Persian Gulf because of the region's geostrategically critical location, near the Middle East, Central Asia,

eastern Africa and South Asia. If the United States were denied access to the Persian Gulf, its ability to influence events in many other key regions of the world would be greatly diminished.[526]

Although Pollack's work was an outstanding example of the CFR's 2002–2003 push for a war on Iraq, it was not the only one. In the same 2002 issue of *Foreign Affairs* that featured Pollack's article arguing for war was an article by Sebastian Mallaby called "The Reluctant Imperialist: Terrorism, Failed States and the Case for American Empire." At the time the article appeared, Mallaby was a journalist for the *Washington Post*, but within a year he had been hired to join the CFR's Center for Geoeconomic Studies as a Senior Fellow in international development. British-born, Mallaby was the son of a British diplomat and attended Eton College, first among the elite boys' schools, later graduating from Oxford University. Mallaby took an approach characteristic of the British imperial tradition in the article he wrote for *Foreign Affairs*, arguing that due to terrorism and failed states the United States should more openly become an imperialist power:

The logic of neoimperialism is too compelling for the Bush administration to resist. The chaos in the world is too threatening to ignore. . . . A new imperial moment has arrived, and by virtue of its power America is bound to play the leading role. The question is not whether the United States will seek to fill the void created by the demise of European empires but whether it will acknowledge that this is what it is doing. Only if Washington acknowledges this task will the response be coherent. The first obstacle to acknowledgment is the fear that empire is infeasible.[527]

In the May–June 2002 *Foreign Affairs* two additional war-related pieces appeared, both touting the military side of the issue. Secretary of Defense Donald Rumsfeld's "Transforming the Military" argued for the "need for preemptive offense" on the part of the U.S. military. Eliot A. Cohen, a CFR member and strategic studies professor at Johns Hopkins University, wrote that the United States now had a "unique, world-historical role" and future "defense" requirements must "begin with the capacity to project effective military power rapidly to most locations on the planet."[528]

Other CFR leaders reinforced the growing consensus. In an August 1, 2002, op-ed piece published in *Newsday*, Council Senior Fellow Michael Mandelbaum argued that the conclusion that Saddam Hussein must be removed from power through war "is reasonable," adding that such an outcome might revolutionize the entire Persian Gulf region, overthrowing current regimes, and putting America in command:

While prewar American commitments to a continuing presence in Iraq, to preserving the country's territorial integrity, to the decentralization of power and to an appropriate disposition of the country's oil will help to broaden the anti-Hussein coalition, they will probably not suffice to win the support of three of Iraq's neighbors. The current governments of Iran, Syria and Saudi Arabia are likely to resist a war against Hussein on the unstated grounds that the removal of one brutal, unpopular and illegitimate Mideast government would set a precedent that would jeopardize the stability of other, similar regimes—specifically theirs. So it might. The overthrow of Saddam Hussein might indeed set in motion forces that would threaten the rule of the Islamic clergy in Tehran, the Assad family in Damascus and the Saudi tribe on the Arabian Peninsula. Insofar as such a scenario is plausible, it provides yet another reason for the Bush administration to move to replace the present government of Iraq.[529]

Yale law professor and CFR Senior Fellow for International Organizations and Law Ruth Wedgwood attempted to answer those who felt that preventative war was illegal by arguing in the *National Law Journal* under the heading "Strike at Saddam Now," that Saddam Hussein

still aspires to dominate the region; he still wants a 900-kilometer missile, nuclear weapons and remote means to deliver Iraqi stockpiles of chemical and biological reagents. . . . Much has been written about the American doctrine of "pre-emptive self-defense." The idea has broader footing than some may suppose. The UN Charter explicitly recognizes (in Article 51) the right of every nation to act in its own self-defense when it is the victim of an armed attack. . . . One need not wait until the enemy's mobilized troops have crossed the border in order to respond.[530]

Other Council leaders, who clearly wanted a preemptive war on Iraq, supported these views. In a December 2002 interview, Council member Rachel Bronson, who was the CFR's director of Middle East Studies and an Olin Senior Fellow, made the following pro-war comments in response to a question from fellow CFR staff member Bernard Gwertzman:

Q. *That's been your view all along? Not only that war is inevitable, but that we should launch it?*

A. Yes. It is strategically sound and morally just. The Middle East is a strategic region for us. It is where oil does play into all this. . . . It is about stability in the region. Saddam has been very destabilizing. . . . Strategically trying to get rid of one of the most destabilizing forces in the Middle East is a good idea. But the moral aspect doesn't get as much play as it should. . . . When Secretary Albright said it was not us causing the suffering of the Iraqi people, but Saddam, technically she was right. And everyone in the region agreed; but what they couldn't understand was why we pursued a policy knowing that Saddam would use it to his advantage to torture his people. We were complicit. We have to get rid of this monster. He is our Frankenstein.[531]

Another CFR leader sanguine about the prospects for war was CFR vice president and Director of Studies Lawrence J. Korb, who pointed out that the United States actually made a profit on the last war on Iraq. In an interview with Bernard Gwertzman, Korb made the following comments:

Q. *Everyone remembers the allied land invasion in 1991 to liberate Kuwait that lasted three days. What kind of military action will we have this time? Will it also be a quick one?*

A. I think if there is a military action and it occurs during the winter and you get support from countries in the region it will be over in less than a month. What you will have this time is simultaneous air and ground operations.

Q. *Can the United States afford this? How much will this cost?*

A. If you talk about cost, you have the incremental cost of the operation. We have a $400 billion annual defense budget. You won't have to buy much new equipment. For a one-month war, counting the buildup under way, you are talking about an incremental cost of about $50 billion. . . . The Persian Gulf campaign in today's dollars cost $80 billion.

Q. *That was essentially paid by the Saudis, right?*

A. The last war was actually paid for by the Saudis, the Germans, and the Japanese. We actually made a profit on that war. Nobody likes to admit that. When you look at the incremental costs of the war and what we collected, we actually collected more than the costs of the war. What we did after the war was over was make the books come out even. . . . We actually collected more than we . . . spent.[532]

While many CFR leaders, members, and staff were actively promoting a war on Iraq during 2001, 2002, and early 2003, at least a few were critical, offering another point of view, a perspective that was disseminated, but not as widely or frequently as the pro-war position. One key dissenter was Council member G. John Ikenberry, professor of geopolitics and global justice at Georgetown University. Unlike Pollack, Mandelbaum, Wedgwood, Bronson, and Korb, Ikenberry was not a CFR staff member, so apparently he was not as swept up by the imperialist pro-war visions that were manifestly circulating at the Council's New York headquarters. He offered a clear critique, one that was printed in the September–October 2002 *Foreign Affairs*, arguing that the Bush administration had developed a "neo-imperial grand strategy" that threatened

> to rend the fabric of the international community and political partnerships at a time when that community and those partnership are urgently needed. It is an approach fraught with peril and likely to fail. It is not only politically unsustainable but diplomatically harmful. And if history is a guide, it will trigger antagonism and resistance that will leave America in a more hostile and divided world. . . . America's . . . imperial strategy could undermine the principled multilateral agreements, international infrastructure, and cooperative spirit needed for the long-term success of nonproliferation goals.
>
> The specific doctrine of preemptive action poses a related problem: once the United States feels it can take such a course, nothing will stop other countries from doing the same. Does the United States want this doctrine in the hands of Pakistan, or even China or Russia? Moreover . . . overwhelming American conventional military might, combined with a policy of preemptive strikes, could lead hostile states to accelerate programs to acquire their only possible deterrent to the United States: WMD. . .
>
> Another problem follows. The use of force to eliminate WMD capabilities or overturn dangerous regimes is never simple, whether it is pursued unilaterally or by a concert of major states. After the military intervention is over, the target country has to be put back together. . . . This is not heroic work, but it is utterly necessary.
>
> When these costs and obligations are added to America's imperial military role, it becomes even more doubtful that the neoimperial strategy can be sustained at home over the long haul—the classic problem of imperial overstretch.[533]

Ikenberry's critique and recommendation that the United States stay with a more cooperative multilateral approach—although his perspective turned out to be accurate—was a distinctly minority view in the higher circles of the CFR and U.S. capitalist class, and those who were in charge of setting foreign and military policy in the Bush administration rejected his perspective. A close examination of these policymakers who decided to make war on Iraq, reveals that, with only a few exceptions, they were individuals with close historical and current ties to the Council on Foreign Relations. They reflected the goals and strategic thinking of the majority of those in the highest circles of the American capitalist ruling class.

CFR DECISION-MAKERS AND THE DECISION TO GO TO WAR

Besides the activities of its staff and members who were promoting war, the Council as an organization held no less than thirty-nine separate private meetings on Iraq and the Middle East during 2002–2003. These sessions included one on "Iraq: The War and Oil." Others were led by former CIA director John Deutch discussing the progress of the war, Secretary of Defense Donald Rumsfeld, pro-war senator Joseph I. Lieberman, Undersecretary of Defense Paul D. Wolfowitz, Middle East expert Bernard Lewis, *New York Times* reporter Judith Miller, and numerous CFR member scholars.[534] All of those named above, except Rumsfeld, were current CFR members in 2002.[535] During 2003–2004, Iraq and related issues continued to be a major focus at the Council. The 2004 *Annual Report* stated: "Homeland security, terrorism, and gripping developments in Afghanistan, Iraq, and the greater Middle East have held the country's attention this year. More than forty Council meetings were organized in these areas, and nearly half of those were devoted to the situation in Iraq."[536]

The government's decision to attack and conquer Iraq is covered in depth in two acclaimed full-length books, both published within a few years after this decision. The first to appear was *America Unbound: The Bush Revolution in Foreign Policy* by Ivo H. Daalder and James M. Lindsay.[537] The second was *Rise of the Vulcans: The History of Bush's War Cabinet* by James Mann.[538] All three authors were CFR members when the books came out, and Lindsay was also a Council vice president and the organization's Director of Studies. Their close connections with the Council raise the possibility that the historiography and interpretation of this decision had been decisively and deliberately shaped by the CFR community. But the insider approach to history also ensures that behind-the-scenes events are more fully covered than would be the case for less well connected authors. Mann, for example, conducted "well over a hundred" interviews for his book, many of them with central players in the decision, and lists eighty-nine by name in his acknowledgments. Of these eighty-nine interviewees fully thirty-eight were CFR members, including six former or current CFR directors—Z. Brzezinski, J. Kirkpatrick, C. Powell, B. Scowcroft, G. Shultz, and K. Duberstein—but Mann did not mention the Council connections of these individuals. He wrote his book as "senior writer-in-residence" at the CFR-linked Center for Strategic and International Studies in Washington, stating that two CSIS leaders—director John Hamre and director of its International Security Program Kurt Campbell, both of them Council members—provided "extraordinary support."[539] Mann's index and text mentions the Project for the New American Century, which had close ties to the Council, but the index does not include any references to the CFR.

The index for the Daalder-Lindsay volume also makes no mention of the Council. The acknowledgments in the latter book also leave out any mention of the Council, despite the fact that Lindsay was a top CFR leader. Instead, the focus in the acknowledgments is the support offered by the Brookings Institution, where Daalder was a senior fellow. At Brookings, president Strobe Talbott, a former CFR director, and Council member James Steinberg are listed as providing key support, and three other CFR members, Kenneth Pollack, Michael O'Hanlon, and Tod Lindberg, are also mentioned as among those who made helpful suggestions. Three Council-connected foundations, the Rockefeller Brothers Fund, the Carnegie Corporation, and the William and Flora Hewlett Foundation, provided financial support for the research and writing of the book.[540]

The focus of these two books is on the individuals behind the decision for war. They make no mention of their class and institutional connections, and how such ties might have influenced their individual and collective strategic worldview, agenda setting, and decisions. This "great man" approach to history is taken furthest in the case of Daalder and Lindsay, who assert that "George W. Bush led his own revolution" and "remade American foreign policy."[541] Both books are, however, useful in naming and discussing the key decision makers for war during the early 2001 to early 2003 period. These decision makers can be divided into three groups.

The first group was made up of the top leadership. Daalder and Lindsay call them the "War Council"; Mann calls them the "Vulcans." Eight people are mentioned as key by all three authors: President Bush, Vice President Cheney, Secretary of State Powell, National Security Adviser Rice, Defense Secretary Rumsfeld, CIA head Tenet, Undersecretary of Defense Wolfowitz, and Undersecretary of State Richard Armitage.[542] All of the eight except Bush and Armitage had at one time in their careers been members of the CFR. Five of the eight (Cheney, Powell, Rice, Tenet, and Wolfowitz) were current, dues-paying CFR members in 2002.[543] Cheney was a former Council director, Powell was a future director, and Rice had spent a year in the mid-1980s working at the CFR as an International Fellow, presided over Council meetings and served on at least one committee of the board of directors. Cheney, Rumsfeld, and Wolfowitz were also involved in the Project for the New American Century.

The second group was made up of eight leading deputies and staff people, aides who took orders from the top leadership, were spokespeople, and often wrote the position papers, memos, and orders that went out after being approved and signed by the top leadership. These included Deputy National Security Adviser Steven Hadley, Cheney's Chief of Staff I. Lewis Libby, Undersecretary of Defense Douglas Feith, Trade Director Robert Zoellick, State Department Policy Planning Director Richard N. Haass, UN ambassador John Negroponte, Undersecretary of State Paula J. Dobriansky, and Zalmay Khalilzad, the National Security Council staffer in charge of Iraq and Afghanistan policy.[544] All eight of these individuals were members of the CFR in 2002.[545] Zoellick was a former director of the Council, Dobriansky had been a vice president, Washington office director and a Senior Fellow at the CFR, and Haass became president of the organization in 2003. Libby, Zoellick, Dobriansky, and Khalilzad were also part of the Project for the New American Century. Haass later wrote an insider history of the 1991 and 2003 U.S. invasions of Iraq, confirming who the main and subordinate policymakers were, and stating that he was on the fence personally, "60/40 against going to war," but did not resign over the issue since his disagreement "was not fundamental," and it might impair the functioning of the government.[546]

The third or "outside" group consisted of five in-and-outer "wise men" types, former top government officials, most of them having worked for the George H. W. Bush administration during 1989–93. These well-connected and powerful individuals were, in 2002, either outside the government or part of advisory bodies with little formal power. Former secretaries of state James A. Baker and Lawrence S. Eagleburger, former national security adviser Brent Scowcroft, former assistant secretary of defense Richard Perle, and former CIA director R. James Woolsey made up this group. All five were CFR members in 2002, and Scowcroft had been a director of the Council in the 1980s.[547] Perle and Woolsey were also part of the Project for the New American Century.

Baker, Eagleburger, and Scowcroft were somewhat skeptical of war, while Perle and Woolsey pushed for it. This division within the outside group provided the only semi-serious public debate by members of the American governing class over the wisdom of an invasion.[548]

In sum, then, twenty-one individuals mentioned in the Daalder and Lindsay and Mann books were important in the decision to invade and conquer Iraq. Eighteen of the twenty-one, a stunning 85.7 percent, were Council members at the time the decision was made in 2002. Several (Cheney, Rice, Scowcroft, Dobriansky, Haass) had been unusually active in CFR activities as directors or Fellows. A lesser number of these key players (nine of twenty-one, or 42.9 percent) a number of them also CFR members, were leaders of the other, more public, pro-war lobbying group, Project for the New American Century. The CFR and its members had played the central role in shaping policies and making decisions that resulted in a war on Iraq.

The UN and the U.S. Congress were afterthoughts as far as these leaders were concerned. The debate over the war, such as it was, basically ended in August–September of 2002 when Bush and the top leadership, at the urging of the mild skeptics, agreed to present the case to the UN and Cheney made his speech to the Veterans of Foreign Wars.[549] When the UN refused to agree to authorize the war, the administration decided to go to war anyway. Cheney's speech, reviewed below, was the first public statement of the neoliberal geopolitical war aims of the Bush administration. The Congress passed a resolution in October of 2002 authorizing a war on Iraq. CFR members like Christopher J. Dodd, Dianne Feinstein, John F. Kerry, Joseph I. Lieberman, John D. Rockefeller IV, and Robert G. Torricelli voted for the war resolution in the Senate, while two other Council members, Bob Graham and Jack Reed, voted no. Kerry stated in 2004 that he did not regret his vote in favor of war. [550]

IMPERIALIST GOALS: THE DEVELOPMENT OF WAR AIMS, 2001–2003

The 2001–2003 years of government service of Secretary of the Treasury Paul O'Neill has been documented in great detail by Ron Suskind in his book *The Price of Loyalty: George W. Bush, the White House and the Education of Paul O'Neill.* O'Neill himself read the final manuscript and verified its factual accuracy.[551] Suskind recounts that in early 2001 O'Neill reviewed at top-level government meetings documents that Rumsfeld's Defense Intelligence Agency had prepared, documents that O'Neill said mapped

> oil fields and exploration areas ... listing companies that might be interested in leveraging the precious asset. One document, headed "Foreign Suitors for Iraqi Oilfield Contracts," lists companies from thirty countries—including France, Germany, Russia and the United Kingdom—their specialties, bidding histories, and in some cases their particular areas of interest. An attached document maps Iraq with markings for "super-giant oilfield," "other oilfield," and "earmarked for production sharing," while demarking the largely undeveloped southwest of the country into nine "blocks" to designate areas for future exploration. The desire to "dissuade" countries from engaging in "asymmetrical challenges" to the United States ... matched with plans for how the world's second largest oil reserve might be divided among the world's contractors made for an irresistible combination.[552]

The desire to be in charge of dividing up Iraq's oil wealth among favored and not favored nations and giant oil corporations was a part of the overall picture, but closely connected and even more important was the geopolitical aspect, the quest for world power. In his August 26, 2002, speech to the Veterans of Foreign Wars, Vice President Richard B. Cheney outlined the reasons for invading Iraq and taking over that country, warning that failure to do so would have grave consequences:

> Armed with an arsenal of ... weapons of terror, and seated atop ten percent of the world's oil reserves, Saddam Hussein could then be expected to seek domination of the entire Middle East, take control of a great portion of the

world's energy supplies, directly threaten America's friends throughout the region, and subject the United States or any other nation to nuclear blackmail. Simply stated, there is no doubt that Saddam Hussein now has weapons of mass destruction.[553]

Of course, Cheney was mistaken about Saddam's supposed arsenal, but he indirectly expressed the geopolitical economic goals of the Bush administration: it wanted to make America the dominant power in the Middle East. Instead of Saddam taking control of the "great portion of the world's energy supplies" and subtly or overtly blackmailing any power who needed that energy, the United States would try to do so.

War aims for an imperial power especially involve forcibly determining the shape of the peace following victory. The first war aim of America in Iraq was to relocate population and resources (oil in this case) into its own sphere of interest. The second war aim was to convert Iraq into a neoliberal paradise for U.S. and other multinational corporations. In mid-2002 the Council, together with the James A. Baker III Institute for Public Policy at Rice University, established a twenty-three-member planning group to help formulate what should be American war aims and the political and economic rules for a postwar Iraq. The co-chairs were Edward P. Djerejian and Frank G. Wisner, both CFR members. One of the project directors was the Council's director of Middle East Studies, Rachel Bronson, and members included Senior Fellows Kenneth Pollack and Richard Murphy, as well as corporate leaders (Boeing, PFC Energy), university professors (Princeton, Yale, Vermont), a Naval War College professor, a Senate Committee on Foreign Relations staffer, and representatives from Cambridge Energy Research Associates, the Brookings Institution (CFR member Martin S. Indyk), the James Baker III Institute for Public Policy (CFR member Ann Myers Jaffe), and nine other staffers from the CFR. The Council was the dominant force within the planning group. In late 2002 the CFR produced—jointly with Rice—the report titled *Guiding Principles for U.S. Post-Conflict Policy in Iraq*.[554] Since the Baker Institute is in Texas and James A. Baker III, besides being a CFR member, was a trusted Bush family lawyer, this collaboration undoubtedly increased the report's weight in the eyes of the Bush administration.

The report stated that the establishment of a "U.S. coordinator for Iraq" was an "urgent" task, a suggestion on which the Bush administration soon followed through.[555] The body of this CFR report included a section called "The Lure of Oil: Realities and Constraints," as well as an addendum called "Oil and Iraq: Opportunities and Challenges," which was almost as long as the rest of the report. The report had this to say about the "lure" of Iraqi oil: "Iraq has the second largest proven oil reserves in the world (behind Saudi Arabia), estimated at 112 billion barrels, with as many as 220 billion barrels of resources deemed probable. Of Iraq's seventy-four discovered and evaluated oil fields, only 15 have been developed. Iraq's western desert is considered to be highly prospective but has yet to be explored."[556]

In the report's sections focusing on oil, lip service is given to Iraq's control of its own oil, though in fact the report argues that national control of Iraqi oil must be scrapped and an economy based on "free market economics" and a "level playing field for all international players to participate" be created. The report suggests that the UN Secretary-General should "investigate ways that oil companies could be allowed to invest in Iraq."[557] In short, the CFR, both as an organization and as a community of members, had much to do with the preliminary development of U.S. war aims in Iraq, which conformed to the Council's neoliberal geopolitical worldview, and stress on the central role of oil. This importance was, of course, downplayed, ensuring the slight public discourse on the origins and aims of the war. This led to Alan Greenspan's later comment: "I am saddened that it is politically inconvenient to acknowledge what everyone knows: the Iraq war is largely about oil."[558]

THE WAR AND FINALIZATION OF WAR AIMS

The U.S. war of neoliberal conquest began in March and was over in April of 2003. At the same time an internal bureaucratic battle took place within the U.S. government over control of Iraq policy, with the Department of Defense emerging victorious. The Coalition Provisional Authority (CPA), under Defense, assumed responsibility for postwar planning and setting war aims.

General Jay Garner, who was not a member of the CFR, was initially put in charge of running Iraq, but lasted for only a few weeks. The quick victory had resulted in delusional thinking among American policymakers in New York and Washington with regard to having absolute power in Iraq. Garner was evidently seen as someone who wanted to allow too much democracy in Iraq, and who wanted to compromise too much with Iraqis. Garner favored elections in ninety days, for example, along with a quick transition to Iraqi political and economic control. In a later interview he stated his views: "I don't think [Iraqis] need to go by the U.S. plan, I think that what we need to do is set up an Iraqi government that represents the freely elected will of the people. It's their country . . . their oil."[559]

In late April and early May of 2003 the U.S. press began to report on the Council- dominated Bush administration's grand neoliberal plans for the Middle East generally and Iraq specifically. One article appeared in the May 1, 2003, *Wall Street Journal*:

The Bush Administration has drafted sweeping plans to remake Iraq's economy in the U.S. image. Hoping to establish a free-market economy in Iraq following the fall of Saddam Hussein, the U.S. is calling for the privatization of state-owned industries such as parts of the oil sector, forming a stock market complete with electronic trading and fundamental tax reform. Execution of the plan—which is expected to be complicated and possibly contentious—will fall largely to private American contractors working alongside a smaller team of U.S. officials. The initial plans are laid out in a confidential 100-page U.S. contracting document titled "Moving the Iraqi Economy From Recovery to Sustainable Growth." The consulting work could be valued at as much as $70 million for the first year. . . .

The document provides the most detailed look to date at the ways U.S. officials contemplate restructuring an economy that had been almost entirely government-run, and long mired in a slump aggravated by wars and international sanctions. It is likely to intensify already-sharp international criticism of Washington's unilateral actions in Iraq. Treasury Department officials, who helped draft the document, maintain that the plan reflects a broader vision for Iraq's future economy. . . .

For many conservatives, Iraq is now the test case for whether the U.S. can engender American-style free-market capitalism within the Arab world. In a February address, President Bush spoke of "a new Arab charter that champions internal reform, greater political participation, economic openness and free trade." A new regime in Iraq, he said, "would serve as a dramatic and inspiring example of freedom for other nations in the region." On the economic side, the . . . plan serves as a detailed road map for achieving that end. The proposals for possible mass privatization of Iraqi industry are likely to be the most controversial. The document—first drafted in February and circulated among financial consultants—calls for liquidating some insolvent Iraqi companies, while assessing others for possible sale. Some state companies might be sold through "a broad-based mass privatization program," which could distribute ownership vouchers to ordinary Iraqi citizens, similar to a program used in Russia in the mid-1990s.

The document says that the contractors would help support "private sector involvement in strategic sectors, including privatization, asset sales, concessions, leases and management contracts, especially in the oil and supporting industries" that dominate Iraq's business activity. Any attempt at privatizing Iraq's oil industry, which controls the world's largest petroleum reserves after Saudi Arabia, would be a gargantuan business deal. It could be contentious, especially if assets wind up in the hands of foreign oil companies. In the Mideast and Europe, there is widespread belief—despite White House denials—that the U.S. invaded Iraq to get control of its oil.[560]

For the CFR leadership, part of U.S. war aims had to include nation-building, and in his 2003 outgoing message Council president Leslie H. Gelb both supported and offered a mild critique of the Bush administration's approach in Iraq. Gelb stated that he approved of Bush's "very tough minded, tough in action policies, good for him and good for us," adding that the "obsessions" of tyrants and terrorists "can be cured almost always and only by putting them behind bars or into graves." But Gelb also added this: "The Bush team finds the rigors of cooperating with others and nation-building to be a goal too far, an interest not worth pursuing at high cost. The costs would be excessive, however, only if we failed to pursue a policy of cooperation, compromise and nation-building alongside the cocked guns and swagger. It is in the melding of these two strains of policy that the Council can do some good."[561]

BREMER TAKES OVER IMPLEMENTATION OF WAR AIMS,
MAY–SEPTEMBER 2003

L. Paul Bremer III was educated at the Kent School, Phillips Academy, Yale, and Harvard. After working in the Foreign Service and as an assistant to Henry A. Kissinger and Alexander M. Haig in the State Department, he was appointed ambassador to the Netherlands. He later resigned from the Foreign Service to become the managing director of the consulting firm of Kissinger and Associates (1989–2000). By 1990 he had applied and been accepted as a member of the CFR.[562]

On May 11, 2003, General Jay Garner was summarily fired and replaced by Bremer as President Bush's special envoy and Civil Administrator of the Coalition Provisional Authority in Iraq. Bremer's mandate was to act as a dictator, issuing edicts that would implement the hard-line neoliberal economic program to remake Iraq's economy, society, and politics in a manner that would benefit American and other multinational corporations and the various national capitalist classes, especially the U.S. capitalist class that owned the bulk of assets of these companies. He began by immediately canceling Garner's plan for an interim Iraqi government. He followed this up with orders abolishing the Ba'ath Party, banning party members from public office, and dissolving the Iraqi Army. These orders made an estimated 450,000 Iraqis unemployed, depriving them of their jobs and income. Bremer and the U.S. occupation had, almost immediately, created millions of enemies since these men's family members were also affected by these laws. Many of them had access to guns and knew how to use them. Bremer then turned his attention to the task of the neoliberal economic transformation of the Iraqi economy. Over the next four months (mid-May to mid-September 2003), Bremer issued a number of economic edicts establishing Iraq as a test case for rapidly turning a state planned economy to a market driven, globalized neoliberal economy. Bremer's major orders were:

- Order 12: suspending all trade restrictions, including tariffs and customs duties, until December 31, 2003
- Order 37: establishing a 15 percent flat tax
- Order 39: rewriting foreign investment laws in favor of foreign multinational corporations, allowing 100 percent foreign ownership except in the oil sector, privatizing 200 state-owned Iraqi enterprises, and allowing unrestricted, tax-free repatriation of profits out of Iraq
- Order 40: allowing foreign banks to purchase up to 50 percent of an Iraqi bank[563]

Bremer's chief economic adviser for these laws was yet another CFR member, M. Peter McPherson, who had become a Council member in 1987.[564] McPherson had been head of the Agency for International Development in the Reagan administration and had also headed the Overseas Private Investment Corporation, a government-supported organization that mobilizes private capital to invest in and profit from "emerging" markets. McPherson went on to become a deputy secretary of the treasury under Reagan, where he worked on the Canadian-U.S. free trade agreement. Later he was an executive vice president at Bank of America, where he worked on the North American Free Trade Agreement. When he left that position, he became president of Michigan State University. Under Bremer, McPherson was director of economic policy for the Office of Reconstruction in Iraq. He also helped establish a central bank and a new currency for the country. His attitude toward the role of the Iraqi state is illustrated by his support for theft as a way to privatize state assets, offering his view of the "shrinkage" of the state as follows: "I thought the privatization that occurs sort of naturally when somebody took over their state vehicle, or began to drive a truck that the state used to own, was just fine."[565]

EFFECTS ON THE IRAQI PEOPLE

As could have been predicted by anyone without the ideological and self-interest blinders imposed by a strong belief in the American imperial geopolitical project and the ideology of neoliberalism, the effects of the Bremer-McPherson free market economic program—approved by Bush, the Vulcans, and others in Washington—on the Iraqi people were catastrophic. Bremer told a special meeting of the World Economic Forum meeting in Jordan that he would "set in motion policies which will have the effect of reallocating people and resources from state enterprises to more productive private firms." He added that these state enterprises were "inefficient" so their privatization was "essential for Iraq's economic recovery."[566] This resulted in mass unemployment, which reached as high as 50–60 percent during the summer of 2003.[567] As a result, large numbers of Iraqis came to the conclusion that this was simply another form of colonialist and imperialist pillage. Naomi Klein summed up the reality as follows:

> After the toppling of Saddam Hussein, Iraq badly needed and deserved to be repaired and reunited, a process that could only have been led by Iraqis. Instead, at precisely that precarious moment, the country was transformed into a cut-throat capitalist laboratory—a system that pitted individuals and communities against each other, that eliminated hundreds of thousands of jobs and livelihoods and that replaced the quest for justice with rampant impunity for foreign occupiers . . . a very capitalist disaster, a nightmare of unfettered greed in the wake of war.[568]

This neoliberal capitalist disaster imposed by the CFR was one that the Iraqi people could not tolerate, so they began to rebel and attack both the occupiers and those Iraqis who collaborated with them. The U.S. military and intelligence services under Bush and Rumsfeld responded, as occupiers always do, with repression, in this case including picking up tens of thousands of Iraqis and subjecting them to various levels of torture to gain information about who was part of the resistance. To defend the neoliberal free market model and attempt to salvage American hegemonic goals, during the first three and a half years of the occupation, an estimated 61,500 Iraqis were captured and imprisoned by U.S. forces, and many were tortured.[569]

BARBARISM: THE ATTEMPTED SUPPRESSION OF THE IRAQI RESISTANCE, 2003–2005

In article after article in 2003 and 2004 the *New York Times* discussed how the American military, organized to successfully fight conventional wars and lacking adequate intelligence, became frustrated with the guerrilla war that they had been forced into fighting. For example: "On the streets of Baghdad, and in the angry cities west and north of the capital . . . the United States has a hard time isolating the guerrillas who stalk its troops, plant bombs on the roads and launch mortars on its bases." Looking for solutions, the government began consultations with at least two CFR "experts." The first was Lawrence J. Korb, a former Reagan administration official and director of national security studies at the CFR. In November 2003 Korb was flown into Iraq by the Pentagon with other unnamed "experts" to devise solutions.[570] Another Council expert brought into Iraq was CFR Senior Fellow Arthur C. Helton, who was killed in the bombing of the UN headquarters in Baghdad in August of 2003.[571]

As American military and intelligence forces faced increased opposition and casualties during 2003 and early 2004, the Bush administration doubled down, deciding on a harder line with more troops, tougher tactics, and a giant embassy.[572] When Bremer left Iraq in mid-2004, he was replaced by London-born John Negroponte, the new U.S. ambassador, who had become a CFR member in 1982.[573] Negroponte's father was a Greek shipping magnate who had emigrated to the United States, and John was sent to the best schools—Buckley, Phillips Exeter, and Yale. John Negroponte went into the Foreign Service, working at the American Embassy in Saigon during the war on Vietnam, and later became U.S. ambassador to Mexico, the Philippines, and Honduras. It was in the last post during the Reagan years of 1981–85 that Negroponte became known as an enabler of human rights abuses. John MacGaffin, a CIA associate director for clandestine operations, described Negroponte as "a guy who plays hardball. He's a man who understands the whole range of counterintelligence, intelligence and covert action."[574] Negroponte was a strong supporter of the murderous contra war against Nicaragua and played a central role in it, working closely with the CIA and the Honduran military as well as playing host to contra leaders the Reagan administration set up in Honduras, to attack Nicaragua.[575] Jack Binns, a former U. S. ambassador to Honduras told the *New York Times* that he believed Negroponte "was complicit in abuses; I think he tried to put a lid on reporting abuses and I think he was untruthful to Congress about those activities."[576] Negroponte became known as a "veteran of dirty wars" and undoubtedly was sent to Iraq to help organize the massive violence seen as necessary to destroy the insurgency.[577]

A central part of the coercive structure built up to reinforce the planned American domination of Iraq was construction of the largest and most expensive embassy in world history on one bank of the Tigris River in Baghdad. Construction began in 2005 for a facility larger than Vatican City, six times the size of the United Nations compound in New York, and ten times larger than any other U.S. embassy worldwide. When completed at an estimated cost of $700 million, it was the size of a small city, with 16,000 employees, 5,500 of them security personnel. It consisted of twenty fortified structures on 104 acres (the size of about eighty football fields), including six apartment buildings, two giant office structures, a commissary, a cinema, retail and shopping areas, restaurants, water treatment facilities, electric power station, wastewater treatment facilities, an Olympic-size swimming pool, a gym, and club. It held by far the largest CIA station in the world.[578] Unlike other embassies, which are designed to facilitate interaction with local people, the purpose of this massive compound was not only for defense, but also to overawe and impress the Iraqis with the might of the newly dominant imperial power. It forcefully illustrated the continued strong commitment of the Bush administration and men like Negroponte to American war aims in Iraq and the larger Middle East region, with all the larger implications about neoliberalism, oil, and world power. What it actually showed to the Iraqi people, however, was who really exercised power in their country, and it succeeded only in stimulating resistance.

Returning to Iraq in June 2004, at almost the exact same time as Negroponte, was yet another Council member, General David H. Petraeus, called "the most celebrated U.S. military figure of his generation."[579] An intellectual as well as a general, Petraeus earned a PhD from Princeton in the 1980s with a dissertation called *The American Military and the Lessons of Vietnam.* Known as an expert on counterinsurgency, he and another general oversaw the publication of an army field manual called *Counterinsurgency.* He became a member of the CFR and officially joined their network at about the same time he got his doctorate.[580] Petraeus has been an active Council member, co-chairing an independent task force, for example.[581] Petraeus was sent to Iraq to provide the military leadership needed to defeat the resistance, which could only be done, he believed, with Iraqi troops. Indicative of the power he was given, PBS's *Frontline* reported on October 21, 2014, that Petraeus distributed at least $400 million in cash to persuade Iraqi resistance groups to end their armed struggle. President Bush apparently was not informed of the payment of this illegal bribe money, yet Petraeus and the others involved have not been investigated for violations of law.

Petraeus became the first commander of the Multi-National Security Transition Command Iraq. As commander of this group, Petraeus supervised lower-rank officers who were training units like the Special Police Commandos of the Iraq Ministry of Interior to provide security once the American role was reduced. One of his subordinates was Colonel James Steele, who had been selected for a senior job by Undersecretary of Defense and CFR member Paul Wolfowitz.[582] Steele, then an Enron executive, was a retired special forces officer and, like Negroponte, a veteran of the "dirty wars" in Central America. Steele had been in charge of the U.S. Special Forces group training the front-line battalions that committed massive human rights abuses, torture, and death squad activity in El Salvador's civil war, in which upward of 70,000 were killed, many of them kidnapped and murdered by the government forces Steele was training. Steele was thus an expert in organizing a counterinsurgency campaign involving local forces, having honed his skills training torture and murder squads in El Salvador. *Newsweek* later belatedly reported in January of 2005 that the United States was considering "The Salvador Option" in Iraq.[583]

Petraeus assigned Steele to be the main adviser training a group within the Interior Ministry called the Special Police Commandos, and stated that this key unit "would receive whatever arms, ammunition and supplies they required."[584] These commandos soon became known as the group guilty of many if not most of the mass torture and murder of Iraqi civilians that took place during the next few years. While in Iraq, reporter Peter Maass interviewed Steele and others (but apparently not Petraeus), for his article "The Way of the Commandos," which appeared in the May 1, 2005, *New York Times Magazine*. At first, Steele would not allow the reporter to visit a detention center where Steele was an adviser, but eventually relented and took Maass into the prison. Once inside, Maass entered another world, a chamber of horrors. He reported that he saw about 100 detainees, hands bound behind their backs, most of them blindfolded; "to my right, outside the doors, a leather jacketed security official was slapping and kicking a detainee. . . . A detainee was led out with fresh blood around his nose. . . . One desk had bloodstains running down its side."[585] Maass wanted to interview one detainee, but while doing so, "a man began screaming in the main hall. . . . It was not an ecstatic cry; it was chilling, like the screams of a madman, or of someone being driven mad. Steele left the room" and when he "returned the shouts had ceased." Maass heard one U.S. soldier at the center say that he had just seen a detainee "hanging from the ceiling by his arms and legs like an animal being hauled back from a hunt."[586]

In a 2013 *Guardian* (UK) article titled "Revealed: Pentagon's Link to Iraqi Torture Centers" reporters concluded that Petraeus and Steele were behind the commando units implicated in the large-scale torture and murder of detainees.[587] This article also pointed out that the detention centers had video cameras purchased by the U.S. military, which the Iraqi commandos used to film tortured detainees for a TV program shown on the U.S.-funded al-Iraqiya national TV station. This program, called *Terrorism in the Grip of Justice*, showed victims of torture confessing to all manner of crimes. This was shown to terrorize both common criminals and those resisting U.S. control of Iraq, as well as illustrate to the Iraqi public the supposed depraved nature of the detainees. General Petraeus saw the TV program and called up the head of the Special Police Commandos, demanding not that the torture and murder stop, but that they stop showing the torture victims on TV.[588] The Iraqi commander complied, indicating that Petraeus had command authority over those doing the torturing, just as Steele did at the detention center. *Guardian* reporters concluded: "The long-term impact of funding and arming this paramilitary force was to unleash a deadly sectarian militia that terrorized the Sunni community and helped germinate a civil war that claimed tens of thousands of lives. At the height of that sectarian conflict, 3,000 bodies a month were strewn on the streets of Iraq."[589] The purpose of this carnage was to destroy the resistance leadership and their followers. Torture was used to gather intelligence about who should be captured, forced to give information, and later often murdered. As Petraeus expressed it in one of his writings on counterinsurgency: "Intelligence is the key to success."[590]

Petraeus was not the only Council-connected general at the center of U.S. aggressive operations in Iraq. Stanley A. McChrystal was an Army colonel in 1999 when he was selected by the CFR's Military Fellow Selection Board, headed by none other than Richard B. Cheney, to spend a year at the Council's headquarters to, in the words of the CFR's *Annual Report,* "broaden . . . [his] understanding of foreign affairs."[591] He was then elected to Council membership in 2001.[592] After making close connections within the CFR, the colonel was soon promoted to general and commander of the Joint Special Operations Command (JSOC) from 2003 to 2008. JSOC carried out assassinations in Iraq and Afghanistan, working its way through "kill lists" of people who were targeted, then captured or killed in night raids on their homes or kidnapped off the street. JSOC also conducted torture at a secret U.S. Army base in Iraq called Camp NAMA. Journalist Jeremy Scahill later wrote that "a lot of JSOC's dirty business went down is a small cluster of buildings nestled in a corner of a Saddam-era military base near Baghdad International Airport . . . Camp NAMA."[593] Human Rights Watch concluded that torture at Camp NAMA was "part of a regular-ized process of detainee abuse."[594] McChrystal often personally directed special operations in Iraq, and was reported to have frequently visited the Camp NAMA torture site.[595] After an exposé of the war crimes that occurred at Camp NAMA, dozens of lower-rank soldiers were prosecuted and convicted of torture, but the commander was promoted.[596] After lobbying by Petraeus, President Obama put General McChrystal in charge as commander in Afghanistan in 2009. Scahill concludes that McChrystal was one of the key players in the transformation of the JSOC into a global hit squad.[597] Stanley A. McChrystal retired from the Army after being removed from his Afghanistan command in June of 2010. He was soon hired by Yale University as a Senior Fellow, teaching a graduate-level course on "Leadership in Operation." He was also brought onto several corporate and strategic advisory boards, including JetBlue Airways, Navistar International, Siemens Government Systems, and a licensed arms dealer called Knowledge International. With access to the high salaries, stock options, and other perks that corporate directors have, it is likely that McChrystal will soon be a member of the capitalist class himself.

A final piece of evidence illustrating that those highest in the U.S. chain of com-mand had a significant measure of responsibility for the horror in Iraq during those years was what happened when regular U.S. troops or National Guard stumbled onto one of the torture/detention centers, which happened a number of times during the years of civil war in Iraq. The first documented instance took place on June 29, 2004. Oregon Army National Guard troops were startled to observe men in plainclothes beating blindfolded and bound prisoners in the enclosed grounds of the Iraqi Interior Ministry. They swept into the yard and found dozens of detain-ees who stated that they had been beaten, starved, and deprived of water for three days. The *Seattle Times* reported what happened next:

In a nearby building, the soldiers counted dozens more prisoners and what appeared to be torture devices: metal rods, rubber hoses, electrical wires and bottles of chemicals. Many of the Iraqis, including one identified as a 14-year-old boy, had fresh welts and bruises across their backs and legs. The soldiers disarmed the Iraqi jailers, moved the prisoners into the shade, released their handcuffs and administered first aid. Lt. Col. Daniel Hendrickson of Albany, Ore., the highest-ranking American at the scene, radioed for instructions. But in a move that frustrated and infuriated the guardsmen, Hendrickson's superior officers told him to return the prisoners to their abusers and immediately withdraw. It was June 29—Iraq's first day as a sovereign country since the U.S.-led invasion. . . . The U.S. Embassy in Iraq confirmed the incident occurred and disclosed for the first time that the United States raised questions about the June 29 "brutality" with Iraq's interior minister. It said it would be "inappropriate" to discuss "details of those diplomatic and confidential conversations."[598]

John Negroponte was then, as U.S. ambassador, at the top of the chain of command in Iraq, and David Petraeus was near the top of the military command structure. Evidently neither ever did anything to save these and thousands of other prisoners from abuse, apparently believing, as so many in the U.S. power structure did, that American interests were served by torture and murder. Both men soon went on to higher office, Negroponte as the first director of National Intelligence and Petraeus as chief of Central Command and later as CIA director. Petraeus resigned from this last post in November 2012 after his extramarital affair with his biographer, Paula D. Broadwell, surfaced. Petraeus had also shared confidential official data with Broadwell. It turns out that Broadwell is also a fellow CFR member, having been elected as a term member in 2008, likely with Petraeus's support. Following his resignation from both the CIA and the U.S. Army, Petraeus was hired by the CFR-connected Wall Street private equity firm KKR to head up their Global Institute. KKR's co-CEO, Henry R. Kravis, was a director of the Council from 2006 to 2012.[599] Petraeus's new job illustrates how important the Council network can be for individuals; his connections allowed him to transition into an interesting and lucrative position on Wall Street.

A MIDCOURSE CORRECTION: THE 2006 IRAQ STUDY GROUP

Throughout 2005 it was increasingly clear that the Bush administration's Iraq policy was failing, and the number and strength of critics was growing. Those who had promoted and made the decision for war began to leave their government positions in early 2005. It was Secretary of State Colin Powell and his deputy, Richard

Armitage, who left first, in early 2005. Within the inner circle of decision makers, Powell had been the most skeptical about the war on a realistic, pragmatic basis, but ended up strongly supporting it.[600] It was therefore ironic that he and Armitage were the first to desert the sinking ship. Stronger war hawks Wolfowitz, Feith, and Libby all left the administration between June and October of 2005. Rumsfeld and Rice, with Cheney and Bush himself, were still holding on as 2006 began.

With a November 2006 midterm election looming, Republicans in Congress and the Bush policy team began a consultation process early that year aimed at reaffirming existing policies while quieting dissent, trying to disarm critics enough to win the election. The means used to accomplish both goals was to set up a "fresh eyes," "bipartisan blue ribbon" task force that would meet, call upon capitalist-class "wise men" and experts for advice, try to develop consensus within this group, then issue a report that offered possible "new" but likely not significantly different policies. The ten-member Iraq Study Group (ISG) fulfilled this mandate from the time it was appointed in March 2006 to when its report was issued in December of that year.

More often than not, "blue ribbon" task forces are dominated by Council-connected individuals, illustrating the power and reach of the CFR network. The ISG was no different. The ten members were evenly divided between Republicans and Democrats, co-chaired by former secretary of state and secretary of treasury James A. Baker III (Republican) and former congressman Lee Hamilton (Democrat). The eight other original members were four Republicans: former Supreme Court justice Sandra Day O'Conner, former CIA director Robert M. Gates, former New York mayor Rudy Giuliani, and former senator Alan K. Simpson. In addition to Hamilton, the four other Democrats were Lazard Freres managing director and Clinton adviser Vernon E. Jordan Jr., former congressman Leon E. Panetta, former Secretary of Defense William J. Perry, and former senator Charles S. Robb. In 2006, four of the five Democrats (all except Panetta) and two of the Republicans (Baker and Gates) were current CFR members, and O'Connor was a former member.[601] Therefore seven of the ten original members of the ISG were current or former members of the Council. Two of the original ten members—Giuliani and Gates—dropped out before the report was complete. In May Giuliani resigned, and was replaced by former attorney general Edward Meese III. In November, right after the Republican defeat in the election, Gates became secretary of defense, replacing Donald Rumsfeld. CFR member and former secretary of state Lawrence Eagleburger replaced Gates on the ISG.

Besides having a total of eight Council members on the ISG, more than a majority (twenty-three, or 53.5 percent) of the forty-three "former officials and experts" interviewed to solicit their opinions on what to do about Iraq were CFR members.

Nine of the twenty-three Council members interviewed were current or former directors of the CFR, including former former CFR president Gelb, former secretaries of state Albright, Christopher, Kissinger, Shultz, and Powell, as well as former national security advisers Brzezinski and Scowcroft.[602] Many of the experts on the working group panels were also Council members. In sum, the ISG members of the CFR dominated the ISG, and their conclusions reflected what leading members of the Council and the larger capitalist ruling class were thinking about U.S. policy in Iraq and the way forward as of late 2006.

The work of the Iraq Study Group was facilitated especially by the U.S. Peace Institute, which had been proposed under the Carter administration but not implemented until 1984, when Ronald Reagan decided that it was the right year to sign a law creating this organization. The president of the Peace Institute in 2006 was CFR member Richard H. Solomon, who was a former Department of State official (Director of Policy Planning, Assistant Secretary of State, ambassador to the Philippines). The idea behind the Institute was to resolve conflicts without violence, but it became involved in Iraq only as an afterthought, when the situation was already characterized by mass violence. Three other organizations also collaborated in the work of the ISG. These were the James A. Baker III Institute for Public Policy, the Center for the Study of the Presidency, and the Center for Strategic and International Studies. The leaders of each of these three other organizations, who signed on to the ISG Report, were Edward P. Djerejian (Baker Institute), David M. Abshire (CSP), and John J. Hamre (CSIS). All three were members of the CFR in 2006.[603]

The ISG Report of December 6, 2006, representing a consensus of CFR and capitalist-class opinion, was a milestone in the evolution of U.S. policy. It reaffirmed the long-standing belief in the importance of Iraq and its oil reserves, seen as "critical" to U.S. national interests:

Iraq is vital to regional and even global stability, and is critical to U.S. interests. It runs along the sectarian fault lines of Shia and Sunni Islam, and of Kurdish and Arab populations. It has the world's second-largest known oil reserves. It is now a base of operations for international terrorism, including al Qaeda. Iraq is a centerpiece of American foreign policy, influencing how the United States is viewed in the region and around the world.[604]

In terms of recommendations, the ISG's Recommendations 62 and 63 focused on privatizing the all-important oil sector:

Since the success of the oil sector is critical to the success of the Iraqi economy, the United States must do what it can to help Iraq maximize its capability. . . .

As soon as possible, the U.S. government should provide technical assistance to the Iraqi government to prepare a draft oil law that . . . creates a fiscal and legal framework for investment. Legal clarity is essential to attract investment. . . . Expanding oil production in Iraq over the long term will require creating corporate structures. . . . The United States should encourage investment in Iraq's oil sector by the international community and by international oil companies. The United States should assist Iraqi leaders to reorganize the national oil industry as a commercial enterprise. . . . There is no substitute for private-sector job generation.[605]

The illegal imposition of neoliberal policies in all aspects of Iraq's economy, something that had been a central aspect of U.S. policy since the beginning of the war and occupation, was thus reaffirmed by the CFR-dominated ISG at the end of 2006. But they stepped back from a longer-term goal of making Iraq a military colony and a central base in a U.S.-dominated Middle East. Diplomatic and "national reconciliation" efforts to bridge the Sunni-Shia divide were stressed, along with a takeover of the war by the new Iraqi Army. Other U.S. military bases in the region were to be used to patrol the Persian Gulf region, although a short term "surge" of U.S. troops in Iraq might be needed if it helped the process of forcing the Iraqi Army taking over primary responsibility for security:

As additional Iraqi brigades are being deployed, U.S. combat brigades could begin to move out of Iraq. By the first quarter of 2008, subject to unexpected developments in the security situation on the ground, all combat brigades could be out of Iraq. At that time, U.S. combat forces in Iraq could be deployed only in units embedded with Iraqi forces. . . . Even after the United States has moved all combat brigades out of Iraq, we would maintain a considerable military presence in the region, with our still significant force in Iraq and our powerful air, ground, and naval deployments in Kuwait, Bahrain, and Qatar, as well as an increased presence in Afghanistan. . . . Because of the importance of Iraq to our regional security goals . . . we considered proposals to make a substantial increase (100,000 to 200,000) in the number of troops in Iraq. We rejected this course . . . adding more American troops could conceivably worsen those aspects of the security problem that are fed by the view that the U.S. presence is intended to be a long-term "occupation." We could, however, support a short-term redeployment or surge of American combat forces to stabilize Baghdad, or to speed up the training and equipping mission. . . . We believe that our recommended actions will give the Iraqi Army the support it needs. . . . The United States should not make an open-ended commitment to keep large numbers of American troops deployed in Iraq.[606]

Although no timetable was set for withdrawal, and the possibility of a troop surge was supported, the recommendations of the Iraq Study Group nevertheless represented a move back toward the political center, toward a less doctrinaire, less hegemonist, and more realist balance of power approach to the Middle East and the world. The fact that their suggestions were implemented testified to the continuing influence of the Council on U.S. Iraq policy. Once the midterm election resulted in a serious defeat for the Republicans, Rumsfeld resigned (December 18, 2006). Robert M. Gates, a longtime active member of the CFR and part of the Iraq Study Group, took his place. With the neocons in retreat, Gates was influential in implementing the new realist ruling-class consensus on Iraq policy: the attempt to achieve victory through a lower-profile war and occupation.

A CASE OF IMPERIAL OVERSTRETCH: THE SUCCESS OF THE IRAQI RESISTANCE AND SEMI-WITHDRAWAL

As late as the fall of 2011, U.S. officials were quoted as still planning a major increase in diplomatic and cultural programs in Iraq, the building blocks of "soft power," by establishing branch consular-type offices across that nation, as part of "the largest diplomatic mission since the Marshall Plan."[607] In 2011 the State Department estimated that it would spend "$3 billion over the next five years on its private security contracts to protect its massive embassy complex in Baghdad alone."[608] The main event of 2011, however, was the U.S. military withdrawal from Iraq. This happened after many months of trying and failing to negotiate an agreement with the Iraqis that would override the one signed by Bush to withdraw all U.S. troops by December 31, 2011. Resistance to continued U.S. occupation was strong in both Iraq and the United States. Iraqi political leaders had to push the Americans out because of the strong nationalist popular sentiment in Iraq that wanted the occupiers gone. Prime Minister Nouri al-Malaki wanted to agree to all the conditions needed to keep U.S. troops in Iraq, but his government would have fallen had he done so. Almost all uniformed U.S. troops left the country. Private security guards and Marines were left to guard the giant U.S. embassy.

GIANT FAILURES, SOME "SUCCESS"

The failure in Iraq marked the end of the brief, post–Cold War U.S. unipolar moment. In Iraq the limits of American military and geopolitical power were pitilessly revealed. The biggest long-term impact of the invasion was not to implant U.S. power in the center of the Middle East, but to upend the balance of power in one of the most combustible regions in the world, catapulting the Shia majority into power in Iraq, and reigniting the simmering inter-Muslim conflict between

Sunni and Shia in the Arab heartland. That conflict is still being played out in Iraq, as well as other nearby nations. These developments can be seen, at least partly, as the unintended consequences of the distruction of the regional balance of power created by the U.S. invasion and occupation of Iraq. The rise of the Islamic State in Iraq and the Levant (ISIL) in Syria, Iraq, Libya and other countries is but one example. The strength of this military and political organization is symptomatic of a larger disorder, loose in many parts of world due to neoliberal geopolitical policies, but especially in the Middle East. This is the chaos and alienation created by U.S. intervention and attempted domination that has seriously corrupted and weakened the social and political fabric of a number of nations. As usual, CFR leaders are pushing their type of "solutions" to the situation created by the rise of ISIL and the Syrian civil war. Their people, Council members like John F. Kerry, Ashton Carter, and General John R. Allen—Allen was appointed in September 2014 by President Obama in to oversee the war on ISIL—are still crafting and executing U.S. policy there.[609]

The U.S. intervention and occupation has also left a legacy of ecological destruction. The Iraqis have been left with a natural landscape devastated by war and the use of extremely toxic munitions, the long-term consequences of which are only beginning to be assessed. Immediately after the March–April 2003 invasion of Iraq, experts at the Pentagon and the United Nations estimated that 1,100 to 2,200 tons of depleted uranium munitions were used during the initial attack on Iraq.[610] These munitions are extremely effective in their destructive power but leave a dangerous residue. To cite but one example of reports on the effects of such weapons, the German newspaper *Der Spiegel* had a long investigative article on the massive level of birth defects and infant deaths found in Basra, where the United States and British had used depleted uranium. Cause and effect is often difficult to prove in such cases, but many well-informed observers believe that there is a causal relationship between the poor health and frequent deaths of infants and the use of these weapons.[611]

The politics of Iraq ten years after the U.S. invasion were reviewed in a lengthy *Financial Times* article in March 2013, which noted that the Green Zone was still the

> heart of political power, of plotting and intrigue, and is the home to the prime minister's office and parliament. Still surrounded by blast walls, but its entry points now controlled by Iraqi forces, the Green Zone is a world apart from the chaos of the city. The US embassy, the largest US mission in the world, is here . . . with its apartment blocks for staff, sports facilities including tennis and basketball courts, and even a power station. In a fitting image of the US's declining influence . . . the 10,000 staff—mostly contractors—who work

here and across the other missions in Iraq—are being slashed to 5,000–6,000 by the end of the year.[612]

The Iraqi government is reportedly made up of "greedy politicians struggling for control of the state. For this political class, sectarianism and patronage are the only means of survival." One Iraqi woman indicated that life in 2013 was no better than under Saddam: "They're keeping people busy with cars, electronics and mobiles and they give us no services, no security or jobs and no housing…. We had one oppressive regime but now we have 100 political parties that are oppressive. We can express ourselves but so what? No one is listening."[613]

If the American power grab for world hegemony has largely failed in Iraq, the second U.S. war aim, imposing on Baghdad a neoliberal capitalist regime, including new rights for the oil majors, was more of a "success." Speaking of the surreal situation of checkpoints and explosions alongside increased shopping opportunities, the *Financial Times* commented:

The banality of violence is part of a strange combination of simultaneous progression and regression. Baghdad's potholed streets are crumbling, with only rare signs of the new infrastructure. Residents still receive only a few hours of electricity a day. Many young people are unemployed, while others take up three jobs to make ends meet. But the facades of old shops have been covered with shiny hoardings advertising the glut of consumer goods now available, from mobile telephones to flat-screen televisions. Iraq's factories are still idle but there are several new malls under construction, as well as fancy car dealerships and private banks.[614]

Two of the newest private banks that expanded into Iraq beginning in 2009 are JPMorgan Chase and Citigroup, both corporate members of and closely interlocked with the CFR.[615] In June of 2013 the *Financial Times* reported on Citigroup's activities in Iraq:

In the past decade, the bank has already been catering to investors and large companies operating in Iraq, offering products such as trade finance, cash management and investment banking services through its regional hub in Dubai, its Iraq desk in Amman and via London. Citi's move to establish a physical foothold in the market comes as major international oil groups as well as industrial and construction companies are looking to invest in Iraq. This oil-driven growth will turn the country into one of the largest oil exporters globally within the next decade and into a $2tn. economy by 2050, Citigroup's economists estimate.[616]

The emerging neoliberal economic structure also offers speculative financial opportunities for individuals who have wealth and expect to get much wealthier. As the author of the article pointed out: "An old Iraqi friend who lives in London but visits Baghdad almost every month, is starting an investment fund to buy stocks on the Iraqi exchange. She says Iraq needs so much reconstruction and infrastructure that an economic boom is inevitable." [617]

Meanwhile, the persistence of both the U.S. government and the major multi-national oil companies has begun to result in some successes for these corporations in Iraq. The resistance of the Iraqi people to privatization of the country's oil and gas wealth prevented the national parliament from passing a hydrocarbon law that would allow foreign control. But both the Iraqi central government under al-Malaki and the Kurdistan regional government did not let this legal shortcoming stop them. Beginning in 2008, both governments began to negotiate and sign contracts with major and some smaller oil corporations. The contracts with the central government were designed to circumvent the legislative stalemate and allow big oil to get an initial foothold in Iraq. The first step was memorandums of agreement, reportedly signed by forty-six different companies although only a few got actual contracts. Among these are the very biggest majors and some smaller state-owned firms: ExxonMobil and Occidental (U.S.), Royal Dutch Shell (British-Dutch), Total SA (French), Eni (Italian), China National Petroleum/ PetroChina, BP (Britain), Petronas (Malaysia), Lukoil (Russia), Statoil (Norway), Gazprom (Russia), TPAO (Turkey), and Korea Gas.[618] Some of those thus far shut out of the main Iraqi oil fields, including Chevron, Hess, and Hunt Oil, have signed oil contracts to work in Iraqi Kurdistan. Of these above-mentioned oil corporations now benefiting from the murderous conquest of Iraq, eight are corporate members of the CFR: ExxonMobil, Chevron, Hess, BP, Eni, Shell, Total SA, and Occidental.[619]

Many others who favored war are also benefiting today. Zalmay Khalilzad for example, a CFR member and Project for the New American Century activist who pushed for war as head of the National Security Council's staff of experts on Iraq in 2002, later became U.S. ambassador to Iraq (2005–2007). After he left the government, Khalilzad founded an investment advisory and consulting firm called Gryphon Partners that focuses on assisting clients "in markets throughout the Middle East and Central Asia." Khalilzad is the president of the company and states on the company's website that he "maintains close ties with high-level leadership throughout the Middle East and Central Asia, and is regularly called upon to provide strategic advice to numerous heads of state."[620]

Many in the CFR and the capitalist think tank world have an attitude toward the Iraq War, money, and oil that is exemplified by Council member Stephanie Sanok who works at the CFR-connected Center for Strategic and International Studies: "We are still sinking a lot of money into this and we are still trying to get our oil dividend."[621] These capitalists certainly do not want to give up their "oil dividend," built on the lives and treasure of rank-and-file Iraqi and American people. They ignore the immorality and lack of elemental ethics and humanity imposed by a catastrophic and criminal war, with the massive destruction, displacement, kidnapping, torture and murder visited upon the Iraqi people. Though estimates vary, the respected British medical journal *The Lancet* conducted a study and estimated that about 650,000 Iraqis were killed; an unknown, but vast number wounded; and millions displaced from their homes. Almost 8,000 U.S. citizens were killed (almost 4,500 service personnel and at least 3,400 contractors) and over 100,000 wounded.[622] To speak of the lack of an "oil dividend" in light of such an ocean of human suffering is telling.

Also illustrative is the refusal of the Obama administration, dominated by members of the CFR, to uphold the rule of law in regard to the actions of many Bush administration personnel in kidnapping and torture in Iraq and elsewhere during this period. The UN's special rapporteur for human rights stated in April of 2009 that since the United States had committed itself to the UN Convention Against Torture, it was obliged to investigate and prosecute any violations. Otherwise, he pointed out, the Nazi principle of "I was only following orders" would be endorsed. President Obama, stating "nothing would be gained" from such investigations, exempted Bush, Cheney, their lawyers and other officials from any liability, reaffirming in effect the Nazi principle.[623]

7

THE CFR AND THE EMPIRE
OF NEOLIBERAL GEOPOLITICS:
CASE STUDIES

Neoliberalism is the immediate and foremost enemy of genuine participatory democracy, not just in the United States but across the planet.

—NOAM CHOMSKY

You can't fight power if you don't understand it.

—MUMIA ABU JAMAL

The case studies in this chapter are meant to concretely illustrate the
range, scope and power of the Council on Foreign Relations and the
ways it has utilized its membership, connections, and policy-planning
studies to create, expand, and maintain the American neoliberal geopolitical
empire. Because the number of studies, reports, books, memos, articles, interviews, testimony, op-eds, briefs, podcasts, and videos that the Council has produced during the last several decades is very large, only a small but relevant sample can be discussed here.

Two types of case studies are presented. The first focuses on non-conflictive
relations with the more developed nations, in general, the world's North. The general theme is integration and cooperation into the neoliberal geopolitical world
order, although in the cases of the Ukraine as well as the seas around China, geopolitical conflicts between states threaten to block U.S. neoliberal goals. The second
type focuses on the often conflict-ridden relations with largely powerless countries
in the world's South. The general theme is domination, control, and exploitation

by the United States, its Northern allies, and associated private corporate interests, resulting in the creation of an informal empire, often by forcing nations into the dominant system.

RENEWING THE ATLANTIC PARTNERSHIP

The U.S. war for oil, geopolitical position, and a neoliberal Iraq created conflict with some European states, most notably France and Germany, both of which actively opposed the American invasion and war aims as stated by prominent members of the George W. Bush administration. This gave rise to a level of unease and concern on the part of the leadership of the Council, since the alliance between the United States and Western Europe, by far the two richest parts of the world, was viewed as central to the U.S. informal empire, the neoliberal geopolitical hegemonic bloc running the world. The danger of growing disunity in this alliance was, in part, considered by a CFR Independent Task Force that issued a 2004 report titled *Renewing the Atlantic Partnership*. Council president Richard N. Haass set the context for the work of this ITF as follows:

The Atlantic alliance has been a critical component of the international system for the last five decades. Through joint efforts to pursue shared interests, the United States and its European allies succeeded not just in containing the Soviet threat (and in fostering conditions that contributed to the ultimate demise of the Soviet Union itself) but also in liberalizing the global economy and extending democratic governance to Europe's east and beyond. The transatlantic relationship is now under serious strain. The end of the Cold War, Europe's continuing integration, and the new array of threats confronting the West have led Americans and Europeans alike to question the durability and utility of the Atlantic alliance. The transatlantic rift that opened over the war in Iraq significantly intensified these concerns.[624]

The ITF was set up with financing from four European and one U.S institution: Eni, the largest Italian industrial corporation, a major transnational oil company with about 76,000 employees working in seventy-nine nations; the Fundacion Juan March, the family foundation operated by the March banking family, one of the wealthiest families in Spain; the French Fondation pour la Science et la Culture; the German Marshall Fund of the United States, founded in 1972 with funds from the German government to strengthen transatlantic relations; and the U.S.-based Merrill Lynch investment firm.[625]

Two prominent individuals, Henry A. Kissinger and Lawrence H. Summers, headed up this task force. Both were "in-and-outers" with experience as high government officials (secretary of state and secretary of the treasury, respectively), as well as extensive connections to the private worlds of big corporations and academe, as chair of Kissinger Associates and president of Harvard University, respectively. Both were long-term members of the CFR, and Kissinger was a onetime director. Charles A. Kupchan, a Council Senior Fellow and director of European studies, was director of the ITF and primary author of its report.

In accordance with the usual CFR practice, the ITF was composed of a large group of very experienced and well-connected individuals who worked to produce a consensus document. The group had twenty-six members and included five Europeans, one each from Britain, France, Germany, Italy, and Poland. Giuliano Amato was a member of the Italian Senate; Thierry de Montbrial was the founder and president of the French Institute of International Relations; Timothy Garton Ash was a British historian at Oxford University and on the board of the European CFR, the first pan-European think tank; Josef Joffe was editor of Hamburg's *Die Zeit*; and Andrzej Olechowski was a leader of Civic Platform, a centrist Polish political party.[626]

Every one of the twenty-one U.S. ITF members were members of the Council, and fully six were current or former directors. These six were Kissinger, former secretary of defense Harold Brown, former chairman of the Council of Economic Advisers Martin S. Feldstein, former national security adviser Brent Scowcroft, Princeton University Dean Anne-Marie Slaughter, and former national economic adviser and corporate executive Laura d'Andrea Tyson. These and other U.S. members of this ITF had a wealth of connections to powerful political, economic and intellectual networks. Four had been U.S. ambassadors to a number of European nations: Reginald Bartholomew to Spain, NATO and Italy, Richard R. Burt to Germany, Stuart E. Eizenstat to the European Union, and Felix G. Rohatyn to France. International lawyer and former State Department official Thomas E. Donilon later became President Barack Obama's second national security advisor. Nine were professors at top universities: three at Harvard, three at Georgetown, and one each at Yale, Princeton, and the London School of Business.[627]

The general theme of the ITF report was the need to improve and increase transatlantic communication, and stressed that, though the United States was, in the words of Council president Haass, the "indispensable nation," the European nations were "indispensable allies." There were five other, more specific, priorities for the United States and Europe that would also help form the basis for relationships with other parts of the world. The first of these was to establish new guidelines or "rules of the road" for the use of military force. This was key to resolving the central issue dividing the United States and some key nations of Europe in regard to Iraq. The CFR-dominated group assured the Europeans that "preemption" as a policy "would be reserved for special cases and not be the centerpiece of U.S. strategy." The group suggested that in return the Europeans would agree that preemption would not be ruled out in principle, thus coming to "common ground" on this issue.[628] It is noteworthy that the Council group felt that it could make such a commitment, illustrating that it considers itself the real power, the definers of the national ruling-class interest of the United States.

Another recommendation was to develop "compatible policies toward states that possess or seek to possess weapons of mass destruction, that harbor terrorists or support terrorism, and that seek through these means to challenge the international order that Europeans and Americans have created and must sustain."[629] This recommendation was, of course, largely aimed at Iran, but was also hypocritical, because U.S. military and intelligence agencies have supported and harbored terrorists when convenient. U.S.-supported terrorists have frequently attacked Cuban civilians and tourists visiting Cuba, for example, and American use of Special Operations Forces, bombing campaigns, and drones in the global South could properly be labeled "terrorism."

A third policy that the ITF promoted was to "build a common approach to the greater Middle East." The report stressed the geopolitical economic importance of the Middle East to the rest of the world and the need to cooperate on four issues:

The region contains the globe's greatest concentration of oil and natural gas. It poses potent threats from international terrorism and the proliferation of weapons of mass destruction. The region faces a rapidly rising youth population—for example, roughly 50 percent of Saudi Arabia's population is under the age of twenty—but have economies ill suited to providing gainful employment. Europe's proximity to the greater Middle East and its growing Muslim population make these issues all the more urgent. The transatlantic community must tackle four central issues, the first of which is Iraq. . . . Europeans and Americans must set aside narrow political and economic ambitions in the region and jointly shoulder responsibility for stabilizing the country. NATO, already demonstrating its value in Afghanistan, is a natural successor to the current international military presence in Iraq.

If a substantial increase in financial and military support from Europe is to be forthcoming, the United States must be prepared for greater European participation in the political management of Iraq. . . . Iran is a second issue. Iran is experiencing considerable internal debate over the direction of its domestic politics and foreign policy. Americans and Europeans should coordinate their policies—if possible, with Russia as well—to ensure that Iranians fully understand how the international community will react to their decisions regarding proliferation, support for terrorism, and democracy. The importance of encouraging political reform in Iran and neutralizing potential threats should give Europe and the United States a strong incentive to act in unison. A third issue is the Israeli-Palestinian conflict. The widespread perception in Europe that the United States one-sidedly favors Israel weakens support for American foreign policy in Europe. Meanwhile, many American policymakers see European policy toward the dispute as reflexively pro-Palestinian. Both sides need to make an effort to achieve a common position. The United States needs to define more precisely its concept of a Palestinian state; Europe must take more seriously Israel's concern for security. A fourth area for transatlantic cooperation in the greater Middle East concerns the area's long-term economic and political development. Many countries in the region have lagged behind the rest of the world in moving toward democratic societies and market economies. Educational systems are in many instances not providing the skills needed for competing successfully in the modern world; women often are denied basic rights and opportunities. The rigid and brittle societies that result breed widespread frustration and disaffection— social characteristics conducive to radicalism and terrorism. Such societies are also prone to state failure, civil war, or both. Tackling these challenges requires a concerted effort by Europe and the United States, one comparable to the effort waged during the Cold War to assist and win over much of the developing world. Such an undertaking requires considerable resources over a sustained period. It also requires astute public diplomacy.[630]

A fourth policy area involved recommendations that revolved around NATO and the future geographical expansion of the transatlantic security "partnership." As America draws down its military forces stationed in Europe, the ITF recommended that NATO continue to serve as the "primary forum" for transatlantic cooperation on international security. Also important was promoting "reform" in eastern and southeastern Europe and continuing the NATO-related momentum of initiatives that involve Turkey, Ukraine, and Russia. This was part of what the report called "adjusting to new geopolitical realities . . . the alliance must find the appropriate balance between a new emphasis on out-of-area missions and its traditional focus on European security. . . . NATO must increasingly concern itself with threats emanating from outside Europe."[631]

The fifth and final policy, related to expanded and neoliberalized trade, will be discussed in more detail below. The ITF report summarized these recommendations as follows:

Security cooperation requires economic cooperation. It follows, then, that Europeans and Americans must work together, not just to liberalize

U.S.-European trade, but also to ensure the successful completion of the current round of world trade negotiations. High-level consultations designed to produce a common approach to the Doha round are essential. Europeans and Americans must also pursue a long-term strategy for fostering economic growth and political liberalization in the developing world. Specific elements of such a strategy should include eliminating trade barriers with developing regions.[632]

TRADE AND INVESTMENT: EXPANDING AND INTEGRATING THE NEOLIBERAL EMPIRE

From an early date in his study of capitalism, Karl Marx recognized the tendency toward universalization inherent in capitalism, pointing out in 1857–58 that "the tendency to create the world market is directly given in the concept of capital itself. Every limit appears as a barrier to overcome," and "capital must . . . strive to tear down every spatial barrier to . . . exchange, and conquer the whole earth for its market."[633] A major goal of the CFR since its founding in 1921 has been encouraging the internationalization of economic life through the continual liberalization of national and global trade and investment rules, favoring corporations and their wealthy owners over the sovereignty of nations. During the past four decades, CFR leaders and members have continued this tradition. They have been instrumental in making and implementing the neoliberal policies of the capitalist class. This is further illustrated by the number of U.S. Trade Representatives who have been connected to the Council. From Carter to Obama there have been a dozen permanent U.S. Trade Representatives. Eight of the twelve have been Council members, and three of these, Carla A. Hills, Charlene Barshefsky, and Robert Zoellick, have been CFR directors. The current (2014) U.S. Trade Representative is longtime Council member Michael Froman, who is a former CFR Senior Fellow who served for a decade on the Council's Studies Committee (2001–2011), and has also been a Trilateral Commissioner.[634] Another "in-and-outer," Froman has had a long career in the U.S. government (in the Treasury Department and as an adviser to the National Security Council and National Economic Council) and with Citigroup, where he was a managing director, working closely with Robert Rubin. Froman's Deputy Trade Representative, Miriam Sapiro, is also a CFR member.[635]

As part of its "Renewing America Initiative," in 2011 the CFR sponsored an Independent Task Force on U.S. Trade and Investment Policy. Co-chairs Republican Andrew H. Card and Democrat Thomas A. Daschle led the task force members responsible for the report. Card, who is not a Council member, served in important positions in the Reagan and Bush administrations, as president and

CEO of the American Automobile Association, and on the boards of Union Pacific Corporation and the U.S. Chamber of Commerce. Daschle, a former U.S. senator and CFR member, is a senior adviser to the multinational law firm DLA Piper and serves on several policy boards, including the Center for American Progress, the Blum Foundation, and a General Electric corporate advisory board. Two Council staff members, Edward Alden and Matthew J. Slaughter, both Senior Fellows, directed the project and drafted the report. The remaining eighteen task force participants included nine CFR members. One of them, James W. Owens, former chair and CEO of Caterpillar, was a Council director. Another task force member, Laura D'Andrea Tyson, a professor at the University of California, Berkeley, and a board member of Morgan Stanley, AT&T, CB Richard Ellis, and other major international corporations, was a former Council director. The rest of the ITF members included a former U.S. ambassador to Canada, James J. Blanchard; a former U.S. secretary of agriculture, Daniel R. Glickman,; several former congressmen, senators, and governors—Blanchard, Glickman, Harold E. Ford Jr., Trent Lott, William M. Thomas, William F. Owens; lawyers, nonprofit leaders, and academics involved in trade and investment issues; policy intellectuals from Brookings, the Scowcroft Group, Aspen Institute, and the University of Denver's Institute of Public Policy Studies; and two labor representatives, Leo W. Gerard of the United Steelworkers and Andrew L. Stern of the Service Employees International Union.

Trade and investment policy brings together the geopolitical/geoeconomic and neoliberal currents in U.S. foreign policy. The report of the Independent Task Force on Trade and Investment Policy stated that expanding and deepening global economic networks through open markets is a "major strategic instrument" of U.S. foreign policy, preventing conflict and creating prosperity through economic growth. Task force leader members made major claims for the importance of U.S. policy on this issue, stating that the resulting increase in profits and economic growth had reduced poverty and helped the United States become wealthier.[636]

This ITF report concluded that the Doha Round of the WTO negotiations has been a "failure" and a "significant setback for U.S. trade policy." The danger was that the other biggest international players, the EU and China, were politically and economically outflanking the U.S. by pursuing

more ambitious bilateral and regional trade-negotiating agendas. The EU has entered into negotiations with India, with the countries of the Association of Southeast Asian Nations (ASEAN), as well as with South Korea and Canada, and China has pursued trade links throughout the Asia-Pacific region. . . . For the United States, these deals . . . tilt the global market in favor of its largest competitors, leaving U.S.-based production at a disadvantage. The United States needs a more flexible and varied negotiating strategy that can yield greater market opening in the sectors and countries that promise the largest economic gains. The Task Force believes that the United States should revitalize its trade-negotiating agenda by focusing on the biggest markets and sectors that have the greatest potential for increasing U.S. production of goods and services and for creating additional employment and income in the United States.[637]

The consensus of this ITF was, therefore, that the United States "cannot afford to be left behind" and "needs to get beyond the Doha talks." One way to move forward was to pursue the Trans Pacific Partnership (TPP). This trade and investment agreement, under negotiation in 2013–15, would unite twelve Pacific Basin nations, including the United States, Japan, Canada, Mexico, Malaysia, Singapore, and Australia into a NAFTA-like economic union. The TPP was promoted by the CFR as an "extremely promising initiative.... The TPP could emerge as the vehicle for more comprehensive trade liberalization in the Asia-Pacific region." To that end the ITF recommended in 2011 that the United States "should work to bring Japan and other interested regional participants into the negotiations as soon as possible," something that was accomplished two years later.[638] Council activists, such as former Obama national security adviser Thomas Donilon, argued that due to its size the TPP was a potential "game changer" and the "economic lynchpin of U.S. rebalancing strategy in Asia."[639] What was left out of the discussion was the impact on local and national laws by the TPP and similar trade deals. These so-called free trade agreements are actually investor protection pacts that strip governments of the power to regulate corporate activities and allow corporations to sue governments and taxpayers and collect payments based on laws that supposedly curtail their current or future profits. For example, the Swedish energy giant Vattenfall is currently suing Germany for 3.7 billion euros over Germany's moratorium on nuclear power, arguing that their future profits will be impacted.[640] TPP would also give international firms access to U.S. federal government contracts and likely result in the export of jobs to low-wage nations. The cumulative effect of the race to the bottom on regulations, wages, and working conditions resulting from these free trade policies is an important source of the growing inequality in the United States and other developed nations. These policies overrule democratic laws that protect workers, consumers, and ecologies so that corporate power can expand and profits grow. The fact that such agreements continue to be negotiated by both Democratic and Republican administrations illustrates once again the undemocratic power of the CFR and the corporate capitalist class over our collective future.

The TPP negotiations are, however, not the only major regional trade and investment talks now under way. On February 12, 2013, President Obama announced during his annual State of the Union Address that the United States would pursue another agreement outside the Doha Round: the Transatlantic Trade and Investment Partnership (TTIP) with the European Union. The goal is similar to the TPP—to remove trade and regulatory barriers, set common standards, and possibly open state enterprises and government procurement policies to competition, creating a more closely integrated transatlantic economy. The TTIP is very ambitious, wanting nothing less than the largest trade and investment negotiations ever undertaken. If successful, it would create the biggest free trade zone the world has ever known. First round talks between U.S. Trade Representative and active Council member Michael Froman and EU Commissioner for Trade Karel De Gucht began in July 2013.

Using IMF statistics, the countries involved in the TTIP produce 49 percent of global GDP; if Japan's current GDP is added, the figure reaches 57.6 percent, not counting the smaller nations involved in the TPP talks. The combined size of the economies involved in the ongoing TPP and TTIP negotiations thus amounts to over 60 percent of the world economy. The potential geopolitical and geoeconomic implications of either of these agreements are serious enough for China, but together would open the door to the possibility of a full-scale export disaster for that nation, with all the attendant ramifications for employment, domestic stability, and role in the world. In a May 21, 2013, speech at the CFR, EU Commissioner De Gucht stated that China especially is going to "sit up and take notice" of the decision to launch the TTIP talks, but he also stressed that the purpose was not to unite against anyone, just to encourage China and others to adopt similar approaches. But at least one active CFR member, Vali Nasr, formerly a Council Adjunct Senior Fellow for Middle East Studies and now dean of the Johns Hopkins School of Advanced International Studies, sees a clear U.S. geopolitical and geoeconomic aim to these trade negotiations: to outflank and weaken China. Nasr was quoted in the *Financial Times* as stating that the United States "is trying to block off the two biggest areas of global gross domestic product from what Washington considers its main rival."[641]

While the United States has been pursuing these two trade deals with major geopolitical implications, it is significant that China has taken notice and been active in the same field. In November of 2012, China was centrally involved in beginning negotiations for it own free trade agreement, this one including sixteen Asian-Pacific nations. This agreement—the Regional Comprehensive Economic Partnership (RCEP)—so far includes all of the ten Association of Southeast Asian Nations (ASEAN) countries, plus China, India, Japan, South Korea, Australia, and New Zealand. Seven of the sixteen members of this developing trade bloc—Japan, Australia, New Zealand, Malaysia, Singapore, Vietnam, and Brunei—are also part of the TPP. But clearly the United States will dominate the TPP and China will dominate the RCEP, intensifying the developing competitive rivalry as each side tries to further its own vision and national economic interests. The consensuses among the parties that both the TPP and RCEP will depend upon are still under construction, but it appears that the two trade pacts have similar goals, focused on more open trade and investment. One apparent difference in emphasis is that the RCEP appears be more interested in economic interdependence, with attention to development gaps and facilitating mutual engagement in regional supply chains in order to create a unified market.

The rapid development of a new economic landscape in Asia and worldwide—including the likely creation of partly exclusive geoeconomic trading blocs—whose complexities and related national security issues will be managed by competing national states is likely to create contradictions and conflicts that could become serious. Illustrative of this are current disagreements between a rising China and other states over control and use of the East China and South China Seas.

CHINA POLICY

Council studies and recommendations on specific U.S.-China policy were being developed at the same time as trade policy discussions were ongoing. In April 2007 the CFR published the result of almost a year and a half of work, an Independent Task Force report titled *U.S.-China Relations: An Affirmative Agenda, A Responsible Course.*[642] The U.S.-China ITF was co-chaired by Carla A. Hills and Dennis C. Blair. Its overall purpose was to assess developments both in China and in U.S.-Chinese relations since 1972 and to put forward a new strategy to govern future bilateral relations. In his foreword to the report, Council president Richard A. Haass expressed how important this topic was, reflecting a consensus view that China's rise is one of the most important developments in world history:

> No relationship will be as important to the twenty-first century as the one between the United States, the world's great power, and China, the world's rising power. China's development is directly transforming the lives of one-fifth of the world's population and is otherwise influencing billions more. China's rapid economic growth, expanding regional and global influence, continued military modernization, and lagging political reform are also shifting the geopolitical terrain and contributing to uncertainty about China's future course. After thirty-five years of "engagement," the United States and China have a relationship that was truly unimaginable two generations ago. At the same time, there are some Americans who believe that China's strategic interests are incompatible with those of the United States.[643]

The choice of Hills and Blair as co-chairs for this task force clearly indicates the neoliberal and geopolitical thrust of the resulting report. A CFR director who became co-chair of the Council in 2007, Hills has, since the 1970s, been an important neoliberal voice promoting free market, free trade, pro-foreign investment regimes worldwide (she was centrally involved in creating NAFTA) while running a consulting business specializing in the related task of helping U.S. corporations expand abroad. She was a cabinet-level government official in the Ford and Bush I administrations. Blair, a sixth-generation naval officer, attended a private Episcopal boarding school, the Naval Academy, and Oxford University on a Rhodes Scholarship. He eventually became Admiral Blair, and commander-in-chief of the U.S. Pacific Command. Following his retirement from the Navy in 2002, he became president and CEO of the Institute of Defense Analysis, a federally funded research and development center, and taught military strategy at the U.S. Army War College and Dickinson College. In 2009 he became the Obama administration's Director of National Intelligence.

Both Hills and Blair today continue to be leaders of the National Committee on U.S. China Relations (NCUSCR), Hills as the longtime chair of this organization and Blair as a board member. The thirty members of the U.S.-China ITF included nine NCUSCR board members, and fully 80 percent (24 out of 30) belonged to the Council or were CFR staff in 2007. Besides Hills, other top CFR leaders on this ITF included former vice chair and longtime director Maurice R. Greenberg, a billionaire who headed the American International Group (insurance) for many years, as well as former Council president Winston Lord and former director Harold Brown. Lord and Brown had served in high government positions in the Nixon, Ford, and Carter administrations. A Kissinger protégé, Lord was a special assistant to Kissinger, director of the State Department's policy planning staff, an assistant secretary of state, and U.S. ambassador to China. Brown was Carter's secretary of defense, then joined the financial firm of Warburg Pincus and also became a trustee at the Center for Strategic and International Studies.

The majority of the other task force members consist of "in-and-outers," and therefore have a multitude of past and ongoing connections. These include networks linked most prominently to national and transnational finance capital; to private think tanks and consultancies; to the U.S. government, especially the National Security Council and the State, Treasury and Defense Departments; and to top American and Asian universities. Just to list the connections of the ITF members to finance capital yields the following: Evercore Partners, the Blackstone Group, Lehman Brothers, Promontory Financial Group, Goldman Sachs, Evergreen Holdings, Federal Reserve Bank of New York, Carlyle Asia, and Albright Capital Management. Many of these companies have direct economic interests relating to China. Group members also include professors or visiting scholars from Harvard, Princeton, Yale, Stanford, Swarthmore, George Washington, Institute of International Policy Studies (Tokyo), Tsinghua University (Beijing), Jiaotong University (Shanghai), City University of Hong Kong, Johns Hopkins, University of Washington, Hamilton College, Chinese Academy of Social Sciences, Foreign Affairs College (China), Columbia, Barnard College, and the University of Pennsylvania. The connections of group members to think tanks and consulting organizations besides the CFR and NCUSCR are also impressive: U.S.-China Business Council, Asia Society, Eurasia Group, Brookings Institution, Business Council, Business Roundtable, National Foreign Trade Council, British-American Business, National Foreign Trade Council, U.S.-Japan Business Council, Kamsky Associates, China Institute of America, Nixon Center, Peterson Institute for International Economics, RAND, Korea Society, Institute for Defense Analyses, Center for Strategic and International Studies, Council for Security Cooperation in the Asia Pacific, Henry L. Stimson Center, U.S. Institute of Peace, Armitage International, and the Albright Group.[644]

The work of this distinguished and extremely well-connected CFR group focused on both further spreading neoliberalism to China through economic engagement/integration, and the overlapping geopolitics and geoeconomics of China's rising power in the East Asian region especially.

Sino-American Economic Engagement

In general, with a few minor dissents from a few of its members, the ITF saw Sino-American relations since the 1970s as "positive" and China's behavior as somewhat mixed but benign overall. Terms like "growing adherence to international rules, institutions and norms" and becoming "more attentive to U.S. views" were applied to China. The central strategy—the "affirmative agenda" and "responsible course"—recommended by the task force was to work toward integrating China more fully into the global economic community, thus making it a responsible stakeholder in the system. This would involve "a blend of engaging China on issues of mutual concern, weaving China into the fabric of international regimes on security, trade, and human rights, and balancing China's growing military power."[645]

The ITF identified two economic issues of specific concern, China's "rampant theft" of intellectual property rights (IPR) from U.S. firms, costing them billions, and the undervaluing of Chinese currency, which makes Chinese goods cheaper in U.S. markets, and contributes to the large U.S. trade deficit. The task force concluded that on the issue of IPR, Chinese efforts to address U.S. concerns "have been sorely inadequate." These were, however, the strongest words against Chinese behavior in the report. The ITF concluded that on the issue of currency "the value of the yuan is not a major cause of the U.S. trade deficit with China."[646]

Finally, a major ITF recommendation was close Sino-U.S. cooperation on energy and the global environment. The report argued that because the two countries are the largest consumers of energy and largest emitters of greenhouse gases, "the fate of the planet depends on the success of efforts by the United States and China to curb harmful emissions and work together . . . to demonstrate that environmental protection and economic growth are not mutually incompatible." The report went on to state that the United States should set an example, touting that it was "a world leader in many of the relevant technologies," specifically mentioning new nuclear power reactors that China was purchasing in part from a Westinghouse subsidiary, "clean" coal technology, solar power, hybrid and hydrogen automobiles, energy-efficient light bulbs and systems to reduce industrial emissions.[647] As will be discussed below, there are gross inadequacies in this and the CFR's general approach to ecological problems, including, but not limited to, global warming.

The Geopolitical Side of U.S.-China Policy

The ITF began its analysis of the geopolitical side of U.S.-China policy by discussing China's military modernization program:

China's military modernization has two main drivers, one with a clear operational objective (Taiwan) and the other with a clear strategic objective (to build a modern military because China will be a modern power). In its 2005 report to Congress on China's military, the Pentagon found that China is emphasizing preparations to fight and win short duration high-intensity conflicts along China's periphery, particularly in the East and South China Seas, where long-standing territorial disputes hold the potential for conflict and where trade routes are of growing importance. Longer term, China's military strategy will be shaped by its growing dependence on imported oil, the presence of unstable regimes on its western and northeastern borders, and Beijing's lingering concerns about a U.S.-led containment strategy. In the 2006 Quadrennial Defense Review, the Pentagon concluded, "Of the major and emerging powers, China has the greatest potential to compete militarily with the United States and field disruptive military technologies that could over time offset traditional U.S. military advantages." In January 2007, then Director of National Intelligence John D. Negroponte testified to Congress that China's modernization is driven by its aspirations for great power status and said it would continue even if the Taiwan problem were resolved. One manifestation of China's great power aspirations is its active space program. China became the third country to put a person in space in 2003, and Beijing has established the goal of putting a person on the moon by 2024. China's investments in space systems—commercial space launch vehicles, surveillance satellites, and telecommunication satellites—all have dual-use applications. The 2006 Quadrennial Defense Review reports that China's space, air, and missile capabilities now pose a coercive threat to potential adversaries in contested areas around China. . . . China's emerging military capabilities will complicate the strategic environment confronting U.S. forces for decades to come.[648]

Despite China's growing military strength, this ITF assessed the military/geo-political balance as decisively favoring the United States and its allies, even along its borders, but especially away from that zone, since China "lacks many of the instruments of force projection, including long-range bombers, aircraft carriers, large airborne units, and the logistics capability to support and sustain combat forces beyond its borders."[649] The ITF concluded its overall assessment of the military/geopolitical situation as follows (emphasis in original):

> The principal area in which the mission sets of the United States and China currently come into potential conflict is Taiwan. China can damage Taiwan with missiles, but it can only take and hold Taiwan if it can win and sustain control of the space, air, and waters around Taiwan—a difficult task without U.S. intervention, and nearly impossible should the United States intervene in a China-Taiwan war. *The Task Force finds that as a consequence of its military modernization, China is making progress toward being able to fight and win a war with Taiwan (absent U.S. intervention), and it is also beginning to build capabilities to safeguard its growing global interests.* The mere existence of these capabilities—including anti-satellite systems—poses challenges for the United States. China does not need to surpass the United States, or even catch up with the United States, in order to complicate U.S. defense planning or influence U.S. decision-making in the event of a crisis in the Taiwan Strait or elsewhere. *Looking ahead as far as 2030, however, the Task Force finds no evidence to support the notion that China will become a peer military competitor of the United States. By virtue of its heritage and experience, its equipment and level of technology, its personnel, and the resources it spends, the United States enjoys space, air, and naval superiority over China. The military balance today and for the foreseeable future strongly favors the United States and its allies.*[650]

Although the ITF saw the balance of military power as fundamental and suggested "shifting the balance" of U.S. naval forces from the Atlantic to the Pacific, it also advocated combining balance of power with "concert of power" tactics, not only to sustain U.S. superiority, but also to maintain and enhance U.S. alliances in East Asia, such as with Japan, while at the same time promoting dialogue, transparency, and coordination with China.

The CFR and U.S.-China Rivalry in the Western Pacific

In the years since the 2007 ITF on China policy was published, the Council has continued to closely monitor the slowly maturing U.S.-China conflict in the Western Pacific, specifically in the East and South China Seas. The disputes grow out of a number of key facts.

- The East and South China Seas are seen as both economic and strategic zones by a number of powers—most prominently China, Japan, the Philippines, Vietnam, and the United States—with fish, potential oil and gas resources, tourism, guano, and strategic position (coastal defense, large trade flows, and safe passage to the open Pacific Ocean) all at stake.
- For decades the United States has been the dominant naval and military power in the region and at least since 1992 has had the strategic objective of preventing the emergence of a rival superpower. Furthermore, it is now "pivoting" to Asia; for example, beginning to station military forces in northern Australia.
- The United States has defense treaties, which it has pledged to uphold, with Japan and the Philippines.
- The United States asserts that international waters and the right of free navigation for all begins at twelve miles from the landmass of a given nation, meaning that most of these two seas are open waters.
- China, the key rising world and regional power, is assertive of what it sees as its rights and claims a 200-mile-wide "exclusive economic zone" in the South China Sea, stating that the military forces of other nations are not free to enter this zone without express permission.
- China is rapidly ramping up its military spending and military forces. According to the CFR website, China's military spending increased 175 percent between 2003 and 2013. This spending resulted in the launching of China's first aircraft carrier in 2012, with another carrier currently under construction.
- China and Japan have both claimed the small Diaoyu/Senkaku Islands in the East China Sea, creating an ongoing conflict over them.
- China and various other Southeast Asian nations claim the long stretch of archipelagos in the South China Sea that comprise hundreds of islets, including, most prominently, the Paracels and Spratleys. There has been a long history of military and non-military skirmishes between various parties over these territories. China currently occupies the Paracels, but their rights are contested by Vietnam.

The forty-five or so islands making up the Spratleys are occupied by six different nations—China, Taiwan, Vietnam, Malaysia, Brunei, and the Philippines—all with tendencies to contest the rights of each other to the islands they hold.[651]

The Council has been observing this entire developing situation carefully and has a special multimedia section on its website, described as an "infoGuide," that outlines the danger involved as follows:

Thousands of vessels ply the East and South China Sea waters, from fishing boats to coastal patrols and naval ships. Increasingly frequent clashes between China and its neighbors heighten the risk that miscalculations by sea captains or political leaders could trigger an armed conflict, which the United States could be drawn into through military commitments to allies Japan and the Philippines. Policy experts believe that a crisis management system for the region is crucial.[652]

Longtime Council member Kurt Campbell undoubtedly reflected current CFR thinking about the dangers involved in the situation in a 2013 op-ed piece in the *Financial Times*. Campbell is an "in-and-outer" who has served as a presidential adviser, on the National Security Council staff, as a Deputy Assistant Secretary of Defense, and most recently as an Assistant Secretary of State for East Asian and Pacific Affairs (2009–13). In between government service he has worked as a Harvard professor, a director of the Aspen Strategy Group, CEO of the Center for New American Security, a senior vice president and director of international security programs at the Center for Strategic and International Studies, and chairman and CEO of the Asia Group. In his *Financial Times* piece, Campbell focused on the tensions between China and Japan over the Diaoyu/Senkaku Islands, stating that the situation has created the fear of world war: "a feel of 1914 in the air. Just as with tensions between European armies at the turn of the last century, both Tokyo and Beijing are absolutely certain of the rightness of their positions . . . both believe that with a little further pressure, the other side is on the verge of blinking and backing down . . . both sides underestimate the risks of the crisis."[653]

Council leaders have attempted to reduce the risks and prevent escalation through behind-the-scenes diplomacy, likely combined with warnings to both sides. In October of 2012, as tensions were rising between China and Japan over these islands, four former national security officials from both Democratic and Republican administrations visited Japan and China with the approval of Secretary of State Hillary Clinton. Three of them—Joseph S. Nye Jr., James B. Steinberg, and Steven J. Hadley—were longtime CFR members, and Nye was a Council director. The fourth, Richard L. Armitage, although not a CFR member, has long been a close ally of longtime Council director Colin Powell, and has co-chaired at least one CFR Independent Task Force (No. 65, on Pakistan and Afghanistan).[654] Although none of them held a government position at the time, they were quickly put in touch with the highest government officials in both nations, speaking first with Japanese prime minister Yoshihiko Noda, then flying to Beijing the next day to speak with Chinese vice premier Li Keqiang.[655] What they said to each leader was not reported, but in an interview afterward, Armitage indicated a clear tilt toward Japan, stating that, though the United States does not take an official position on who has a legal right to the islands, "we're not neutral when our ally is a victim of coercion or aggression or intimidation," and adding that the U.S.-Japan Security Treaty means that the United States "has responsibilities for the defense of the Senkakus."[656] Reinforcing American support for Japan, Armitage used the Japanese, not the Chinese, name for the islands.

Elizabeth C. Economy, a CFR Senior Fellow and Director of Asia Studies and a leading Council China expert, suggested in October 2013 that China's policy toward nations like the Philippines that are in conflict with China over the islands of the South China Sea is moving from "peaceful rise" to "bullying." Once the Philippines appealed to the UN to settle the dispute, China disinvited Philippine president Benigno Aquino to a business investment summit in Nanjing. China is now attempting to handle any disputes through bilateral diplomacy, in order to keep the United States out of any conflicts with the smaller nations and therefore more easily control the situation.[657] Disputes in this part of the world continue to raise the specter of catastrophic great-power conflict, making clear that the current neoliberal geopolitical global order has serious contradictions.

UKRAINE: NEOLIBERALISM, GEOPOLITICS, AND CONFLICT

Since the fall of the USSR in the early 1990s, there has been a drive on the part of the U.S. and European capitalist class, led by CFR people and CFR-connected organizations, to economically and strategically penetrate the former states that were part of the Soviet bloc. The goal is the full integration of these nations into the U.S.-dominated neoliberal geopolitical empire. The most important of these countries is Ukraine, due to its size, resources (including shale gas resources), level of development, and geographic position in the heart of eastern Europe. It lies in a key position for east-west gas transportation for example. CFR leader Zbigniew Brzezinski, in his 1997 work *The Grand Chessboard*, wrote that Ukraine is one of Eurasia's "vital geopolitical pivots," suggesting that both the EU and NATO should expand to include Ukraine within a "reasonable time frame." He added the warning that "if Moscow regains control over Ukraine, with its 52 million people and major resources as well as access to the Black Sea, Russia automatically again regains the wherewithal to become a powerful imperial state, spanning Europe and Asia."[658] Brzezinski has been centrally involved in promoting recognition of the importance of Ukraine among the higher circles of the U.S. power structure. In 1994 he and the CFR-connected Center for Strategic and International Studies established an American-Ukrainian Advisory Committee of nineteen members, ten from the United States. Besides Brzezinski, the U.S. group included five other CFR members, among them Henry A. Kissinger, Frank Carlucci, and George Soros, along with the CEOs or chairs of major multinational corporations with actual or potential interests in eastern Europe such as Archer-Daniels Midland, Morrison-Knudsen, Westinghouse Electric, the Carlyle Group, and *Forbes* magazine. They suggested policies to the U.S. government, including U.S. training for Ukrainain military officers as well as,promoting free enterprise and privatization programs in Ukraine. Their goals included an eventual "redefinition of Russia" through changes in Ukraine. To promote their plans, they also met, during the Clinton administration, with Deputy Secretary of State and former CFR director Strobe Talbott.

Since the 1990s, a prime means to further the aim of bringing Ukraine into the Western orbit has been the funding of "civil society" groups in that nation by the National Endowment for Democracy (NED). As pointed out in chapter 3, NED and the CFR are heavily interlocked, with ten CFR members serving on the NED board of directors, including two current Council Senior Fellows. NED has put a high priority on funding Ukrainian groups, and NED's president, Carl Gershman, even called the country "the biggest prize."[659] As a result, NED has spent a vast amount funding private groups in Ukraine; in 2013 alone NED spent millions on sixty-five different projects in the country. This was part of a larger U.S. government effort that resulted in $5 billion being spent in Ukraine since 1991.[660] Large amounts have also come from private sources. For example, George Soros reportedly donated over $100 million to Ukrainian non-governmental organizations. The NGOs favored with this largess were those that could promote neoliberalism in the country and orient it to the West.

The geopolitical aspect has been the imperialist expansion of NATO to include nations on the borders of Russia. The CFR began to debate and develop ruling-class consensus on this topic early, announcing in its 1995 *Annual Report* that "we have plunged into the issue of whether NATO should expand eastward." The chair of this study group was former secretary of defense Harold Brown, and included people like former and future CFR directors Richard C. Holbrooke, Joseph S. Nye Jr., and Anne-Marie Slaughter.[661] The January 1995 report of this group concluded: "NATO should move swiftly and with determination to put itself in a position to admit new members, and prospective entrants should take steps now to prepare themselves for full membership."[662] The Council conducted a follow-up study in

1996, with Senator Richard Lugar as chair and State Department official Victoria Nuland as project director. Nuland's husband, Robert W. Kagan, is a longtime CFR member who later became a Senior Fellow for International Economics at the Council.[663] The resulting report was titled *Russia, Its Neighbors, and an Enlarging NATO*.[664] Finally, another study group was formed in 2000, with Zbigniew Brzezinski as chair and Senior Fellow Ronald D. Asmus as project director. Asmus, who had been a key adviser to Secretary of State Madeleine K. Albright, produced a CFR book, *Opening NATO's Door*, which came out in 2004.[665] This book was called the "definitive account" of NATO's expansion, which had as its main aim binding America and eastern Europe closer together.[666]

As the process of enlargement took place during the 1999–2009 period, Moscow complained bitterly, arguing that this process was threatening core Russian national interests. This was especially true in the case of Ukraine, yet the CFR and the NATO alliance pushed forward. At its summit in April of 2008 the NATO alliance considered admitting Ukraine, but due to the opposition of France and Germany, they postponed the decision, asserting in a statement that eventually both Georgia and Ukraine "will become members of NATO."[667]

In 2013–14 the conflict between the West and Russia over Ukraine's future became more serious, with each side pushing harder to bring Ukraine into its own sphere. The neoliberal economic stakes were outlined clearly by the U.S. ambassador to Ukraine in a speech of September 3, 2013, when he stated in clear geoeconomic language that "Ukraine . . . has the opportunity to become the eastern frontier of a large European economic space at the same time that it serves as Europe's gateway to the Eurasian heartland and Europe's gateway to one of the most dynamic economic regions of the world which stretches all the way to Shanghai and Vladivostok."[668] Both sides offered economic "association" deals designed to tie Ukraine to one of the two competing blocks. When President Viktor Yanukovich chose the Russian counteroffer to the negotiated agreement with the EU in November 2013, anti-government demonstrations led to a coup in February of 2014. It is clear that Washington backed the coup, and State Department official and CFR-connected Victoria Nuland and CFR member Senator John S. McCain both traveled to Kiev and participated in anti-government demonstrations. The new government in Kiev included Arseniy Yatsenyuk as its prime minister, a man evidently chosen by Nuland.[669] Yatsenyuk—who has been a speaker at both the CFR and at least one Trilateral Commission meeting—has extensive ties to Western corporations and institutions that are now penetrating Ukraine through his Open Ukraine Foundation, whose partners include NATO, the National Endowment for Democracy, U.S. State Department, the German Marshall Fund, and Chatham House. One of the corporations that "partners" with Yatsenyuk and his foundation is Horizon Capital, which promotes foreign investment in Ukraine. CFR member Jeffrey C. Neal is a founding partner of Horizon.[670] The new government in Kiev was not only pro-Western and anti-Russian, it also included at least four neo-fascists in high-ranking positions.[671] Responses to this right-wing coup included an armed rebellion by local people in the Crimea and eastern Ukraine, clearly encouraged and supported by Russia, including the use of Russian Special Forces. This resulted in a civil war between Kiev and its eastern provinces with dangerous implications for the future of peace in Europe due to the involvement of great powers on each side. Gradually escalating Western-imposed sanctions on Russia was another result, also undermining the globalized European economy.

The stakes in this conflict are especially high for Russia, since its people have suffered greatly in the past when several aggressors were able to invade their territory through Ukraine. Sergey Karaganov, a Russian who was a member of the Council's International Advisory Board from 1995 to 2005, highlighted the importance of this issue for Russia in an opinion piece in the *Financial Times*.[672] It is noteworthy that a Russian leader close to the CFR in the past, and who describes himself as a "Europhile," could strongly warn that the West's strategy of

sanctions . . . war of disinformation, and the reinvigoration of NATO as a military force . . . is a strategy that rests on misunderstanding and miscalculation. The misunderstanding is that this is, at root, a stand-off over Ukraine. To Russians, it is something far more important: a struggle to stop others [from] expanding their sphere of control into territories they believe are vital to Russia's survival. . . . Westerners need to understand how their governments made a potential foe out of what was once an aspiring ally. Russia will not yield. This has become a matter of our nation's life and death. A lasting peace in Europe is a noble aim. It can be achieved only through mutual respect and an accommodation of legitimate interests.[673]

This book was completed in early 2015, so the end results of these developments are unknown. But it is already clear that the CFR-led attempt to impose neoliberalism and Western geopolitical interests regarding Ukraine has helped create a serious and dangerous conflict between the West and Russia in the heart of Europe. Since both the Western allies and Russia possess nuclear weapons, some have compared the situation to the nuclear standoff during the 1962 Cuban missile crisis.[674] This conflict has also led to Russia strengthening its ties to China, which may have long-range implications for the geopolitics of the twenty-first century.

Capitalist Geopolitics as an Existential Threat to Humanity

The current geopolitical tussles between the West and Russia over Ukraine's future and the conflict between the United States and China in the Western Pacific are prime examples of the existential danger to humanity posed by today's imperial geopolitics. Each side is striving for military advantage, spending huge sums of money, and wasting resources that could and should be used for the advancement not the destruction of humanity. The current military strategies being followed by China and the United States in East Asia are instructive. China is focusing on developing an anti-naval surveillance and missile capability in order to attain greater maritime control in the Western Pacific through being able to attack American or other ships operating near its borders. At the same time, the United States is asserting its right to have its ships patrol near China, something many Chinese view as humiliating. The United States also has an alliance system with Japan and other nations in East Asia that are potentially in conflict with China over the seas and small islands in the area. Conflict could result in America being drawn into a war with China through these allies, similarly to the way the various parties to the First World War were drawn into war during 1914.

To counter the Chinese missile threat, the United States has developed the "AirSea Battle" concept. In the event of a conflict, America plans to attack Chinese surveillance and missile sites in depth through a massive bombing campaign. This is obviously a formula for rapid escalation, possibly preventing diplomatic intervention. The Chinese could quickly conclude that their nuclear weapons were at risk and decide that they must use or lose these weapons, possibly leading to an all-out nuclear war.[675] The results of such a war are impossible to fully foresee, but to use the word *catastrophic* for humans and the planet's larger ecological web of life would likely be an understatement.

THE COUNCIL AND ISRAEL

Many people within the U.S. foreign policy, military, and business communities, as well as critics who are outside these power structures, believe that the United States-Israel alliance mainly benefits Israel, contributing little or nothing to American national interests. They doubt the wisdom of the current close relationship. Leading policymakers at the CFR believe differently and have argued that Israel is a key strategic asset for the United States. This was the subject of a 2011 paper written by two CFR members, Robert D. Blackwill and Walter B. Slocombe. Blackwill had stints in government in the Department of State, as an adviser to George W. Bush, as a presidential envoy to Iraq, and as U.S. ambassador to India. He was also a counselor for the Council's studies program. Blackwill's service to the Bush administration in Iraq illustrates the high regard many have for him. He was reportedly brought into the administration in 2003–2004 to "take charge of" and "reshape" Iraq policy.[676] In 2013 Blackwill was the Henry A. Kissinger Senior Fellow for U.S. foreign policy at the CFR. Slocombe, who has been a CFR member for over thirty-five years, is a Washington lawyer who has a lengthy record of government service, especially in the Pentagon and also in Iraq in 2003.

Blackwill and Slocombe began their analysis with two concepts—that the United States and Israel share key values and that America has a moral responsibility to protect the Jewish state. The shared values include democratic norms, common roots in Judeo-Christian culture and civilization, and the right of all nations to live in security. They add U.S. national interests as a third leg:

> We believe that the United States and Israel have an impressive list of common national interests; that Israeli actions make substantial direct contributions to these U.S. interests; and that wise policymakers and people concerned with U.S. foreign policy, while never forgetting the irreplaceable values and moral responsibility dimensions of the bilateral relationship, should recognize the benefits Israel provides for U.S. national interests.[677]

Blackwill and Slocombe identify U.S. interests in the Middle East as including:

- ensuring the free flow of oil and gas at reasonable prices;
- opposing the spread of Iranian influence, including its partners;
- combating terrorism and the radical Islamist ideology from which it originated;
- preventing the proliferation of weapons of mass destruction, especially nuclear weapons;
- promoting an orderly process of democratic change and economic development in the region.

They then examine Israel's national interests, stating that "there is no other Middle East country whose definition of national interests is so closely aligned with that of the United States." Although they acknowledge disputes, Blackwill and Slocombe assert that more frequent have been instances "when the two sides have worked together successfully for over more than thirty years to achieve shared policy objectives, especially the series of peace treaties and agreements that have been an anchor of U.S. influence in the region."[678] The two authors also note that Israel continues to be helpful through joint training and the sharing of military experience, intelligence and counterintelligence, and military and security technology such as cyber defense. In any case, the authors argued that the United States "can have strong and productive relations with Arab and Muslim nations while sustaining its intimate collaboration with Israel," concluding their paper with recommendations on how to develop an even deeper level of cooperation.[679]

THE GLOBAL SOUTH

The great Latin American writer Eduardo Galeano pointed out that "in the outskirts of the world the system reveals its true face."[680] So it is with the Council's relationships with the global South, those who inhabit what President George W. Bush infamously and contemptuously called the "dark corners" of the world. A frequent theme of CFR writing on the global South has been racist at its core. They associate the South's realities—those of the "other"—with a lawless frontier land, a wild zone in an increasingly dangerous world, a situation caused, moreover, by the supposed inferiority of the peoples of the South. This analysis has been used to justify U.S. intervention supposedly to set things right, renewing colonial practices of domination through the use of violence, dispossession, and exploitation. This desire to intervene to dominate another society flows from a deeply rooted sense of superiority, exceptionalism, and mission, traceable to the Manifest Destiny concepts of the nineteenth century. The desire to intervene and transform is part of capitalism and the neoliberal ethos, and is directly related to the drive to exploit people and nature in order to accumulate capital. This makes the global South a geopolitical and geoeconomic space to be penetrated, conquered, restructured, and transformed. This results in the subversion of national sovereignty in many countries of the South.

Harvard professor and CFR member Samuel P. Huntington's work follows this theme: the world of the South lacks law and order and a future of "sheer chaos" is a possibility.[681] As we saw in chapter 5, Council Senior Fellow Max Boot's work expresses similar ideas. These and other analyses conveniently ignore the central historical role of Western colonialism and, more recently, the role of neoliberalism and geopolitical power struggles in weakening traditional economy, community, and society, as well as governments, helping to create "failed" states and opening the way to Western violence, dispossession, and exploitation of the peoples of the South.

One result of the long history of colonial exploitation, a legacy that has continued today with the current neoliberal and geopolitical domination of the global South, is the destitution of its people, who constitute the poorest one-third of the world's approximately seven billion people. Dickens-like poverty characterizes the lives of these two and a half billion people whose constant companions are low wages, hopeless debt, unemployment, lack of health care, dangerous working conditions, sickness, high infant morality, few educational opportunities, and early death. A few facts paint a damming picture of the world under the reign of neoliberal geopolitics today, a planet where vast numbers of people live in dire poverty and have no chance to develop their human potential:

- Over three billion people live on less than $2.50 a day, and 80 percent of the world's population lives on less than $10 a day.
- One billion children are living in poverty.
- Over 8 million children under the age of five die every year, more than a third of them due to malnutrition; about half are in South Asia, but the highest mortality rates are in Africa, where many countries have child mortality rates of between 20 and 30 percent.
- Worldwide, 842 million people do not have enough to eat.

Political, economic, and social democracy are lacking in any real sense, and rank-and-file attempts to change their situation by organizing unions or revolutionary parties and organizations are almost always met with violent repression, organized by local ruling classes in cooperation with the main imperial powers, led by the United States. The Council on Foreign Relations, as a main formulator of the strategic capitalist-class interests of the United States, which is carried into the government through multiple channels, has an important role in maintaining this system of violence, dispossession, and exploitation through military as well as economic and diplomatic means. Aspects of the use of military power in the global South include the increasing use of stealth elite units called Special Operations Forces, as well as drones to conduct clandestine and overt attacks. Examples of economic exploitation include genetically engineered agriculture, the plight of garment workers in Bangladesh, health care privatization in Malaysia and the Ebola crisis in West Africa. The policies of the CFR on these issues are discussed below.

The CFR and the Use of Special Operations Forces

The Council has close relationships with and strongly supports the American national security apparatus, the "deep state," playing a major strategic planning, directing, and supervising role through its members' commanding presence in the federal government, especially the Department of Defense, NSA, and CIA. CFR members like Janet Napolitano and Jeh Charles Johnson have also been prominent in the management of the Department of Homeland Security. Weapons manufacturers like Lockheed Martin, DynCorp International, Boeing, General Electric, Northrop Grumman, and Raytheon, as well as intelligence technology producers like Palantir Technologies, have all been corporate members of the Council.[682] These corporations also have many directors who are CFR members.

As part of its dialogue on the future of the deep state, in April 2013 the Council published its Special Report No. 66 by Linda Robinson on *The Future of U.S. Special Operations Forces*. Robinson is a Council member and well connected to the CFR and its network. In her career she has had appointments not only at the Council, where she was an Adjunct Senior Fellow for U.S. national security and foreign policy in 2011–12, but also at *Foreign Affairs* magazine, RAND corporation, the Wilson Center, Harvard University, International Institute for Strategic Studies, the Merrill Center for Strategic Studies at Johns Hopkins, and *U.S. News and World Report*.[683] With this kind of background, she was well qualified to accurately reflect the views of the capitalist class on this topic. To make sure she got everything right, she also had an advisory committee that reviewed the outline of her report at an early stage, as well as the draft report itself, offering "insightful comments that greatly improved the final product."[684] This advisory committee consisted of fourteen individuals, ten of them CFR members. Two others, Stephen D. Biddle and Max Boot, were Council Senior Fellows. The group was chaired by longtime CFR member James F. Dobbins, a former ambassador, an expert in nation-building, and the head of international security policy at RAND Corporation. In 2013 he was President Obama's special representative for Afghanistan and Pakistan. The committee also included an Army major general, a retired Air Force colonel, professors at the Naval War College and U.S. Military Academy, a former congressman, a foundation executive, and several individuals from other think tanks.

In her data-gathering phase, Robinson conducted over sixty interviews with military officers of the U.S. Joint Special Operations Command (which also supplied data for her report), congressional staff members, academic experts, and members of the U.S. government's interagency policy community. All subjects were granted anonymity to ensure frank and full responses. She was able to gather an impressive amount of information on the U.S. military's rapidly expanding special operations forces. Its over 66,500 personnel had been reorganized into one command in 1987 after the failed hostage rescue operation in Iran. Special Operations Forces are active in as many as a hundred countries in a given year, making them the U.S. military's elite and likely most important troops. [685] Their widespread use appears to be the wave of the future, as the United States looks for more ways to exert its power and control in a world bursting with revolt against the injustice and oppression characteristic of neoliberal corporate globalization.

Robinson's theoretical framework follows the U.S. military's own lexicon, which divides special operations into two distinct categories. The first approach is the *Direct Approach/Surgical Strike*. These are unilateral raids, mainly manhunting operations that aim to kill or capture individuals or destroy groups judged to be threats to the United States and its policies. Such raids often amounted to a "dozen or more a night" in recent years in Afghanistan and Iraq, making the total number of such raids at least in the multiple thousands in these two nations alone. The most famous of such operations was the assassination of Osama bin Laden in 2011. Robinson calls such operations a "global game of whack-a-mole" and critiques their "tactical and episodic" nature, preferring "deliberate campaigns that can achieve lasting outcomes." Robinson also wrote an op-ed piece in USA Today, April 8, 2013, titled "Special Ops Global Whack-a-Mole."[686]

The second method is Indirect Approach/Special Warfare. This is the policy that Robinson and the Council strongly argue for in this report. It encompasses a multiplicity of longer-term, complex political-military activities, including humanitarian work such as medical aid, building schools or drilling wells, combined with training, advising, and conducting joint military operations with armies, militias, tribes, police, and civil defense forces. The goal is both to physically destroy the opposition as well as shape and influence political environments and populations, countering longer-term threats to stability.

Robinson cites two examples of successes of the indirect approach/special warfare option. She states in her introduction that the "indirect approach has been successfully applied over the past decade in Colombia and the Philippines, where small numbers of army, navy, air force, and marine special operators have worked with indigenous counterparts to greatly diminish the threats to both countries, as part of a multifaceted country assistance program."[687] In the case of Colombia, Robinson is referring to the fact that in recent years the Colombian army, with a large amount of U.S. assistance, apparently including many special operations, has gone on the offensive against the left-wing guerrilla armies of the FARC (the Revolutionary Armed Forces of Colombia) and the ELN (the National Liberation Army). What she and CFR intellectuals generally fail to consider is the ocean of injustices that led the FARC and ELN to begin an armed rebellion in the first place. The vast repression by the Colombian oligarchy that led to this situation goes back for decades. During "La Violencia" of 1948–58, for example, an estimated 200,000–300,000 people were killed, with more than double that number wounded and over a million displaced. Much of this violence was organized and financed by large landowners and other members of the Colombian oligarchy to seize peasant lands and repress the people's aspirations for a more just society. When elections were eventually held, it became routine for center and left candidates to be assassinated by rightist death squads, and thousands of liberal and progressive candidates for public office were murdered. In 1990, for example, every single one of the center and left candidates for president of Colombia was assassinated. The results of such "elections" were obviously illegitimate. To a large extent, insurrectional warfare became the only means to defend oneself and express one's political goals. The correct approach, generally ignored by CFR intellectuals, is to demand and use U.S. power to enforce legitimate free elections under international supervision, not treat opponents as "terrorists."

In her study, Robinson put forth a typical set of recommendations:

- Increase the amount of resources going to the long-term direct approach/special warfare category of special operations.
- Create a unity of command for all operations whenever possible. She added that "this should become standard procedure in new theaters such as Yemen and Africa."
- Assure consistent long-term funding for special operations in a given country to achieve lasting effects over time.
- Encourage the conventional military to support the more agile, small-footprint special operations with airlift, aviation, logistics, intelligence, surveillance, and reconnaissance assistance.
- Produce strategic-minded leaders and a "doctrine for special operations that describes how special operations forces achieve decisive or enduring impact through the surgical application of force coupled with long-term campaigns . . . affecting the political level of war."[688]

Robinson concludes:

Enacting these changes will be difficult, not only because of bureaucratic inertia but also because there is such a limited view of what special operations forces are. They are the country's premier precision raiders, vital in meeting urgent contingencies as killing or capturing terrorists, rescuing hostages, and securing weapons of mass destruction. Those capabilities are essential and must be maintained. The recommendations here are additive, to raise the game of special forces in enabling and operating with partners in a range of political-military activities, and thereby improving other countries' means to secure themselves.[689]

The CFR's evaluation of and suggestions for improvement in U.S. special operations policies ignores the unknown but large number of innocent civilians killed or wounded in these undeclared wars by the deep state, as documented in various publications and in Jeremy Scahill's movie and book *Dirty Wars*. Clearly, treating a large part of the world as a battlefield and engaging in thousands of secret nighttime military attacks on as many as a hundred different nations in a given year (one of the informants in *Dirty Wars* says the number is "only" seventy-five nations) is an out-of-control, grossly abusive program in violation of international norms and law. These attacks, using drones and highly trained elite troops, amount to a program of launching death squads who work from a "kill list" that has targeted and killed even U.S. citizens without the pretense of due process. Robinson and her sponsor, the CFR, conclude that these activities are "essential" and "must be maintained." But those in the fields of fire of these activities are likely to increase their resistance to these violations of their humanity and national sovereignty and find supporters worldwide. This makes a future of endless war and the common ruination of the contending parties more likely.

The CFR and Drone Strikes

In 2003 the Pentagon had only fifty drone aircraft, by 2013 it had about 7,500.[690] During this period, but especially since 2009, when the Obama administration came into office, the JSOC, along with the CIA, have jointly operated a murderous program of drone strikes against targets in several third world nations as mentioned below. These attacks have killed thousands of people, some on "kill lists" of supposed terrorists personally vetted by President Obama, often based on questionable intelligence, and an unknown but large number of them completely innocent civilians. Estimates for Pakistan, Yemen, and Somalia by the Bureau of Investigative Journalism result in totals of 3,857 killed, 743 of them civilians. There are also other nations targeted for U.S. drone strikes, including Afghanistan, Iraq, Libya, and possibly the Philippines that are excluded from these totals.[691] Two key questions can be posed: even for those deemed terrorists by Obama and the U.S. government and on a "kill list," what legal or other right does Obama, and Bush II before him, to be judge, jury, and executioner of thousands of people, and are these actions "defensive measures," or are drone strikes simply terrorist attacks and war crimes via remote control?

In early 2013 the Council published a Center for Preventative Action report—funded by the Carnegie Corporation—recognizing some of the problematic aspects of drone warfare and calling for reforming this program in order to assure that it can be maintained in the face of mounting domestic and international criticism. The report's author, Micah Zenko, is the Douglas Dillon Fellow in the Center for Preventative Action at the CFR. He is also a veteran of Harvard's Kennedy School, the Brookings Institution, the Congresssional Research Service, and the Office of Policy Planning at the Department of State. He had the assistance of a twenty-one-member advisory committee—eleven of them Council staff or CFR members—that Zenko stated "was an invaluable resource" for the completion of his study. The twenty-one included eight university professors from leading universities (including Harvard, Georgetown, Virginia, and Cornell), three media leaders, two retired military officers, including Council member and retired general Stanley A. McChrystal, two from other key think tanks, and two lawyers from leading law firms (such as Arnold & Porter). Zenko conducted over sixty interviews "with current and former civilian and military officials from the U.S. government."[692]

Zenko and the CFR believe that drone strikes have two major risks that require reforms to resolve. First, domestic and international pressure could result in operational restrictions. In Zenko's words:

In the United States, the public and policymakers are increasingly uneasy with limited transparency for targeted killings. If the present trajectory continues, drones may share the fate of Bush-era enhanced interrogation techniques and warrentless wiretapping—the unpopularity and illegality of which eventually caused the policy's demise. Internationally, objections from host states and other counterterrorism partners could also severely circumscribe drones effectiveness. Host states have grown frustrated with U.S. drone policy, while opposition by nonhost partners could impose additional restrictions on the use of drones. Reforming U.S. drone strike policies can do much to allay concerns internationally by ensuring that targeted killings are defensible under international legal regimes.[693]

Second, drone use will likely spread, potentially creating an unmanageable situation with drones used irresponsibly—as if U.S. drone use has been somehow "responsible"—and on a much greater scale:

The second major risk is that of proliferation. Over the next decade, the U.S. near-monopoly on drone strikes will erode as more countries develop and hone this capability. . . . In this uncharted territory, U.S. policy provides a powerful precedent for other states and nonstate actors that will increasingly deploy drones with potentially dangerous ramifications. Reforming its practices could allow the United States to regain moral authority in dealings with other states and credibly engage with the international community to shape norms for responsible drone use.[694]

Therefore, Zenko and the Council issued a series of recommendations that needed to be implemented in order to be able to continue the advantages of drone strikes without negative consequences such as the possible long-term undermining of legal regimes, loss of state sovereignty for some nations and impunity for others:

The Obama administration can proactively shape U.S. and international use of armed drones in nonbattlefield settings through transparency, self-restraint, and engagement. . . . To better secure the ability to conduct drone strikes, and potentially influence how others will use armed drones in the future, the United States should undertake the following specific policy recommendations.

- Limit targeted killings to individuals who U.S. officials claim are being targeted . . . and bring drone strike practices in line with stated policies.
- Either end the practice of signature strikes or provide a public accounting of how it meets the principles of distinction and proportionality that the Obama administration claims.
- Review current policy whereby the executive authority for drone strikes is split between the CIA and JSOC, as each has vastly different legal authorities, degrees of permissible transparency, and oversight.
- Provide information to the public, Congress, and UN special rapporteurs . . . on what procedures exist to prevent harm to civilians.
- Never conduct nonbattlefield targeted killings without an accountable human being authorizing the strike.
- Congress . . . should demand regular White House briefings on drone strikes and how such operations are coordinated with broader foreign policy objectives
- Congress . . . should hold hearings . . . on the short- and long-term effects of U.S. targeted killings.
- Explicitly state which legal principles apply—and do not apply—to drone strikes and the procedural safeguards to ensure compliance to build broader international consensus.
- Begin discussions with emerging drone powers for a code of conduct to develop common principles for how armed drones should be used outside a state's territory, which would address issues such as sovereignty, proportionality, distinction, and appropriate legal framework.[695]

The text of the Zenko/CFR report and its recommendations help us answer the two questions posed above. First, in the text of the report, Zenko reveals that U.S. drones have reportedly targeted "on multiple occasions . . . children, individuals attempting to rescue drone strike victims and the funeral processions of deceased militants." The U.S. military also has a collateral damage estimate methodology for the death of innocent civilians. The CIA also employs this methodology, which is, tellingly, "known as the 'bug splat.'"[696] The use of such language to refer to the innocent people murdered by U.S. drones illustrates the level of depravity some U.S. officials have sunk to in recent years, and how people in the third world are routinely dehumanized so that the neoliberal geopolitical empire of exploitation, violence, and chaos can continue to operate.

Second, information in the text and the recommended reforms make it clear that the killing of thousands of people by drones has been out of control, is illegal, grossly immoral, and that such actions amount to war crimes by the Bush II and Obama administrations, crimes that Zenko and the Council want to be able to continue, although with some limited restrictions to try to prevent blowback and harm to long-term U.S. interests.

The CFR and Genetically Engineered Agriculture

Genetically engineered agriculture is a form of dispossession, since one of its key goals is to deny the world's farmers their right to freely produce and save the seeds they need to continue to farm. Instead, farmers are forced to purchase genetically modified seeds, which often have a built-in anti-life "terminator" gene that are put into the seeds by monopoly corporations like Monsanto and DuPont. This process undermines and destroys the use value of saved seeds, substituting profit-making exchange value instead. Genetically engineered agriculture also inserts pesticides into the seeds, so the resulting plants are resistant to both insect pests and large doses of poisons applied to kill surrounding weeds. Since these poisons are inside the plant itself, they cannot be washed off, and consumers, including humans, animals, and insects like bees ingest them.

Many governments and millions of people believe that the genetically modified organisms (GMOs) that result from this form of agriculture are unhealthy for human consumption. Attempts to require labeling so that people can make an informed choice have been fiercely resisted by Monsanto, Dupont, and other giant corporations profiting from genetically engineered agriculture. For example, a 2012 ballot proposition in California to require labeling was opposed by a $25 million blitz of advertising by Monsanto, DuPont, General Mills, Kraft Foods, Coca-Cola, Cargill, Con Agra, PepsiCo, Dow, Syngenta, Bayer, and other corporations, resulting in a victory for these corporations.[697] Coca-Cola and PepsiCo are corporate members of the CFR.[698]

In 2002 the Council published an almost fifty-page study titled *Sustaining a Revolution: A Policy Strategy for Crop Engineering* by David G. Victor and C. Ford Runge.[699] Victor was an Adjunct Senior Fellow in Science and Technology at the CFR, and Runge was a Council member and a professor at the University of Minnesota, heading up commodities and trade policy at its Center for International Food and Agricultural Policy. Although written by these two authors, the report was "based on cogent and careful deliberations of a Council on Foreign Relations Study Group."[700] Examining the extremely complex issues surrounding the manipulation of basic life forms like seeds as well as making recommendations for the future required a larger and more diverse study group than is usual for the CFR. This study group had sixty-two members. The largest sectors were CFR members and staff, followed by representatives from corporations, universities, nonprofits, government, foundations, and farmers. The biggest single bloc of individuals were from the biggest of the corporations, nonprofits, and universities directly involved in genetically engineered agriculture: DuPont, Monsanto, Bayer, Emergent Genetics, Cargill, Syngenta, the Council for Biotechnical Information, Rockefeller University, and the GIC Group, an agribusiness consulting firm. In sharp contrast, only one representative was from an organic farming advocacy body (Oregon Tilth). Finance capital was also well represented in this study group, with executives from JPMorgan Chase, Morgan Stanley, UBS Warburg, ATP Capital, and Cross Atlantic Partners. The U.S. government representatives were from the Department of Agriculture, the National Intelligence Council, Environmental Protection Agency, the Naval Academy, and the Department of Justice. A final significant sector of the study group had Minnesota connections, especially the University of Minnesota. David L. Aaron, a CFR member, Bilderberg Group participant, and former high government official (Deputy National Security adviser during the Carter administration), and employed in 2002 by the Minneapolis-based international law firm Dorsey & Whitney (whose clients include the food giant Cargill Corporation), chaired the study group. In sum, the study group was anchored by people from the CFR and corporations that were conducting genetic engineering for profit, together with individuals from finance and investment firms who are interested in guiding their investors to where capital can most rapidly accumulate as this field develops. Various helpers from the nonprofit, university, government, and foundation communities rounded out this group.

With the goal of formulating a long-term policy to sustain genetically engineered agriculture, and a study group heavily weighted toward support of crop engineering, it is no surprise that the CFR report completely endorses what the authors call an "agricultural revolution," arguing that significant benefits can be achieved with proper regulatory oversight, protection of the intellectual property created by innovators, and containment of international conflicts over engineered food.[701] These authors begin by stating that the period since the 1970s marked a watershed in the long history of agriculture, but unnamed "detractors" are contesting this "revolution":

An agricultural revolution is unfolding. For more than ten thousand years, farmers have improved crops by letting nature do the breeding. . . . Today, however, new techniques based on discoveries made in the 1970s but applied commercially in just the last decade make it possible to breed crops with much greater precision and power. The most controversial and pivotal of these techniques are "transgenic": they empower scientists themselves to actually engineer new crops by splicing together particular genes, rather than relying solely on the random and uncertain crosses that are the hallmark of traditional crop breeding. For some, the transgenic revolution is a horror. Tinkering with nature's order, these detractors argue, is human arrogance and will backfire when spliced genes disrupt the ecosystems on which life depends. For others, plant engineering is a Promethean step in a logical progression of crop breeding techniques. . . . Plant engineering can also make it possible to control crop diseases and pests with precision, reducing the need for the blanket-spraying of hazardous and costly pesticides and herbicides that has been the norm in industrial agriculture.

We side with the optimists but are concerned that today's debate over genetically engineered crops has drifted away from reality, driven by short-sighted tactics rather than strategic thinking. On the one side, some advocates of transgenics are so eager to see the method deployed that they pretend engineered crops are no different from earlier agricultural innovations; in fact, differences do exist, and some of them are substantial enough to require new types of regulatory oversight. On the other side meanwhile, a vocal minority of detractors has amplified risks in an all-out assault on the very concept of crop engineering.[702]

Key biotechnologies form the basis for genetically engineered agriculture, among them transgenic tools that allow the altering of the genetic code of plants, inserting genes that code for particular properties such as resistance to pests or to herbicides and pesticides, such as "Roundup Ready" soybean seeds. These tools can also be used to prevent saving of seeds by inserting terminator genes into the genes of some seeds, allowing corporations to assert exclusive rights to particular genes. The symbolism of using terminator genes to enhance capitalist profits and property rights over life forms is telling. It clearly illustrates the priorities involved in the entire genetic engineering project. Victor and Runge and their CFR study group favor the "intellectual property rights" that are created this way: "Governments have thus far resisted pressure to ban terminator technologies— and rightly so. . . . Our conclusion is that the fundamental elements of intellectual property policy are sound. The countries that are the major centers of innovation were right to extend patent protection to crops and other plants."[703] Victor and Runge, and behind them the CFR study group, do see some dangers however, centered on the lax regulatory systems in what they label "developing countries." They cite China as a key example:

After the United States, China is probably the second most active hub of innovation in crop engineering, yet, despite recent improvements, the Chinese system for overseeing field trials and approving novel crops is lax and opaque. This state of affairs poses dangers to all nations because some of the risks from improperly regulated biotechnology, such as gene flow, affect the entire world's heritage of biological diversity. The bigger danger, however, may be to public confidence. The entire industry of genetic engineering relies on the reputations that form around the technology. Real and prominent failures due to poor regulation will be extremely harmful.[704]

These two CFR authors correctly note that the activities of the biotech industry might threaten the biological diversity of our planet, a fact that should lead to a focus on how to end the entire genetic engineering project. But they do not come to this conclusion; instead, they see the bigger danger as a potential public loss of confidence, which might in some way lead to restrictions on this industry.

Victor and Runge also recognize that private sector solutions to the plight of the poorest people of the world are inadequate; they favor public investment that will preserve both market forces and private power:

Nor will private-market solutions solve the agricultural development problem. Two billion people dispersed over extremely large areas with very low purchasing power and few of the modern legal institutions necessary for encouraging private investment do not provide propitious conditions for a purely private-sector solution. Rather, the trick to solving these development problems is to find solutions that lift standards of living while not perpetuating dependence on public aid—i.e., public investment programs that do not extinguish the private sector.[705]

A final aspect of the dispossession characteristic of genetically engineered agriculture are the limitations put on national sovereignty by trade regimes like the World Trade Organization that are also managing trade in genetically modified food. Traditionally, trade rules were limited to non-discrimination and limits on tariffs and quotas. The WTO goes well beyond this tradition, however, in that it attempts to involve itself in domestic law and practice by applying trade law to production methods, including stopping nations from applying food safety standards for imported goods and preventing the labeling of GMOs for what they are. This CFR report argues that the best strategy to overcome European resistance to U.S. exports of GMO foods is to avoid a formal WTO trade dispute process, attempt to maintain dialogue, and work around existing conflicts. In their words: "In matters involving food safety, which often arouse strong public passions, a clear decision from the WTO does not guarantee compliance. Rather, it can often redouble public convictions that international institutions are stealing their sovereignty. Victories in WTO battles can lose the war. With bigger matters at stake—care is needed to skirt such land mines."[706]

This CFR report ends as follows: "We have argued that sustaining investment in crop engineering will require a complex array of policies. . . . A conscious and deliberate strategy, rather than a wistful hope for light at the end of the tunnel, is needed to carry this innovation toward its ultimate and promising future."[707]

The supposedly "promising future" touted by this Council report can already be seen in the plight of India's cotton farmers, almost all of whom are forced to purchase cotton seeds from Monsanto, which—and according to award-winning author and ecological activist Dr. Vandana Shiva—controls 95 percent of India's cotton seed supply. Bt cotton, a type of GMO seed, has become the "intellectual property" of Monsanto, which makes profits from its near monopoly. One of the members of this CFR study group, Monsanto's Judith A. Chambers, a vice president of the corporation, was involved in the expansion of Monsanto into India.[708] The high costs of seeds, chemicals, and pesticides to fight off the increased vulnerability to pests and disease created by cotton monocropping, has worsened an existing debt trap for Indian farmers. One result of this debt trap is increased farmer suicides in India, which, according to official statistics from India's National Crime Records Bureau, saw the tragic number of more than 199,000 farmer suicides in the 1997–2008 period. The documentary film *Bitter Seeds* tells the story of Monsanto's central role in this massive wave of farmer suicides in India. The causes of farmer suicides is undoubtedly complex, but two official Indian research organizations, the Indian Council of Agricultural Research and the Central Cotton Research Institute, issued an advisory in 2012 stating that "cotton farmers are in a deep crisis since shifting to Bt cotton. The spate of farmer suicides in 2011–2012 has been particularly severe among Bt cotton farmers."[709]

The systemic pesticides, such as neonicotinoids, produced by Monsanto and other genetic engineering corporations and spread onto farms worldwide have also been directly linked to Colony Collapse Disorder in bees, threatening this key pollinator of many crops, thus endangering global agriculture.

The larger issues involved with the genetic engineering of agriculture are the complete subjugation of nature to human needs and will; increased pesticide use; the largely uncontrolled altering of the reproductive capacities of entire species of plants; and the seeds of life coming under the private ownership of giant monopoly corporations whose central goal is increased accumulation of capital. As seen in India and with bees, this is the road to dispossession, disempowerment, and death, and must be opposed with all the power of global people's movements. The clear alternative is smaller-scale, democratically organized organic agriculture, proved to increase crop yields through education, improving soil fertility, maintaining beneficial habitats and insects, composting, intercropping, and crop rotation. This is the way forward for humanity, ditching corporate-controlled large-scale pesticide and GMO habits in favor of this healthy alternative.

Neoliberal Exploitation: Garment Workers in Bangladesh

Neoliberalism, like its direct ancestor, competitive capitalism, causes a race to the bottom in pay and working conditions for hundreds of millions of workers in the global South, with similar conditions being gradually imposed on workers worldwide. This results in the gradual imposition of a system of generalized economic apartheid, in which the inequality of wealth, income, and power is extreme. The ruthless exploitation of garment workers, the great majority of them women, in Bangladesh is one example of neoliberalism at work. Bangladesh is an "export powerhouse," with "Made in Bangladesh" labels commonplace in many U.S. and European stores.[710] Bangladesh apparel exports are based on foreign investment, ultra-cheap labor, and a neoliberal "investment-friendly" government at the service of foreign and domestic bosses. The result is horrible conditions similar to those in the early Industrial Revolution, and Bangladesh has been called the "most dangerous place in the world" for garment workers. Over three and a half million workers work ten to fifteen hours a day, six days a week, for a minimum wage of $37/month (about $1.25/day), in often dangerous working conditions, and severe repression of any attempt to organize the workforce to promote the interests of the rank and file.[711] Special government paramilitary police, called the "Rapid Action Battalion," together with intelligence agencies like the National Police Intelligence Service, closely watch industrial areas and workers who try to organize. Numerous instances of threats, beatings, firings, and blacklistings, as well as cases of torture and murders of worker-organizers, amounting to corporate-inspired terrorism, have been documented. The case of worker-organizer Aminul Islam, once a worker at the Shasha denim garment factory, who was first arrested and tortured by the National Police Intelligence Service in 2010, then was found murdered in April 2012, surely because he was an organizer, is one such example. Another danger faced by the workers is building collapse or fire in their workplaces, which are often unsafe and have locked doors with no emergency exits. In late November 2012 a fire in a factory producing clothing for Walmart, Disney, Sears, and others killed 112 workers.[712] In April 2013 at least 1,127 workers died in the collapse of an unsafe building.[713] Such incidents are a form of industrial homicide, one product of a system of production that puts profit first, above the lives of the workers who produce the profit. The neoliberal mantra of suppression of the right to organize strong and democratic unions, which could demand appropriate safety measures, thus has deadly consequences. The *New York Times* reported that Walmart, an anti-union corporation, was directly responsible for blocking a 2011 effort to improve fire safety in Bangladesh, its representative arguing that it was not "financially feasible" to do so.[714] This from a corporation owned by a U.S. family whose net worth is over $100 billion. Walmart is a corporate member of the Council.[715]

Following the cheating of workers out of some of their already minuscule wages, the workers protested in March 2012. In response, the special police fired rubber bullets at the workers and beat them with cane poles, knocking some unconscious. Returning to work afterward, one seamstress who had been beaten unconscious said that she had no choice but to return, as she was her family's only breadwinner. "I am helpless," she cried, "We have to get food."[716] Meanwhile, U.S. and European shoppers at stores like Walmart, Sears, Disney, The Gap, Target, J.C. Penney, Kohl's, Levi Strauss, and Carrefour purchase Tommy Hilfiger, Calvin Klein, Nike, Puma, Adidas, H&M clothing and other products, commodities whose production history is steeped in the exploitation and repression of workers half a world away.[717] Many commodities, especially clothes made in Bangladesh, have relationships of power and violence hidden in them; if these commodities could talk, what tales of exploitation, terror, and oppression they could tell.

As could be expected, the CFR has not only played a key role in creating the overall system of neoliberal exploitation; a number of its members also have a direct role in implementing the system in Bangladesh. The Tommy Hilfiger and Calvin Klein product lines, produced in Bangladesh and exported to the United States, are owned by PVH Corporation, one of whose current (2012) directors is longtime (over twenty years) CFR member Rita M. Rodriguez.[718] In 2010 Rodriguez was also a Visiting Fellow at the Peterson Institute for International Economics, indicating that her CFR ties are close. She is a Cuban-born immigrant, an expert in international finance, a former professor at the University of Illinois and Harvard University, who was appointed to the Board of Directors of the Export-Import Bank by President Reagan in 1982. Both presidents Bush I and Clinton reappointed her to this board, making her one of its longest-serving members ever (1982–1999). Interestingly, she currently also co-directs a program at Georgetown University called the Woodstock Theological Center's Global Economy and Cultures Project, and is on the advisory board of Woodstock's "Arrupe Program in Social Ethics for Business." This is yet another example of the deep corruption of religion and business "ethics" during our current neoliberal era.

Other direct CFR connections to the exploitation of these garment workers include Disney, Target, and Levi Strauss, all of which sell clothes made in Bangladesh.[719] Three of Disney's ten 2012 governing board members. John S. Chen, Monica C. Lozano, and Sheryl K. Sandberg; two of Target's board, James A. Johnson and Anne M. Mulcahy; and Robert D. Hass, a board member and part of the owning family of Levi Strauss, are all members of the Council.[720]

Following the horrific garment factory collapse and massive loss of life of April 2013, Western firms were pressured to improve safety conditions. Some U.S. firms, including Walmart, refused to sign on to a stronger safety plan that required independent safety inspections of factories. Instead, they signed on to an initiative launched by a Washington nonprofit called the Bipartisan Policy Center (BPC) to develop a weaker plan, an effort that was immediately called a sham by labor advocates. Six of the sixteen directors of the Bipartisan Policy Center are Council members, and the two individuals most directly involved in developing a Walmart-inspired plan for Bangladesh—former U.S. senators George J. Mitchell and Olympia J. Snowe, are both CFR members, and Mitchell is also a former Council director.[721] In August 2013 the BPC organized the "Alliance for Bangladesh Worker Safety," with the founding members all North American apparel companies and retailers, and a nine-person board of directors headed by CFR member and former congresswoman Ellen O. Tauscher. While Walmart, Target, the Gap, VF Brands, and the Bangladesh Garment Manufacturing and Exporters Association all have representatives on the so-called Alliance for Bangladesh Worker Safety, there is not one workers' representative. This fact exposes this group and its plan as a clever attempt to fool people into thinking something is being done to improve safety and conditions, as pointed out by Scott Nova, executive director at the Worker Rights Consortium. Nova said that the Alliance's program is "no different than what companies have been doing without success for decades."[722]

The CFR and Privatization of Health Care in Malaysia

In 1988 the CFR published, as a Council on Foreign Relations book, *The Promise of Privatization: A Challenge for U.S. Policy*, edited by Council member, Harvard professor, and World Bank consultant Raymond Vernon. To explore the issue of privatization of state-owned enterprises, which aims at expanding private capital accumulation through transfer of public sector assets and functions to the private, for-profit capitalist sector, the CFR assembled a large study group consisting of Vernon as chair, two co-directors, and sixty-three members. Not surprisingly, one conclusion was that the U.S. government was a strong supporter of privatization, pointing out that in 1986 Reagan's Agency for International Development ordered "each of its overseas missions to generate at least two privatization projects in the succeeding year."[723] Vernon's book paints a more subtle picture of the role of the IMF and World Bank, stating on the one hand that "the 1980s may well go down as a decade-long open season for assaults on state-owned enterprises in developing countries. Both the World Bank and the IMF have made a contribution to these assaults." On the other hand, the book points out that generally the bank's structural adjustment loan programs pushed privatization only as part of a package of market-oriented "reforms aimed at steering borrowing members toward more open and liberal economic policies."[724] In the case of poorer nations, pushing and demanding was substituted for "steering" such nations:

The data also suggest an unevenness of attention to privatization in World Bank lending programs. . . . If the Bank's record is a reliable indicator, the ability of international institutions to push privatization increases with the borrower's level of desperation. The experiences of Togo and Guinea suggest the lengths to which international agencies can go in bringing influence to bear on poorer countries.[725]

As could be expected, corporations close to the CFR are also mentioned as benefiting from specific instances of privatization. In June 1985, for example, Morgan Guaranty Trust (now part of JPMorgan Chase) was awarded a contract by the Turkish government. This contract, paid for by a loan from the World Bank, was to prepare a document titled "Privatization Master Plan" that laid out a set of recommendations on what should be privatized and how to do it.[726]

With privatization firmly established as key part of the CFR's neoliberal world order, many Council members aggressively began to push for openings that would benefit them financially. For example, in the 1995 CFR *Annual Report*, Council member Virginia A. Kamsky, president of Kamsky Associates, a consultancy specializing on Asia, wrote about how the CFR meetings program helped her connect with a powerful leader to open doors for privatization of kidney dialysis in Malaysia:

I met the prime minister of Malaysia, Mohamad Mahathir, at the Council. We . . . started talking about . . . how in Malaysia they'd decided to attempt privatization in select sectors, starting with cardiac care. Then about two years ago, I was asked by a company to assist with building kidney dialysis clinics throughout Asia. The company wanted to start in Malaysia, but had been told by the Ministry of Public Health that there was no privatization in Malaysia. But I knew there was. Coincidentally, I got an invitation to a Council lunch for Mahathir two weeks later. I reminded him that we'd met before, and he remembered our conversation. I told him I'd been working throughout Asia in kidney dialysis, and asked if Malaysia might consider dialysis privatization. He told me to talk to his people at the embassy. Now I'm working on a project—privatization of kidney dialysis throughout Malaysia. It's not a done deal yet, but Mahathir said to me, "I like the idea, why don't you come, and I'll set up meetings for you." And he did. I've been to Malaysia since that lunch seven or eight times on this one project. All that came out of a lunch at the Council. And the prime minister has taken a personal interest in our efforts.[727]

The privatization of any aspect of health care, especially in a relatively poor nation, is inherently pernicious because health care as a private, capital-accumulating industry will inevitably strive to achieve maximum profits and long-term growth, whatever the cost to the population. This contradicts the true proper role of the state in providing for the welfare of all the people and the promotion of an equitable distribution of benefits within public budgetary constraints. The capitalist social forces dominant at the CFR, represented in this case by Ms. Kamsky, naturally want to expand their possibilities of accumulation by making private and more costly what had formerly been a public service. What in fact happened in Malaysia was the spread of private clinics to supply dialysis machines and treatment to deal with a steady rise in end-stage kidney failure, at least partly due to a lack of proper diet and exercise. By 2005 almost a third of dialysis in Malaysia took place in expensive private clinics. But since most people in need could not afford the high cost, the government and private non-government charity organizations had to step in to prevent large numbers of people from dying due to lack of treatment, and these two together still provided about two-thirds of the treatment in Malaysia as of 2005. The privatization of dialysis in Malaysia had apparently only succeeded in increasing the profits of Ms. Kamsky and other foreign capitalist investors, and did not improve the health of the people or reduce the need for government spending on dialysis.

The Council's Neoliberal System and Ebola in Liberia

The CFR-promoted system of capitalist neoliberal geopolitics has helped create a threat to humanity in the form of the Ebola pandemic coming out of West Africa, with Liberia the hardest hit. In 2012, Council member Richard Downie, on the staff of the CFR-connected Center for Strategic and International Studies, wrote a study outlining how to rebuild Liberia's health care system, which had been seriously impacted by the civil wars there during the 1989–2003 years.[728] In his study, *The Road to Recovery: Rebuilding Liberia's Health System*, Downie offers a number of recommendations, among them:

> . . . engage the private sector more effectively. The United States should come up with creative ways of involving the private sector more fully in Liberia's health system. . . . The private for-profit health care sector is growing in Liberia and should be harnessed. USAID is in the early stages of engaging with this sector . . . using private companies . . . to deliver therapy treatments for malaria patients.[729]

This typically neoliberal prescription of privatization puts the private interests of wealthy investors above the public interests of those who are sick and cannot afford to pay high prices for health care. It also illustrates how this system deliberately weakens the states as well as unions of workers in the impoverished and formerly colonized nations of the global South in order to increase the relative power of multinational corporations and the nation-states of the global North. These weak states are forced to open up their economies, cut public services, including expenditures on public health, in order to qualify for IMF, World Bank, and other loans. They must also privatize such public services to allow wealthy foreign investors to buy up public assets in order to profit and accumulate capital as well as wipe out unions to create a typical neoliberal goal: a "favorable investment climate." As poverty becomes rampant, people rely more on unconventional sources of food, such as wild animals, "bush meat," whose consumption can result in the infection and spread of viruses such as Ebola. This combination of lack of an adequate public health infrastructure and poor people without unions to protect their rights at work, lacking proper sanitation, and eating bush meat, leaves these nations, especially in Africa, vulnerable to deadly outbreaks such as the Ebola epidemic in West Africa during the summer and fall of 2014. The Director General of the World Health Organization, Dr. Margaret Chan, stated in October 2014 that this developing crisis was not only a vast human tragedy, but was "unquestionably the most severe acute public health emergency in modern times . . . a crisis for international peace and security" due to potential state failure, putting the population of large parts of the world at risk.[730]

When this outbreak began, the entire nation of Liberia, a nation settled during the nineteenth century by ex-slaves from the United States, reportedly had only fifty-one doctors for a nation of about four million people. More Liberian doctors were working in the United States than in their home country. About 25 percent of the nation's grossly inadequate health facilities were already owned by the private sector, organized to serve the relatively well-off population. As this is written in October of 2014 Liberia has been hit hardest by Ebola, with thousands dead, the health system overwhelmed, and the virus spreading rapidly and likely out of control. Some people do survive this infection but the mortality rate is as high as 70 percent. The lack of an adequate public health infrastructure due to the weakness of small states in the CFR-inspired neoliberal geopolitical world order is imposing a very steep cost in Liberia, Sierra Leone, and Guinea in West Africa, with the possibility of a regional and even global spread of this disease with potentially catastrophic consequences. Despite the fact that the Ebola virus has been known for decades, no preventative or curative vaccine has ever been developed because the profit-seeking big pharmaceutical companies of the North decided that the people who needed such a vaccine were too poor to pay for it, so they would have to go without. This is yet another example of the moral bankruptcy, irrationality, and inhumanity of the neoliberal geopolitical "free market" capitalist system, where poor people are condemned to die because they cannot pay the lords of the world as much as they demand. The United States and the rest of the world's most powerful governments apparently cannot fully recognize that in our interconnected neoliberal geopolitical world all are potentially vulnerable to pandemic viruses, and "broken health care systems" need to be repaired on an urgent basis.[731] Tellingly, it was only the small country of Cuba, upholding the ideals of socialism, that sent hundreds of volunteer doctors to West African nations to couragously try to contain the spread of the epidemic, something that the *New York Times* called "impressive . . . it should be lauded and emulated."[732]

8

FIDDLING WHILE THE EARTH SLOWLY BURNS: THE COUNCIL AND THE ECOLOGICAL CRISIS, 1990–2014

You are lost if you forget that the fruits of the earth belong to all and the earth to no one.

—JEAN-JACQUES ROUSSEAU

We're finally going to get the bill for the Industrial Age. If the projections are right, its going to be a big one: the ecological collapse of the planet.

—JEREMY RIFKIN

We could have saved the earth but we were too damned cheap.

—KURT VONNEGUT, JR.

One of the central contradictions of the current capitalist neoliberal geopolitical system is the global ecological crisis, an ongoing and still maturing critical situation for humanity and other life-forms. As is the case with so many issues, the Council on Foreign Relations has worked hard to define the issues and set the climate of opinion on at least one aspect of this crisis, climate change. The CFR, like the broader capitalist class, does not want to view the global ecological crisis holistically, because that would suggest that a holistic solution is called for. Rather, a piecemeal approach is preferred, so that the entire system of capitalist neoliberal geopolitics is not called into question. Since 1990 the Council has organized a number of study and discussion groups devoted to this topic, but they have not successfully found the market-based solutions they have been seeking. Their efforts amount to a kind of denial of the seriousness of this issue.

At the beginning of the era that is the focus of this book, 1976, the carbon dioxide level in the earth's atmosphere was about 330 parts per million. In 2013 this level had reached about 400 ppm. In 1990, a little less then halfway through this period, the Council on Foreign Relations published a book titled *Sea Changes: American Foreign Policy in a World Transformed,* edited by CFR Vice President and Director of Studies Nicholas X. Rizopoulos.[733] Council chairman Peter G. Peterson wrote the foreword, and eleven of the sixteen authors responsible for chapters in the book were CFR members.[734] The book, suggested and funded by Peterson himself, focused mainly on providing an interpretation of the origins and long-term meaning of the stunning transformations that took place in 1989–90, when the Soviet Union collapsed, Germany was reuniting, South Africa's apartheid system was falling, and the Sandinistas were ousted from power in Nicaragua. But Peterson in his introduction and two authors in the text of the book also identified ecological-environmental concerns as part of what Peterson called "the new global issues" of what was seen as a more internationalist future.[735] This review of capitalism and the ecological crisis as of 1990 was a landmark since it put the U.S. capitalist class and the Council itself on notice that this topic was a serious one and needed to be put on the agenda for policy decision and implementation.

The two authors that had important sections in this CFR book on ecological issues were Robert L. Heilbroner and Roger D. Stone. Historical economist Heilbroner was a CFR member in 1974 but had dropped out by 1975.[736] In *Sea Changes,* he pointed out the "looming confrontation of capitalist dynamics with the limits of ecological tolerance," arguing:

> The magnitude, irreversibility, and potentially disastrous aspects of this challenge are by now familiar. In broad outline, the challenge emerges from a perceptive rise in global mean temperatures of between 1.5 and 4.5 degrees Celsius over the next half-century. This rise is mainly the consequence of the steady addition of carbon dioxide to the ecosphere, where it catalyzes the atmosphere into a "greenhouse" that traps heat. There is disagreement as to the expected magnitude or speed of arrival of the greenhouse effect, but not as to its ultimate seriousness. If the present rate of increase of carbon emissions is not reduced, the effect could assume life-threatening proportions. . . . The supreme challenge . . . concerns the rate at which we can reduce the carbon emissions at the center of the heat problem. That reduction, in turn, can be attained only by large-scale abandonment of fossil fuels . . . the use of gas, oil, and coal must be gradually, but in the end drastically, curtailed. . . . Such a reduction would threaten the

historic thrust of all modern socioeconomic orders, and of capitalism in particular. . . . Solar and geothermal . . . adjustments are unquestionably within the existing technical capacity of modern society. . . . The challenge is whether capitalist societies will develop the political will to make them. Here the obstacles derive in part from adversely affected business interests, and in part from the resistance of the consuming public itself. It would be foolhardy to underrate the power of these counterforces.

Even this, however, is not a full measure of the difficulty of the problem. . . . It is the nature of the ecological threat that it respects no national boundaries. The greenhouse effect must be tamed for the entire world or for none of it. All advanced capitalisms must therefore bring the heat problem under control together, for the Western nations are responsible for 75 percent of all carbon emissions . . . the industrial (capitalist) West must shift to a pollution-free energy technology. Such a shift may be triggered by limited disasters, but its actual implementation will require a very large degree of government intervention. . . . The guidance of economic activity by considerations of profit alone becomes too hazardous to allow. . . . The allocational role accorded to the market is certain to be drastically reduced. . . . The radical changes in the world's social and natural environment imply radical changes in the setting within which economic activity must be carried on. Can capitalism absorb such drastic institutional restructurings?[737]

In effect, Heilbroner was questioning the very future of capitalism, and arguing that in order to save humanity and the planet the entire neoliberal capitalist free market project must give way to a "very large degree" of state influence.

Roger D. Stone, who was both the Whitney H. Shepardson Council Fellow and a CFR member, also had a chapter on the looming environmental crisis.[738] Stone quoted a 1989 World Bank study that referred to the global warming situation as "potentially catastrophic" because of the cumulative and irreversible effects of loading the atmosphere with carbon dioxide.[739] But in his article "A Look at the Environmental Crisis," Stone also recognized that atmospheric pollution was only part of a much larger problem:

The multiple environmental pressures on the surface of the planet constitute a crisis. Desertification worldwide proceeds at the rate of an Ireland (6 million hectares) a year, with devastating consequences for affected farmers and pastoralists. While human populations and food security problems grow rapidly, soil erosion and depletion are causing rain-fed croplands to become ever less productive. Tropical deforestation has reached the point where many once heavily wooded countries (the Philippines, for example) have practically no forest left. The assault is not only causing accelerating losses in biological diversity but also weakening already fragile economies. . . . A senior World Bank economist attributes 25,000 deaths a day to the direct and indirect effects of water shortages (caused largely by deforestation) and acute water pollution. The increasing scarcity of fuelwood affects 1.5 billion people. While 2 billion people depend on seafood as their principal source of protein, severe downturns have occurred in many inshore fisheries. Oil spills, toxic pollution from agricultural chemicals or poorly managed waste disposal, industrial disasters such as Bhopal and Chernobyl, the environmental tragedy of Eastern Europe—all form part of the deepening imprint of human misuse upon the earth's surface.[740]

THE FIRST VICTOR STUDY GROUP, 1998–2001

Despite the strong statements of Heilbroner and Stone about the looming planetary emergency in 1990, a review of CFR *Annual Reports* and publications from the early and mid-1990s indicates that their warnings were ignored. There were no study groups or publications on the topic until 1998. This could be because, as Heilbroner pointed out, solving the ecological crisis meant questioning the future use of fossil fuels and capitalism itself, something the Council and its leadership clearly did not want to face. Finally, in January of 1998, David G. Victor was hired for the CFR staff as the "Robert W. Johnson Jr. Fellow in Science and Technology." That same year he became project director for a study group whose focus was not to look at changing socioeconomic structures and arrangements, but rather to look for technological solutions, having as a goal to "examine policies that could reduce global warming by spurring the development of new technologies."[741] The study group was further described as follows in the 1998 CFR *Annual Report*:

With U.S. industry accounting for one-fifth of annual global emissions of 22 billion tons of carbon dioxide—the leading cause of global warming—this study group is exploring U.S. policies that directly target the development and deployment of less carbon-intensive energy technologies. Since cutting emissions will require massive technological change toward clean, carbon-free fuels, the group set its sights on long-term technological solutions for the United States and other industrial countries as well as the developing world. Products will include an options paper for U.S. policy as well as a detailed monograph.[742]

The focus of the Victor study group illustrated that the CFR's initial organizational response to the larger ecological crisis focused more narrowly on global warming and the search for technological rather than the necessary socioeconomic transformation of capitalism. The capitalist drive for constant growth and accumulation on a finite planet, an important part of this drive involving the massive burning of fossil fuels, was ignored in favor of the search for potential technological fixes. This conclusion is reinforced by the choice of the chair for the Victor study group as well as the book that resulted from Victor and the group's efforts. The chair was Rodney W. Nichols, then president and CEO of the New York Academy of Scientists.[743] A Council member, Nichols had spent much of his career with Rockefeller University, as a vice president and on the university council's board. Nichols has also served on the boards of the Federation of American Scientists and the conservative Manhattan Institute. More important, Nichols was a consultant to Shell Technology Ventures, a subsidiary of CFR corporate member Shell Oil Company, one of the major oil multinationals. On its website, Shell Technology Ventures states that it "invests in companies across the energy sector to speed up the development and deployment of new technologies which complement our business." Thus the study group's search for new technologies, supposedly to reduce planet-threatening global warming, was complementary to the search for additional profit/accumulation opportunities for monopoly corporations like Shell Oil.

The CFR and Princeton University Press published Victor's book, *The Collapse of the Kyoto Protocol and the Struggle to Slow Global Warming*, in 2001.[744] In it, Victor offers little in the way of technological fixes, instead focusing on what he views as the inevitable failure of the 1997 accords on reducing global warming: "As the aggrieved and inconvenienced exit, the trading system will unravel." He reaffirmed the decision by the Clinton and Bush II administrations not to join the Kyoto Protocol, stressing that the way forward involved "channeling market forces toward sensible projects."[745] Victor elaborated as follows:

> Pressure for new thinking must begin with the United States government, which largely created the conventional wisdom that pure textbook emission trading is the best approach and has been the single most influential country in the negotiations to create global warming agreements. The United States has rightly held firm in requiring the use of market-based mechanisms to ensure that abatement of greenhouse gases is cost effective. Wrongly, it has advocated trading as the only market-based approach.[746]

Victor's solution, as of 2001, was a hybrid system—join emissions trading with emission taxes to gain the best of both market-based schemes. Adaptation to some of the effects of global warming—flooding from storm surges and higher sea levels—and, of course, investments in "geoengineering," such as mirrors in space to reflect sunlight, are also mentioned in the Victor book.[747]

THE SECOND VICTOR STUDY GROUP, 2004

The second Council study group on this topic, resulting in a 2004 report, *Climate Change: Debating America's Policy Options,* also authored by David G. Victor, was in the form of a Council Policy Initiative. The CFR organizes this type of study group when an important issue exists, but it seems unlikely that clashing views within the CFR and U.S. power structure generally can by compromised enough to reach a consensus. Therefore, alternatives are presented both in order to set the framework and agenda for future policymaking and encourage debate with the parameters—the "range of options"—set by the Council. In his foreword to the report, CFR president Richard N. Haass outlined the problems:

> Climate change is among the most complex problems on the foreign policy agenda. Even with a mounting consensus that humans are causing a change in the world's climate, experts are divided on the severity of the problem and the necessity and nature of policy responses. Practically any course of action implies that today's societies will incur costs as they deviate from the status quo, and any benefits of their efforts will accrue mainly in the distant future. Such intergenerational bargains are always hard to strike.
>
> Compounding the difficulty is the reality that this problem is truly global in scope. A few nations—led by the United States, which is responsible for one-quarter of the effluent that is linked to global warming—account for most emissions. Yet in a global economy some measure of global coordination will be required to ensure that some do not ride free on the efforts of others. This issue thus involves all the factors that make it hard to construct successful foreign policy: highly complex yet uncertain scientific knowledge, widely diverging interests, and the need for effective international arrangements.
>
> In the United States, climate change has become a lightning rod. On one side is a sizable minority that dismisses most or all of the science. There are as well those who view the threats of climate change with such seriousness that nothing less is required than a prompt and complete reorganization of the modern industrial economy—away from the use of fossil fuels . . . and toward some alternative energy future. Bridging this divide will likely prove impossible, and generating a middle position that a credible majority supports will take considerable time. Yet the longer we wait, the more urgent the issue becomes as the concentrations of so-called greenhouse gases build in the atmosphere.
>
> Ever since withdrawing from the Kyoto Protocol in 2001, the United States has incurred widespread criticism for its stance on climate change. But what should guide the federal and state governments as they struggle to

craft practical policies on this issue? This is a question more easily asked than answered. As a result, the Council has chosen to tackle this issue by sponsoring a Council Policy Initiative (CPI) rather than seek an unlikely consensus on this highly divisive question.[748]

The 2004 group, called an Advisory Committee (AC), consisted of fourteen members, only two of them CFR members. One of these was, however, Council vice president and director of studies James M. Lindsay. Lindsay had previously worked on the staff of the National Security Council as well as at Brookings. In 2008 he was a principal author of a Department of Defense–funded multimillion-dollar project (part of its Minerva Research Initiative) to study "Climate Change, State Stability and Political Risk in Africa."

Seven of the fourteen AC members were corporate-connected, either in terms of their career history, or latest occupation. Two of these were oil company representatives, from the very largest corporations, Walter F. Buchholtz of ExxonMobil and Chris Mottershead of British Petroleum. Another individual, Connie Holmes, was from the National Mining Association, representing, among others, the U.S. coal mining industry. Also representing corporate interests was Dale E. Heydlauff, senior vice president for environmental affairs for the American Electric Power Service Corporation. This corporation was, in the early twenty-first century, the largest consumer of coal and the third-largest consumer of natural gas in the United States, and one of the largest emitters of CO_2 in the nation. Another AC member, Diane Wittenberg, spent much of her career as an employee of Edison Electric, an industry representative for many electric utility coal users. The final two corporate-connected individuals were Jacques DuBois from Swiss RE, the 150-year-old giant multinational re-insurance company, and Dan Reicher of New Energy Capital, a recently established consultancy promoting and attempting to profit from "green capitalism."

The remaining half of the study group members represented an assortment of corporate-connected nonprofits, David Hawkins from the Natural Resources Defense Council and Paul Portney of Resources for the Future, and university professors specializing in environmental issues like the environment and free trade, climatology, carbon capture, and geoengineering—Jeffrey A. Frankel of Harvard, Stephen H. Schneider from Stanford, and M. Granger Morgan of Carnegie Mellon.

Additional details on several of these study group members are useful for understanding its final report. Particularly important was the presence of the ExxonMobil representative Walter F. Buchholtz, who was a longtime lobbyist for Big Oil's biggest player. Many years before, and a few years after this period, Council corporate member ExxonMobil, with chair and CEO Lee Raymond, a CFR member, leading the way, was a prime supporter of climate skepticism. Recognizing the reality of climate change and the need to cut CO_2 emissions would obviously affect ExxonMobil, since its profits largely depend upon burning the products it produces, resulting in the pumping of tens of millions of tons of CO_2 into the environment. So its own economic self-interest, including hundreds of billions of investments and annual income, involved denying the need to put any limits on the use of fossil fuels.[749] So ExxonMobil donated at least $730,000 to and dispatched its lobbyist Buchholtz to become an adviser and board member for the Heartland Institute, a free-market think tank. In May of 2012 *The Economist* called Heartland "the world's most prominent think tank promoting skepticism about man-made climate change."[750] ExxonMobil's most recent biographer pointed out that the corporation was "more aggressive than all but a handful of peer companies" in supporting "fringe activists," arguing that the resulting cooking of science about climate change amounted to "disinformation."[751]

British Petroleum, represented on the study group by Chris Mottershead, a thirty-year veteran of the company that is also a corporate member of the CFR, had a slightly better position on these issues, but not a fundamentally different one than ExxonMobil. BP's "beyond petroleum" mantra was simply a public relations gambit, and its actual investments in renewable and alternative energy systems were minuscule.[752]

The inclusion on the AC of representatives from the largest of producers and consumers of coal in the form of the National Mining Association and American Electric Power is also telling. This was recognition that the U.S. government and investors in the coal industry hold an estimated $30 trillion worth of coal, by far the largest and most valuable supply of any nation on earth. Downgrading the value of this resource by imposing limits on its consumption and radically increasing renewables to begin to try to limit global warming would obviously seriously impact a substantial sector of the U.S. capitalist class.

The AC also had several academics and nonprofit representatives who favored weak reformist actions like improved fuel economy standards, energy-efficient building standards, promotion of alternative fuels, and vehicles using new technology, as well as cap-and-trade "market-based" programs to limit emissions. For example, the AC included Portney, the president of Resources for the Future, a nonprofit that is known for being a key driver of market-based environmental policies as a "solution." This nonprofit operates on funds from governments, corporate-related foundations, as well as corporate donations, including the U.S. EPA, the Ford Foundation, Gates Foundation, Robert Wood Johnson Foundation, Packard Foundation, Alcoa Foundation, ExxonMobil, Chevron, Goldman Sachs, American Electric Power, Duke Energy, and Toyota.

As a result of bringing together the members of this AC under the direction of David Victor, three alternative policy options were presented that the United States could pursue. These had the function of attempting to set the strategic framework for acceptable market-based policies for the future, none of which if implemented would actually seriously limit fossil fuel consumption. The first, and most modest, policy option reflected the climate skeptic position and advocated for investment in science and technology, adaptation to climate change, voluntary emission reductions, and a rejection of any binding international agreement like Kyoto. The second suggested that Kyoto should be reinvigorated and a global system of emission trading created in a top-down fashion within a multilateral framework. The third approach focuses on creating a step-by-step "bottom-up" process to create an international emission trading system through creating national markets for new low-emission technologies in the United States and other countries.[753]

THE NATIONAL SECURITY SIDE OF CLIMATE CHANGE

Following a hiatus of three years, the Council had a different study group on an aspect of climate change during each of the three years beginning in 2007. Two of these reports focused on the national security and geopolitical aspects of this issue: *Climate Change and National Security: An Agenda for Action* (2007) and *The Canadian Oil Sands: Energy Security vs. Climate Change* (2009). The third report was focused on the broader topic of overall policy and will be discussed below.

The 2007 report was in the form of a Council Special Report (CSR) commissioned by the CFR studies program. CFR member and Research Fellow Joshua W. Busby, a professor at University of Texas at Austin, formerly at Brookings, Harvard, and Princeton, authored the report. A fifteen-person advisory committee, ten of them Council members, guided his work. The most prominent member of this committee was R. James Woolsey, a former director of the CIA. Four other members were drawn from the national intelligence community and the military. Two were from top corporations Alcoa and Lehman Brothers, three from foundations, two from other think tanks, two were academics, and one was a lawyer.

The conclusions of Busby and his advisory group were based on the overall goal of a "broader strategy of geopolitically informed climate policy."[754] These were summed up in the report as follows:

The concentrated impacts of climate change will have important national security implications, both in terms of the direct threat from extreme weather events as well as broader challenges to U.S. interests in strategically important countries. Domestically, extreme weather events made more likely by climate change could endanger large numbers of people, damage critical infrastructure (including military installations), and require mobilization and diversion of military assets. Internationally, a number of countries of strategic concern are likely to be vulnerable to climate change, which could lead to refugee and humanitarian crises, and, by immiserating tens of thousands, contribute to domestic and regional instability.[755]

Beyond generalizations, Busby and his group also had specific proposals on such issues as the need to support more research on climate vulnerability; the need for deft diplomacy with China, India, Indonesia, Brazil, and the Democratic Republic of the Congo to promote engagement on climate issues; and institutional reforms such as building a cadre of climate change–focused officials at the Pentagon.[756]

The second Council Special Report in this series on the ecological crisis was on the tar sands of Canada, also called "oil sands," which also looked at the geopolitical side: energy security versus climate change. The Advisory Committee for this study, written up by CFR Senior Fellow Michael A. Levi, consisted of twenty-two individuals, sixteen of them CFR members. "In and outers" dominated the list of participants, with fully half of the group having engaged in at least several occupations, usually beginning in the executive branch of the U.S. government, then work in the academic, corporate, consulting, or nonprofit worlds.

One prime example of an in-and-outer on this AC was former CIA director John M. Deutch, who was appointed head of the CIA after years of working in the Energy and Defense Departments, and as Provost and Dean at the Massachusetts Institute of Technology. Then he was invited to serve on a number of corporate boards, including Citigroup, Raytheon, Cummins, and Schlumberger and also became a member of the Trilateral Commission. Another example is Energy Secretary Ernest Moniz. A longtime member of the MIT faculty, Moniz then worked in the executive office of the president and as undersecretary of energy in the Clinton administration. He became Obama's second energy secretary in 2013. A third leading example is energy and commodity expert Edward L. Morse. Following teaching at Princeton, Morse joined the CFR as a senior research fellow. After several years at the Council, Morse was appointed to work on international energy policy at the Department of State. Then Morse entered the corporate world, occupying leading roles at a succession of top corporations, including Phillips Petroleum, PFC Energy, Hess Energy Trading, Lehman Brothers, Credit Suisse, and Citigroup. For the last two finance capitalist corporations, Morse headed up their commodities research departments.

Another key in-and-outer on this AC was the lawyer Gordon D. Griffin, who began his career as legislative director and chief counsel to U.S. Senator Sam Nunn. Following law practice and involvement in Democratic Party political campaigns (he was a major contributor to the political campaigns of both Bill and Hillary Clinton), Griffin was appointed U.S. ambassador to Canada, where he served from 1997 to 2001. After 2001 he joined the multinational law firm of McKenna Long and Aldridge, becoming chair of their public policy and international departments. He has also served on a number of corporate boards, among them the Canadian Imperial Bank of Commerce and Canadian Natural Resources, which has major tar sands interests. McKenna Long and Aldridge is also a lobbyist for Transcanada and the Keystone XL pipeline being built to transport tar sands oil to U.S. refineries. Transcanada is known to have paid at least $190,000 to the McKenna firm to lobby for them in Washington.

The next largest group after the in-and-outers on this AC were oil company representatives from ExxonMobil, Chevron, Enron, and Belfer Petroleum. David P. Bailey was manager for climate policy for ExxonMobil and their "in-house specialist" on tar sands.[757] Kathleen Cooper spent over a decade with ExxonMobil as chief economist. Lisa B. Berry was vice president and general manager of government affairs at Chevron; she coordinated Chevron's successful lobbying efforts in Congress to thwart the Chinese attempt to acquire Unocal, which Chevron later took over. Peter Tertzakian began his career with Chevron, later becoming a leader of ARC Financial Corporation. Robert A. Belfer was the founder of Belco Petroleum, which later merged into Enron. Belfer then became a director and part of the central owning group of that corporation. When Enron collapsed, Berfer lost in the neighborhood of a billion dollars.[758]

Others on this AC included journalists, a few academics, a financier, Ruth Greenspan Bell of the World Resources Institute, and a leading consultant, Scott Nyquist of McKinsey.

Levi's report begins by pointing out that Canada ranks second, behind only Saudi Arabia, in oil reserves, partly due to tar sands, which are estimated to contain nearly 1.7 trillion barrels of oil, about 170 billion of which can be extracted under current economic and political conditions.[759] Doing the math on the approximate current dollar value of this resource—170 billion barrels times $50 a barrel—results in the figure of $8.5 trillion. With this kind of potential wealth involved, and with numerous individuals closely connected to this potential profit stream on the AC, it is no wonder that after an analysis of all aspects of the problem, including economic values, geopolitical aspects, as well as the serious environmental impacts, Levi's report concludes that rapid tar sands development should continue, adding, of course, some meaningless rhetoric about the need to pay attention to "climate concerns":

> The preceding sections make clear that oil sands production delivers energy security benefits and climate change damages, but that both are limited. A healthy balance is possible. Global economic conditions along with Canadian policy will be the main determinants of the oil sands' future, but U.S. policy will play a critical role. For the near future, the economic and security

value of oil sands expansion will likely outweigh the climate damages that the oil sands create— but climate concerns cannot and must not be ignored, and will become more important over time. U.S. policymakers should balance the two goals by working with Canada to promote strong incentives to cut the emissions associated with each barrel produced from the oil sands, without directly discouraging production itself. . . . Since the oil sands are a limited piece of the energy and climate puzzles, any policies will need to be embedded in a much broader strategy to cut global emissions and to increase U.S. energy security.[760]

Levi also warned that "obsession over the tar sands would be a dangerous distraction" and that therefore the United States "should resist attempts to use U.S. environmental regulations to block permitting of oil-sands-related pipelines or refineries on climate grounds."[761]

Developing the "broader strategy to cut global emissions" was the job of Independent Task Force No. 61 that had an even larger and more prestigious group as its Advisory Council.

INDEPENDENT TASK FORCE REPORT NO. 61: CLIMATE CHANGE AND CAP-AND-TRADE LEGISLATION IN THE U.S., 2008–2010

In June 2008 an ITF issued a report called *Confronting Climate Change: A Strategy for U.S. Foreign Policy*. It had a broader aim than prior reports, nothing less than setting the agenda and fixing a strategy for U.S. domestic and foreign policy on this key issue. The introduction to the 2008 report indicated that, at least by 2008, the CFR as an organization had at last "gotten it" and recognized the serious, planetary-wide problem presented by climate change (emphasis in original):

> Climate change poses a stark challenge to the United States and the world. A series of careful and widely respected studies, including most prominently those of the Intergovernmental Panel on Climate Change (IPCC), have raised consistently troubling and increasingly loud alarms about dangerous climate change. The newest report of the IPCC, published in 2007, concluded that "most of the observed increase in global average temperatures since the mid-twentieth century is very likely due to the observed increase in anthropogenic greenhouse gases concentrations." Those increased concentrations—primarily of carbon dioxide (CO_2)—result mainly from the burning of fossil fuels, such as coal and oil, and from deforestation as well as other changes in how people use land. The IPCC found that this human-caused warming is likely already altering ecosystems, weather and sea levels. Many

of those signals may still be faint today but, if the world continues on course, they are expected to become far stronger.

To many, the temperature changes often predicted by experts may not sound like much. Yet they would have wide-ranging consequences that would unfold over the coming years, decades, and centuries. In fact, the likely effects of climate change resulting from unchecked greenhouse gas emissions extend well beyond temperature. They have the potential to affect life in a panoply of ways, endangering coastal populations, reducing the availability of fresh water, increasing damage from storms and wildfires, changing grow-ing patterns and productivity, shifting the geographical range of disease, and straining biodiversity. These effects, bad enough alone, could also be classic "threat-multipliers," intensifying conflict and stoking instability in some of the most fragile parts of the world.

To be sure, the litany of long-term effects—not all of them certain to be negative for all societies, but on balance deeply harmful for the planet and the United States—cannot be predicted with anything approaching preci-sion. The climate system is extremely complex and can be highly sensitive. Some observers have used the resulting uncertainty as an excuse for delay or inaction. Those uncertainties, however, imply the disturbing possibility of much greater buildup of greenhouse gases in the atmosphere and more severe changes in the climate, making it hard to rule out the possibility of climate impacts that could be much worse than most experts' assessments of what is likely.

The Task Force finds that the likely effects associated with unchecked climate change are large and demand serious U.S. attention, both because they would deeply affect the welfare of Americans and of people around the world, and because they could have adverse impacts on international security. It also finds that the chance, however small, of far more extreme impacts is reason for strong and urgent concern.

Reducing the risks of dangerous climate change requires limiting the buildup of greenhouse gases in the atmosphere. In turn, that requires efforts to cut the emissions of greenhouse gases and to increase the removal of greenhouse gases from the atmosphere.[762]

The ITF organized by the Council to develop a consensus and begin work on policy implementation was both unusually large and included powerful people as well as leading intellectuals. The ITF had twenty-nine individuals, nineteen of them (65.5 percent) CFR members or staff. In sharp contrast to the 2004 study group, this ITF was dominated by eighteen in-and-outers. They included three who had served or were soon to serve at the cabinet level of the federal government: former treasury secretary Lawrence H. Summers; future agriculture secretary Thomas A. Vilsack; and former chief of Environmental Protection Agency William K. Reilly. Two state governors were also included, Vilsack of Iowa and George E. Pataki of New York, who served as co-chairs. Financier James D. Wolfensohn, a former head of the World Bank, was a member, as was Timothy E. Wirth, a former congressman and senator from Colorado. ITF member and university president Shirley Ann Jackson, a director of IBM, Marathon Oil, and FedEx, was also a director of the CFR. Corporate executives who had never served in government were a much smaller percentage of this ITF than had been the case in 2004. Only five of the twenty-nine (17.2 percent) were business leaders of this type. They were top people, however, and included the chair or CEO of BP, Deere, Lehman Brothers, and Dominion (an electric utility that is a heavy user of coal).

A number of the in-and-outers on this ITF had also landed in top corporate positions after government service. Billionaire CFR director David M. Rubenstein had served in the Carter administration, for example, then was a founder of the Carlyle Group, a leading private equity firm with international reach. ITF member Kenneth B. Mehlman, also served in Republican administrations (Bush I and II), then joined the CFR-connected private equity firm of KKR. Mark R. Tercek was an academic who later helped lead Goldman Sachs. The ranks of this ITF also included two leading academics, Sally M. Benson of Stanford and Stephen W. Pacala of Princeton, with expertise in the environmental sciences. One union leader, Lawrence R. Scanlon of AFSCME, and one individual from the non-profit world, Jonathan Lash, president of the corporate funded-World Resources Institute, an environmental think tank, were also in the group. Two leaders of for-profit private consulting firms rounded out the body. One of these, the Lindsey Group, was a Republican-connected Washington for-profit advisory organization that follows macroeconomic trends and events in order to see how they influence investment opportunities in world economic and financial markets. The second one, Christensen Global Strategies, a Democrat-connected group led by Aimee R. Christensen, advised clients seeking to profit from the global challenges resulting from climate change, ecosystem degradation, and resource scarcity. CFR Senior Fellows Michael A. Levi and David G. Victor were project director and senior adviser, respectively. Funding for the project came from Rubenstein, the Rockefeller Foundation, and the MacArthur Foundation.

This 2008 task force report included findings of fact and recommendations about policy, strategy and tactics. Among these was the conclusion that about three-fourths of all greenhouse gases were being emitted by a relatively few nations: the United States, China, India, Brazil, Indonesia, Russia, Japan, and the countries of the European Union.[763] Another conclusion was that in order for the United States to be a credible world leader on climate change, it needed to have a strong domestic policy on this issue, stating that "U.S. strategy for confronting climate change must begin at home."[764] Not surprisingly, given Council sponsorship and the makeup of the ITF, the policy recommended was a market-based one:

A "cap-and-trade" system that begins reducing emissions now and that sets a course for cuts between 60 percent and 80 percent from 1990 levels by 2050; those targets should be periodically revisited and revised as necessary. This system would let the market find opportunities to reduce emissions and remove greenhouse gases from the atmosphere at the lowest possible cost.[765]

Also recommended were "complementary steps to help market forces function more effectively and to seize the many opportunities to align the goal of slowing climate change with other policy objectives." The task force rejected carbon taxes because they believed that the "political momentum" was behind cap-and-trade and its near-term adoption was "much more" likely, therefore avoiding delays in adopting a national program to reduce emissions. In a concluding section, the ITF recommended that the president or vice president of the United States should take a strong leadership position and make climate change and energy challenges generally a personal priority.[766]

CFR connections with the incoming Obama administration and the Democratic Congress were generally strong, and there were also two task force members (Vilsack and Summers) in prominent positions at the top of the administration. So cap-and-trade legislation was introduced in the Congress in 2009. This legislation passed the House in June that year in a close vote, which saw heavy Republican opposition and a few of the more liberal Democrats refusing to vote for it, considering it too weak. The bill got stalled in the Senate, however, and was dropped from the agenda in 2010 without a vote. By this time the Republican Party was completely against cap-and-trade legislation, and the Democrats did not have the 60 votes in the Senate needed to stop a potential filibuster. Prominent among the reasons for the total Republican refusal to support cap-and-trade was the fact that despite the support of the ITF and its prominent list of participants, the corporate world of the United States was deeply split on this issue, with powerful sectors strongly opposed. Oil and gas corporations and electric public utilities were central players in the opposition movement that influenced the Senate to deadlock. These two groups alone spent well over $500 million on lobbying the Congress and the Senate during the key January 2009 to June 2010 period when this legislation was being considered. Five of the top seven spenders on lobbying to stop cap-and-trade during this period were ExxonMobil, ConocoPhillips, Chevron, BP, and Shell, all of them longtime corporate members of the CFR. The U.S. Chamber of Commerce, its top leaders interlocked with the CFR, also weighed in against cap-and-trade. Supporters could not counter the power of these and other leading corporations. Even the relatively weak provisions of the cap-and-trade approach recommended by the Council-organized ITF were too much for corporations mainly interested in maintaining their power and continuing to accumulate capital at the expense of the earth's life-giving ecologies. They were not convinced that the changes would yield the "incentives for new industries . . . new markets that will arise at home and abroad for low-carbon technologies" that would make up for the potential losses these corporations faced.[767]

ACCEPTING ADAPTATION: A RENEWED FOCUS ON OIL AND GAS, 2011–2013

The CFR's eternal interest in fossil fuels again came to the fore after the failure to achieve capitalist-class unity on cap-and-trade agreement in the U.S. Senate. Along with this came an acceptance that climate change would accelerate. Council president Richard N. Haass's chapter on energy in his 2013 book *Foreign Policy Begins at Home* is revealing in this regard: "Oil is so important" that it "has had an enormous impact on U.S. foreign policy." The United States has fought "multiple wars in the Middle East . . . in part . . . to ensure that a strategic commodity would not be controlled by individuals or regimes hostile to U.S. interests."[768] He acknowledges that oil and other fossil fuels contribute to climate change, and expresses interest in taking steps to slow climate change as long as this does not constrain economic growth. The fear of low economic growth is strong in Haass's work; he states that the consequences of "prolonged low growth" are "potentially dire," threatening the fabric of American society if growth were to be low for an extended period. Haass believes that absent robust growth "social and economic mobility will atrophy and class frictions will increase, leaving the population focused inward." To assure necessary economic growth and avoid possible "class frictions," Haass and the Renewing America Initiative advocate reducing the statutory federal tax rate on corporations and "fast track" authority to cement pro-corporate trade policies like the Trans Pacific Partnership, and welcome fracking of shale formations, mining of tar sands, building the Keystone XL pipeline to transport dirty oil to U.S. refineries, and the construction of more nuclear power plants.[769] This is part of a general belief that nothing can be done about climate change because to do so would constrain the economic growth that is a mainstay of capitalism:

> In the case of climate change, there is near-universal acceptance among the world's governments of the scientific evidence that burning fossil fuels

is causing measurable change in the earth's climate, something that in turn will affect not just average temperatures but agriculture output, species survival, insect and disease prevalence, severity and frequency of tornadoes and hurricanes, and flooding in coastal areas. But taking the kinds of steps that would have a meaningful effect on carbon emissions has proven impossible, given that any such pact would constrain economic activity (anathema to developed countries suffering from low or no economic growth) and slow the extension of access to energy and electricity to literally hundreds of millions of people in developing countries.... The result is that the world will face a future in which significant climate change is a reality.... The policy debate will come to focus less on mitigation and more on how best to adapt to altered conditions or even geoengineering, a controversial approach bordering on science fiction.[770]

Haass thus admits and accepts that climate chaos is in the offing due to capitalism's need for constant growth and therefore higher emissions.

OCEANS IN PERIL

The destruction of the oceans is also well advanced, as pointed out in a 2013 article in the CFR's *Foreign Affairs*. Alan B. Sielen points out the scientific facts about the alarming ongoing destruction of the world's oceans, but offers only weak recommendations to solve this very serious problem:

Of all the threats looming over the planet today, one of the most alarming is the seemingly inexorable descent of the world's oceans into ecological perdition. . . . Sea life is now in peril. Over the last 50 years—a mere blink in geologic time—humanity has come perilously close to reversing the almost miraculous biological abundance of the deep. Pollution, overfishing, the destruction of habitats, and climate change are emptying the oceans and enabling the lowest forms of life to regain their dominance. The oceanographer Jeremy Jackson calls it "the rise of slime": the transformation of once complex oceanic ecosystems featuring intricate food webs with large animals into simplistic systems dominated by microbes, jellyfish, and disease. In effect, humans are eliminating the lions and tigers of the seas to make room for the cockroaches and rats. The prospect of vanishing whales, polar bears, bluefin tuna, sea turtles, and wild coasts should be worrying enough on its own. But the disruption of entire ecosystems threatens our very survival, since it is the healthy functioning of these diverse systems that sustains life on earth. . . .

The oceans' problems start with pollution, the most visible forms of which are the catastrophic spills from offshore oil and gas drilling or from tanker accidents. Yet as devastating as these events can be, especially locally, their overall contribution to marine pollution pales in comparison to the much less spectacular waste that finds its way to the seas through rivers, pipes, run-off, and the air. For example, trash—plastic bags, bottles, cans, tiny plastic pellets used in manufacturing—washes into coastal waters or gets discarded by ships large and small. This debris drifts out to sea, where it forms epic gyres of floating waste, such as the infamous Great Pacific Garbage Patch, which spans hundreds of miles across the North Pacific Ocean. The most dangerous pollutants are chemicals. The seas are being poisoned by substances that are toxic, remain in the environment for a long time, travel great distances, accumulate in marine life, and move up the food chain. . . .

Then there are the nutrients, which increasingly show up in coastal waters after being used as chemical fertilizers on farms, often far inland. . . . Another cause of the oceans' decline is that humans are simply killing and eating too many fish. A frequently cited 2003 study in the journal *Nature* by the marine biologists Ransom Myers and Boris Worm found that the number of large fish—both open-ocean species, such as tuna, swordfish, and marlin, and large groundfish, such as cod, halibut, and flounder—had declined by 90 percent since 1950. . . .

The problem is not just that we eat too much seafood; it's also how we catch it. Modern industrial fishing fleets drag lines with thousands of hooks miles behind a vessel, and industrial trawlers on the high seas drop nets thousands of feet below the sea's surface. In the process, many untargeted species, including sea turtles, dolphins, whales, and large sea birds (such as albatross) get accidentally captured or entangled. Millions of tons of unwanted sea life is killed or injured in commercial fishing operations each year. . . .

As if all this were not enough, scientists estimate that man-made climate change will drive the planet's temperature up by between four and seven degrees Fahrenheit over the course of this century, making the oceans hotter. Sea levels are rising, storms are getting stronger, and the life cycles of plants and animals are being upended. . . .

On top of all these problems, the most severe impact of the damage being done to the oceans by climate change and ocean acidification may be impossible to predict. The world's seas support processes essential to life on earth. These include complex biological and physical systems, such as the nitrogen and carbon cycles; photosynthesis, which creates half of the oxygen that humans breathe and forms the base of the ocean's biological productivity; and ocean circulation. . . . These complex processes both influence and respond to the earth's climate, and scientists see certain recent developments as red flags possibly heralding an impending catastrophe. . . . Solutions will also require broader changes in how societies approach energy, agriculture, and the management of natural resources. Countries will have to make substantial reductions in greenhouse gas emissions, transition to clean energy, eliminate the worst toxic chemicals, and end the massive nutrient pollution in watersheds.[771]

Here we have an article in the CFR's own magazine that says that ongoing impacts to the ocean "threatens our very survival" and as such possibly heralds "impending catastrophe." The CFR's study group work, Haass's book and the CFR's Renewing America Initiative represent, in many respects, the best thinking that these capitalist-class rulers are capable of. Why then are they obviously promoting only business as usual? Their paralysis is a result of their class interest, part of their deep connection to the short-term, unplanned nature of neoliberal capitalism and its dominant monopoly finance corporations, which include many fossil fuel corporations. The strong sense of solidarity among capitalists also means that they feel the need to stick together, and therefore they are blind to alternatives that would seriously impact their system. It is telling that the president of the CFR, a key leader of the Renewing America Initiative, can acknowledge a serious global warming problem, yet conclude that this or the general ecological crisis facing our planet and all its life forms, including those living in the oceans, does not rise to the level of an "existential threat." Nor does he see nuclear war or pandemics as existential threats. He limits use of this term to domestic social and economic challenges and relations with other states, concluding that no such threats exist.[772] Instead, Haass and the Council want to continue to dominate the U.S. government and pursue the twin neoliberal geopolitical paths that have characterized its framework for policy for decades. In fact, a continuance of CFR domination of the state and continuing to implement these two policy frameworks creates a major existential threat to all of humanity and our ability to survive as a species on this planet.

NEOLIBERAL CAPITALISM'S IMPACT ON
THE EARTH'S ECOLOGIES

The CFR, its leaders and as an organization, has been blind to key facts. There is no long-term economy or human well-being without nature, and continued high levels of carbon emissions and other impacts from carbon-based industrial development will result in serious, irreversible impacts. The awful truth is that a serious existential threat does in fact exist, a threat to the future of all higher life-forms, developing directly out of the current predatory neoliberal capitalist system's need for constant growth, for maximum profit in minimum time. Profit-seeking is not a rational mode of operation—it plainly leads to the generalized ruin of nature and life by disrupting the earth's biosphere and ecosystems.

As a global system, neoliberalism actively promotes massive world production and long-distance trade, which includes the making of shoddy and useless products, unnecessary advertising, and unneeded packaging to sell such products, along with transportation to markets that increase the use of fossil fuel, development of which, no matter how polluting, is encouraged. Our current rulers, led by the CFR, have given their full support to fracking, tar sands mining, deep underwater drilling, mountaintop removal, and the Keystone XL pipeline. Nor is the Council against the sea of human poverty and oppression created by global capitalism in its older and newer variants. The CFR's newest program, the Renewing America Initiative, which makes a shift to controlling the U.S. domestic agenda as well as foreign policy, is obviously a continuation of the attempt to benefit capital, and continue an attack on the working class.

Historical emissions of global warming gases from burning fossil fuels and cement manufacturing have been concentrated in a few nations, led by the United States, China, and Russia. If Brazil, India, United Kingdom, and Germany are included, these seven account for 60 percent of total emissions historically.[773] These nations, plus a few others like Japan, Canada, and France, are also the countries that have the largest number of what could be called heavy consumers: the capitalist-class individuals and families with their business and vacation trips, private jets, yachts, numerous cars, and multiple grand-scale homes. There is a direct correlation between wealth and emissions: one estimate of the consumption habits of the wealthier segment of the world's population found that the richest 7 percent are responsible for 50 percent of the globe's CO_2 emissions, with the poorest 50 percent responsible for only 7 percent.[774]

During the neoliberal geopolitical era since the mid-1970s world energy consumption has approximately doubled. Since the late 1990s, and despite the Kyoto Accord—which must be seen primarily as a public relations effort—carbon dioxide emissions have been increasing every year, reaching a record of 36 billion tons in 2013, with emissions from China growing the fastest.[775] It is increasingly obvious that to preserve a habitable biosphere, we immediately need massive investments in solar, wind, geothermal, and other alternative energy systems so that fossil fuel use can be phased out as rapidly as possible. But the truly vast infrastructure of investment in fossil fuels and the multiple trillions of assessed value in fossil fuel production sites prevents the national and world capitalist class from taking this route; they are, in fact, continuing gigantic subsidies to the fossil fuel corporations. The International Energy Agency estimated that there were $544 billion in subsidies globally for fossil fuel consumption in 2012 alone.[776] Renewable energy subsidies were much smaller.

Solutions to this problem have been developed. Scientists have shown that renewables can provide all the energy humanity requires, but the existing socio-economic system and power structure and resulting social relations so far has prevented humanity from taking the steps needed for its own survival.[777]

THE CFR'S CLIMATE STUDIES: COMPLACENCY AND DENIAL

This review of the Council's long efforts to produce reports and books on the climate crisis clearly illustrate that the Council, like the world capitalist class generally, cannot be relied upon to develop any serious proposals in regard to what is happening to our climate and the very serious implications for our planet and its life-forms. The capitalist system that the CFR represents cannot think holistically, and is incapable of addressing climate heating, let alone the wider ecological crisis. Complacent and intent on keeping their system of profit and accumulation going, they prefer to create illusions, convincing attentive publics that something serious is being done about this serious threat to our collective future. The reliance on ExxonMobil representatives in several of the CFR study groups is indicative of the overall approach, as this corporation has been the leader and a chief funder of the climate change denial movement.[778] The Council, speaking through its study groups, has argued that human-caused global warming is happening, and that something should be done. But that something has only been the promotion of a weak cap-and-trade program. This was as far as the CFR was willing to go as of 2014, while continuing to strongly support fracking and the exploitation of the dirty oil of the Canadian tar sands. One reason why the Council has failed is clear: it is a capitalist-class organization dedicated, first and foremost, to corporate prosperity and expansion, as this is the continuing source of the wealth and power of this class, a class for itself. These are many of the same corporations most responsible for the ecological crisis. A November 2013 study by Richard Heede, published in the magazine *Climate Change*, detailed the top ninety entities: private investor corporations, state-owned companies, and nation-state entities that have been responsible for fully 63 percent of global carbon emissions during the period 1854–2010.[779] Five of the top six, and six of the top nine private and state-owned entities on the list are large transnational corporations that are corporate members of the CFR. These are, in the order listed in Heede's study, the top corporate emitters: Chevron, ExxonMobil, Saudi Aramco, BP, Shell, and Conoco Phillips.[780] A number of other top emitters, such as Total, Anglo-American, Eni, Occidental, Marathon, and Hess, are also corporate members of the Council, but lower down in the list of the leading ninety. This illustrates a key fact about the CFR network:

it has very close connections to the top global oil corporations. It should be added that, in the case of domestic and foreign coal companies, a number of which are in the top ninety, the ties to the CFR are much weaker and indirect. In addition, the coal corporations are not corporate members of the Council.

The facts of the global ecological crisis are ones that a capitalist-class organization like the CFR do not want to face: to save the planet and its existing life-forms, fossil fuel mining and burning has to be severely restricted by government fiat. This conclusion goes against the entire neoliberal free-market monopoly finance capitalist world order that the CFR has sponsored. If such restrictions are put in place, however, capitalism as we know it will be, at minimum, substantially impacted. The final chapter presents the case for a different, fully democratic system, a new civilization that could successfully preserve nature and affirm all forms of life.

CONCLUDING REFLECTIONS: CAPITALIST-CLASS RULE VS. DEMOCRACY AND THE PUBLIC INTEREST

Radical criticism of the given, even in advance of having blueprints for an alternative, can be a material force, because it can seize the mind of the masses of people. There is no greater responsibility for intellectuals.

—JOEL KOVEL

There's a time when the operation of the machine becomes so odious—makes you so sick at heart—that you can't take part. You can't even passively take part. And you've got to put your bodies upon the gears and upon the wheels, upon the levers, upon all the apparatus, and you've got to make it stop.

—MARIO SAVIO

We shall require a substantially new manner of thinking if mankind is to survive.

—ALBERT EINSTEIN

If we, as a human species, are to overcome the existential threats to our collective future, nation-states controlled by the people will have to be a central part of this necessary struggle. In this book we have discussed the ways that the CFR, an agent of the capitalist class, controls the U.S. state in an undemocratic fashion, implementing policies in the interest of the capitalist class, not the people at large. The Council consists of a combination of the wealthiest of the old and new plutocratic families and their corporations, families, and the private organizations that have no formal, legal, or political power per se. They need the state to wield coercive and management power in their interest, the interest of the possessing class. Management of the system involves using the strength of the state to create profit opportunities and provide legitimacy, including the illusion of democracy. Police, the army, and prisons provide protection against the inevitable discontent of the dispossessed and exploited classes. In addition, leading elements of the capitalist class in general, and the financial sector in particular, depend on explicit and implicit government guarantees against market losses in a supposedly "free market" system. Taxpayer bailouts of "too big to fail" companies are frequent occurrences in recent history—witness the 2008 economic crisis and its aftermath—illustrating the power of the capitalist class in getting the government to do its bidding, and use public resources to assure its own private profit. All too often the economic risks of the private enterprise system are socialized, and the gains privatized, resulting in the destruction of the public interest and general welfare.

Seeing the state as an organ of class rule, intertwined with the CFR and the capitalist class, allows us to see the reality of the term "ruling class," a class for itself that forms its own economy, society, and politics that is part of the whole but above it, ruling over it, even to the extent of sometimes standing above the law. The CFR is at the center of this ruling class, as well as being a critical transmission belt between the capitalist class, its professional-class helpers, and a colonized state, using multiple means to assure that the state serves, first and foremost, the needs of monopoly finance capitalism, and not the needs of the people and the planet. This is how the class struggle from above, the ongoing class war of the 1 percent against the working-class majority, is waged. The essentials of the status quo are preserved through force as well as through ideological hegemony and a constant process of co-optation of many of the better-educated and active elements of the working and professional classes.

This book's focus on the CFR helps expose the phoniness of American "democracy," a corrupt system in which the needs and avarice of the capitalist class are dominant, a desire to accumulate more and more wealth in all of its forms. Behind this avarice is a passion for power over others, an unquenchable thirst for conquest, to rule over more and more human beings in order to exploit their labor power, to keep them imprisoned in an immoral slave-like division of labor, often including low wages, poor conditions, and work insecurity. This division of labor puts the capitalist at the top, making decisions about the lives of the workers, as well as plundering the surplus value/profits and, as folk wisdom puts it, "laughing all the way to the bank." This focus on the Council and its activities also provides important advance knowledge about developing trends in ruling-class thinking, intelligence that can be useful to working people as they confront the capitalists in their daily and longer-term struggles.

At the more individual level, the "in-and-outers" (part of the revolving door between private institutions and the government), very often CFR members who almost always remain members while serving in government, academic life, or in the private sector business world, are a kind of double agent, serving the interests of the capitalist class and its corporations while in "public service," then leaving, often to reap the benefits of their decisions after returning to top corporate or other lucrative positions. Their membership in the Council informs all who want to see that such an individual is "reliable," someone who will make decisions in conformity with the needs and interests of the capitalist class and neoliberal geopolitics.

These facts and analyses have a crucial bearing on the often mentioned, but mistaken, "relative autonomy of the state" theory of state power and governmental decision making.[781] This theory and its proponents assert that the state bureaucracy in the United States is normally relatively independent of a ruling capitalist class and has the autonomy to make decisions that are in the interest of the system as a whole. The advocates of this view have failed to consider that market and private trade associations are not the only important social relationships among the top capitalists and their relationships to government. The capitalist class also has the deep state—made up of the CFR and related organizations especially—to formulate and coordinate their overall strategic interests and insert them into the government. The Council and its larger network of interlocked institutions plays a central role in training and selecting the capitalist-class and professional-class leaders who occupy the highest levels of state power.

Leo Panitch and Sam Ginden argue that it cannot be said that the state is "captured" by Wall Street because the Treasury and the Fed are concerned with strengthening their own management and regulatory capacities. An example they give to prove their "relative autonomy" theory is Secretary of the Treasury Timothy F. Geithner's statement on the need for regulation of Wall Street, which supposedly offers "a remarkably clear example of the relative autonomy of the state." Geithner addressed the issue at a June 2011 meeting of bankers, saying: "The success of the Dodd-Frank Act will depend on a sustained effort to improve the level of expertise in the regulators charged with oversight and to ensure there are enough 'cops on the street.'"[782] As we have seen throughout this book, the regulatory "cops on the street" are in fact usually closely connected to the CFR and capitalist class and make decisions based on their direct understanding of the needs of big capital. As we have seen in Geithner's case, his entire career has been as a leader and agent of the capitalist class and the Council: as a member and employee of the CFR, as a staff member at Kissinger Associates, as an adviser to the chair of the Council, as a member of the Trilateral Commission and the Bilderberg Group, as New York Fed bank president, and as president of Warburg Pincus. As treasury secretary, his highest number of phone calls were to top CFR leaders and capitalists like director

Lawrence D. Fink and chair Robert E. Rubin. Finally, he is quoted in the Council's 2014 *Annual Report* as saying, when he was treasury secretary: "You don't go to speak to the Council; you go to get advice."[783] To argue that Geithner's actions represent a "remarkably clear example" of the relative autonomy of the state is clearly mistaken, as is this overall theory in the U.S. case.

When in-and-outers like Geithner make policy they consider first and foremost the needs of their own class of wealthy owners and their corporations, and consult with the leaders of this class to get advice about how to handle key issues. The task of these key players and the CFR itself is to generalize the overall longer-term systemic strategic interests of the capitalist class and make decisions based upon the resulting consensus. The potential and actual power of government is too strong for the capitalist class not to want to heavily influence or control its decisions. The CFR and its network also develop the new policy initiatives needed for the state to be able to cope with and stay ahead of changing world and national circumstances. It is the Council and the class it represents, not the state, that is the organization with relative autonomy from the great majority of people and that small part of the capitalist class not well represented in its ranks.

The above analysis refers, of course, to the United States during what could be called normal times and conditions. During such periods the U.S. federal government, together with the in-and-outers from the CFR, amount to nothing less than the managing committee of the capitalist ruling class. Abnormal times, rare situations of societal stress, are different. Situations of actual or threatened civil war, depression, and intense class struggle, rapid change and crisis, make it more difficult for the dominant sector of the capitalist class to influence the conflicts and struggles that arise. It is during such abnormal times that the state can become more autonomous from the capitalist ruling class and can more independently embody the preservation instincts of the overall system, and make and execute decisions needed based on the historical situation.[784] To recount two concrete examples from U.S. history, during both the Civil War of 1861–65 and the Great Depression of 1933–39, Abraham Lincoln and Franklin D. Roosevelt respectively assumed unusual powers in order to save the overall system. These two exceptional situations represented the relative autonomy of the state from the ruling capitalist class. But even in these unusual circumstances the interests of the propertied plutocracy were, in large measure, preserved. For example, during the threatening environment of the Civil War and its aftermath, the rebel landowners of the former slave-owning South were generally allowed to keep their property after losing the war. They were also allowed to, in effect, re-enslave most of their powerless former slaves as a sharecropping agricultural labor force. During the Great Depression, workers' struggles threatened the system and this led to Roosevelt and the state granting some labor and other rights in the form of the Wagner Act, the Social

Security Act, and other laws over the opposition of one sector of the capitalist class. But the overall property rights of the capitalists were fully upheld, even during this intense crisis.

The Council and allied organizations are not, however, the only avenue used by the capitalist class to influence the U.S. state. As documented by many critical thinkers, another is a corrupted political process, a "Dollarocracy" that regularly elects the candidates who have the most money to spend on their campaigns for office, with the decisive amounts coming from the capitalist plutocracy, a number of them members of the CFR.[785] The Council and allied organizations also supply numerous expert advisers to their favored politicans, and the CFR-connected major media give friendly attention to these plutocratic-connected candidates. [786]

The facade of democracy, and the false consciousness associated with this ruse, is thus another part of the overall picture. Electing representatives who are increasingly selected and fully funded by the capitalists only disguises the reality of a system run by and for the dictatorship of big capital. These two routes together allow the capitalist class, especially the financial sector, to control the U.S. state and influence it to do its bidding, with increasingly dire results for both the rank and file and the ecologies that all life on earth depend upon. In the relatively few cases in which the U.S. capitalist class fails to succeed in their policy aims, it was usually due to direct class struggle from below, and resulting adjustments made by the capitalist class, not to any supposed "relative autonomy of the state" from the capitalist ruling class and its own special interests.

The United States and other nation-states will only become autonomous from the power of the capitalist class through the direct action and electoral action— where electoral systems are truly democratic—of the mass of the people. The section at the end of this chapter provides suggestions on how to build this necessary majoritarian movement, focusing on the looming ecological crisis.

THE ECOLOGICAL CRISIS AND NEOLIBERAL GEOPOLITICAL MONOPOLY FINANCE CAPITALISM

As we saw in chapter 8, the CFR has primarily focused its studies only on climate change, when the ecological crisis is actually much broader, extending to the entire human-environment interaction. As Fred Magdoff and John Bellamy Foster pointed out in March 2010:

One of the latest, most important, developments in ecological science is the concept of "planetary boundaries," in which nine critical boundaries/ thresholds of the earth system have been designated in relation to: (1) climate change; (2) ocean acidification; (3) stratospheric ozone depletion; (4)

the biogeochemical flow boundary (the nitrogen cycle and the phosphorus cycles); (5) global freshwater use; (6) change in land use; (7) biodiversity loss; (8) atmospheric aerosol loading; and (9) chemical pollution. Each of these is considered essential to maintaining the relatively benign climate and environmental conditions that have existed during the last twelve thousand years (the Holocene epoch). The sustainable boundaries in three of these systems—climate change, biodiversity, and human interference with the nitrogen cycle—may have already been crossed.[787]

When one stops to ask why these planetary boundaries are being crossed, one must fully understand the nature of the predatory economic system of neoliberal financial monopoly capitalism that currently dominates the globe. Such an understanding exposes the CFR's entire enterprise as a kind of pathology and a form of higher immorality, lacking any real social or moral bearing. The Council and other organs of the global capitalist ruling class qualify as massive failures when it comes to tackling the real problems of our age; they are dinosaurs pulling us all into the gyre of destruction, racing toward extinction. Their overriding interest is in the expansion of neoliberal geopolitics, always wanting to expand, speed up, and deepen the capitalist accumulation machine, continuing to prosper in darkening times, never considering the obvious trajectory of history. Capitalism in its neoliberal geopolitical variant operates like a religious compulsion, but is now a doomsday machine, characterized by reckless excess, unable to consider the precautionary principle and the long term. They fail to recognize that it is impossible to have an ever-growing economy on a finite planet, with a finite amount of pure air, water, rich soil, forests, and other natural resources. Left to its own logic, capitalism will undercut and destroy the foundations for its own existence; in short, ecological sustainability is incompatible with neoliberal geopolitical capitalism as promoted by the CFR. The system of neoliberal, geopolitical capitalism has brought on a global ecological crisis whose magnitude is so vast that it dwarfs any problem that past humanity has ever had to deal with. That catastrophic consequences are in the offing should now be beyond debate. The capitalist system threatens the entire web of life by gradually but inexorably destroying a stable biosphere, climate system, and our oceans.

In reality, this descent into climate hell has already begun; witness the increasing extreme weather events: record storms killing thousands, the advance of deserts, both heat and cold waves, massive fires, drought, floods, melting ice, and rising oceans. A 2014 study by Rutgers University and National Oceanic and Atmospheric Administration scientists concluded that these unusual weather events, including extreme cold in some places due to the "polar vortex" shifting south, are due to an increasingly erratic jet stream, caused in turn by global warming. One year will see an unusually warm winter, another year an unusually cold winter, one year a record number of tornadoes, another year a record lack of tornadoes; one place will have record flooding and another will suffer an epic drought.[788]

The global ecological crisis is deeply rooted in the logic of capitalist profit and accumulation. Capitalism promotes the processes, relationships, and outcomes that are the opposite of what is needed for an ecologically and biologically sound, just, and harmonious society. Capitalism's main driving force is the imperative of production and exchange for profit. "Expand or die" are the watchwords of this anti-ecological system. Forests and entire ecosystems are commodified and demolished, the oceans, waterways, and nature generally treated as a sewer for the disposal of capitalist industrial waste. The very biochemical processes of the entire planet are altered. Capitalism is therefore a cancerous system, an angel of death, a death for all prepared by the fragmentation and destruction of ecosystems through alienation from nature. This alienation begins with the separation from the worker of the means of production, including land, which also separates the worker from the means of life. The objects produced by labor are taken over by the capitalist and become alien to and independent of the producers. The worker is then forced down to the level of a mere commodity, separated from his or her own natural life force. The resulting alienated labor is fundamental to capitalism, acting as it does on the principles of exploitation of human labor, conversion of nature into commodities, and exchanging those commodities into capitalist value. Capitalism pushes on in an endless pursuit of more and more production, profit, and accumulation on a larger and larger scale, domestically and worldwide. Yet human and other life species live on a finite planet, which by definition ultimately has limited resources. Once limits to growth are reached, capitalism begins to flounder, creating crisis.

Economic limits must now be set within natural ones, resources must be conserved and shared, pollution must be cleaned up, and adequate health care dispensed. Democratic planning and state power, not the market, are necessary to enforce limits on fossil fuel mining and burning, restrictions that—because the use of fossil fuel is so ubiquitous—will end the rule of capital. Here we even find at least one current member of the Council advocating this type of radical measure to try to solve the looming threat to humanity and other life-forms. James K. Galbraith is an economist and a professor at the University of Texas. He became a CFR member in 2007.[789] His father, the economist John Kenneth Galbraith, was also a CFR member. In 2008 James K. wrote in his book *The Predator State* that the threat of global warming was so serious that

the problem of technological planning and disaster management will soon become the central security issue facing every part of the planet. And it will

become so in a way that must necessarily remove a central element of economic life—control over the sources and uses of energy—from the purview
of private corporations and place it under public administration. Indefinitely.
That is the reality of climate change if we are going to manage climate change
and not simply succumb to it.[790]

Needless to say, Galbraith's view is not popular within the CFR and the larger
capitalist class, yet it represents the truth. Capitalism is a system characterized
by commodities in motion, most of them moved, directly or indirectly, by fossil
fuels (gasoline, diesel, natural gas, coal, oil, electricity). Therefore what needs to
be faced is that the needed large-scale abandonment of fossil fuels, "leaving the
coal in the hold, the oil in the soil and the gas under the grass," would end capitalism as we know it, and this is why climate denialism is still being promoted on a
large scale, along with a "head in the sand" market-based approach on the part of
the CFR, allied organizations, and a large part of the U.S. political economic and
media establishment. This ruling class insists on assuming that capitalism can go
on forever, therefore posing all discussions of the ecological crisis within a framework of how to preserve capitalism. To break with this order, and win a future for
humanity and other life-forms, this refusal must be coupled with an affirmation, an
outline of an alternative future. What is necessary is the revolutionary transcend-
ing of this system and substituting a completely democratic—in both economic
and political aspects of life—humane, rational, and scientific ecosocialist system
that promotes solidarity between humans and harmony with the earth's ecologies. Such a future can only be the democratic work of millions of people, and it is
the greatest challenge humanity has ever faced. Here we can only suggest starting
points for the needed ongoing great debate for our collective future.

ALTERNATIVES: WHAT IS TO BE DONE?

The neoliberal geopolitical system of capital faces what John Bellamy Foster calls
an epochal crisis, "the convergence of economic and ecological contradictions
in such a way that the material conditions of society as a whole are undermined,
posing the question of a historical transition to a new mode of production."[791]
Although we are at a critical moment in human history, fast approaching the
reality of ecological collapse, we are also on the verge of a global mass democratic awakening and uprising. The system of neoliberal geopolitics, run by
unelected, non-democratic forces, can only be changed by massive rebellion
and direct struggle aimed at putting full democracy, human development, and
ecological restoration at the center of political and economic life, not profit and
accumulation.

Only mass social movements worldwide can now save the people and the planet. We know for certain where—if left unchecked—the current system is headed, what road it is on. If we stay on that road a dystopia awaits, so we must block the road and create a new pathway for humanity. People need to begin by arming themselves with education and then unify, organize, and act on that education. The path to survival requires us to act now in time to avert catastrophe. Such essential changes on a crash basis, similar to a war emergency, only more serious, have never been attempted before in human history, and will be fiercely resisted by the powers that be both within and outside the CFR circle. We need education, science, engineering, but most of all resistance to the existing neoliberal geopolitical system, which has to be completely overthrown and transcended as a mode of production. In its place we need a society characterized by full, participatory democracy, localism instead of globalism, freely associated labor by the producers, a cooperative economy, long-term planning, a much larger and more powerful public sector, and peaceful resolution of conflicts instead of capitalist-class tyranny and war.

No full blueprint is possible for a society of an ecological commons, such as is being described here, together with freely associated labor; the actions of the workers/producers themselves must create such a fundamental transformation from below or it will not be brought into existence. Society-wide and global solutions to the capitalist-created ecological crisis would have to be discussed and decided democratically on a massive scale; there is and can be no master plan. But intellectuals who consider themselves of, by, and for the working class have a responsibility to offer preliminary proposals, a brief catalogue of ideas and possibilities that might be helpful to encourage thought, debate, and material action by the rank and file. Below, suggestions at three different levels will be offered: characteristics of the movements we want; suggestions for a transitional program; and the nature of the longer-term goal of a constantly advancing and improving ecosocialist civilization.

ANOTHER WORLD IS POSSIBLE

Characteristics of Our Movement

The anthropologist Margaret Mead once said: "Never doubt that a small group of thoughtful, committed citizens can change the world. Indeed it is the only thing that ever has."[792] Our genius as human beings is that we can dream and envision a world that has never existed. We have to overcome illusions and capitalist brainwashing to dedicate ourselves to a long-term, difficult yet beautiful journey, a struggle for a humane, sane, holistic world of ecological balance, one that will save the planet and all of its life-forms. We must create inclusive spaces where broad sectors of the people, especially youth, can cooperatively come together as part of that effort. Interculturality and the recognition of humanity's oneness must be central, welcoming all cultures, races and ethnicities, forms of knowledge, philosophies, and religions to participate democratically in making real and concrete the slogan "Another world is possible." Our movements must be like a loving family working together in solidarity: altruistic and generous; moral and spiritual; radically collective and egalitarian, based on mutual aid, creativity, community, and grassroots democracy. We need to feel bonded together as part of one struggle for a higher form of being and society—in resistance to capitalist ecocide, with a social justice ethic—offering a responsible, life-serving alternative to the current self-destructive course toward predictable planetary catastrophe that humanity is currently on.

Suggestions for a Transitional Reform Program: For All and the Welfare of All

In our involvement in real-world struggle, revolutionaries must maintain a difficult and contradictory balance. We need to join struggles for ecological reforms and yet not slide into suggesting that capitalism with these reforms could create a just society and avoid ecological catastrophe.

Although this is a complex question that can only be worked out through experience, a revolutionary transitional ecosocialist program—a set of political positions put forth in order to present our vision of a better world and to push forward and unite the various political struggles—will help us maintain this balance by linking immediate demands to a revolutionary democratic vision.

The basic elements in an ecosocialist transitional program aim to end neoliberal alienation, empowering the working class in the service of sustainable, ecologically based human development with an emphasis on the local, the collective, the community, and including more free time for people for its own sake.

Transitional demands like these have to be part of an explicitly class-conscious revolutionary program, one that envisions a society that overcomes capitalist class rule, exploitation, the oppression of women, people of color, and other groups, creating full equality and taking rapid strides to reestablish a balanced metabolism between society and nature.

The elements of a transitional program such as those listed below could be paid for by ending geopolitical-linked military spending, corporate bailouts, and corporate welfare, and increased progressive taxes on the wealthy, all carried out by an active, ecologically oriented and fully democratic state:

- *Ecosystems*—nature valued for its own sake as the ultimate source of all life; an end to destruction of habitats; a massive effort to restore and re-create damaged ecosystems, including tree planting on a gigantic scale.
- *Food and Agriculture*—a crash program to wipe out hunger and malnutrition worldwide, ending the tragic daily massacre of tens of thousands of people by starvation in the predatory capitalist neoliberal geopolitical world; promoting self-sufficient diversified organic local food production and distribution (gardens in the cities); actively supporting farmers to convert to decentralized ecological agriculture; banning GMOs as harmful to humans and other living things; and transitioning to a communal system of user rights and responsibilities instead of land ownership in giant parcels.
- *Jobs*—an end to exploitation and private capital accumulation worldwide through collective ownership of the main means of production and a rapid transition to control by the associated workers as subjects working for themselves, leading to a full-employment economy based on sound ecological principles.
- *Transportation*—creating large-scale, free, and efficient public transportation networks.
- *Technology*—use of computers, the Internet, and other instruments to have a global movement of working people establishing a harmonious, self-governing, post-capitalist world through information, connection, and organization.
- *Politics*—decentralized organization, direct democracy from below is the goal, inclusive and transparent.
- *Housing*—rehabilitate existing housing, including solar upgrades and weatherproofing, build new housing through the creation of a public entity, training workers to build and maintain houses.
- *Health Care*—a human right and public good, not a commodity to make profit on; therefore universal health care must be guaranteed by the state in a single-payer, "medicare for all" or similar free and all-inclusive socialized system with preventative care an important component. The pharmaceutical industry should be a public sector service industry, not for private profit, so that vaccines can be developed for all of the neglected diseases of poverty like Ebola.
- *Culture*—a shift to more free time and less consumerism means an increase in the level of cultural development by and for the people, with more music, dance, and the arts.
- *Education*—a public school system dedicated to the creative, all-round development of every student and free to all from preschool to graduate school.
- *Peace*—end geopolitical rivalries, develop a peaceful, cooperative foreign policy instead of imperialist wars and interventions based on the needs of the capitalist system; national defense based on a mobilized population, closing

foreign bases, converting the armed forces to a defensive force also trained in
ecological restoration practices.

- *Advertising*—substitute a simple listing of services and products for the massive and wasteful (now about $450 billion annually worldwide) current adver-
tising/propaganda system, since ads are simply a means for capitalists to colo-
nize and dominate our minds in service to more and more consumption.
- *Retirement*—improve the current Social Security system by making it more
generous.
- *Community*—foster strong local communities through stressing cooperation,
use value, and barter on the local level, not exchange value and long-distance
trade.
- *Fossil Fuels*—rapid phasing out of these fuels in favor of clean energy sources
through large investments in solar, wind, and geothermal; making ownership
and control of all fossil fuel sources a public utility controlled by the people.

Limiting the use of the world's proven fossil fuel reserves would likely result
in many trillions of dollars of investment losses, however, subtracting massive
amounts from what are now counted as the private capitalist assets of corporations, governments, families, and individuals. Speaking of coal alone, as mentioned above, one estimate puts the value of U.S. coal reserves—about a third
under U.S. government ownership, the remainder private/corporate—at $30 tril-
lion, the most valuable supply of any nation on earth. U.S. natural gas reserves'
estimated worth is $3.1 trillion. Other nations would have to be involved in any
attempt to save our planet and humanity by limiting the burning of fossil fuels,
and here the values are also large. Just to cite a few examples: Saudi Arabia's oil
reserves are estimated to be worth $31.5 trillion; Canada's oil reserves at $21 trillion; Russia's natural gas reserves at $19 trillion; Iran's oil reserves at $16.1 trillion;
Iraq's oil reserves at $13.9 trillion; and Venezuela's oil reserves at $11.7 trillion.[793]
Putting fossil fuels under public ownership and control would obviously seriously
impact capitalist interests and would be strenuously resisted by the corporations
and leading plutocratic families that benefit from the existing system.

An Ecosocialist Civilization

In an ecosocialist civilization, living beings would come together in the matrix of
nature to form interdependent webs of life: ecosystems. Such a society would be
characterized by the logic of life: full human development, completely outside the
imperatives of commodification, profit, and capital accumulation. Production for
use (use value) instead of for sale (exchange value) would be central, together with
an emphasis on nature valued for itself, part of a commons benefiting all.

Ownership and ecologically sustainable production would be social, organized by the workers for maximum public benefit and the satisfaction of community needs. Such a civilization would focus on full development of the potential of every human being but stop growing when basic needs are met. For example, technological advances in production would be used to shorten work hours rather than to produce more, leading to more free time for truly fulfilling activities, and allow greater variety in how we spend our lives. Organizing cooperatives would be central to implementation.

A sustainable and just society would also eliminate the distinction between productive and reproductive labor by socializing domestic labor (such as childcare, cooking, and laundry) and organizing cooperatives. This would be a more efficient way to fulfill people's needs and would further women's liberation, combating the gendered division of labor in society. In a democratically planned and ecologically rational society, many of the lifestyle changes that individualist environmentalism points to as necessary would occur, but as part of a social process of liberation, not as a forced sacrifice or imposed by moralistic principles.

Such an economy would be characterized by freely associated labor of the cooperating workers/producers, organized in councils. It would neither need nor allow advertising to entice people to consume more and more. It would restore and protect ecologies—natural life-support systems—and respect the limits of natural resources, taking into account the needs of future generations. It would make decisions on long-term societal requirements, fostering a culture of cooperation, sharing, love, hope, compassion, reciprocity, and responsibility to community. It would run as much as possible on current energy (solar, wind, geothermal, and biomass) instead of fossil fuels. It would promote fully democratic mass-participatory political and economic decision making for local, regional, and multiregional coordination bodies, aiming at common prosperity for all, not excessive wealth for the few.[794]

Such a civilization of collective control of the means of production and democratic planning of production and exchange can only be brought into being by an ecosocialist revolution.

John Bellamy Foster summed up the goal of such a revolution as follows:

What is clear is that the long-term strategy for ecological revolution throughout the globe involves the building of a society of substantive equality, i.e., the struggle for socialism. Not only are the two inseparable, but they also provide essential content for each other. There can be no true ecological revolution that is not socialist; no true socialist revolution that is not ecological.[795]

Foster points out that the forces to create such a new system of social justice and ecological sanity are now coming together, offering a way out of what is an epochal crisis:

> The objective conditions are . . . emerging that are creating the potential for a larger material alliance against the system. This will likely take the form of a co-revolutionary struggle, in the sense suggested by David Harvey, embodying an alliance of gender, race, class, indigenous and environmental movements.
>
> All of this depends of course on the rise to prominence of an environmental working class (and ecological peasantry) capable of initiating a broad, counter-hegemonic struggle for the fulfillment of human needs in line with the fundamental biogeochemical processes of the planet—a world of substantive equality and ecological sustainability. There is no doubt that this is an objective necessity and . . . will increasingly become a subjective one as well. Yet, there is no certainty as to the future of humanity. The very continuation of the human species along with most . . . other "higher" forms of life is now in doubt. The future and even survival of humanity thus rests as never before on the revolutionary struggle of humanity itself. [796]

Ecosocialist thinkers worldwide have developed three manifestos—starting points for discussion, mobilization, and action—furthering this revolutionary struggle. They obviously do not exhaust the possibilities, but all are international in scope and represent the best beginnings for the discussion at this point in time.[797]

There are signs that opposition to capitalism is beginning to go mainstream. A battle of worldviews is under way as we reinvent the commons, a system by and for everyone. More and more, former politically neutral scientists are recognizing the need for resistance as an existential necessity, since the ecological crisis represents a threat to our species' existence. Radical de-growth strategies, especially in the wealthy nations of the triad, are no longer optional, and calls for revolutionary change are spreading.[798]

Do Humans Have a Future? Whose Future?

The Council on Foreign Relations represents the theoretical expression, the personification, of a form of social organization that cannot plan for the long term, or in any way change the eco-destructiveness of its system—capitalism—that always bring forth behaviors in its own corrupt and ethically bankrupt image.

We need a moral, political, and economic antidote to the hegemony of an irresponsible capitalist class led by the CFR. This alternative is expressed through valuing nature and humanity, and their undeniable interconnectedness. A stress on the intrinsic value of nature differentiates ecosocialism from the other socialisms of the past. Ecosocialism challenges the fatal compromises that prior socialisms made with industrialism, resulting in impacts to nature and peoples, especially indigenous peoples.

The new road for humanity must also have the overarching goal of all-sided development for every member of the human family everywhere in the world, rather than the obscene commitment to unlimited wealth and unlimited power of the few over the many. Equality, scientific rationality, common prosperity, collective ownership, ecological values and practice, equitable distribution of income and wealth, and full participatory direct democracy, as well as humanity as protagonists and subjects of our collective destiny through organizations of freely associated labor are the interests of the vast majority—the working class. These interests must be asserted in revolutionary ways for humanity to survive. Ecosocialism represents these emancipatory objectives of a fundamentally different social order; we must strive for it by building the unified, combative international mass movements and organizations of, by, and for the working class. To the CFR and others steeped in the status quo, this will sound too radical, just as the U.S. abolitionists fighting slavery during the mid-nineteenth century were seen as strange people who were willing to violate the laws of "property" and upend the economy of Southern plantations and the cotton trade. But we must recognize the emergency we are in and that the current status quo in regard to fossil fuel use is a death sentence for our children and grandchildren because our house, our elegant planet, is slowly burning down. The real danger we face is underreaction, not overreaction. The capitalists investing in and promoting fossil fuel use and seeing geopolitical advantage in more production must be bluntly asked: How will your stocks do as the ocean dies? when massive crop failures and heat waves kill millions of people? when monster storms and rising seas wipe out coastal areas? when planetary climate chaos makes billions of people desperate? Taking care of our planet before it spirals into chaos makes good sense for everyone.

The fragile fabric of planetary life will not be able to take many more years of the kind of wanton destruction of nature it has suffered at the hands of the CFR-inspired capitalist empire. If we as a species stay on our current path, relatively soon a time will come when the effects will be so severe that we will lose the ability to creatively plan for and implement our own future. We will have only severely degraded ecosystems remaining when planetary forces we cannot control are being unleashed. The slide into an unknown but surely unpleasant fate for ourselves, our children, and grandchildren will then become inevitable. But the promise of humanity resides within itself, and this trend does not have to become our destiny.

We must recognize that we have nothing to lose by revolting and engaging in direct action except the dismal spectacle of observing a dying planet, constantly made uglier by continuing injustice and ecocide. We have a world to gain, the chance to save our beautiful earth and its many life-forms, including humanity itself. Humanity can have a future if we take that future into our own hands by asserting the people's inherent right to alter our current destructive and undemocratic system, which is contrary to the needs and welfare of all.

APPENDIX: CFR OFFICERS AND DIRECTORS, 1921–2013

Isaiah Bowman	1921–50	Charles M. Spofford	1955–72	Graham T. Allison Jr.	1979–88
Archibald Cary Coolidge	1921–28	Adlai E. Stevenson	1958–62	Richard L. Gelb	1979–88
Paul D. Cravath	1921–40	William C. Foster	1959–72	William D. Ruckelshaus	1979–83
John W. Davis	1921–55	Caryl P. Haskins	1961–75	James F. Hoge Jr.	1980–84
Norman H. Davis	1921–44	James A. Perkins	1963–79	William D. Rogers	1980–90
Stephen P. Duggan	1921–50	William P. Bundy	1964–74	George P. Shultz	1980–82
John H. Finley	1921–29	Gabriel Hauge	1964–81	Lewis T. Preston	1981–88
Edwin F. Gay	1921–45	Carroll L. Wilson	1964–79	Walter B. Wriston	1981–87
David F. Houston	1921–27	Douglas Dillon	1965–78	Warren Christopher	1982–91
Otto H. Kahn	1921–34	Henry R. Labouisse	1965–74	Alan Greenspan	1982–88
Frank L. Polk	1921–43	Lucian W. Pye	1966–82	Robert A. Scalapino	1982–89
Whitney H. Shepardson	1921–66	Robert V. Roosa	1966–81	Harold Brown	1983–92
William R. Shepherd	1921–27	Bill Moyers	1967–74	Stanley Hoffmann	1983–92
Paul M. Warburg	1921–32	Alfred C. Neal	1967–76	Juanita M. Kreps	1983–89
George W. Wickersham	1921–36	Cyrus R. Vance	1968–76,	Brent Scowcroft	1983–89
Allen W. Dulles	1927–69		1981–87	Clifton R. Wharton Jr.	1983–92
Russell C. Leffingwell	1927–60	Hedley Donovan	1969–79	Donald F. McHenry	1984–93
George O. May	1927–53	Najeeb E. Halaby	1970–72	B. R. Inman	1985–93
Wesley C. Mitchell	1927–34	Bayless Manning	1971–77	Jeane J. Kirkpatrick	1985–94
Owen D. Young	1927–40	W. Michael Blumenthal	1972–77,	Charles McC. Mathias Jr.	1986–92
Hamilton Fish Armstrong	1928–72		1979–84	Ruben F. Mettler	1986–92
Charles P. Howland	1929–31	Zbigniew Brzezinski	1972–77	Peter Tarnoff	1986–93
Walter Lippmann	1932–37	Elizabeth Drew	1972–77	James E. Burke	1987–95
Clarence M. Woolley	1932–35	George S. Franklin	1972–83	Richard B. Cheney	1987–89,
Frank Altschul	1934–72	Marshall D. Shulman	1972–77		1993–95
Philip C. Jessup	1934–42	Martha Redfield Wallace	1972–82	Robert F. Erburu	1987–98
Harold W. Dodds	1935–43	Paul C. Warnke	1972–77	Karen Elliott House	1987–98,
Leon Fraser	1936–45	Peter G. Peterson	1973–83,		2003–2008
John H. Williams	1937–64		1984–2007	Glenn E. Watts	1987–90
Lewis W. Douglas	1940–64	Robert O. Anderson	1974–80	Thomas S. Foley	1988–94
Edward Warner	1940–49	Edward K. Hamilton	1974–83	James D. Robinson III	1988–91
Clarence E. Hunter	1942–53	Harry C. McPherson Jr.	1974–77	Strobe Talbott	1988–93
Myron C. Taylor	1943–59	Elliot L. Richardson	1974–75	John L. Clendenin	1989–94
Henry M. Wriston	1943–67	Nicholas deB. Katzenbach	1975–86	William S. Cohen	1989–97
Thomas K. Finletter	1944–67	Paul A. Volcker	1975–79,	Joshua Lederberg	1989–98
William A.M. Burden	1945–74		1988–99	John S. Reed	1989–92
Walter H. Mallory	1945–68	Franklin Hall Williams	1975–83	Alice M. Rivlin	1989–92
Philip D. Reed	1945–69	Theodore M. Hesburgh	1976–85	William J. Crowe Jr.	1990–93
Winfield W. Riefler	1945–50	Lane Kirkland	1976–86	Thomas R. Donahue	1990–2001
David Rockefeller	1949–85	George H.W. Bush	1977–79	Richard C. Holbrooke	1991–93,
W. Averell Harriman	1950–55	Lloyd N. Cutler	1977–79		1996–99,
Joseph E. Johnson	1950–74	Philip L. Geyelin	1977–87		2001–2009
Grayson Kirk	1950–73	Henry A. Kissinger	1977–81	Robert D. Hormats	1991–2004
Devereux C. Josephs	1951–58	Winston Lord	1977–85	John E. Bryson	1992–2002
Elliott V. Bell	1953–66	Stephen Stamas	1977–89	Kenneth W. Dam	1992–2001
John J. McCloy	1953–72	Marina v.N. Whitman	1977–87	Maurice R. Greenberg	1992–2002,
Arthur H. Dean	1955–72	C. Peter McColough	1978–87		2004–2009

Karen N. Horn	1992–95	Joseph S. Nye Jr.	2004–2013	**VICE CHAIRMEN**
James R. Houghton	1992–96	Fareed Zakaria	2004–	**OF THE BOARD**
Charlayne Hunter-Gault	1992–98	Peter Ackerman	2005–	Grayson Kirk 1971–73
Donna E. Shalala	1992–93	Charlene Barshefsky	2005–2010	Cyrus R. Vance 1973–76,
Paul A. Allaire	1993–2002	Stephen W. Bosworth	2005–2009	1985–87
Robert E. Allen	1993–96	Tom Brokaw	2005–	Douglas Dillon 1976–78
Richard N. Cooper	1993–94	David M. Rubenstein	2005–	Carroll L. Wilson 1978–79
E. Gerald Corrigan	1993–95	Frank J. Caufield	2006–2010	Warren Christopher 1987–91
Alton Frye	1993	Ann M. Fudge	2006–	Harold Brown 1991–92
Leslie H. Gelb	1993–2001,	Alberto Ibargüen	2006–2013	B. R. Inman 1992–93
	2002–2003	Henry R. Kravis	2006–2012	Jeane J. Kirkpatrick 1993–94
Rita E. Hauser	1993–97	James W. Owens	2006–	Maurice R. Greenberg 1994–2002
Theodore C. Sorensen	1993–2004	Colin M. Powell	2006–	Carla A. Hills 2001–2007
Garrick Utley	1993–2003	Christine Todd Whitman	2006–	William J. McDonough 2002–2003
Carla A. Hills	1994–	Sylvia Mathews Burwell	2007–2013	Robert E. Rubin 2003–2007
Helene L. Kaplan	1994–96	Stephen Friedman	2007–	Richard E. Salomon 2007–2013
Frank G. Zarb	1994–96	Jami Miscik	2007–	David M. Rubenstein 2012–
Robert B. Zoellick	1994–2001	Alan S. Blinder	2008–	
Les Aspin	1995	J. Tomilson Hill	2008–	**HONORARY**
Mario L. Baeza	1995–2001	Shirley Ann Jackson	2008–	**VICE CHAIRMAN**
Peggy Dulany	1995–2003	George Rupp	2008–2013	Maurice R. Greenberg 2002–
Jessica P. Einhorn	1995–2005	David G. Bradley	2009–	
Louis V. Gerstner Jr.	1995–2005	Donna J. Hrinak	2009–	**PRESIDENTS**
Hannah Holborn Gray	1995–98	Penny S. Pritzker	2009–2013	John W. Davis 1921–33
William J. McDonough	1995–2004	Frederick W. Smith	2009–	George W. Wickersham 1933–36
George J. Mitchell	1995–2005	John P. Abizaid	2010–	Norman H. Davis 1936–44
Frank Savage	1995–2002	Mary McInnis Boies	2010–	Russell C. Leffingwell 1944–46
George Soros	1995–2004	Pamela Brooks Gann	2010–	Allen W. Dulles 1946–50
Lee Cullum	1996–2006	Thomas H. Glocer	2011–	Henry M. Wriston 1951–64
Vincent A. Mai	1997–2003	Eduardo J. Padrón	2011–	Grayson Kirk 1964–71
Warren B. Rudman	1997–2005	Peter B. Henry	2012–	Bayless Manning 1971–77
Laura D'Andrea Tyson	1997–2007	Muhtar Kent	2012–	Winston Lord 1977–85
Roone Arledge	1998–2002	Margaret G. Warner	2012–	John Temple Swing* 1985–86
Martin S. Feldstein	1998–2008,	Zoë Baird	2013–	Peter Tarnoff 1986–93
	2009–	R. Nicholas Burns	2013–	Alton Frye 1993
Bette Bao Lord	1998–2003	Steven A. Denning	2013–	Leslie H. Gelb 1993–2003
Michael H. Moskow	1998–2008	Laurence D. Fink	2013–	Richard N. Haass 2003–
Diane Sawyer	1998–99	Ruth Porat	2013–	
John Deutch	1999–2004			**PRESIDENT EMERITUS**
Robert E. Rubin	2000–	**CHAIRMEN OF THE BOARD**		Leslie H. Gelb 2003–
Andrew Young	2000–2005	Russell C. Leffingwell	1946–53	
Henry S. Bienen	2001–2011	John J. McCloy	1953–70	**HONORARY PRESIDENTS**
Kenneth M. Duberstein	2001–2012	David Rockefeller	1970–85	Elihu Root 1921–37
Joan E. Spero	2001–2011	Peter G. Peterson	1985–2007	Henry M. Wriston 1964–78
Vin Weber	2001–2011,	Carla A. Hills		
	2012–	*(Co-Chairman)*	2007–	**EXECUTIVE**
Fouad Ajami	2002–2012	Robert E. Rubin		**VICE PRESIDENTS**
Jeffrey L. Bewkes	2002–2006	*(Co-Chairman)*	2007–	John Temple Swing 1986–93
Ronald L. Olson	2002–2010			Michael P. Peters 2002–2005
Thomas R. Pickering	2002–2007	**CHAIRMAN EMERITUS**		Keith Olson 2012–
Helene D. Gayle	2003–2008	Peter G. Peterson	2007–	
Richard N. Haass	2003–			**CHIEF FINANCIAL OFFICERS**
Richard E. Salomon	2003–2013	**HONORARY CHAIRMEN**		Kenneth Castiglia 2009–2011
Anne-Marie Slaughter	2003–2009	John J. McCloy	1970–1989	Keith Olson 2012–
Madeleine K. Albright	2004–	David Rockefeller	1985–	
Richard N. Foster	2004–2009			* pro tempore

Source: CFR.org, March 3, 2013.

BIBLIOGRAPHY

Listed here are the most important sources consulted in the writing of this study. Not all sources are included below, but all are accounted for in the endnotes.

Archival and Web Sources

For any understanding of the CFR the organization's *Annual Reports* are key sources. During the period 1976–2014 these reports range from nearly 100 pages to about 200 pages in length.

Another central source of information about the CFR is its website, CFR.org. Recent *Annual Reports*, numerous Independent Task Force and other reports, interviews, blogs, biographies, organizational information, up-to-date analyses of current events and other data can be found on this extensive website.

A third important source is the CFR's in-house journal, *Foreign Affairs*. It often features articles by Council leaders, staff and members (who are not always identified as such). *Foreign Affairs* website: www.foreignaffairs.com.

Newspapers

Newspaper reports relating to the CFR and its members are cited in the notes, so will not be listed in this bibliography.

Books, Journal Articles, and Reports

Ajami, Fouad. "The Sentry's Solitude," *Foreign Affairs* 80/6 (November–December 2001).

Alden, Edward, and Matthew J. Slaughter. *U.S. Trade and Investment Policy* (New York: Council on Foreign Relations, 2011).

Ali, Tariq. *The Obama Syndrome: Surrender at Home, War Abroad* (London: Verso, 2010).

Allegretto, Sylvia A. *The State of Working America's Wealth, 2011* (Washington, D.C.: Economic Policy Institute Briefing Paper #292, 2011).

Allen, Michael P. *The Founding Fortunes* (New York: E. P. Dutton, 1987).

Alsop, Stewart. *Nixon and Rockefeller: A Double Portrait* (New York: Doubleday, 1960).

Amin, Samir. *The Implosion of Contemporary Capitalism* (New York: Monthly Review Press, 2013).

Bain, Foster. *Ores and Industry in the Far East* (New York: Council on Foreign Relations, 1927).

Baran, Paul A., and Paul M. Sweezy. *Monopoly Capital: An Essay on the American Economic and Social Order* (New York: Monthly Review Press, 1966).

Blackwill, Robert D., and Meghan L. O'Sullivan. "America's Energy Edge: The Geopolitical Consequences of the Shale Revolution," *Foreign Affairs* 93/2 (March–April 2014).

Blackwill, Robert D., and Walter B. Slocombe. *Israel: A Strategic Asset for the United States* (Washington, D.C.: Washington Institute for Near East Policy, 2011).

Boot, Max. *The Savage Wars of Peace: Small Wars and the Rise of American Power* (New York: Basic Books, 2002).

Bowman, Isaiah. *The New World: Problems in Political Geography* (Yonkers-on-Hudson, NY: World Book Co., 1928).

Brookings Institution. *Iraq Index: Tracking Variables of Reconstruction & Security in Post-Saddam Era* (Washington, D.C.: Brookings Institution, 2009).

Brzezinski, Zbigniew. *Game Plan: A Geostrategic Framework* (New York: Atlantic Monthly Press, 1986).

———. "A Geostrategy for Eurasia," *Foreign Affairs* 76/5 (September–October 1997).

———. *The Grand Chessboard: American Primacy and Its Geostrategic Imperatives* (New York: Basic Books, 1997).

Busby, Joshua. *Climate Change and National Security: An Agenda for Action* (New York: Council on Foreign Relations, 2007).

Campbell, John Franklin. "The Death Rattle of the Eastern Establishment," *New York*, September 20, 1971.

Camps, Miriam, and Catherine Gwin. *Collective Management: The Reform of Global Economic Organizations* (New York: Council on Foreign Relations and McGraw-Hill, 1981).

Carroll, William K. *The Making of a Transnational Capitalist Class: Corporate Power in the 21st Century* (London: Zed Books, 2010).

Chatterjee, Pratap. *Iraq, Inc.: A Profitable Occupation* (New York: Seven Stories Press, 2004).

Cleveland, Harold van B., and Ramachandra Bhagavatula. "The Continuing World Economic Crisis," *Foreign Affairs* 59/3 (1980).

Cohen, Elliot. "A Tale of Two Secretaries," *Foreign Affairs* 81/3 (May–June 2002).

Coll, Steve. *Private Empire: ExxonMobil and American Power* (New York: Penguin Group, 2012).

Conant, Melvin A. *The Oil Factor in U.S. Foreign Policy, 1980–1990* (Lexington, MA: A Council on Foreign Relations Book, D. C. Heath, 1982).

Constitution Project. *Report of The Constitution Project's Task Force on Detainee Treatment* (Washington, D.C: The Constitution Project, 2013).

Crain, Andrew D. *The Ford Presidency: A History* (Jefferson, NC: McFarland, 2009).

Credit Suisse. *Global Wealth Data Book* (Zurich: Credit Suisse Research Institute, 2010).

Crozier, Michael J., Samuel P. Huntington, and Joji Watanuki. *The Crisis of Democracy: Report on the Governability of Democracies to the Trilateral Commission* (New York: New York University Press, 1975).

Daalder, Ivo H., and James M. Lindsay. *America Unbound: The Bush Revolution in Foreign Policy* (Hoboken, NJ: John Wiley, 2005).

Davies, James B., Susanna Sandstrom, Anthony Shorrocks, and Edward Wolff. *World Distribution of Household Wealth* (Santa Cruz, CA: Center for Global, International and Regional Studies, University of California, 2007).

Djerejian, Edward P., and Frank G. Wisner, Rachel Bronson and Andrew S. Weiss. *Guiding Principles for U.S. Post-Conflict Policy in Iraq* (New York: Baker Institute for Public Policy of Rice University and the Council on Foreign Relations, 2003).

Downie, Richard. *The Road to Recovery: Rebuilding Liberia's Health System* (Washington: CSIS Global Health Policy Center, 2012).

Draper, Hal. *Karl Marx's Theory of Revolution*, vol. 1: *State and Bureaucracy* (New York: Monthly Review Press, 1977).

Fifield, Russell H. *Southeast Asia in United States Policy* (New York: Council on Foreign Relations, 1963).

Fishlow, Albert, Carlos F. Diaz-Alejandro, Richard R. Fagen, and Roger D. Hansen. *Rich and Poor Nations in the World Economy* (New York: Council on Foreign Relations and McGraw-Hill, 1978).

Florida, Richard. "What Is the World's Most Economically Powerful City?," *The Atlantic*, May 8, 2012.

Foster, John Bellamy. "Why Ecological Revolution," *Monthly Review* 61/8 (January 2010).

———. "The Age of Monopoly–Finance Capital," *Monthly Review* 61/9 (February 2010).

———."The Financialization of Accumulation," *Monthly Review* 62/5 (October 2010).

———. "The Epochal Crisis," *Monthly Review* 65/5 (October 2013).

Foster, John Bellamy, Robert W. McChesney, and R. Jamil Jonna. "The Internationalization of Monopoly Capital," *Monthly Review* 63/2 (June 2011).

Freeland, Chrystia. *Plutocrats: The Rise of the New Global Super-Rich and the Fall of Everyone Else* (New York: Penguin Press, 2012).

Frye, Alton. *Humanitarian Intervention: Crafting a Workable Approach* (New York: Council on Foreign Relations, 2000).

Galbraith, James K. *The Predator State* (New York: Free Press, 2008).

Galeano, Eduardo. *Days and Nights of Love and War* (London: Pluto Press, 2000).

Greenspan, Alan. *The Age of Turbulence: Adventures in a New World* (New York: Penguin Press, 2007).

Greider, William. *Secrets of the Temple: How the Federal Reserve Rules the Country* (New York: Simon and Schuster, 1989).

Grim, Ryan. "Priceless: How the Federal Reserve Bought the Economics Profession," *HuffingtonPost.com*, May 25, 2011.

Grose, Peter. *Continuing the Inquiry: The Council on Foreign Relations from 1921 to 1996* (New York: Council on Foreign Relations, 2006).

Guha, Ranajit. *Dominance Without Hegemony: History and Power in Colonial India* (Cambridge, MA: Harvard University Press, 1998).

Haass, Richard N. *The Reluctant Sheriff: The United States after the Cold War* (New York: Council on Foreign Relations, 1997).

———. "What to Do with American Primacy," *Foreign Affairs* 78/5 (September/October 1999).

———. *War of Necessity War of Choice: A Memoir of Two Iraq Wars* (New York: Simon and Schuster, 2009).

———. *Foreign Policy Begins at Home: The Case for Putting America's House in Order* (New York: Basic Books, 2013).

Harvey, David. *A Brief History of Neoliberalism* (Oxford: Oxford University Press, 2005).

Heaton, Herbert. *A Scholar in Action: Edwin F. Gay* (Cambridge, MA: Harvard University Press, 1952).

Hirsh, Michael. "Tough Diplomacy," *Newsweek,* February 16, 2005.

Horton, Scott. "The Guantánamo 'Suicides': A Camp Delta Sergeant Blows the Whistle," *Harper's,* March 2010.

Huntington, Samuel P. *The Clash of Civilizations and the Remaking of the World Order* (New York: Simon and Schuster, 1996).

Ikenberry, G. John. "America's Imperial Ambition," *Foreign Affairs* 81/5 (September–October 2002).

Iraq Planning Group. *Choosing Victory: A Plan for Success in Iraq,* Phase 1 Report (Washington, D.C.: American Enterprise Institute, 2007).

Iraq Study Group. *Iraq Study Group Report: The Way Forward: A New Approach* (Washington, D.C.: American Peace Institute, 2006).

Jacobson, Mark Z., and Mark A. Dlucchi. "A Path to Sustainable Energy by 2030," *Scientific American,* November 2009.

Jannuzi, Frank Sampson. *U.S.- China Relations: An Affirmative Agenda, A Responsible Course, Report of an Independent Task Force* (New York: Council on Foreign Relations, 2007).

Jabber, Paur, Gary Sick, Hisahiko Okazaki, and Dominique Moisi. *Great Power Interests in the Persian Gulf* (New York: Council on Foreign Relations, 1989).

Jeffers, H. Paul. *The Bilderberg Conspiracy: Inside the World's Most Powerful Secret Society* (New York: Kensington Publishing, 2009).

Jones, Geoffrey, and Mary Rose. *Family Capitalism* (New York: Routledge, 2012).

Juhasz, Antonia. "Capitalism Gone Wild," *Tikkun* 19/1 (January–February 2004).

Kinzer, Stephen. *Overthrow: America's Century of Regime Change from Hawaii to Iraq* (New York: Times Books, 2006).

Klein, Naomi. *The Shock Doctrine: The Rise of Disaster Capitalism* (New York: Henry Holt, 2007).

———. *This Changes Everything: Capitalism vs. the Climate* (New York: Simon and Schuster, 2014).

Korten, David C. *When Corporations Rule the World* (West Hartford, CT: Kumarian Press, 1995).

Krugman, Paul. *The Accidental Theorist: And Other Dispatches from the Dismal Science* (New York: W. W. Norton, 1998).

Kupchan, Charles A. *Reviving the Atlantic Partnership* (New York: Council on Foreign Relations, 2004).

Lambrecht, Bill. *Dinner at the New Gene Café: How Genetic Engineering Is Changing What*

We Eat, How We Live, and the Global Politics of Food (New York: St. Martin's Press, 2001).

Levi, Michael A., and David G. Victor. *Confronting Climate Change: A Strategy for U.S. Foreign Policy* (New York: Council on Foreign Relations, 2008).

Levi, Michael A. *The Canadian Oil Sands: Energy Security vs. Climate Change* (New York: Council on Foreign Relations, 2009).

Lundberg, Ferdinand. *America's 60 Families* (New York: Citadel Press, 1946).

————. *The Rich and the Super-Rich* (New York: Lyle Stuart, 1968).

Maass, Peter. "The Way of the Commandos," *The New York Times Magazine,* May 1, 2005.

McChesney, Robert W. "This Isn't What Democracy Looks Like," *Monthly Review* 64/6 (November 2012).

McGann, James G. *Think Tanks and Policy Advice in the United States: Academics, Advisors and Advocates* (New York: Routledge, 2007).

————. *The Global "Go-To Think Tanks": The Leading Public Policy Research Organizations in the World* (Philadelphia: Think Tanks and Civil Societies Program, University of Pennsylvania, 2010).

Madrick, Jeff. *Age of Greed: The Triumph of Finance and the Decline of America, 1970 to the Present* (New York: Alfred A. Knopf, 2011).

Magdoff, Fred. "Ecological Civilization," *Monthly Review* 62/8 (January 2011).

Magdoff, Fred, and John Bellamy Foster. "What Every Environmentalist Needs to Know about Capitalism," *Monthly Review* 61/10 (March 2010).

Maheshvarananda, Dada. *After Capitalism: Economic Democracy in Action* (San German, PR: InnerWorld Publications, 2012).

Mallaby, Sebastian. "The Reluctant Imperialist: Terrorism, Failed States, and the Case for American Empire," *Foreign Affairs* 81/2 (March–April 2002).

Mandelbaum, Michael. "U.S. Must Plan Post-Hussein Iraq," *Newsday,* August 1, 2002.

————. *The Case for Goliath: How America Acts as the World's Government in the Twenty-first Century* (New York: Public Affairs, 2005).

Mander, Jerry. "Privatization of Consciousness," *Monthly Review* 64/5 (October 2012).

Mann, James. *Rise of the Vulcans: The History of Bush's War Cabinet* (New York: Penguin Books, 2004).

Markey, Daniel S. *U. S. Strategy for Pakistan and Afghanistan* (New York: Council on Foreign Relations, 2010).

Marx, Karl. *The Portable Karl Marx,* selected, translated in part, and with an Introduction by Eugene Kamenka (New York: Penguin Books, 1983).

Maxwell, Kenneth. "The Other 9/11: The United States and Chile, 1973," *Foreign Affairs* 82/6 (November–December 2003).

Mead, Walter Russell. *Power, Terror, Peace and War: America's Grand Strategy in a World at Risk* (New York: Alfred A. Knopf, 2004).

Mearsheimer, John J. "Why the Ukraine Crisis Is the West's Fault," *Foreign Affairs* 93/5 (September–October 2014).

Medvetz, Thomas. *Think Tanks in America* (Chicago: University of Chicago Press, 2012).

Menshikov, S. *Millionaires and Managers* (Moscow: Progress Publishers, 1969).

Moritz, Charles. *Current Biography Yearbook* (New York: H. W. Wilson, 1972).

Murphy, Richard W. *Differentiated Containment: U.S. Policy Toward Iran and Iraq* (New York: Council on Foreign Relations, 1997).

Neikirk, William R. *Volcker: Portrait of the Money Man* (New York: Congdon & Weed, 1987).

Newman, Peter C. *Bronfman Dynasty: Rothschilds of the New World* (Toronto: McClelland & Stewart, 1978).

Nichols, John, and Robert W. McChesney. *Dollarocracy: How the Money and Media Complex Is Destroying America* (New York: Nation Books, 2013).

Nye, Joseph S., Jr. *Soft Power: The Means to Success in World Politics* (New York: Public Affairs, 2004).

Packer, George. *The Unwinding: An Inner History of the New America* (New York: Farrar, Straus and Giroux, 2013).

Panitch, Leo, and Sam Gindin. *The Making of Global Capitalism: The Political Economy of American Empire* (London: Verso, 2012).

Peterson, Peter G. *The Education of an American Dreamer...* (New York: Hachette Book Group, 2009).

Petraeus, David H. "Learning from Counterinsurgency: Observations from Soldiering in Iraq," *Military Review* (January–February 2006).

Phillips, Kevin. *Wealth and Democracy: A Political History of the American Rich* (New York: Broadway Books, 2002).

Pollack, Kenneth M. "Next Stop Baghdad?," *Foreign Affairs* 81/2 (March–April 2002).

———. *The Threatening Storm: The Case for Invading Iraq* (New York: A Council on Foreign Relations Book, Random House, 2002).

———. "Securing the Gulf," *Foreign Affairs* 82/4 (July–August 2003).

Rice, Condoleezza. *No Higher Honor: A Memoir of My Years in Washington* (New York: Crown Publishing, 2011).

Rizopoulos, Nicholas X., ed. *Sea Changes: American Foreign Policy in a World Transformed* (New York: Council on Foreign Relations Press, 1990).

Robinson, Linda. *The Future of U.S. Special Operations Forces* (New York: Council on Foreign Relations, 2013).

Rockefeller, David. *Memoirs* (New York: Random House, 2003).

Rothkopf, David J. "The Ultimate Lagging Indicator," *Foreign Affairs* 77/1 (January–February 1998).

Rumsfeld, Donald. "Transforming the Military," *Foreign Affairs* 81/3 (May–June 2002).

Sanders, Barry. *The Green Zone: The Environmental Costs of Militarism* (Oakland, CA: AK Press, 2009).

Scahill, Jeremy. *Dirty Wars: The World Is a Battlefield* (New York: Nation Books, 2013).

Schick, Elizabeth A. *Current Biography Yearbook* (New York: H. W. Wilson, 1997).

Shelton, Hugh. *Without Hesitation: The Odyssey of an American Warrior* (New York: St. Martin's Press, 2010).

Shepardson, Whitney H. *Early History of the Council on Foreign Relations* (Stamford, CT: Overbrook Press, 1960).

Shoup, Laurence H. *The Carter Presidency and Beyond: Power and Politics in the 1980s* (Palo Alto, CA: Ramparts Press, 1980).

———. "Corporate Gold: The Presidential Election 2008," *Z Magazine* 21/2 (February 2008).

Shoup, Laurence H., and William Minter. *Imperial Brain Trust: The Council on Foreign Relations and U.S. Foreign Policy* (New York: Monthly Review Press, 1977).

Sielen, Allan. "The Devolution of the Seas: The Consequences of Oceanic Destruction," *Foreign Affairs* 92/6 (November–December 2013).

Sigmund, Paul E. "The 'Invisible Blockade' and the Overthrow of Allende," *Foreign Affairs* 52/2 (January 1974).

Sklair, Leslie. *The Transnational Capitalist Class* (Malden: MA: Blackwell, 2001).

Social Register Association. *Social Register, 1930* (New York: Social Register Association, 1929).

Stone, Diane, and Andrew Denham, eds. *Think Tank Traditions: Policy Research and the Politics of Ideas* (Manchester, UK: Manchester University Press, 2004).

Suskind, Ron. *The Price of Loyalty: George W. Bush, the White House, and the Education of Paul O'Neill* (New York: Simon and Schuster, 2004).

Tama, Jordan. *Terrorism and National Security Reform: How Commissions Can Drive Change during Crises* (Cambridge: Cambridge University Press, 2011).

Treaster, Joseph B. *Paul Volcker: The Making of a Financial Legend* (New York: John Wiley, 2004).

Vernon, Raymond, ed. *The Promise of Privatization: A Challenge for U.S. Policy* (New York: Council on Foreign Relations, 1988).

Victor, David G. *The Collapse of the Kyoto Protocol and the Struggle to Slow Global Warming* (Princeton: A Council on Foreign Relations Book, Princeton University Press, 2001).

———. *Climate Change: Debating America's Policy Options* (New York: Council on Foreign Relations, 2004).

Victor, David G., and L. Ford Runge. *Sustaining a Revolution: A Policy Strategy for Crop Engineering* (New York: Council on Foreign Relations, 2002).

Wedgwood, Ruth. "Strike at Saddam Now," *National Law Journal,* October 28, 2002.

Williams, Chris. *Ecology and Socialism* (Chicago: Haymarket Book, 2010).

Wolff, Edward N. "Recent Trends in Household Wealth in the United States: Rising Debt and the Middle-Class Squeeze—an Update to 2007," Levy Economics Institute Working Paper No. 589, Bard College, 2010.

Woodward, Bob, and Carl Bernstein. *The Final Days* (New York: Simon and Schuster, 1976).

World Economic Forum, *The World Economic Forum: A Partner in Shaping History, the First 40 Years, 1971–2010* (Geneva: World Economic Forum, 2009).

Wright, Ronald. *A Short History of Progress* (Cambridge, MA: Da Capo Press, 2004).

Wriston, Walter. *Risk and Other Four Letter Words* (New York: Harper and Row, 1986).

Zeitlin, Maurice, and Richard E. Ratcliff. *Landlords and Capitalists: The Dominant Class of Chile* (Princeton: Princeton University Press, 1988).

Zenko, Micah. *Reforming U.S. Drone Strike Policies* (New York: Council on Foreign Relations, 2013).

NOTES

1. Paul A. Baran and Paul M. Sweezy, *Monopoly Capital: An Essay on the American Economic and Social Order* (New York: Monthly Review Press, 1966); John Bellamy Foster, "The Financialization of Accumulaion," *Monthly Review* 62/5 (October 2010).

2. See David Rothkopf, *Superclass: The Global Power Elite and the World they are Making* (New York: Farrar, Straus and Giroux, 2008).

3. CFR, *Annual Report 2000*, 18; *Annual Report 2007*, 13. Hereafter CFR, *AR* date, and page.

4. Dada Maheshvarananda, *After Capitalism: Economic Democracy in Action* (San German, PR: InnerWorld Publications, 2012), 292.

5. Samir Amin, *The Implosion of Contemporary Capitalism* (New York: Monthly Review Press, 2013), 9, 45–48.

6. CFR, *AR* 1994, 12.

7. CFR, *AR* 2007, 13.

8. CFR, *AR* 2014, 6, 81–88.

9. Peter Grose, *Continuing the Inquiry: The Council on Foreign Relations from 1921 to 1996* (New York: Council on Foreign Relations, 2006), 8.

10. Whitney H. Shepardson, *Early History of the Council on Foreign Relations* (Stamford, CT: Overbrook Press, 1960), 16.

11. CFR, *AR* 2013, 31–33.

12. Laurence H. Shoup and William Minter, *Imperial Brain Trust: The Council on Foreign Relations and U.S. Foreign Policy* (New York: Monthly Review Press, 1977), 16–17, 104–5.

13. Social Register Association, *Social Register, 1930* (New York: Social Register, 1929).

14. Herbert Heaton, *A Scholar in Action: Edwin F. Gay* (Cambridge, MA: Harvard University Press, 1952), 51.

15. Grose, *Continuing the Inquiry*, xiii–xiv.

16. Shoup and Minter, *Imperial Brain Trust*, 20.

17. Grose, *Continuing the Inquiry*, 27–28.

18. Ibid., 1.

19. Isaiah Bowman, *The New World: Problems in Political Geography* (Yonkers-on-Hudson, NY: World Book Co., 1928), 14.

20. Foster Bain, *Ores and Industry in the Far East* (New York: Council on Foreign Relations, 1927).

21. Shoup and Minter, *Imperial Brain Trust*, 117–87.

22. Grose, *Continuing the Inquiry*, 41–42.

23. CFR, *AR* 1951, 2.

24. William P. Bundy, *The History of Foreign Affairs,* 1994, 3, available at www.cfr.org.

25. Ibid., 6.

26. Grose, *Continuing the Inquiry,* 41.

27. Shoup and Minter, *Imperial Brain Trust,* 200–201.

28. Ibid., 207–12; Grose, *Continuing the Inquiry,* 43–44.

29. Russell H. Fifield, *Southeast Asia in United States Policy* (New York: Council on Foreign Relations, 1963), 4–5.

30. Shoup and Minter, *Imperial Brain Trust,* 233–38.

31. Ibid., 240–49; Grose, *Continuing the Inquiry,* 49–53.

32. John Franklin Campbell, "The Death Rattle of the Eastern Establishment," *New York,* September 20, 1971, 47–51.

33. CFR, *AR* 1970, 82–93.

34. Ferdinand Lundberg, *America's 60 Families* (New York: Citadel Press), 19.

35. Stewart Alsop, *Nixon and Rockefeller: A Double Portrait* (New York: Doubleday, 1960), 41.

36. Sylvia A. Allegretto, *The State of Working America's Wealth, 2011* (Washington, D.C.: Economic Policy Institute Briefing Paper # 292, 2011), 6, 8, 14.

37. *Financial Times,* May 6, 2012, 2.

38. See G. William Domhoff, ucsc.edu/ whorulesamerica/power/wealth, 2012; Edward N. Wolff, "Recent Trends in Household Wealth in the United States: Rising Debt and the Middle Class Squeeze—An Update to 2007," Levy Economics Institute Working Paper No. 589, Bard College, 2010.

39. *Financial Times,* May 6, 2012, 4.

40. WealthInsight, World City Millionaire Rankings, May 2013;

available at www.theguardian.com/ news/datablog/2013/may/08/ cities-top-millionaires-billionaires.

41. Richard Florida, "What Is the World's Most Economically Powerful City?" *The Atlantic,* May 8, 2012; *Financial Times,* October 2, 2014, 15.

42. See the richest.com at www. nbcnews.com/10richest presidents.

43. CFR, *AR* 2007, 71.

44. Ibid.

45. David Rockefeller, *Memoirs* (New York: Random House, 2003), 138–39.

46. Ibid., 83.

47. Ibid., 88.

48. Ibid., 215.

49. *New York Times,* October 20, 2003, F8.

50. Rockefeller, *Memoirs,* 247–48.

51. Ibid., 258.

52. Ibid.

53. Ibid., 264, 272–76, 282, 301–2.

54. Ibid., 311, 369.

55. Ibid., 154.

56. Daniel Schafer, "Rockefellers and Rothschilds Unite," *The Independent* (London), May 31, 2012; Tom Bawden, "Transatlantic Alliance between Rothschilds and Rockefellers for Wealth Management," *Financial Times,* May 29, 2012.

57. CFR, *AR* 2013, 43, 54.

58. Peter G. Peterson, *The Education of an American Dreamer . . .* (New York: Hachette Book Group, 2009), 44–51.

59. Charles Moritz, *Current Biography Yearbook* (New York: H. W. Wilson, 1972), 350.

60. Peterson, *The Education,* 125–26.

61. Ibid., 128.

62. Ibid., 156–206.

63. Ibid., 124.

64. Ibid.

65. Ibid., 91.

66. Ibid., 309.

67. Elizabeth A. Schick, *Current Biography Yearbook* (New York: H. W. Wilson, 1997), 473.

68. George Packer, *The Unwinding: An Inner History of the New America* (New York: Farrar, Straus and Giroux, 2013), 223.

69. Tariq Ali, *The Obama Syndrome: Surrender at Home, War Abroad* (London: Verso, 2010), 90.

70. Eric Dash & Louise Story, "Rubin Leaving Citigroup; Smith Barney for Sale," *New York Times,* January 9, 2009.

71. *Politico,* April 8, 2010. See www. politico.com/news/stories 0410/35515.html.

72. Robert Rubin, "Slaying the Dragon of Debt: Fiscal Politics and Policy Since the 1970s" (Berkeley: University of California Regional Oral History Project, Bancroft Library, 2011).

73. CFR, *AR* 2007, 71.

74. John Caher, "Greenberg AIG Case Headed to State Court of Appeals," *New York Law Journal,* July 18, 2012.

75. *Financial Times,* February 28, 2012, 15.

76. *Financial Times,* March 23–24, 2013, 3.

77. *Financial Times,* March 1, 2013, 7

78. *Financial Times,* March 9–10, 2013, 1; March 23–24, 2013, 3.

79. CFR, *AR* 2007, 71.

80. Leslie H. Gelb, *Power Rules: How Common Sense Can Rescue American Foreign Policy* (New York: HarperCollins, 2009).

81. *Financial Times,* May 25–26, 2013, 2.

82. See www.forbes.com/profile/ richard–haass/; Richard N. Haass, *The Opportunity: America's Moment to Alter History's Course* (New York: PublicAffairs, 2005).

83. See blogs.ft.com/the–a– list/2013/04/09/thatcher.

84. See www. laurenceshoup.com for more details about many other individual CFR directors during the 1976–2014 era.

85. CFR, *AR* 1987, 87.

86. CFR, *AR* 1978, 75; 1987, 167; 1995, 125–26; 2003, 88; 2006, 65.

87. CFR, *AR* 1995, 107; 1997, 96; 2000, 108; 2006, 60.

88. www.forbes.com/profilemartin– feldstein/.

89. CFR, *AR* 2014, 33; www. rockefeller.edu/pubinfo/roster. pdf; americanassembly.org/people/ trustee/steven-stamas.

90. See WealthInsight World City Millionaire Rankings, May 2013.http:ftalphaville.ft.com/ files/2013/05/world-cities-wealth- briefing.pdf.

91. CFR, *AR* 2011, 31–52; 2012, 33–54. A list of over 125 of the most prominent, most powerful, and most well known of the Council's capitalist-class members can be found at www.laurenceshoup.com. They are listed by name together with available information about wealth level and connections. This list is indicative and instructive, but by no means definitive. The list includes prominent capitalist members listed in the *Annual Reports* of 2011 and 2012 only.

92. CFR, *AR* 1999, 6.

93. CFR, *AR* 1981, 20.

94. Ibid., 91–92.

95. CFR, *AR* 1986, 101.

96. CFR, *AR* 2014, 32.

97. CFR, *AR* 2011, 24.

98. CFR, *AR* 2012, 26; 2013, 30; 2014, 32.

99. CFR, *AR* 1984, 12.

100. CFR, *AR* 2011, 28.

101. CFR, *AR* 2014, 5.

102. CFR, *AR* 2011, 30.

103. Ibid., 28.

104. CFR, *AR* 2014, 39.

105. Ibid.

106. Steve Clemons, www. huffingtonpost.com/steve–clemons/theimpact-today-and-tomo_b_786578.html..

107. CFR, *AR* 1977, 4.

108. CFR, *AR* 1978, 14, 75–77.

109. CFR, *AR* 1980, 14.

110. CFR, *AR* 1980, 74–75, 82.

111. CFR, *AR* 1981, 6.

112. CFR, *AR* 1983, 12.

113. CFR, *AR* 1981, 88–89; 1982, 97–98.

114. CFR, *AR* 1984, 94.

115. *Newsweek*, October 2, 1972, 40.

116. CFR, *AR* 1985, 104; 1988, 113.

117. CFR, *AR* 1987, 43, 84.

118. CFR, *AR* 1988, 103.

119. CFR, *AR* 1990, 60; 1991, 41.

120. Condoleezza Rice, *No Higher Honor: A Memoir of My Years in Washington* (New York: Crown, 2011).

121. CFR, *AR* 1990, 105–6.

122. Ibid., 15.

123. CFR, *AR* 1993, 7.

124. Ibid., 7.

125. Ibid., 10, 13.

126. CFR, *AR* 1994, 23–24; 1995, 7.

127. CFR, *AR* 1981, 6; 1994, 24, 100; 1995, 87–88.

128. CFR, *AR* 1995, 36.

129. CFR, *AR* 1996, 45.

130. Ibid., 11.

131. CFR, *AR* 1997, 85.

132. Ibid., 64.

133. CFR, *AR* 1998, 80.

134. CFR, *AR* 2014, 6.

135. CFR, *AR* 1996, 79.

136. CFR, *AR* 1997, 6.

137. Ibid., 7, 13.

138. CFR, *AR* 1999, 69.

139. CFR, *AR* 2001, 15.

140. Ibid., 52–53.

141. CFR, *AR* 2005, 40–43.

142. CFR, *AR* 1981, 6; 2007, 10, 27.

143. CFR, *AR* 2007, 9, 41.

144. Ibid., 13.

145. Pew Research Center, *America's Place in the World 2013*, 46, 53, 70. www.people-press.org/files/legacy-pdf/12-3-2013.

146. Ibid., 65.

147. Ibid., 73–74.

148. Ibid., 76.

149. CFR, *AR* 2014, 65.

150. Ibid., 63.

151. *Financial Times*, Special Report, November 21, 2011, 1.

152. *Financial Times*, December 22, 2011, 16.

153. Ibid.

154. "Fortune 500: America's Largest Corporations," *Fortune*. May 3, 2010.

155. *Financial Times*, November 27, 2011, 1.

156. Ibid.

157. CFR, *AR* 2005, 44.

158. Ibid., 45.

159. CFR, *AR* 2012, 15.

160. CFR, *AR* 2005, 45.

161. CFR, *AR* 2008, 46.

162. CFR, *AR* 2010, 8.

163. CFR, *AR* 2011, 5; lists of the Council's corporate membership as of 1993 and 2011 can be found at laurenceshoup.com.

164. CFR, *AR* 2008, 12.

165. CFR, *AR* 2012, 18.

166. CFR, *AR* 2014, 8.

167. CFR, *AR* 2012. 18.

168. Ibid., 8.

169. Ibid., 18.

170. CFR, *AR* 1978, 5.

171. CFR, *AR* 1987, 19.

172. CFR, *AR* 1996, 13.

173. Ibid., 79.
174. CFR, *AR* 2013, 78–80.
175. CFR, *AR* 1989, 60.
176. CFR, *AR* 1975, 3.
177. CFR, *AR* 1976, 1–2; 1982, 13.
178. CFR, *AR* 1976, 1–2.
179. CFR, *AR* 1977, 5, 65.
180. Ibid., 65.
181. See www.foreignaffairs.com/about-us.
182. Ibid.; CFR, *AR* 1982, 13; 1988, 13; 2000, 55.
183. See www.foreignaffairs.com/about-us/advertising/circulation.
184. CFR, *AR* 1994, 10.
185. CFR, *AR* 1977, 7.
186. CFR, *AR* 2000, 55.
187. CFR, *AR* 2014, 29.
188. CFR, *AR* 1982, 16–17, 20.
189. CFR, *AR* 1980, 15, 53.
190. CFR, *AR* 1989, 12.
191. CFR, *AR* 1998, 15.
192. CFR, *AR* 1997, 29–30; 1998, 15; 2011, 4.
193. CFR, *AR* 2001, 6.
194. CFR, *AR* 1997, 34.
195. CFR, *AR* 1994, 7.
196. CFR, *AR* 1997, 23.
197. CFR, *AR* 2001, 6.
198. Ibid., 7.
199. Ibid.
200. Ibid.
201. Ibid.
202. CFR, *AR* 1998, 15.
203. Ibid.
204. CFR, *AR* 1997, 29–30.
205. CFR, *AR* 2000, 18.
206. CFR, *AR* 1999, 8.
207. CFR, *AR* 2002, 8.
208. CFR, *AR* 2001, 13.
209. CFR, *AR* 2005, 82–83.
210. Ibid.
211. CFR, *AR* 2002, 7, 10, 25.
212. Ibid., 25.
213. Ibid., 6, 32.
214. CFR, *AR* 2003, 6–7.

215. Ibid., 9.
216. Ibid., 10.
217. *New York Times,* June 5, 2003, A11.
218. *New York Times,* September 9, 2003, B2.
219. Ibid.
220. CFR, *AR* 2004, 17.
221. Ibid., 20.
222. CFR, *AR* 2005, 17.
223. Ibid., 17–18.
224. Ibid., 24.
225. CFR, *AR* 2007, 28.
226. Ibid., 8, 27.
227. Ibid., 13.
228. CFR, *AR* 2009, 13; 2010, 10; 2011, 14.
229. CFR, *AR* 2008, 15; 2010, 16.
230. CFR, *AR* 2008, 15; 2010, 8; 2011, 8.
231. CFR, *AR* 2011, 17.
232. Ibid., 13.
233. Ibid., 10–11.
234. CFR, *AR* 2012, 11.
235. Ibid., 16.
236. Ibid.
237. See CFR *Experts Guide,* at www.cfr.org/thinktank/experts.
238. Ibid.
239. CFR, *AR* 1976, 23; 1982, 11, 28, 38; 1984, 10; 1986, 39; 1991, 29, 38; 1994, 61; 1998, 54, 56, 61, 68; 2002, 45, 46, 49; 2003, 40.
240. *Financial Times,* September 30, 2013, 11.
241. CFR, *AR* 2014, 36.
242. CFR, *AR* 1976, 11.
243. Ibid., 13–32.
244. CFR, *AR* 1986, 23–26.
245. Ibid., 24.
246. Ibid., 23.
247. Ibid.
248. Ibid.
249. CFR, *AR* 1996, 12, 54.
250. CFR, *AR* 2006, 32.
251. Ibid., 32–33.
252. Ibid., 36–39.
253. Ibid., 40–43.

254. Ibid., 44–45.
255. CFR, *AR* 2001, 6.
256. CFR, *AR* 1987, 101.
257. CFR, *AR* 1989, 132.
258. Ibid.
259. Ibid.
260. CFR, *AR* 1990, 134.
261. See www.cfr.org/thinktank/iigg/ mission.
262. CFR, *AR* 2011, 9.
263. Ibid.
264. Edward Alden and James M. Lindsay, www.cfr.org/competitiveness/ renewing–america.
265. Richard Haass, *Foreign Policy Begins at Home: The Case for Putting America's House in Order* (New York: Basic Books, 2013).
266. Diane Stone and Andrew Denham, eds., *Think Tank Traditions: Policy Research and the Politics of Ideas* (Manchester, UK: Manchester University Press, 2004), 289.
267. Ibid., 286–88.
268. *Financial Times,* July 8, 2013, 1; CFR, *AR* 2013, 79.
269. CFR, *AR* 1996, 155; 2001, 9; 2005, 66.
270. *Financial Times,* October 12, 2012, 1, 5.
271. *Washington Post,* November 24, 2008, A13.
272. *Financial Times,* November 18, 2013, 21.
273. CFR, *AR* 1977, 1.
274. CFR, *AR* 2011, 30.
275. CFR, *AR* 1998, 5.
276. CFR, *AR* 1994, 150; 1996, 163; 1998, 28.
277. CFR, *AR* 2002, 82; 2003, 89; 2004, 65–66.
278. CFR, *AR* 2013, 41.
279. CFR, *AR* 1994, 146; 1995, 148.
280. www.state.gov/s/p/fapb/.
281. http://en.wikipedia.org/wiki/ Project on National Security Reform; CFR, *AR* 2012, 71.

282. Jordan Tama, *Terrorism and National Security Reform: How Commissions Can Drive Change during Crises* (Cambridge: Cambridge University Press, 2011), 199–205.
283. James G. McGann, *Think Tanks and Policy Advice in the United States: Academics, Advisors and Advocates* (New York: Routledge, 2007).
284. James G. McGann, *The Global "Go–To Think Tanks": The Leading Public Policy Research Organizations in the World* (Philadelphia: Think Tanks and Civil Societies Program, University of Pennsylvania, 2010), 36.
285. Ibid., 25.
286. McGann, *Think Tanks and Policy Advice,* 23.
287. CFR, *AR* 2005, 86.
288. McGann, *Think Tanks and Policy Advice,* 75–139.
289. CFR, *AR* 2007, 94–111.
290. Quotes about the think tanks discussed in the following section are from the websites or *Annual Reports* of these organizations.
291. The Brookings Institution *Annual Report* (Washington, D.C.: Brookings Institution, 2011).
292. Ibid., 1.
293. Richard N. Haass, "Toward Greater Democracy in the Muslim World, " available at wwwCFR.org/ democratization/toward–greater– democracy–muslim–world, 2002.
294. CFR, *AR* 1995, 148; 2013, 47.
295. Alton Frye, *Humanitarian Intervention: Crafting a Workable Approach* (New York: Council on Foreign Relations, 2000), ix; CFR, *AR* 2000, 144; 2013, 41.
296. www.aei.org/about; see also http:// en.wikipedia.org/wiki/American Enterprise Institute.
297. *Financial Times,* February 15–16, 2014, Life and Arts, 1.

298. Peterson, *The Education,* 327.

299. See Maurice Zeitlin and Richard E. Ratcliff, *Landlords and Capitalists: The Dominant Class of Chile* (Princeton: Princeton University Press, 1988); Michael P. Allen, *The Founding Fortunes* (New York: E. P. Dutton, 1987); Geoffrey Jones and Mary Rose, *Family Capitalism* (New York: Routledge, 2012); S. Menshikov, *Millionaires and Managers* (Moscow: Progress Publishers, 1969); Ferdinand Lundberg, *America's 60 Families* (New York: Citadel Press, 1946); Ferdinand Lundberg, *The Rich and the Super Rich* (New York: Lyle Stuart, 1968).

300. CFR, *AR* 2007, 48.

301. CFR, *AR* 2008, 46–47.

302. *Financial Times,* July 8, 2012, 15; CFR, *AR* 2012, 55–56.

303. *Fortune,* May 3, 2010, F-33.

304. CFR, *AR* 2007, 74.

305. *Financial Times,* March 5, 2012, 16.

306. CFR, *AR* 2007, 74.

307. *Financial Times,* April 10, 2012, 18.

308. *Financial Times,* March 22, 2013, 23.

309. *Financial Times,* March 8, 2014, 5.

310. *Financial Times,* July 8, 2013, 15.

311. CFR, *AR* 2007, 74.

312. *San Francisco Chronicle,* June 11, 2013, D4; June 2, 2013, A14.

313. *Financial Times,* October 24, 2013, 22.

314. *Financial Times,* March 8, 2014, 5.

315. *Financial Times,* January 17, 2014, 12.

316. CFR, *AR* 2013, 61.

317. Ibid., 32.

318. *Financial Times,* March 8, 2013, 5.

319. Ibid.

320. Ibid.

321. *Financial Times,* March 1, 2013, 14.

322. Ibid.

323. Bob Woodward and Carl Bernstein, *The Final Days* (New York: Simon and Schuster, 1976), 194–95.

324. *Financial Times,* September 23, 2014, 8.

325. Hugh Shelton, *Without Hesitation: The Odyssey of an American Warrior* (New York: St. Martin's Press, 2010), 2.

326. CFR, *AR* 2013, 46, 54, 56.

327. See www.ricehadleygates.com.

328. CFR, *AR* 1998, 38–49.

329. CFR, *AR* 2013, 51.

330. CFR, *AR* 2011, 40–41.

331. Ibid.

332. Additional information is available at www.laurenceshoup.com.

333. CFR, *AR* 1981, 151; 1997, 138; 2000, 152.

334. *Financial Times,* November 11, 2011, 9.

335. Chrystia Freeland, *Plutocrats: The Rise of the New Global Super-Rich and the Fall of Everyone Else* (New York: Penguin Press, 2012), xiv.

336. See www.bilderbergmeetings.org.

337. See Paul H. Jeffers, *The Bilderberg Conspiracy: Inside the World's Most Powerful Secret Society* (New York: Kensington Publishing, 2009), 2.

338. Rockefeller, *Memoirs,* 411.

339. Ibid., 412.

340. CFR, *AR* 2013, 31–33; David C. Korten, *When Corporations Rule the World* (West Hartford, CT: Kumarian Press, 1995), 137.

341. Rockefeller, *Memoirs,* 416.

342. Ibid., 416–17.

343. Michael J. Crozier, Samuel P. Huntington, and Joji Watanuki, *The Crisis of Democracy: Report on the Governability of Democracies to the Trilateral Commission* (New York: New York University Press, 1975), 106, 113.

344. Ibid., 65–67, 113.

345. See http//trilateral.org/ go.cfm?do=Page.View&pid=6.

346. Ibid.; CFR, *AR* 2012, 27–28.

347. See http//trilateral.org/.download/ file/TClist_2_15pdf.

348. The Trilateral Commission (North America) *Annual Report,* 1984–85, 23–25.

349. William K. Carroll, *The Making of a Transnational Capitalist Class: Corporate Power in the 21st Century* (London: Zed Books, 2010), 44.

350. Klaus Schwab, "A Breakdown in Our Values,"*The Guardian,* January 6, 2010.

351. World Economic Forum, *The World Economic Forum: A Partner in Shaping History, the First 40 Years, 1971–2010* (Geneva: World Economic Forum, 2009), 229.

352. Ibid., 88, 111, 113, 115, 124, 140, 152, 163, 171, 178, 197–98, 203, 207, 226, 232, 245, 256.

353. *Financial Times,* January 17–18, 2015, 3.

354. Henry Blodget, "The Truth about Davos, " wwwbusinessinsider.com/ costs–of–davos–2011–1, January 26, 2011.

355. World Economic Forum, *The World Economic Forum,* 253; CFR, *AR* 2010, 51–52.

356. www.crisisgroup.org/en/about. aspx.

357. CFR, *AR* 2009, 19.

358. See www.CFR.org/about/people/ global_board_of_advisors.html.

359. Data are from wwwCFR.org and CFR, *AR* 1995, 86; 1996, 108; 1997, 27–28; 1999, 102; 2000, 116; 2001, 83; 2002, 83; 2003, 90; 2004, 67; 2005, 67; 2006, 67; 2007, 74; 2008, 73; 2009, 19; 2013, 2 2014, 71.

360. *Financial Times,* September 13, 2013, 15.

361. See www.worstpolluted.org/docs/ TopTenThreats2013.pdf.

362. *Financial Times,* October 16, 2014, 1.

363. *Financial Times,* April 27–28, 2013, Life and Arts, 19.

364. CFR, *AR* 2014, 71.

365. *Financial Times,* May 20, 2013, 21.

366. Leslie Sklair, *The Transnational Capitalist Class* (Malden, MA: Blackwell, 2001), 282–87.

367. Ibid., 283.

368. *Financial Times,* June 23–24, 2012, 10.

369. *Financial Times,* May 22, 2013, 15.

370. *The Economist,* August 2, 2014, 49.

371. *Financial Times,* February 11, 2014, 6; Vibhuti Agarwal, "Inquiry into Tata Tea over Labor Issues," *Wall Street Journal,* February 13, 2014.

372. *Financial Times,* May 28, 2013, Arab World, 4.

373. CFR, *AR* 2012, 47.

374. *Financial Times,* April 13–14, 2013, 7.

375. Ibid.

376. *Financial Times,* May 24, 2013, 16.

377. Carroll, *The Making of a Transnational Capitalist Class,* 143.

378. Ibid., 144.

379. *Financial Times,* December 7, 2012, 3.

380. CFR, *AR* 2012, 55–56.

381. See Council of Councils Overview at cfr.org /projects/world/council– of–councils.

382. CFR, *AR* 2013, 69.

383. Ibid.

384. CFR, *AR* 1981, 63.

385. John Bellamy Foster, Robert W. McChesney, and R. Jamil Jonna, "The Internationalization of Monopoly Capital, " *Monthly Review* 63/2 (June 2011): 21.

386. David Harvey, *A Brief History of Neoliberalism* (Oxford: Oxford University Press, 2005), 10–11.

387. Ibid., 2.

388. *Financial Times,* December 4, 2012, 9.

389. *Financial Times,* March 20, 2014, 16.

390. Harvey, *A Brief History of Neoliberalism,* 54–55.

391. See Wolff, "Recent Trends in Household Wealth…"

392. Freeland, *Plutocrats,* 35; Credit Suisse, *Global Wealth Data Book* (Zurich: Credit Suisse Research Institute, 2010) 20–23, 78, 93.

393. James B. Davies, Susanna Sandstrom, Anthony Shorrocks, and Edward Wolff, "World Distribution of Household Wealth" (Santa Cruz, CA: Center for Global, International and Regional Studies, University of California, 2007), 7–8.

394. *San Francisco Chronicle,* January 22, 2014, C3.

395. Credit Suisse, *Global Wealth Data Book,* 81.

396. Harvey, *A Brief History of Neoliberalism,* 159.

397. *Financial Times,* December 31, 2013, 5.

398. See Naomi Klein, *The Shock Doctrine: The Rise of Disaster Capitalism* (New York: Henry Holt), 2007.

399. Kenneth Maxwell, "The Other 9/11: The United States and Chile, 1973," *Foreign Affairs* 82/6 (November–December 2003): 151.

400. See U.S. CIA Declassified Documents Relating to the Military Coup in Chile, 1970–1976, Project Fubelt, NationalSecurityArchive, www2.gwu.edu/~nsarchiv/NSAEBB/NSAEBB8/nsaebb8i.htm; and http://en.wikipedia.org/wiki/Project_FUBELT.

401. Stephen Kinzer, *Overthrow: America's Century of Regime Change from Hawaii to Iraq* (NewYork: Times Books, 2006), 182.

402. Paul E. Sigmund, "The 'Invisible Blockade' and the Overthrow of

Allende, " *Foreign Affairs* 52/2 (January 1974); CFR, *AR* 1974, 107.

403. See Sigmund, "The 'Invisible Blockade.'"

404. Klein, *The Shock Doctrine,* 86–87.

405. CFR, *AR* 1976, 33; Albert Fishlow, Carlos F. Diaz–Alejandro, Richard R. Fagen, and Roger D. Hansen, *Rich and Poor Nations in the World Economy* (New York: Council on Foreign Relations and McGraw-Hill, 1978), xi.

406. CFR, *AR* 1976, 33.

407. Fishlow et al., *Rich and Poor Nations…,* ix–x.

408. Ibid., 56, 63, 65, 78.

409. Ibid., 71–72.

410. Miriam Camps and Catherine Gwin, *Collective Management: The Reform of Global Economic Organizations* (New York: Council on Foreign Relations and McGraw-Hill, 1982), 2.

411. CFR, *AR* 1976, vi, 136–37; 1978, 119; 1981, 141; 1986, 2; 2002, 2; 2011, 25–26.

412. CFR, *AR* 2011, 25–26.

413. Jeff Madrick, *Age of Greed: The Triumph of Finance and the Decline of America, 1970 to the Present* (New York: Alfred A. Knopf, 2011), 10, 20, 24–25.

414. Walter Wriston, *Risk and Other Four-Letter Words* (New York: Harper and Row, 1986), viii, x.

415. Alan Greenspan, *The Age of Turbulence: Adventures in a New World* (New York: Penguin Press, 2007), 52.

416. Ibid., 81; CFR, *AR* 1978, 119.

417. Andrew D. Crain, *The Ford Presidency: A History* (Jefferson, NC: McFarland, 2009), 41, 202.

418. Greenspan, *The Age of Turbulence,* 71, 82.

419. Laurence H. Shoup, *The Carter Presidency and Beyond: Power and Politics in the 1980s* (Palo Alto, CA: Ramparts Press, 1980), 173, 186–87.

420. *Business Week*, April 10, 1978, 126.

421. Joseph B. Treaster, *Paul Volcker: The Making of a Financial Legend* (New York: John Wiley, 2004), 38; William R. Neikirk, *Volcker: Portrait of the Money Man* (New York: Congdon & Weed, 1987), 78–79.

422. Greenspan, *The Age of Turbulence*, 84.

423. William Greider, *Secrets of the Temple: How the Federal Reserve Rules the Country* (New York: Simon and Schuster, 1989), 47.

424. *New York Times*, July 26, 1979, 16; *Financial Times*, September 21–22, 2013, 7.

425. Leo Panitch and Sam Gindin, *The Making of Global Capitalism: The Political Economy of American Empire* (London: Verso, 2012), 172.

426. Greenspan, *The Age of Turbulence*, 86; Madrick, *Age of Greed*, 161–62; Greider, *Secrets of the Temple*, 430.

427. Harold van B. Cleveland and Ramachandra Bhagavatula, "The Continuing World Economic Crisis," *Foreign Affairs* 59/3 (1980): 594, 604.

428. Alan Greenspan, "The Reagan Legacy," remarks presented at the Ronald Reagan Library, Simi Valley, CA, April 9, 2003, www.federalreserve.gov/BoardDocs/speeches/2003/.../default.htm.

429. Alan Greenspan, Testimony before the Senate Committee on Banking, Housing and Urban Affairs, February 26, 1997, federalreserve.gov/boarddocs/hh/1997/february/testimony.htm.

430. Panitch and Gindin, *The Making of Global Capitalism* , 435n8.

431. CFR, *AR* 2011, 25.

432. Greenspan, *The Age of Turbulence*, 86–87, 282.

433. Madrick, *Age of Greed*, 225.

434. Klein, *The Shock Doctrine*, 268.

435. Ryan Grim, "Priceless: How the Federal Reserve Bought the Economics Profession," *HuffingtonPost.com*, May 25, 2011.

436. Panitch and Gindin, *The Making of Global Capitalism*, 249.

437. Ibid., 228.

438. Karl Marx, *The Portable Karl Marx*, selected, translated in part, and with an introduction by Eugene Kamenka (New York: Penguin Books, 1983), 209.

439. Panitch and Gindin, *The Making of Global Capitalism*, 252–54.

440. Madrick, *Age of Greed*, 243.

441. Ibid., 226, 240, 248.

442. Credit Suisse, *Global Wealth Data Book*, 20–23, 72–75 , 81, 93–94.

443. *Financial Times*, October 31, 2013, 2.

444. Transcript of the launch of the Maurice R. Greenberg Center for Geoeconomic Studies, February 15, 2002, www.cfr.org/.../launch-maurice–r–greenberg–center–geoeconomic–studies.../

445. CFR, *AR* 1975, 105; 2013, 31.

446. Zbigniew Brzezinski, *Game Plan: A Geostrategic Framework for the Conduct of the U.S. Soviet Contest* (New York: Atlantic Monthly Press, 1986); *The Grand Chessboard: American Primacy and Its Geostrategic Imperatives* (New York: Basic Books, 1997).

447. Brzezinski, *Game Plan*, xiii–xiv.

448. Ibid., 33.

449. Ibid., 30.

450. Ibid., 30–42, 253.

451. Ibid., 41.

452. Ibid., 48.

453. Ibid., 51.
454. Ibid., 52–53.
455. Zbigniew Brzezinski, "A Geostrategy for Eurasia, " *Foreign Affairs* 76/5 (September–October 1997): 50–51.
456. Ibid., 51–58, 62–64.
457. CFR, *AR* 2000, 143; 2003, 109.
458. Max Boot, *The Savage Wars of Peace: Small Wars and the Rise of American Power* (New York: Basic Books, 2002).
459. Ibid., 410.
460. Ibid., xvi, xx, 284.
461. Ibid., 336, 347, 350, 352.
462. Joseph S. Nye Jr., *Bound to Lead: The Changing Nature of American Power* (New York: Basic Books, 1990); and *Soft Power: The Means to Success in World Politics* (New York: Public Affairs, 2004).
463. CFR, *AR* 1975, 112; 2013 , 32.
464. Nye Jr., *Soft Power*, xvi.
465. Ibid., x, xiii, 6.
466. Ibid., xiii.
467. Ibid., 5.
468. Ibid., x, xiii.
469. Michael Mandelbaum, *The Case for Goliath: How America Acts as the World's Government in the 21st Century* (New York: Public Affairs, 2005).
470. CFR, *AR* 1976, 131; 1988, 58; 1990, 199; 1995, 131, 151; 2003, 109, 126.
471. Mandelbaum, *The Case for Goliath*, xi–xii.
472. Ibid., xv.
473. Ibid., xv–xvi.
474. Ibid., xvii–xix; 67, 141, 161.
475. Ibid., 24–25, 27.
476. Ibid., 71.
477. Ibid., 49–50.
478. Ibid., 77.
479. Ibid., 200.
480. Ibid., 97, 170–71.
481. Walter Russell Mead, *Power, Terror, Peace and War: America's Grand Strategy in a World at Risk* (New York: Alfred A. Knopf, 2004).
482. CFR, *AR* 1997, 137; 1998, 121.
483. Mead, *Power, Terror, Peace and War*, 214–16.
484. Ibid., 7–9, 19, 21, 23.
485. Ibid., 25–44, 160.
486. Ibid., 25–28, 43.
487. Ibid., 25, 29–36.
488. Ibid., 25, 36–44.
489. Ibid., 44–81.
490. Ibid., 71.
491. Ibid., 196.
492. Haass, *Foreign Policy Begins at Home*, iii.
493. Ibid., 1, 3.
494. Ibid., 16, 21.
495. Ibid., 15–16.
496. Ibid., 78–82, 110, 113.
497. Ibid., 104–5.
498. Ibid., 121.
499. Ibid., 126–27.
500. Ibid., 128, 134–61.
501. CFR, *AR* 2013: 61–62.
502. Steve Pearlstein,"Caterpillar to Unions: Drop Dead," *Washington Post*, August 4, 2012; Alexandra Brown, "GE to Unions: Drop Dead," *Labor Notes,* May 24, 2011.
503. Robert D. Blackwill and Meghan L. O'Sullivan, "America's Energy Edge: The Geopolitical Consequences of the Shale Revolution, " *Foreign Affairs* 93/2 (March–April. 2014): 109–10.
504. James M.Lindsay, cfr.org/iraq/Lindsay-successful-constitution-vote.
505. CFR, *AR* 1980, 62, 129.
506. Melvin A. Conant, *The Oil Factor in U.S. Foreign Policy, 1980–1990* (Lexington, MA: A Council on Foreign Relations Book, D.C. Heath, 1982), xiii, 3, 29.
507. Paul Jabber, Gary Sick, Hisahiko Okazaki, and Dominique Moisi,

Great Power Interests in the Persian Gulf (New York: Council on Foreign Relations, 1989), 1–2, 16–17, 32.

508. Micah L. Sifry and Christopher Cerf, *The Iraq War Reader: History, Documents, Opinions* (New York: Simon & Schuster, 2003), 399.

509. James Mann, *Rise of the Vulcans: The History of Bush's War Cabinet* (New York: Penguin Books, 2004), 209–10; CFR, *AR* 1990, 197–99, 207.

510. Mann, *Rise of the Vulcans,* 209–10.

511. See http://en.wikipedia.org/wiki/Project_for_the_New_American_Century.

512. Richard N. Haass, *The Reluctant Sheriff: The United States after the Cold War* (New York: A Council on Foreign Relations Book, 1997), 71.

513. Ibid., 73.

514. Richard N. Haass, "What to Do with American Primacy," *Foreign Affairs* 78/5 (September–October 1999).

515. Fouad Ajami, "The Sentry's Solitude," *Foreign Affairs* 80/6 (November–December 2001).

516. Kenneth M. Pollack, "Next Stop Baghdad?," *Foreign Affairs* 81/2 (March–April 2002).

517. Kenneth M. Pollack, *The Threatening Storm: The Case for Invading Iraq* (New York: A Council on Foreign Relations Book, Random House, 2002).

518. Ibid., 425–26.

519. CFR, *AR* 2002, 6.

520. Pollack, "Next Stop Baghdad?"; Pollack, *The Threatening Storm,* xv, xxx.

521. Pollack, *The Threatening Storm,* 337.

522. Ibid., 335–38.

523. Ibid., 338.

524. Ibid., 397.

525. Ibid., xxv, 424.

526. Kenneth M. Pollack, "Securing the Gulf," *Foreign Affairs* 82/4 (July–August. 2003), 3, 4.

527. Sebastian Mallaby, "The Reluctant Imperialist: Terrorism, Failed States, and the Case for American Empire," " *Foreign Affairs* 81/2 (March–April 2002) 6.

528. Donald Rumsfeld, "Transforming the Military," *Foreign Affairs* 81/3 (May–June 2002); Elliot Cohen, "A Tale of Two Secretaries," *Foreign Affairs* 81/3 (May–June 2002).

529. Michael Mandelbaum, "U.S. Must Plan Post-Hussein Iraq," *Newsday,* August 1, 2002.

530. Ruth Wedgwood, "Strike at Saddam Now," *National Law Journal,* October 28, 2002.

531. See www.cfr.org/iraq/us-has-strategically-sound-morally-just-reasons-invade-iraq-says-councils-middle-east-director-rachel-bronson/p5303.

532. See www.cfr.org/iraq/us-still-looking-smoking-gun-justify-overthrow-saddam-hussein.

533. G. John Ikenberry, "America's Imperial Ambition," *Foreign Affairs* 81/5 (September–October. 2002).

534. CFR, *AR* 2003, 40–71.

535. CFR, *AR* 2002, 112, 118, 120, 127.

536. CFR, *AR* 2004, 32.

537. Ivo H. Daalder and James M. Lindsay, *America Unbound: The Bush Revolution in Foreign Policy* (Hoboken, NJ: John Wiley, 2003; rev. ed., 2005).

538. Mann, *Rise of the Vulcans.*

539. Ibid., 373.

540. Daalder and Lindsay, *America Unbound,* 231.

541. Ibid., 15, 231.

542. Ibid., 97; Mann, *Rise of the Vulcans,* 251–53, 332.

543. CFR, *AR* 2002, 111, 122, 125, 127.

544. Daalder and Lindsay, *America Unbound,* 29, 111, 116, 130–133; Mann, *Rise of the Vulcans,* xv–xvi, 251–52, 273, 316–17.

545. CFR, *AR* 2002, 112, 113, 115, 117, 118, 120, 127.

546. Richard N. Haass, *War of Necessity War of Choice: A Memoir of Two Iraq Wars* (New York: Simon and Schuster, 2009), 222–23, 247.

547. CFR, *AR* 2002, 90, 109, 113, 121, 124, 127.

548. Daalder and Lindsay, *America Unbound,* 28–30, 130–133; Mann, *Rise of the Vulcans,* 140, 334–38.

549. Haass, *War of Necessity War of Choice,* 216–18.

550. *New York Times,* January 14, 2004, A15.

551. Ron Suskind, *The Price of Loyalty: George W. Bush, the White House, and the Education of Paul O'Neill* (New York: Simon and Schuster, 2004), ix

552. Ibid., 96.

553. Daalder and Lindsay, *America Unbound,* 135.

554. Edward P. Djerejian, Frank G. Wisner, Rachel Bronson, and Andrew S. Weiss, *Guiding Principles for U.S. Post-Conflict Policy in Iraq,* Report of an Independent Working Group of the Baker Institute for Public Policy, Rice University and the Council on Foreign Relations (New York: Council on Foreign Relations, 2003).

555. Ibid., 4.

556. Ibid., 19.

557. Ibid., 3, 11, 24.

558. Greenspan, *The Age of Turbulence,* 463.

559. Greg Palast, "Unreported: The Zarqawi Invitation, " www. ZCommunications.org, 2006.

560. *Wall Street Journal,* May 1, 2003, 1.

561. CFR, *AR* 2003, 11, 13.

562. CFR, *AR* 1990, 190.

563. Antonia Juhasz, "Capitalism Gone Wild, " *Tikkun* 19/1 (January–February, 2004); Klein, *The Shock Doctrine,* 345–48; Harvey, *A Brief History of Neoliberalism,* 6.

564. CFR, *AR* 1987, 140.

565. Klein, *The Shock Doctrine,* 337.

566. Ibid., 345; http://reliefweb.int/report/Iraq/chief-us-administrator-Iraq-reviews-progress-plans-Iraq-reconstruction, 2003.

567. Brookings Institution, *Iraq Index: Tracking Variables of Reconstruction and Security in Post-Saddam Iraq* (Washington, D.C.: Brookings Institution, 2009).

568. Klein, *The Shock Doctrine,* 351.

569. Ibid., 366.

570. *New York Times,* November 2, 2003, WK1, WK3.

571. *New York Times,* August 20, 2003, A1.

572. Brookings Institution, *Iraq Index,* 2009.

573. CFR, *AR* 1982, 165.

574. Michael Hirsh, "Tough Diplomacy," *Newsweek,* February 16, 2005.

575. Scott Shane, "Cables Show Central Negroponte Role in 80's Covert War against Nicaragua," *New York Times,* April 13, 2005.

576. Scott Shane, "Poker-faced Diplomat, Negroponte Is Poised for Role as Spy Chief," *New York Times,* March 29, 2005.

577. Scott Shane, "Cables Show Central Negroponte Role in 80's Covert War against Nicaragua," *New York Times,* April 13, 2005.

578. *Financial Times,* December 24, 2011, 3.

579. *Financial Times,* November 17–18, 2012, 7.

580. CFR, *AR* 1986, 162.

581. CFR, *AR* 2014, 19.

582. Jeremy Scahill, *Dirty Wars: The World Is a Battlefield* (New York: Nation Books, 2013), 164.

583. *Newsweek,* January 7, 2005.

584. Peter Maass, "The Way of the Commandos," *The New York Times Magazine,* May 1, 2005.

585. Ibid.

586. Ibid.

587. Unsigned, "Revealed: Pentagon's Link to Iraqi Torture Centers," *The Guardian,* March 6, 2013.

588. Ibid.

589. Ibid.

590. David H. Petraeus, "Learning from Counterinsurgency: Observations from Soldiering in Iraq, " *Military Review* (January–February 2006).

591. CFR, *AR* 2000, 51.

592. CFR, *AR* 2001, 119.

593. Scahill, *Dirty Wars,* 147.

594. Ibid., 153.

595. Unsigned, "Camp Nama: British Personnel Reveal Horrors of Secret U.S. Base in Baghdad," *The Guardian,* April 1, 2013.

596. Eric Schmitt and Carolyn Marshall, "In Secret Unit's 'Black Room' a Grim Portrait of U.S. Abuse," *New York Times,* March 19, 2006.

597. Scahill, *Dirty Wars,* 258, 348–49.

598. Mike Francis, "Oregon Guard Unit Told to Return Prisoners to Iraqi Abusers," *Seattle Times,* August 8, 2004.

599. CFR, *AR* 2008, 96; CFR, *AR* 2012, 28.

600. Mann, *Rise of the Vulcans,* 340–342; 350–351.

601. CFR, *AR* 2006, 87, 91, 92, 94, 98–99; 1995, 153.

602. Iraq Study Group, *The Way Forward—A New Approach* (2006), 68–69. See U.S. Institute of Peace website: usip.org/isg/iraq_study_ group_report/_report/…index. html.; CFR, *AR* 2006, 72–73.

603. Iraq Study Group, *The Way Forward,* 64; CFR, *AR* 2006, 86, 90, 92.

604. Iraq Study Group, *The Way Forward,* 9.

605. Ibid., 56–57.

606. Ibid., 49–50.

607. *San Francisco Chronicle,* October 23, 2011, A7.

608. *Financial Times,* March 19, 2013, 4.

609. CFR, *AR* 2012, 33, 40, 43.

610. *Oakland Tribune,* June 15, 2003, 5.

611. Alexander Smoltczyk, "Mystery in Iraq: Are US Munitions to Blame for Basra Birth Defects?,"*Der Spiegel,* December 18, 2012.

612. *Financial Times,* March 16–17, 2013, 2.

613. Ibid., 2, 13.

614. Ibid., 2.

615. *Financial Times,* October 7, 2013, 3; "Western Bank Giants Prepare to Revamp Iraq's Financial Systems," *Wall Street Journal,* January 28, 2009.

616. *Financial Times,* June 24, 2013, 17.

617. *Financial Times,* March 16–17, 2013, 13.

618. *Financial Times,* May 2, 2013, 18; November 29, 2013, 19.

619. CFR, *AR* 2012, 55–56.

620. See www.gryphon-partners.com.

621. *Financial Times,* March 19, 2013, 4.

622. *Oakland Tribune,* March 20, 2013, A11.

623. *San Francisco Chronicle,* April 17, 2009, A11; April 19, 2009, A5.

624. Charles A. Kupchan, *Reviving the Atlantic Partnership* (New York: Council on Foreign Relations, 2004), vii.

625. Ibid., viii.

626. Ibid., 31–37.

627. Ibid.

628. Ibid., viii, 18–19.

629. Ibid., 19.

630. Ibid., 22–23.

631. Ibid., 25–26.

632. Ibid., 26.

633. Ranajit Guha, *Dominance without Hegemony: History and Power in Colonial India* (Cambridge, MA: Harvard University Press, 1998), 14.

634. CFR, *AR* 2001, 82; CFR, *AR* 2011, 23; http://trilateral.org/go.cfm?do=page.view+pld=6.

635. CFR, *AR* 2012, 39, 50.

636. Edward Alden and Matthew J. Slaughter, *U.S. Trade and Investment Policy* (New York: Council on Foreign Relations, 2011), ix, 6.

637. Ibid., 32–33, 35.

638. Ibid., 36–37, 70.

639. Tom Donilon, "The President's Free-Trade Path to Prosperity," *Wall Street Journal,* April 15, 2013.

640. *Financial Times,* March 1–2, 2014, 9.

641. *Financial Times,* September 23, 2013, 9.

642. Frank Sampson Jannuzi, *U.S.-China Relations: An Affirmative Agenda, A Responsible Course: Report of an Independent Task Force* (New York: Council on Foreign Relations, 2007).

643. Ibid., xi.

644. Ibid., 107–16.

645. Ibid., 7, 10.

646. Ibid., 58.

647. Ibid., 93–95.

648. Ibid., 47–48.

649. Ibid., 51.

650. Ibid., 54.

651. CFR.org/asia-and-pacific/china's-maritime-disputes.

652. Ibid.

653. *Financial Times,* June 26, 2013, 7.

654. CFR, *AR* 2002, 115, 121, 122, 125; 2012, 28; Daniel S. Markey, *U. S. Strategy for Pakistan and Afghanistan* (New York: Council on Foreign Relations, 2010), xi.

655. *New York Times,* October 20, 2012: A10.

656. Peter Landers, "U.S. Not Neutral about Japan, Armitage Told Beijing," *Wall Street Journal,* November 29, 2012.

657. Elizabeth C. Economy, "China and Southeast Asia: Take Three," blogs.cfr.org/asia/2013/10/01/china-and-southeast-asia-take-three/.

658. Brzezinski, *The Grand Chessboard,* 46, 52, 121.

659. John J. Mearsheimer, "Why the Ukraine Crisis Is the West's Fault," *Foreign Affairs* 93/5 (September–October 2014), 80.

660. Ibid.

661. CFR, *AR* 1995, 9, 30.

662. See www.cfr.org/nato/should-nato-expand/.

663. CFR, *AR* 1997, 135; 2013, 79.

664. CFR, *AR* 1997, 39.

665. CFR, *AR* 2000, 28; 2001, 35; Ronald D. Asmus, *Opening NATO's Door: How the Alliance Remade Itself for a New Era* (New York: Columbia University Press, 2004).

666. See http://cup.columbia.edu/book/opening-natos-door/9780231127776.

667. Mearsheimer, "Why the Ukraine Crisis Is the West's Fault," 78–79.

668. Geoffrey R. Pyatt, speeches, interviews with Ambassador Geoffrey R. Pyatt, Embassy of the United States, Ukraine, September 3, 2013, http://ukraine.usembassy.gov/speaches/amb-den.html.

669. Mearsheimer, "Why the Ukraine Crisis Is the West's Fault," 80–81.

670. CFR, *AR,* 2013, 52.

671. Mearsheimer, "Why the Ukraine Crisis Is the West's Fault," 80.

672. CFR, *AR* 1995, 86; 2004, 67; 2005, 67; *Financial Times,* September 15, 2014, 9.

673. *Financial Times,* September 15, 2014, 9.

674. *Financial Times,* October 7, 2014,11.

675. *Financial Times,* February 22–23, 2014, Life and Arts, 1–2.

676. *San Francisco Chronicle,* November 6, 2004, A11.

677. Robert D. Blackwill and Walter B. Slocombe, *Israel: A Strategic Asset for the United States* (Washington, D.C.: Washington Institute for Near East Policy, 2011), 2–3.

678. Ibid., 4–6.

679. Ibid., 8–17.

680. Eduardo Galeano, *Days and Nights of Love and War* (London: Pluto Press, 2000), 170.

681. Samuel P.Huntington, *The Clash of Civilizations and the Remaking of the World Order* (New York: Simon and Schuster, 1996), 35.

682. CFR, *AR* 2013, 47, 52, 61–62.

683. Linda Robinson, *The Future of U.S. Special Operations Forces* (New York: Council on Foreign Relations, 2013), 33.

684. Ibid., iv.

685. Ibid., vii, ix, 8–9, 14.

686. Ibid., 3, 11, 14;, Linda Robinson, "Special Ops Global Whack-a-Mole," *USA Today,* April 8, 2013.

687. Robinson, *The Future of U.S. Special Operations Forces,* 3–4, 11–12.

688. Ibid., 15–16, 20–21.

689. Ibid., 27.

690. *Time,* February 11, 2013, 28.

691. Micah Zenko, *Reforming U.S. Drone Strike Policies* (New York: Council on Foreign Relations, 2013), 13, 28n1.

692. Ibid., ix, x, 25, 32–33.

693. Ibid., 3.

694. Ibid., 4.

695. Ibid., 25–27.

696. Ibid., 12, 14.

697. "Monsanto, DuPont Spending Millions to Oppose California's GMO Labeling Law," *Forbes,* August 22, 2012.

698. CFR, *AR* 2013, 61.

699. David G. Victor and C. Ford Runge, *Sustaining a Revolution: A Policy Strategy for Crop Engineering* (New York: Council on Foreign Relations, 2002).

700. Ibid., v.

701. Ibid., 3–11.

702. Ibid., 1–2.

703. Ibid., 25–26.

704. Ibid., 32.

705. Ibid., 35.

706. Ibid., 43–45.

707. Ibid., 46–47.

708. Bill Lambrecht, *Dinner at the New Gene Café: How Genetic Engineering Is Changing What We Eat, How We Live, and the Global Politics of Food* (New York: St. Martin's Press, 2001), 281–82.

709. Zia Hag, "Ministry Blames Bt Cotton for Farmer Suicides,"*Hindustan Times,* March 26, 2012.

710. *International Herald Tribune,* August 25–26, 2012, 8.

711. *International Herald Tribune,* August 25–26, 2012, 8, 11; *Financial Times,* May 4, 2013, 4.

712. *San Francisco Chronicle,* November 26, 2012, A4; *Oakland Tribune,* November 29, 2012, A4.

713. *San Francisco Chronicle,* May 18, 2013, A11.

714. *New York Times,* December 5, 2012.

715. CFR, *AR* 2012, 56.

716. *International Herald Tribune,* August 25–26, 2012, 11.

717. Ibid., 8, 11; *Oakland Tribune,* November 29, 2012, A4.

718. CFR, *AR* 1991, 190; 2013, 54.

719. *San Francisco Chronicle,* May 15, 2013, C3.

720. CFR, *AR* 2012, 36, 40, 42, 45, 46, 50.

721. *New York Times,* May 30, 2013; *San*

Francisco Chronicle June 2, 2013, D2; CFR, *AR* 2012, 28, 46, 51.

722. *San Francisco Chronicle,* August 21, 2013, C1, C5.

723. Raymond Vernon, ed., *The Promise of Privatization: A Challenge for U.S. Policy* (New York: Council on Foreign Relations, 1988), 20.

724. Ibid., 268, 274.

725. Ibid., 269.

726. Ibid., 163–66.

727. CFR, *AR* 1995, 31.

728. CFR, *AR* 2013, 43.

729. Richard Downie, *The Road to Recovery: Rebuilding Liberia's Health System,* Report of the CSIS Global Health Policy Center, 2012, 16. Available at csis.org/publication/road–recovery.

730. *San Francisco Chronicle,* October 14, 2014, A2, A13.

731. *San Francisco Chronicle,* October 18, 2014, A8.

732. Editorial, "Cuba's Impressive role on Ebola," *New York Times,* October 19, 2014.

733. Nicholas X. Rizopoulos, ed., *Sea Changes: American Foreign Policy in a World Transformed* (New York: Council on Foreign Relations, 1990).

734. Ibid., v–x; CFR, *AR* 1991, 176–94.

735. Rizopoulos, *Sea Changes,* viii.

736. CFR, *AR* 1974, 107; 1975, 109.

737. Rizopoulos, *Sea Changes,* 116–18.

738. Ibid., 293; CFR, *AR* 199, 192.

739. Rizopoulos, *Sea Changes,* 140.

740. Ibid., 138.

741. CFR, *AR* 1998, 47.

742. CFR, *AR* 1998, 35.

743. David G. Victor, *The Collapse of the Kyoto Protocol and the Struggle to Slow Global Warming* (Princeton: A Council on Foreign Relations Book, Princeton University Press, 2001), xiii.

744. Ibid.

745. Ibid., xi, x.

746. Ibid., 115.

747. Ibid., 21–22, 114.

748. David G. Victor, *Climate Change: Debating America's Policy Options* (New York: Council on Foreign Relations, 2004), v–vi.

749. Steve Coll, *Private Empire: ExxonMobil and American Power* (New York: Penguin Group, 2012), 78, 493.

750. Unsigned, "Toxic Shock," *The Economist,* May 26, 2012.

751. Coll, *Private Empire,* 185–86.

752. Ibid., 225–26.

753. Victor, *Climate Change,* vi, 6–7, 68–74.

754. Joshua Busby, *Climate Change and National Security: An Agenda for Action* (New York: Council on Foreign Relations, 2007), 19.

755. Ibid., 26.

756. Ibid., 17–22.

757. Coll, *Private Empire,* 547.

758. Leslie Eaton and Geraldine Fabrikant, "Enron's Collapse: the Losers," *New York Times,* December 5, 2001.

759. Michael A. Levi, *The Canadian Oil Sands: Energy Security vs. Climate Change* (New York: Council on Foreign Relations, 2009), 5.

760. Ibid., 27.

761. Ibid., 40.

762. Michael A. Levi and David G. Victor, *Confronting Climate Change: A Strategy for U.S. Foreign Policy* (New York: Council on Foreign Relations, 2008), 11–12.

763. Ibid., 42.

764. Ibid., 3.

765. Ibid.

766. Ibid., 4, 36–37, 92.

767. Ibid., 21.

768. Haass, *Foreign Policy Begins at Home,* 129.

769. Ibid., 8, 130–133, 149–50, 152.
770. Ibid., 50.
771. Allan Sielen, "The Devolution of the Seas: The Consequences of Oceanic Destruction," *Foreign Affairs* 92/6 (November–December 2013).
772. Haass, *Foreign Policy Begins at Home*, 113.
773. *San Francisco Chronicle,* January 16, 2014, 16.
774. Chris Williams, *Ecology and Socialism* (Chicago: Haymarket Books, 2010), 72.
775. *San Francisco Chronicle,* November 24, 2013, C5.
776. International Energy Agency, worldenergyoutlook.org/resources/energysubsidies, 2014.
777. Mark Z. Jacobson and Mark A. Dlucchi, "A Path to Sustainable Energy by 2030," *Scientific American,* November 2009; available at www.scientificamerican.com/.../a-path-to-sustainable-energy-by-2030/.
778. Coll, *Private Empire*, 182–83, 335–40, 535.
779. Richard Heede, "Tracing Anthropogenic Carbon Dioxide and Methane Emissions to Fossil Fuel and Cement Producers, 1854–2012," *Climate Change* 122 (January 2014); available at http://link.springer.com/article/10.1007/s10584-013-0986.
780. See ibid.; CFR, *AR* 2013, 61–62.
781. See, for example, Panitch and Gindin, *The Making of Global Capitalism*, 4, 170, 324; and works by Nicos Poulantzas.
782. Panitch and Ginden, *The Making of Global Capitalism*, 324.
783. CFR, *AR* 2014, 8.
784. See Hal Draper, *Karl Marx's Theory of Revolution*, vol. 1: *State and Bureaucracy* (New York: Monthly Review Press, 1977), 584–87.

785. See Robert W. McChesney, "This Isn't What Democracy Looks Like," *Monthly Review* 64/6 (November 2012); John Nichols and Robert W. McChesney, *Dollarocracy: How the Money and Media Complex is Destroying America* (New York: Nation Books, 2013).
786. Laurence H. Shoup, "Corporate Gold: The Presidential Election 2008," *Z Magazine* 21/2 (February 2008): 29–31.
787. Fred Magdoff and John Bellamy Foster, "What Every Environmentalist Needs to Know about Capitalism," *Monthly Review* 61/10 (March 2010): 5.
788. *San Francisco Chronicle,* February 23, 2014, C7; and www.earthweek.com/2014/ew 140221.
789. CFR, *AR* 2007, 99.
790. James K. Galbraith, *The Predator State* (New York: Free Press, 2008), 169–70.
791. John Bellamy Foster, "The Epochal Crisis," *Monthly Review* 65/5 (October 2013): 1.
792. http://www.brainyquote.com/quotes/quotes/m/margaretme100502.html
793. See "The World's Most Resource Rich Countries," www.247wallst.com./special-report/2012/04/18.
794. Fred Magdoff, "Ecological Civilization," *Monthly Review* 62/8 (January 2011).
795. John Bellamy Foster, "Why Ecological Revolution," *Monthly Review* 61/8 (January 2010).
796. Foster, "The Epochal Crisis," 11.
797. One is the Belem Ecosocialist Declaration (2007); another is the Universal Declaration of the Rights of Mother Earth (2010); the third is the Draft Universal Declaration of the Common Good of Humanity

(2013). All three are available at laurenceshoup.com.
798. Naomi Klein, *This Changes Everything: Capitalism vs. The Climate* (New York: Simon and Schuster, 2014).

INDEX